About Abortion

About Abortion

Terminating Pregnancy in Twenty-First-Century America

Carol Sanger

THE BELKNAP PRESS *of* HARVARD UNIVERSITY PRESS

Cambridge, Massachusetts & London, England · *2017*

First printing

Library of Congress Cataloging-in-Publication Data

Names: Sanger, Carol, author.
Title: About abortion : terminating pregnancy in twenty-first-century America / Carol Sanger.
Description: Cambridge, Massachusetts : The Belknap Press of Harvard University Press, 2017. | Includes bibliographical references and index.
Identifiers: LCCN 2016041934 | ISBN 9780674737723 (alk. paper)
Subjects: LCSH: Abortion—Moral and ethical aspects—United States. | Abortion—Law and legislation—United States. | Abortion—Political aspects—United States. | Abortion—United States—Psychological aspects. | Pregnancy, Unwanted—United States.
Classification: LCC HQ767.15 .S26 2017 | DDC 179.7/6—dc23
LC record available at https://lccn.loc.gov/2016041934

IN MEMORY OF

My father

Marshall Sanger

Colonel, United States Army

1923–2004

AND

To my dear mother

Lila Sanger

Contents

Preface

Any book about abortion necessarily begins *in media res*. This is because the problem of unwanted pregnancy does not start with abortion. Abortion follows pregnancy, whether that pregnancy has been much sought after and highly desired or whether it is the worst thing ever. Pregnancy, in its turn, follows sexual intercourse, whether that intercourse was calculated, casual, or coerced. (Because we live in modern times, pregnancy and so abortion may also follow more technical forms of conception, such as embryo implantation.) To say that abortion falls in the middle of things is to say that abortion is located at a discrete intersection in a woman's life. On one side, there is pregnancy. On the other side is non-pregnancy and the status quo with regard to the number of children: a mother of two remains a mother of two; a girl does not become a mother.

This is not to say that a woman's life necessarily proceeds exactly as it would have had there been no pregnancy and no abortion, though many lives do. For some women, abortion registers as a profound loss, the date or a projected birth date reflected upon, sometimes commemorated, for years to come. For many others, the core reaction is one of relief and the welcome return of the preferred (at least for now) non-pregnant self that almost got away. Still other women experience both relief—the most widely reported emotion following abortion—and some form of regret or wistfulness, not about the decision itself, but because the circumstances around the pregnancy—partner, finances, obligations, plans—were just not right enough to proceed.

In this way every abortion has a context, a set of befores and imagined afters that inform how women's decisions about abortion are made and how they are experienced. It is as though on the chronological spectrum of a woman's life, a notional push pin has been planted on the spot marking the decision. That same pin marks the subject of this book: how women confront and decide about unwanted pregnancy within the complicated structures of constraint—personal, cultural, legal—that frame the issue of abortion in modern America.

Just as individual abortion decisions can be located on a timeline, abortion as an historical practice also has a set of befores and afters. The befores in this larger sense are the hundred or so years when abortion at any stage of pregnancy was a crime in most American states. That regime ended in 1973—this is where the second push pin goes in—when the Supreme Court struck down Texas's criminal abortion statute on the ground that it unconstitutionally interfered with the newly recognized right of women themselves to decide whether to keep or end a pregnancy. Abortion has been legal since, though in many states very hard to come by; thus the second pin has a very wide bandwidth. The "afters" for legal abortion are not yet known.

Abortion is an individual practice, something women engage in one by one, and it is also a social practice, for every abortion involves not only the pregnant woman but something of a supporting cast ("supporting" in the sense of "surrounding"). There are the doctors and nurses who provide care; the friends and partners who know; the friends and partners who don't (or don't quite); the sidewalk protestors or, depending on one's point of view, sidewalk counselors outside clinics who try to persuade women to save their babies and souls by turning around and going home. If each of the 700,000 or so women and girls who terminated a pregnancy in 2015 interacted with only a few others along the way—one nurse, one partner, one pastor, one babysitter for the kids, one good friend, one receptionist—several million more people are involved.

Pulling the camera back a bit further, more players come into view. There are spiritual leaders and media figures who regularly pronounce on the subject; television producers and sponsors who decide whether and how abortion should be portrayed in entertainment programming; and, crucially in the American context, the legislators and judges who regulate the provision of abortion through a vast network of law. With this large a cast, it is easy to see that unlike other medical procedures performed at about the same rate—knee surgery, for example—abortion has a social and political economy of its own: a mix of private decision making and public policy, constitutional rights and statutory constraints, with moral conviction standing firm, for the most part, on both sides of the issue.

In sorting out the furor that is abortion in America, three themes circulate throughout this book. The first is the matter of how abortion is regulated, or abortion law. The second concerns the way abortion is discussed or, as is more often the case, how it is not discussed. I call this abortion talk. The third theme concerns the visual culture of abortion or abortion imagery. The dominant image here is not a pregnant woman—most abortions take place before any "bump" makes its debut—but rather the fetus, which most Americans have come to know through the celebratory sharing of ultrasound scans by happy, expectant parents.

The connections among these three themes—law, talk, and imagery—form the basis of this book's central argument. This is that the secrecy surrounding women's personal experience of abortion has massively, though not irreparably, distorted how the subject of abortion is discussed and how it is regulated. We understand why most women don't talk about abortion in this way: it is too personal, too risky, too stigmatizing. We understand as well what a powerful force fetal imagery has been in the campaign to persuade all of us that terminating a pregnancy is killing a person. The claim that a fetus is a person, or a sort of person, has great appeal, in part because many readers may have felt an intimate bond with their own fetus before its birth. The images that bring about this intimacy are the ultrasound scans that so delight women with wanted pregnancies. How does that same imagery register for women whose pregnancies are or have become unwanted? Consider laws that insist that a woman must have an ultrasound and be offered a look at her unborn child, in the language of the statute, before she may legally consent to an abortion. The requirement confuses wanted with unwanted pregnancies, as antiabortion legislators seem happy to do. The example shows how visual technology has created a visual politics and how antiabortion lawmakers have opportunistically—and brilliantly—seized upon both in their campaign against abortion.

I am a lawyer by training, and so the law-inflected exploration of abortion that follows is in part a matter of disciplinary orientation. But only in part. For lawyer or no, it is not possible to understand the enduring grip that abortion holds on American society without an appreciation of law's role in the scheme. In ways subtle and increasingly overt, the structure of American law helps sustain abortion's place as a vivid—sometimes incendiary—public issue whose legality is not simply contested but sought after as the coveted jewel in the political crown. At present state legislatures cannot forbid abortion entirely, though several have certainly tried. In other attempts to create "abortion-free zones," states have been hacking away at the abortion right in every way they can. The general strategy has been to make abortion harder to get: harder legally, financially, emotionally, and practically. As humorist Jon Stewart observed, "just because a procedure is completely legal doesn't mean it has to be treated that way."

The exact limits on the states' authority to regulate in this area are not yet clear—abortion law remains a work in progress as statutes and regulations are passed, challenged in court, appealed, redrafted, challenged in court again, and so forth. Understanding existing limits requires a sense of the constitutional framework, starting with *Roe v. Wade* in 1973, stopping at *Planned Parenthood v. Casey* in 1992, and ending (for now) at the 2016 case of *Whole Woman's Health v. Hellerstedt*. Each of these cases assessed and adjusted the constitutional boundaries of the state's regulatory authority. Although the twists and turns of constitutional doctrine are crucial background, I focus here on the statutes enacted in light of evolving doctrine. Since the *Casey* case in 1992, laws have been tumbling out of statehouses around the country, framing the action on the ground for women, doctors, and medical staff.

I am particularly interested in the relation between abortion laws and harm to women. In the mid-nineteenth century, concerns about women's physical well-being at the hands of unregulated entrepreneurs led (in part) to the criminalization of abortion. Attention then turned to the harms women suffered when they were unable to get a legal abortion at all: the toll that repeated pregnancies took on women's bodies and the woeful history of physical harm wrought by illegal abortions. More recently, pro-life advocates have expressed concerns about the harms that pregnant women are said to suffer by virtue of abortion's legality: the likelihood of remorse, depression, and guilt about which women must now be warned in a fair number of states before they may consent to the procedure.

Most of these claims about how abortion harms women—some historical, some real, some fanciful—are fairly well known. But there has been little public discussion of the harms caused by abortion regulation, even when women are in the end able to obtain a legal abortion. This omission is problematic if we are after a comprehensive account of the stakes for women in abortion's regulation. The hyper-regulation of abortion—the burdensome requirements placed on providers, patients, and clinics—has been served up less to protect women from the physical or psychological dangers of the procedure than to deter and perhaps to punish them for choosing to terminate their pregnancy, an act that is for some a morally reprehensible killing.

One of the problems with America's ongoing abortion debate is that much of the standard fare has become cartoonish and contrarian. The 1996 movie *Citizen Ruth,* featuring Laura Dern as a glue-sniffing gutter punk in a confused state of pregnancy, captures some of this. Ruth is sought after as a poster child by both pro-life and pro-choice advocates who end up bashing one another with placards as Ruth, who in classic Hollywood abortion-avoidance mode has miscarried, slips away with bribe money from both sides. But while the melee in *Citizen Ruth* is comic, there is real violence surrounding the actual provision of abortion services. Clinics are staked out, sent powdery "anthrax" letters, and bombed. Physicians and clinic workers are regularly threatened and sometimes murdered, and clinic patients are accused of murder as they arrive for their appointments. Against this background of violence, the martial characterization of abortion as war, as struggle, as clash, as battlefield is perhaps inevitable.

But amidst the fog of abortion wars, something has gotten lost. This is the possibility of conversation at a lower decibel by women concerning their own abortion decisions and experiences. We understand why most women don't talk about abortion at the level of individual experience. Yet this form of silence takes a toll on women's well-being; it turns out there is something literal about being "weighed down by a secret."

The silence around abortion has implications not only for how individual women fare but for the rest of us who seek to live in a decent society. Citizens, including Citizen Ruth, are not just the subjects of law. Citizens are also supposed to make law, directly or indirectly, and we cannot advance how we and our representatives think about something—and certainly not how it should be regulated—until we start talking about it. As with other topics that in the past have dared not speak their name—cancer, depression, divorce, being gay—we cannot regulate abortion without a more thorough understanding of the subject. It is hard to imagine the possibility of same-sex marriage when the word "homosexual" was unutterable and the word "gay" meant nothing but cheerful. Support for marriage equality came in great part from people's awareness of and love for the same-sex couples around them. More open talk by women about abortion is particularly important now when so many abortion regulations are premised on the view that it is abortion that harms women and not its regulation.

What might a public conversation look like if we took a collective deep breath, dusted ourselves off, and considered anew the values and topics that constitute "talking about abortion"? I don't quite mean consciousness-raising, though there are worse ideas. If a third of all American women will have had an abortion by age forty-five, most people probably know at least one of them, whether they think they do or not.

In urging that we "dust ourselves off," I am not suggesting that we follow the lyrics exactly and "start all over again," unwinding the basic holding in *Roe v. Wade*. I proceed in this book with abortion's basic legality firmly in place. Even so, there is much to discuss about the shape that regulation has taken since

1973. I want to consider aspects of abortion often avoided or rejected outright in existing conversations. I have in mind the impasse wrought by the faux query to pro-life advocates that "You can't really think an embryo is a person?" or the reproach to those who support legal abortion that abortion is murder straight-out and we are living amidst a Holocaust of the unborn. In the pages that follow I mean to take seriously, though not uncritically, the profound meaning of fetal life for those who oppose legal abortion as well as (on the same terms) the profound meaning of women's lives to those who support the abortion right.

In suggesting that public discussion of abortion would be improved by each side's consideration of central concerns of the other, my claim is not that the issue of abortion would be put to bed if we just showed one another a little more respect. After forty years of contention, disagreement about abortion is unlikely to melt away after just one bucket of courtesy. Nor is my aim some sort of cheerful gesture toward compromise. I doubt that there is any harmonic convergence hovering above waiting to sort out the issue if only we would all just listen more carefully.

Nonetheless, to the extent that there is sense and profit in talking about abortion and its regulation—as there must be in a society that takes both the process of democratic lawmaking and the well-being of citizens seriously—there is more to say. Disagreement about abortion is not at its core a problem of civility, though we do know the damage and intransigence that result from uncivil and fractious exchange. Think of the Republican congressman who shouted "baby-killer" on the floor of the House in 2010 (and at a pro-life legislator no less) as part of the uproar over whether Obama's Affordable Care Act would include coverage for abortion. In a civil society, points of affinity are worth pursuing even if they do not conclusively resolve the bitter debate that abortion has become. Even when the stakes appear intractable, things can sometimes be made better. Pro-choice people are not murderers and pro-life people are not idiots.

This book is neither for abortion nor against it. It is *about* abortion. Its aim is to expose how the law often works to make the lives of women with unwanted pregnancies harder than they have to be. Doing this is a complicated process. It requires untangling religious sources of opposition to abortion from secular objections and identifying cultural factors that persuade citizens into or out of a particular camp. It also requires assessing the costs to women of the present legal regime. Certain costs are fairly straightforward: the increased financial costs of traveling an extra hundred miles to the nearest clinic or paying for a motel while waiting out the forty-eight-hour cooling-off period. Others are harder to get at. Over forty states require girls who want an abortion without telling their parents to appear before a judge and prove they are mature enough to decide about abortion. The stress and humiliation to a pregnant teenager of answering questions about her sex life or explaining her mother's depression are not so easily measured. Because women don't like to talk about their abortion experiences, I have had to dig deep with regard to sources, relying on judicial decisions, statutes, media reports, pop culture references, as well as secondary sources from history, sociology, and anthropology. I have also turned to examples of abortion in literature when evidence or textured discussion is unavailable from traditional sources.

Untangling the various strands in our furious national debate reveals much about the role of abortion in American culture—why, for example, abortion law has taken its present, paternalistic shape concerns shading into punitive intentions. The political flavor of abortion regulation—whether respect for the underlying right or determined opposition to it—changes as administrations change. This partisan structure makes it all the more important that part of why they stay mum and feel bad is because a carefully configured structure of regulation welcomes that very outcome. Looking at the dismantled structure—seeing what holds the whole thing up and for what purposes—offers an opportunity for reconstruction along different lines. We might, for example, find it sensible to replace the current regime of shame and apprehension with the kind of quiet dignity that usually attaches when women and men make important life-changing decisions about such things as who to marry or whether or not to have a child.

1

About Abortion

For the last forty years abortion has embedded itself in American consciousness, American politics, and American culture with remarkable durability and reach. Looking only at the first two decades of this century—from Bush to Obama, to use presidential landmarks—abortion has been central to how Americans conceptualize, debate, and sometimes resolve all sorts of official things: nominations to the Supreme Court, asylum policy, health care reform, high school sex education, and what medical services will be provided to American servicewomen stationed overseas. Abortion has also been at the heart of disputes over what products Walmart keeps on its shelves and whether Super Bowl fans should watch or boycott half-time advertisements. Reliably divisive, the subject is never far out of sight. It stands at the ready to stir the pot or, depending on one's viewpoint, to bring sudden clarity to whatever issue is under discussion.

Each year brings new controversies over something to do with abortion. In 2012, a publishing storm arose over whether a *Doonesbury* strip on abortion law in Texas (Nurse to Patient: "You'll need to fill out these forms. Please take a seat in the shaming room") should be carried on the funnies page, the editorial page, or canceled altogether.[1] In 2014, the crowd-funding site GoFundMe shut down a donation site raising money for an abortion. GoFundMe later clarified its terms of service to ban all fundraising related to abortion, gambling, or sorcery.[2] Miss America 2015 made headlines in the pro-life blogosphere for having interned at Planned Parenthood while a college student. "This will cast a shadow on her entire reign," said Carol Tobias, the president of National Right to Life.[3]

There have been provocative rap video lyrics—the 2005 "Can I Live?" sung by a young black man to his abortion-minded mother as she lies on a clinic

1

table next to a tray of surgical instruments ("Hopefully you'll make the right decision / And don't go through with the Knife incision")[4] as well as pop songs like Nicki Minaj's 2014 "All Things Go" in which she muses on an earlier abortion ("My child with Aaron would be sixteen any minute").[5] There is also the slow creep of abortion into television programming, where, aside from *Maude* ages ago and a few modern exceptions, most unwanted pregnancies become either wanted *(Sex and the City)* or unnecessary *(Girls)* or are aborted because the shows are British *(Prime Suspect)* or Canadian *(DeGrassi High)*.[6] There is also the real-life drama of legislative politics: the all-night filibuster in 2013 by sneaker-clad Wendy Davis on the floor of the Texas Senate opposing a ban on abortion before viability, or the 2011 testimony (via ultrasound) of two fetuses before an Ohio legislative committee supporting a ban after the detection of a fetal heartbeat.

Other abortion controversies bring to the surface long-standing social tensions, such as those around race. In 2011, a huge billboard appeared in Manhattan featuring a pretty black child in a sundress above the caption "The Most Dangerous Place for an African American is in the Womb."[7] Similar billboards ("Black Children are an Endangered Species") went up in Atlanta, all part of a pro-life outreach campaign to minority communities denouncing legal abortion as part of a genocidal plan.[8] (Because nothing is simple when the subject involves abortion, the New York billboard generated a controversy of its own: the child's picture had been taken at an unconnected photo shoot at a modeling agency; her mother demanded an apology for its use in an antiabortion campaign.[9]) More recently, the language of Black Lives Matter has been invoked to challenge pregnant black women considering abortion. A headline captures the message: "Planned Parenthood Kills Over 266 Unarmed Black Lives Each Day."[10]

Abortion for the purpose of avoiding a girl (or boy) raises questions about discrimination on the basis of sex, or at least what some identify as sex discrimination and others consider nothing more than gender preference or "gender balancing" among one's offspring. As one woman who sought a girl by selecting embryos through pre-implant genetic diagnosis stated, "I think it is a personal decision for us and it's really nobody else's business. . . . This is the United States and, and you know we get to do everything else we want to do."[11] There is some evidence that a preference for sons has manifested itself in skewed girl–boy birth ratios within certain immigrant communities.[12] Perhaps in response, in 2013 Kansas and North Carolina joined six other states in criminalizing any abor-

Erin Glockner of Pataskala, Ohio undergoes an ultrasound before the Ohio House Health and Aging Committee, March 2, 2011. Glocker's nine-week fetus, seen on the jumbo screen to the right, and its amplified heartbeat were presented to a packed hearing room as testimony to show the materiality of fetal life.

tion performed for the purpose of sex selection. (Whether such legislation is constitutional is another question.)

Things seem to be about abortion even when the link to abortion is not on first glance entirely apparent: a ban on stem cell research, a bomb at the 1996 Atlanta Olympics, the furor over the vegetative Terri Schiavo, and congressional opposition to protective sex trafficking legislation in 2015 or to Zika prevention funding in 2016. Other asserted connections to abortion are not entirely accurate. Consider the assertion that abortion increases a woman's chance of suicide or the Freakonomics claim that the legalization of abortion in 1973 explains a dip in the crime rate eighteen years later.[13]

There are also disputes over the preliminary question of whether an issue has anything to do with abortion at all. Such an example arose in the seemingly unlikely context of stillbirth. In recent years, states across the country have enacted what are called "Missing Angel Acts," statutes that authorize birth certificates for stillborn infants. The acts resulted from lobbying by bereaved parents who argued that a fetal death certificate, the form of documentation that traditionally accompanied stillbirth, failed to capture the true nature of their loss: it was not a fetus who had died but a child who deserved the same official recognition as any other newborn.[14]

Despite enormous sympathy for the parents, concerns were raised that issuing birth certificates for children who never lived—certificates commemorating life before and in the absence of live birth—might over time play a part in the continuing campaign against abortion. Might, for example, states start issuing or even requiring birth certificates for aborted fetuses? Missing Angel supporters insisted that the legislation had nothing to do with abortion but was only about providing solace to grieving parents.[15] The concern remained, however, that it may no longer be possible to cabin the cultural or political meaning of anything to do with fetal life or death in the United States. Compromises were reached and the language of the acts was clarified so that stillborn birth certificates could be issued only on parental request and never in the case of abortion. Still, however compassionately conceived, Missing Angel Acts may nonetheless deepen cultural familiarity with the fetus as a child, and once established the status may take on a life of its own; four states now provide parents with dependent tax deductions in the year of the stillborn baby's birth.[16] The Missing Angel example illustrates how cautious the subject of abortion has made everyone and how attentive citizens have become to even the possibility of a connection to abortion.

Why is it that so many issues end up having an abortion connection and that, once the connection is found, the issues become so susceptible to ignition? So many things in American public life are about abortion because abortion itself is about so many things—things in which people are invested as matters of faith or family, politics or moral principle, gender commitments or professional identity. This exploration of abortion's "aboutness" begins by setting out the central categories into which abortion falls in order to ground the subject culturally and to show how much is at stake—how much bubbles up—when people talk about or around the issue.

What Abortion Is About

Abortion is, in the first instance, a medical procedure. The term "abortion" refers to the induced termination of a pregnancy. A leading obstetrics textbook defines "induced termination of pregnancy" as "the purposeful interruption of an intrauterine pregnancy with the intention other than to produce a live born neonate, and which does not result in a live birth."[17] Where abortion is legal, this is usually performed by a doctor either surgically (with instruments) or, since the development of the drugs mifepristone and misoprostol in the late 1990s, through induced miscarriage, or "medical abortion." Within the medical, research, and public health communities, abortion remains an important aspect of obstetric care. Doctors and other medical professionals provide abortions to women in countries where it is legal, and they treat them after the fact in countries where it is not. Thirteen percent of all deaths included in maternal mortality statistics worldwide are deaths from unsafe abortions.[18]

The characterization of abortion as a medical procedure is important in nonclinical ways as well. It matters to how abortion is treated at law, for like most other forms of medical care, abortion is subject to regulation as part of the state's general interest in the health and welfare of its citizens. Under the state's "police power," all doctors are licensed and all medical facilities inspected. Of course, the regulation of abortion is not quite the same as that of other medical procedures. Since the development of a robust pro-life movement following the Supreme Court's 1973 decision in *Roe v. Wade*, abortion has become the most regulated medical procedure in the United States, with hundreds of laws pouring out of statehouses yearly.[19]

Abortion is also about rights. In *Roe*, the Supreme Court announced that a constitutional right of privacy was "broad enough to encompass a woman's decision whether or not to terminate her pregnancy."[20] Until then, abortion had not been a right under the federal Constitution; it was simply legal in some states and illegal in others. And where it was illegal, abortion was not about rights or medicine. It was about crime and all that follows from that designation: the surveillance, prosecution, and punishment of abortion providers, though, it is interesting to note, not of women themselves. In many ways, abortion is still about crime even though it is no longer criminal. At the individual level, the furtiveness that often surrounds getting an abortion can make it feel criminal, and as a matter of politics, its legality seems ever up for grabs. Certainly abortion is still associated with crime, as sidewalk protesters plead with abortion patients not to kill their babies and as abortion providers are themselves shot and killed.

Abortion is about other claims to rights as well. Some of *Roe*'s most ferocious opponents are defenders of states' rights who contend that the legal status of abortion should have remained a matter for state legislatures, and not federal courts, to determine.[21] Some combine this with an insistence on democratic principles that all decisions about abortion should be made by legislative institutions, whether federal or state. These views about rights and institutional structure often link up with particular theories of constitutional interpretation, such as textualism and originalism. (Thus as part of their pro-life pledge, the 2012 Republican presidential candidates promised to appoint federal judges "committed to restraint and applying the original meaning of the Constitution.)"[22] Because the word "abortion" is unmentioned in the text of the Constitution, there has been ongoing contestation about which (if any) of the provisions or animating values that *are* in the text provide the clearest and most hospitable accommodation for finding a right to abortion. In *Roe v. Wade,* the Supreme Court found that the right derived from a constellation—a "penumbra" in the Court's inventive phrase—of other explicit provisions that protect aspects of privacy, like the Fourth Amendment prohibition on warrantless searches.[23] This view was resisted by those (including the four dissenting justices) who thought a right to choose abortion was itself an invention unsupported by constitutional text or precedent. In an influential 1973 article, constitutional law scholar John Hart Ely put the matter this way: "[*Roe*] is bad because it is bad constitutional law, or rather because it is *not* constitutional law and gives almost no sense of an obligation to try to be."[24]

Other scholars and jurists, quite secure about the Court's authority and the Constitution's scope regarding abortion, suggest that the right might have been more satisfactorily framed not (or not only) in terms of privacy but in terms of other protected interests, such as sex equality.[25] In cases following *Roe v. Wade,* the Supreme Court itself has used the language of liberty and autonomy to characterize the nature of the right at stake. Others have invoked the First Amendment, prohibiting the establishment of religion by the state, and the Thirteenth, invoking the ban on involuntary servitude. Outside the United States, the abortion right has been successfully defended on such grounds as human dignity, the right to health, and the right to life of pregnant women. These have found support in international treaties such as the Convention of the Elimination of All Forms of Discrimination against Women, the International

Covenant on Civil and Political Rights, and the International Covenant on Economic, Social and Cultural Rights, and in the national constitutions of Colombia, Poland, and Peru.[26]

Doctors too have made rights-based claims about abortion. Some argue that their rights to practice medicine and to freedom of expression are unconstitutionally curtailed by statutes prohibiting certain methods of abortion or requiring them to tell their patients that a fetus is a full human being or that it feels pain.[27] Other doctors claim conscience-based rights not to participate in abortion procedures at all or, while medical students, not to learn how to perform one. Supporting that position, in 1996 Congress enacted the Coats Amendment, which protects training hospitals from losing federal funds if they fail to provide abortion training in obstetric residency programs, as otherwise required by the accrediting board for medical schools.[28] Forty-five states and the federal government have now enacted "conscience clauses" permitting physicians and other medical professionals, such as nurses and pharmacists, to refuse to provide or participate in "abortion services."[29] Yet some physicians now assert conscience-based claims in the other direction, arguing that their moral convictions about *providing* abortion services must also be respected if we are to "take conscience seriously."[30]

Last but so not least, there are important claims made about the rights and interests of the fetus. Indeed, many pro-life supporters would say that abortion is only about an embryo or fetus's right to develop until its natural birth—its right to life—and that the rest is noise. Whether the fetus has constitutional rights or moral rights or any other claim to respect, there is no question about its centrality in any discussion of abortion in the United States today. Fetal life, sometimes just called "life," now competes with—or has perhaps overtaken—pregnancy as the operative essence of what an abortion is about. And although the Supreme Court in *Roe v. Wade* rejected the claim that a fetus is a legal person, the court has since held that states may decidedly take fetal interests into account in regulating abortion and may do so from the moment of conception.[31]

For many people, abortion is about religion. Because America is a religious nation with a robust flow between faith and politics, this category of abortion's "aboutness" matters greatly. For some, abortion is about sin. In the 1995 papal encyclical *Evangelium Vitae* (Gospel of Life), Pope John Paul II declared that the modern world is now engaged in a struggle between a Culture of Life ("unconditional respect for the right to life of every innocent person from conception to natural death") and the Culture of Death ("a veritable structure of sin").[32]

This position has had consequences in the temporal world of politics. In 2005, former Pope Benedict XVI, when still Bishop Ratzinger in his position as Prefect for the Congregation for the Doctrine of the Faith, declared that "a Catholic would be guilty of formal cooperation in evil, and so unworthy to present himself for Holy Communion" were he or she to vote for a candidate because of the candidate's permissive stand on abortion.[33] Thus during the 2004 presidential campaign, the Roman Catholic bishop of Boston urged priests to deny Holy Communion to Senator John Kerry, and the bishop of Colorado extended the ban to Catholics who vote for candidates who support legal abortion.[34] This was a powerful shot across the bow as candidates and voters alike learned that they might place themselves "outside of full communion with the Church and so jeopardize their salvation."[35] During the 2012 presidential campaign, Vice President Joe Biden received a similar warning. In 2016 vice presidential candidate Tim Kaine was not denied communion, despite the urgings of Richmond area priests, though he was accused by the Archbishop of Kansas of being a "cafeteria Catholic" who picks and chooses among the Church's teachings for political convenience.[36]

We do not yet know Pope Francis's position, if any, on Catholic candidates or voters with regard to abortion beliefs or practices. His statements about abortion so far have been that the Church might lessen its obsession with the topic; that abortion is horrific; and that Catholic priests may absolve women who repent the grave sin of abortion.[37] Cathleen Kaveny, professor of law and theology, suggests that Pope Francis's general focus on the context in which abortion (and other sins) take place may situate the Church's stance "on key cultural war issues in the broader frame of Catholic social teaching, which is concerned with the fate of vulnerable persons across the board, whether they are threatened by abortion, loss of income, or geographic catastrophe due to climate change."[38]

Of course, not all religions oppose abortion as a matter of doctrine, and doctrine itself sometimes changes over time. The Roman Catholic Church long held that ensoulment, or the beginning of human life, occurred around the time of quickening; according to Aquinas, ensoulment occurred forty days after conception for boys and ninety days after conception for girls. Only in 1974 was ensoulment relocated to the moment of conception. It is also worth remembering that official doctrine, whether of the Vatican or any other governing theological body, does not always represent the views or practices of ordinary worshippers regarding abortion. There are, for example, Catholics for Choice as well as the less well-known Jewish Pro-Life Foundation.[39] Thus there may be division (and reconciliation) within the laity, or even within a single person, as seen in a 1984 lecture at Notre Dame by former New York governor Mario Cuomo. Cuomo sought to distinguish between private religion and public morality: "The Catholic who holds political office in a pluralistic democracy— who is elected to serve Jews and Muslims, atheists and Protestants, as well as Catholics—bears special responsibility. He or she undertakes to help create conditions under which all can live with a maximum of dignity and with a reasonable degree of freedom; where everyone who chooses may hold beliefs different from specifically Catholic ones—sometimes contradictory to them; where the laws protect people's right to divorce, to use birth control and even to choose abortion."[40]

In the last few decades, strong pro-life convictions have taken hold in such Protestant denominations as the Southern Baptists Convention in Texas and the Lutheran Church Missouri Synod, both formerly agnostic on the issue.[41] (Indeed, for much of the twentieth century, Protestants were unlikely to support any issue that Catholics were for.) The antiabortion turn within some Protestant denominations, particularly among Fundamentalists and Evangelicals, has become a powerful political force as faith-based reasoning has moved more directly into the legislative sphere. Sociologist Robert Wuthnow explains in *Rough Country: How Texas Became America's Most Powerful Bible-Belt State* that the campaign for a moral America in the 1970s and 1980s resulted in religion itself becoming more public, shifting from a focus "on private belief and personal morality to being more about politics and the collective affairs of the nation."[42] Yet there are variations among those of the same denomination. While most Evangelicals oppose abortion absolutely, there is also a movement of "New Evangelicals" who believe that a more tempered opposition to abortion can also be "coherent and Christ-like."[43] The religious terrain for abortion is complicated indeed. I want here simply to acknowledge that abortion in the United States is often and crucially a matter of the ability of organized religion to shape and influence America's political life as well as its spiritual one.

Although often connected to religion, for some abortion is at core a secular matter of morality. Arguments based on morality focus on two initial questions: what is the point at which deliberately ending fetal life is immoral and what is it that makes that particular point the salient one? For some, this point is conception. For others, morally protected personhood sets in later in pregnancy, whether at quickening (around eighteen to twenty weeks), consciousness (a developmental progression of sensory awareness beginning around twenty weeks), or around twenty-four weeks when the fetus acquires sentience by virtue of its neurological development.[44] These characteristics are anchored variously in conceptions of fetal humanity, personhood, and dignity. Wherever the moment is marked, ending fetal life thereafter is regarded as a moral wrong.[45] Philosopher Rosalind Hursthouse warns that "to think of abortion as nothing but the killing of something that does not matter, or as nothing but the exercise of some right or rights one has, or as the incidental means to some desirable state of affairs, is to do something callous and light-minded, the sort of thing that no virtuous and wise person would do."[46] Of course, moral propositions are not always advanced in the measured tones of philosophers. Mississippi Supreme Court Justice Easley put the case rather more forcefully in a 2001 opinion: "Ever since the abomination known as *Roe v. Wade* . . . became the law of the land, the morality of our great nation has slipped ever downwards to the point that the decision to spare the life of an unborn child has become an arbitrary decision based on convenience."[47]

Of course, the invocation of morality does not in itself tip the scale against abortion. Many women regard a decision to have an abortion as the moral thing to do, as do the doctors who perform abortions and did so even when the procedure was illegal.[48] Women's decisions may be complicated calculations, perhaps taken against a background conviction that abortion in general is wrong but that the decision to proceed *in this case* is acceptable—thus one woman's description of her decision to terminate as "wrong but the right thing to do."[49] Other women are content to omit the "wrong" altogether, secure about the moral soundness of their decision without qualification.

But let us return to Mississippi and Justice Easley's characterization of abortion as an "arbitrary decision based on convenience."[50] In singling out "convenience" as the motive for abortion, Justice Easley may have in mind something like the ease or casualness with which an unwanted pregnancy can be erased through abortion, as though it and the sex that led to it had simply never happened. And so we come at last to sex, for whatever else abortion may be about, it is necessarily about sex. Views about sex—with whom, how often, for what purpose—are often tucked into people's views on abortion and so into their views on abortion law. For those who believe that the purpose of sexual intercourse is procreative, sex for any other reason is, as natural law philosopher John Finnis states, "the pursuit of an illusion."[51] In her study of California pro-life abortion activists in the early 1980s, sociologist Kristin Luker found that removing the procreative potential of sex through abortion or contraception was "to turn the world upside down."[52]

In addition to the procreative / non-procreative divide, abortions are sorted according to whether the underlying sex was voluntary or involuntary. In the days when abortion was illegal, states regularly made exceptions for pregnancies resulting from involuntary sex, that is, from rape or incest. The position produces a rather sharp inequality among fetuses, but the exceptions still have currency. In 2012, thirty-two states that as a general matter refuse to pay for abortions for Medicaid patients will do so in cases of rape or incest.[53]

Concern about abortion's relation to sex is especially keen when it comes to pregnant teenagers. There is a social consensus that most teenagers who get pregnant have been a little too frisky (and irresponsible) for their own good and should not be able to have an abortion automatically just because they want one. In contrast to other places—all of Western Europe, say—where teenage sexuality is accepted as developmentally normal, in the United States it is still taken as a sign of trouble, particularly for girls. This explains why a young woman's contraceptive preparedness (carrying a condom) is sometimes regarded as provocative rather than prudent behavior; consider that until 2014 possession of a condom could be introduced in court in New York City as evidence of intent to engage in prostitution.[54] The link to sex also explains why in the 2000s under President George W. Bush's Culture of Life, the subject of contraception was excluded from high school sex education classes in favor of federally funded "abstinence only" programs, as (some) teenagers pledged to save themselves for marriage.[55] It turns out that abstinence programs like The Silver Ring Thing made little difference to teenage pregnancy rates, even in Texas. If too many kids take the pledge, the cachet of virginity diminishes: "Pledging works when it embeds kids in a minority community, when it gives them a sense of unique identity."[56] Texas, the home state of abstinence-only education, experienced a serious uptick in sexually transmitted diseases.[57] There are more costs to unprotected sex than just an unwanted pregnancy.

Sex in America is confusing, for despite our highly sexualized culture, teenage girls aren't really supposed to do it. They are supposed to be the kind of daughters their parents imagine them to be. This explains the popularity of the parental involvement statutes in place across the country, which provide that before a pregnant minor can legally consent to an abortion she must notify or get written consent from one or both of her parents, depending on the state. The idea is that parents should be involved in this difficult moment in their daughter's life, and that law can make that connection happen. Indeed, 67 percent of pregnant minors talk to parents or to some other adult even in the absence of a statute.[58] Yet for girls who are hesitant to bring their parents in, compulsion may not be the best way to bring about the conversation. Nevertheless, that is the law. It seems clear even now that parental involvement statutes reveal anxieties not only about abortion but about teenage sexuality in relation to parental authority. An addendum: to stay on the right side of *Roe* legislatures added an exception: girls may petition the local court for permission instead of involving parents. If the judge finds the girl is sufficiently mature, he grants the petition. If he finds she is not, he rejects the petition and the immature minor marches on to motherhood. (I use the masculine pronoun for judges and others throughout to avoid pronoun confusion, since most pregnant persons are female.)[59]

The widespread enactment of parental involvement statutes illustrates another important feature of abortion in America. It is that abortion is about legislative lawmaking. Since *Roe* was decided by the Supreme Court in 1973, an avalanche of statutes regulating abortion provision, procedures, and practice have poured forth from statehouses, with hundreds more in the planning.[60] In addition to legislative action, abortion has also become the subject of populist lawmaking processes, sometimes called "direct democracy." Personhood amendments and other abortion-related measures regularly appear as initiatives and referenda on state ballots. In November 2008, voters in South Dakota, Colorado, and California were respectively called upon to decide whether all abortions should be banned, whether the word "person" should be defined as starting at conception, and whether parental notification is a good idea. Since then personhood measures have appeared on ballots in Mississippi and North Dakota.[61] Although such measures have yet to succeed, all this voting by legislators and by citizens shows the popular perception and acceptance of abortion as an intensely political subject, one that is unsettled and subject to near perpetual review. Officeholders from school board members all the way up regularly campaign on the issue.

Abortion is not only a political issue but a partisan one. Although there are outliers, to be a Republican office holder, certainly since the Reagan administration, has meant opposing a woman's right to choose abortion; being a Democrat means your party supports that right. One consequence of such encompassing alignment is that abortion-related issues, such as federal funding for Planned Parenthood, now sink or swim legislatively depending on voters' views on other issues that may have nothing to do with abortion, such as the economy, but that get candidates elected along with the party platform.[62] Rank-and-file party members are more diverse in their views on abortion, although the party splits are mirror images of one another: just under 30 percent of Republicans identify as pro-choice and just under 30 percent of Democrats identify as pro-life.[63]

At the federal level, the partisan grip on abortion has resulted in abrupt and destabilizing policy shifts concerning women's reproductive health. Similar partisanship on abortion has emerged in state politics as well.[64] A good federal example is the zigzagging path of abortion provision to servicewomen in military hospitals overseas. Following the decision in *Roe v. Wade,* in 1975 the Department of Defense directed all military medical facilities to provide abortion services to pregnant soldiers who sought them.[65] In 1978, a Republican Congress then prohibited the use of federal funds to pay for abortion except in cases of rape, incest, long-lasting physical damage, or where the soldier's life was at risk. Servicewomen could, however, use privately purchased health care insurance to pay for an abortion.[66] In 1981, a new Republican Congress went further and dropped the rape and incest exceptions; in 1988, the Reagan administration got rid of the private payment option. Soon after taking office in 1993, President Clinton lifted the ban on private payments for abortion in military hospitals provided that the procedure was legal under local law. This was no small problem in Iraq, Afghanistan, or Korea, where in 2010 some 200,000 U.S. troops were stationed.[67] In 1995, Congress again under Republican leadership banned all abortions in military hospitals, except in cases of rape, incest, or life endangerment, and then only if the woman paid for it herself. This returned things to the 1978 status quo. Finally (for now), after years of lobbying by veterans, active service members, and women's groups, and newly focused attention on the endemic problem of sexual assaults in the military, Congress passed the Shaheen Amendment to the 2013 National Defense Authorization Act. This much heralded amendment simply reinstated the right of servicewomen to use their military health care insurance to pay for an abortion, and again only in cases of rape or incest.

Similar partisan to-and-fro has gone on with U.S. aid to the United Nations Population Fund (UNFPA), which funds family planning organizations around the world. From 1985 to 1992, U.S. funding was rescinded under Presidents Reagan and George H. W. Bush on the grounds that the UNFPA supported family planning programs in China, a country deemed to have "a program of coercive abortion or involuntary sterilization." In 1993, President

Clinton reinstated the funding on the grounds that UNFPA did not assist coercive abortions in China; in 2001, President George W. Bush reversed the
Clinton policy; and in 2009, President Obama reversed the Bush reversal.[68]
Present and future administrations will put their own stamp on these and
other issues, such as federal policies regarding stem cell research.

Abortion permeates not only legislative and presidential politics but the judicial branch as well. A candidate's record on abortion (or predictions about
his future record) increasingly figures into his chances for nomination and
appointment to federal or state benches.[69] In states that elect rather than appoint their judges, candidates run on the abortion issue outright. Consider the
campaign slogan for a Kentucky district judgeship: "Jed Deters is a Pro-Life
Candidate."[70] Mr. Deters lost the contest but was censured by the Kentucky
Judicial Commission for ethical violations: his campaign statements had "committed or appeared to commit" him beforehand with respect to issues likely to
come before the court, such as petitions filed by pregnant teenagers in parental
bypass hearings.[71] In upholding Deters's censure, the Kentucky Supreme Court
expressed "no doubt" that Deters had intended to commit himself on pro-life
issues: he had "freely testified that 'any good Catholic is pro-life,' that Kenyon
County has a high percentage of Catholic voters, and that his statement . . .
would 'hopefully' give him a 'distinct edge in the race,' since 'you're in it to win.
You do what it takes.' "[72] The case provides a taste of abortion realpolitik. Whatever one's moral or religious views on abortion, there is also its strategic use if
one is "in it to win."

But abortion is more than a handy item in partisan toolboxes. It is a deeply
personal decision that nearly a million American women make every year as each
confronts a pregnancy that is or has become unwanted. The numbers are meaningful. Almost a third of all women in the United States will have an abortion at
some point in their reproductive lives—that thirty-year stretch in which pregnancy is possible over and over and over again. The number of women who
have thought about abortion is likely much larger; four million women in the
United States have babies each year, and surely some of them will have considered doing otherwise. Even Sarah Palin, pregnant with her fifth child at age
forty-four, acknowledged what she called the "fleeting thought": "I'm out of
town. No one knows I'm pregnant. No one would ever have to know."[73]

Abortion is therefore about all the things women consider as they assess the
place of pregnancy and motherhood in their lives at this particular moment in
time. These considerations include a woman's faith, her finances, and her future.

They may also include an assessment of her relationship with an existing (or non-existing) partner and obligations to the children she already has; more than a third of the women who terminate a pregnancy are mothers already. A decision to keep or to terminate a pregnancy is not about abstract conceptions of motherhood, as in an imagined pregnancy where love and resources and cute baby clothes abound and everything is perfect. It is an unflinchingly concrete calculation about family composition, intimate relations, and self-conception. The calculation may well factor in spiritual or cultural commitments; for some women, these are decisive. Whatever the matrix, pregnancy puts a set of questions on the table. How many children will she mother? Is a particular man going to become a father? What impact will a decision either way have on the shape of her life now, in a year, in ten?

The introduction of motherhood into the mix of what abortion is about leads us to sex (biological sex) and to gender. Abortion implicates both. She gets to make the ultimate decision not only because it is her pregnant laboring body (a matter of sexual difference) but also because of the profound social significance of mothering over time (a matter of gender). As the Supreme Court soberly noted in *Roe,* "maternity, or additional offspring, may force upon the woman a distressful life and future. Mental and physical health may be taxed by child care."[74] In his decision, Justice Blackmun did not use the word "gender" in explaining the relationship between motherhood and stressful lives, nonetheless he offered up the classic example of gendered social arrangements: the assignment of child raising to women. And as we know from social science data and from participant observation, the burdens of child rearing rather than child birthing are what explain the massive differences in how men and women are able to proceed with their adult lives.[75]

To be sure, many men and women prefer traditional gender arrangements, that seemingly natural scheme where men (if no longer quite hunters) and women (no longer hearth-bound gatherers) still occupy distinctive and, for some, appropriate roles. In her study of California abortion activists in the early 1980s, Kristin Luker found that pro-life activists believe that men and women are intrinsically different: women are meant to mother and fathers are meant to support them in that endeavor.[76] For those who feel anxious about the stability of this once reliable boy–girl scheme, abortion can be deeply unsettling. It frees women to act more like men. As the Supreme Court stated so matter-of-factly in *Planned Parenthood v. Casey,* "the ability of women to participate equally in the economic and social life of the Nation has been facilitated by their ability to control their reproductive lives."[77] This equal participation (or at least less unequal participation) is good news for some and less welcome by others. The increased status that results from women's participation in the wage-earning market may translate into a greater measure of authority in the home; women unencumbered by children may become more competitive at work; and so on.[78]

A bolder way to frame the matter is to think about abortion in relation to women's power. There is no question that the right to decide about abortion gives women significant authority over their own lives. But that same authority can also create relationships and obligations for others. Certain men will (or won't) become fathers; certain children will (or won't) acquire siblings; certain family wills will (or won't) be amended. Each potential relationship—new daughter, brother, grandchild—may be regarded as the best news ever or a source of deep dismay. But whatever the reception by others, the basic decision about a new child coming into the family has been entrusted to women as a matter of law.

In addition to creating new relationships and obligations for others, women's authority to decide whether a pregnancy will lead to a birth also has a larger metaphysical sweep. Anthropologist Rayna Rapp has observed that deciding about abortion "forces each woman to act as a moral philosopher . . . adjudicating the standards guarding entry into the human community for which she serves as normalizing gatekeeper."[79] Rapp studied termination decisions following a diagnosis of fetal disability, but her point holds more generally. Control over whether and what kind of new persons will come into being—the gatekeeping of human existence—is powerful stuff indeed. The particularized application of that power explains the opposition to abortion by some disability rights advocates concerned that as prenatal testing becomes ever more refined, whole categories of persons—those with Down syndrome, for example—may simply disappear. But even regarding more ordinary pregnancies, the radical character of this primal gatekeeping may disturb those not used to thinking in terms of women's superior authority.

Most cohabiting and married women discuss unwanted or unplanned pregnancies with their partners, and there is often agreement (or sufficient acquiescence) in the resolution. But as a matter of public accountability, the decision is hers. The decisional task is made the harder for some women by statutes that identify the pregnant woman as a mother before there is a born child. (It is necessary to add the qualifier "born" for clarity's sake since the word "child" is now used prenatally.) Labeling pregnant women as mothers also intensifies the wrongfulness of abortion as a public matter. From a pro-life perspective, abortion is not just a killing but a killing by the victim's *mother,* and the law must do all it can to prevent this hideous maternal practice. So whether or not the decision was in fact made jointly, women, and not their husbands or partners, are held responsible. In this way, public discussion about abortion remains highly gendered.

Each of these characterizations of what abortion is about—medicine, religion, law, politics, sexual culture, parental authority, intimate relationships, gender dynamics, and women's power—provokes its own set of anxieties and controversies. Within medical schools, there are debates about whether abortion should be a required subject or an optional one.[80] Within law, parties argue about how to square a woman's right to choose an abortion with the First Amendment rights of sidewalk protestors urging her not to. Within religion and moral philosophy, theologians and scholars dispute whether conceptions of dignity or personhood are poisoned or refined by the abortion debate. Things get even more complicated when conceptions of abortion from one sphere bump into those from another. These collisions happen all the time and in kaleidoscopic combinations: rights and religions, medicine and morality, commerce and culture, politics and everything.

The classification of abortion as one kind of issue or another matters tremendously for how abortion disputes proceed: who gets to weigh in, the available scope of remedies, the resonances within public discourse, and how interests are balanced. If, for example, opposition to abortion is based on a religious belief, it may benefit from whatever statutory or constitutional rights attach to the protected category of sincerely held religious beliefs. This was the basis of the Supreme Court's 2014 decision in *Burwell v. Hobby Lobby Stores,* challenging the Patient Protection and Affordable Care Act. The Court held that the religious opposition to abortion by the owners of a private, for-profit company exempted the company from having to provide its employees with insurance coverage for contraceptive methods that the owners regarded as abortifacients.[81] Hobby Lobby could not have invoked the protection of the Religious Freedom Restoration Act—the statute on which the owners brought their claim—if they had objected to contraception devices on moral or philosophical grounds. (I put to the side the question of how a for-profit company can have a religion.)

Before advocates can draw upon the full range of structural, social, or doctrinal advantages of a particular category, there must be some consensus about how the category is defined and what conduct it includes. Consider the "morning-after pill," a form of emergency contraception (EC) that if taken within seventy-two hours after unprotected sexual intercourse (and the sooner after, the better) reduces the likelihood of pregnancy by 89 percent. In 2003, a distinguished U.S. Food and Drug Administration (FDA) Advisory Committee recommended by a vote of twenty-four to three that the drug be approved for over-the-counter sales. The committee explained that increased access to EC was likely to prevent at least some of the three million yearly unintended pregnancies and that this, in turn, would prevent some abortions as well.[82] A question arose, however, as to whether emergency contraception was itself a form of abortion. If the drug prevents fertilization (egg and sperm never meet up), as evidence shows that it does, then it is by definition a form of contraception: nothing has been conceived. But if the drug prevents the implantation of an already fertilized egg into the uterine lining (as no evidence shows it doesn't), then the claim was that the morning-after pill disrupts an existing pregnancy and is "nothing other than a chemically induced abortion."[83] (States differ on whether pregnancy begins at fertilization or implantation.) The political furor over whether to classify the drug as contraception or as abortifacient led to a three-year delay—characterized by the Government Accountability Office as a "tortuous and highly irregular process"—in the FDA's eventual over-the-counter approval of EC.[84]

Another example of how categories matter in law is the question of whether abortion is medical in nature or whether it is "medicalized." The latter term refers to the practice of treating non-medical aspects of abortion as though they were medical in order to gain the regulatory benefits of the category.[85] Recall that under its police power the state has significant authority to regulate matters of health, including the practice of medicine. But are required pre-abortion disclosures about the benefits of adoption *medical* in nature so that they fall within the state's permissible regulatory scope? A close cousin of that question was answered in the Supreme Court's 2016 decision in *Whole Woman's Health v. Hellerstedt,* where the Court carefully considered whether certain standards imposed on abortion clinics by Texas had anything to do with improving women's health. The Court found they did not. For now, it is enough to see that defining and characterizing what abortion writ large is about is crucial to how it can be regulated.

Imagery and Ideology

Abortion is about us in still another way. The signs and symbols associated with abortion occupy real physical space, and like the arguments heard on talk radio and talk television, visual cues too influence how Americans have come to think about the subject. Drivers see billboards celebrating fetal life, extolling adoption as an alternative, and urging pregnant women not to smoke. Special pro-life billboard trucks trawl the highways displaying pictures of aborted fetal parts. Cars are festooned with bumper stickers informing motorists that "Abortion Stops a Beating Heart" or that everyone should just "Mind Your Own Uterus."[86] There are official "Choose Life" license plates and license plate holders and special pop-up "cemeteries" where commemorative flags are planted for aborted fetuses.[87] City dwellers are more likely to find their abortion visuals in newsstand headlines and on public transportation. The cover of a 2010 *In Touch* magazine featured Sarah and Bristol Palin holding their respective babies ("We're Glad We Chose Life").[88] In 2012, subway cars in New York and buses in St. Louis displayed placards from the antiabortion "Abortion Changes You" campaign ("A grandchild is missing").[89] Fellow citizens wear tiny fetal feet lapel pins and a few others don "I Had an Abortion" T-shirts.[90]

Babies too are part of abortion's visual presence. Think of the televised Palin baby lovingly passed among the candidate's family members as his mother pledged her support for special needs children during her vice presidential acceptance speech at the 2008 Republican National Convention. And long before a baby's actual birth, ultrasound images create their own zone of affection. These images are now a familiar presence throughout the culture, displayed not only at right to life rallies but on colleagues' desks nestled among snapshots of the other children.[91] Even little kids are socialized into fetal imagery; ultrasound scans are now found in toddler board books such as the charming *Waiting for Baby*.[92]

Seeing—or what one court called "sensory and contemporaneous observance"—has become an important mechanism by which abortion is understood and how it is regulated.[93] As a general proposition, the law puts great trust in seeing directly, or "eyewitness evidence." Seeing something is understood to make the thing observed more real and testimony about it more reliable. Although this has long been true inside the courtroom, lawmakers have begun to recognize the power of seeing outside of court, no longer for purposes of obtaining testimony but rather as a method of persuasion.[94] The best abortion example is mandatory ultrasound statutes now in play in one form

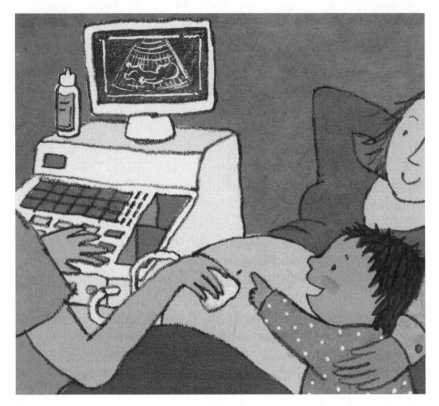

"Is that the baby inside your tummy?" Brightly colored pictures in the twelve-page board book *Waiting for Baby* answer questions posed by a toddler interlocutor about what this new baby will eat, wear, and look like, and what it looks like now.

or another in some twenty-five states. These statutes require doctors to offer pregnant women a look at the ultrasound scan of their unborn child before they may legally consent to the abortion.

A clever move perhaps, yet we should not too readily accept that fetal imagery works just as lawmakers expect it to work (woman sees image, woman changes mind). Sometimes the information imparted by an ultrasound may be the very thing that decides a woman to end, rather than to continue, her pregnancy. Thus while legislators may insist that pregnant women undergo the ultrasound with the hope that the image will stun her into rejecting abortion should she choose to look, responses to a scan depend on a range of factors: the wantedness of the pregnancy, the woman's reproductive history, her resilience, and the narrative she may have constructed around her decision.

Although abortion has been the subject of noisy public debate for some forty years, at more intimate levels, abortion talk remains decidedly muted. For much of the twentieth century and into our own, the experience of abortion was not an easy subject to talk about, whether among friends, within families, or between partners. In a 2010 *Guardian* column, author Lindy West pondered why she never talked about her abortion: "I live in a progressive city, I have a fiercely pro-choice social circle and family, I write confessionally about myself for a living . . . I know about who has a vagina infection, whose boyfriend's penis bends weird, who used to do drugs, who still does. And I know how all of them feel about abortion, policy wise. But I don't know who has had one, and they don't know about mine."[95]

The difficulties of discussing abortion have several distinct causes. There is the immediate provocation of vocabulary: Termination of pregnancy or abortion? Pro-life or anti-choice? Fetus or unborn child? Pregnant woman or mother? The choice of one phrase or the other is not only a matter of political or philosophical commitment but often one of context. Few folks when handed an ultrasound scan by a smiling cousin or colleague are likely to offer congratulations on the friend's *fetus*. To do so isn't in the spirit of the moment; it misses the sense of occasion that news of a wanted pregnancy is meant to convey.

The distinction between "fetus" and "baby" is also crucial when statutory language is at stake, even though political concerns and objectives are now at work. Sometimes the use of a term is negotiated, as in the drafting of the Missing Angel Acts. Other times there is no negotiation. Under George W. Bush's administration, prenatal care was included within federally funded state insurance programs by defining the word "child" to include "an individual under the age of 19 including the period from conception to birth." No question that funding for prenatal care is a good thing. But the statutory language does cultural work beyond eligibility rules when an embryo is identified as the patient for prenatal care, and the mother (who delivers most of the care) drops out. Of course, prenatal life is not always referred to in just one way (embryo) or the other (child), even by the same people or regarding the same pregnancy. The vocabulary of reproduction often progresses in stages. Couples typically move into the language of "baby" as a pregnancy develops, provided that the pregnancy is coming along well. In contrast, couples with histories of miscarriage sometimes distance themselves from the language of "baby" until they are sure this pregnancy will continue.

Another reason that abortion may not be much talked about at a personal level is that it remains a private matter, a woman's business to discuss or not as she chooses. The subject involves intensely personal matters: a woman's beliefs, her commitments, her body, her life. Reticence to talk about an abortion, either before or after the procedure, can well be understood as an exercise in privacy. However, although privacy seems a comfortable and familiar way to think about abortion nondisclosure, I suggest that nondisclosure in the context of abortion may have more in common with secrecy than with privacy. We might think of privacy as the right or the preference to keep something to one's self, whether as a matter of law, tradition, or even etiquette. In contrast, secrecy is differently motivated: it stems less from a preference for privacy than from fear of the consequences of revelation. It is the idea that one *must* conceal something that trips us into the domain of secrecy.

And there is harm aplenty in revealing that a woman is planning or has had an abortion. Many women rightly fear that disclosure puts them at risk for harassment, stigmatization, or the downgrading of reputation, and they are not wrong. As a Fourth Circuit judge observed in a 2002 case involving the confidentiality of medical records, "Women seeking abortions in South Carolina have a great deal more to fear than stigma. The protests designed to harass and intimidate women from entering abortion clinics, and the violence inflicted on abortion providers, provide women with ample reason to fear for their physical safety."[96] Keeping quiet about abortion is often a sensible response as things stand now. It keeps women safe, or at least safer, from the many harms of disclosure. Yet while keeping women safe is a good thing, the silence also works to keep abortion disreputable. Not only does this work a hardship on individual woman, but the reluctance to talk about abortion has an important trickle-up effect. To the extent that women feel unable to talk quietly but openly about the particulars of an abortion—how they got pregnant, the nature of their deliberations, how they negotiated the logistics and the law—the quality of public discussion about abortion is compromised, and this in turn makes informed political discussion less likely.

Much of current abortion regulation operates to punish women for their decision to terminate a pregnancy. This is so even though abortion has not been a crime since 1973, and even then, women themselves were rarely included within criminal abortion statutes.[97] Yet although states can no longer criminalize abortion, a fair number of them have decided to legislate as close to the legal line as possible. In this way non-criminal requirements can create something like sanctions, and this time for women too. A network of rules whose purpose is to persuade pregnant women that what they are doing is wrong can make securing an abortion feel shady and crime-like. Clinics are isolated from the regular medical facilities that provide most other forms of health care. In many communities, strangers fly in to do what is often described as "dirty work." After consenting, women must wait twenty-four or seventy-two hours to consent again. So although abortion now formally falls outside the criminal justice system, its regulation produces a civil law version of what legal sociologist Malcolm Feely identified in the criminal context as "process as punishment."[98] How one is treated along the way to a hearing or trial can be punitive indeed, and the same is so with getting an abortion. Through the treatment of pregnant teens and required description of fetal body parts, the regulation of abortion patients creates circumstances that may fall short of formal retribution but that register as punishment nonetheless.

Even if we accept that the present deluge of abortion regulation is enacted with the genuine interests of women at heart by saving them from the suffering of later learning that they have killed their own unborn kin—the "woman-protective restrictions" that Professor Reva Siegel has decisively parsed—the regulations are still based on a particular conception of women.[99] Much of the regulation takes as its starting point that pregnant women and girls do not exactly understand what they are doing when they decide to end a pregnancy. That is why they must be told when human life starts, that a fetus is a child, that it has a heartbeat and maybe fingernails, and that adoption would work to make everyone happy.

This book is guided by a very different premise. Women—even young women—understand very well what an abortion is. They understand that abortion ends pregnancy and that if they have an abortion, they will not have a baby: that is its very point. The significance of an abortion decision may differ from woman to woman and from girl to girl, but in deciding whether to continue a pregnancy, each will draw upon her own sensibilities, circumstances, and beliefs. But as with other intimate decisions and commitments—who to marry, whether to pray, how to vote, what to do with one's life in matters large and small—women themselves are best able to decide what is at stake. This returns us to the question of what abortion is about. The list is long, and the categories complex and challenging. But they are not impenetrable, and we can begin to unravel them.

2

The Law from *Roe* Forward

On January 23, 1973, the U.S. Supreme Court held that a woman's right to choose abortion was protected under the Constitution. This meant that states could no longer make abortion a crime, as twenty-nine of them still did in one form or another. Before the decision in *Roe v. Wade,* women determined not to continue their pregnancy had a limited range of options. Those with "contacts" could obtain abortions from licensed doctors here and there who performed them surreptitiously, some as a matter of conscience and others as a matter of profit.[1] In states that provided exceptions for pregnancies resulting from rape or that put the mother's life at risk, women could try to bring themselves within one of the exceptions by showing they had reported the rape to the police or because a sympathetic psychiatrist would say they were suicidal. But women whose pregnancies or circumstances were unexceptional had to travel. Organizations like "Jane," the Society for Humane Abortion, and the Clergy Consultation Service helped women navigate these journeys, providing medical referrals, transportation schedules, and sometimes funding.[2] Mexico and Japan were common West Coast abortion "destinations." New York (or Europe for the wealthy) offered legal abortions on the East Coast. New York state was a particular draw in that it had no residency requirement, in contrast to Washington and Colorado where legality extended only to women who already lived in those states. None of these options—"lonely, tragic but . . . necessary pilgrimages"—was surefire or cost-free for the women who took them.[3] Each brought some combination of isolation, ill treatment, high costs, and often enduring shame.[4]

Roe v. Wade changed much of this and quickly. In the year the case was handed down, the number of legal abortions performed in the United States increased from 587,600 to 745,400, a jump of 27 percent from the previous year.[5] The geography of abortion also changed as abortion provision was redistributed across a greater number of states. In 1972, New York reported 300,000 legal abortions; in 1973 the number was 216,000, as women who once had to travel could now turn to facilities and physicians closer to home.[6] There was also a massive decline in maternal mortality and obstetric injury. Thirty-nine illegal abortion deaths were reported in 1972, nineteen in 1973, and three in 1975; emergency rooms saw far fewer cases of sepsis and uterine perforation from illegal abortions.[7] All this shows how differently women were able to proceed with their lives on account of the decision in *Roe v. Wade*.

The legal history leading up to *Roe* began with the English common-law rule that abortion before quickening was not a crime. Historians have detailed how during the mid nineteenth century early abortion was brought within the criminal law as legislatures sought to protect women from dangerous abortifacients and as doctors sought to establish moral and professional authority over abortion by securing it within their exclusive jurisdiction.[8] There is a rich twentieth-century history of a more comprehensive campaign for women's reproductive rights—the legalization of contraceptives, for example—of which abortion became a part.[9] Such scholarship takes us up to and into *Roe* itself: how the case came about, how it was litigated, how the decision was crafted, and the role that it continues to play in America's constitutional jurisprudence, politics, and reputation abroad.[10]

Recognizing the foundational significance of the law's earlier history, this chapter focuses on the progress of abortion law from *Roe* on. Depending on how one counts, the Supreme Court has decided around fifteen significant abortion cases since *Roe v. Wade*. Thus we see what Linda Greenhouse called the "naive optimism" of Justice Blackmun, who scribbled on a draft of the decision that as regards abortion, "it will be an unsettled period for a while."[11]

A trio of cases—*Roe v. Wade* in 1973, *Planned Parenthood v. Casey* in 1993, and *Whole Woman's Health v. Hellerstedt* in 2016—are the pillars of abortion jurisprudence, with subsidiary cases filling in the complete picture, a picture that is shadowed by abortion politics at every turn. Charting that yet unfinished path provides a framework for understanding where abortion law stands now, how it got that way, and what might be imagined for the coming decades.

The discussion here considers not only the legal rules that directly regulate the provision of abortion or what is traditionally considered abortion law, but also nonreproductive areas of law where the fact, or even a hint, of an abortion connection matters to how the law is interpreted and applied. My examples are drawn from immigration, torts, criminal law, and free speech. Within each of these areas, two themes are of special interest. The first concerns cases where an abortion decision is used to punish or reward a litigant. The second concerns how the display of fetal imagery—on the highway, in the workplace, at trial—intersects with other recognized interests and rights.

From *Roe* to *Casey*

The decision in *Roe v. Wade* did more than clear away abortion's basic criminality. It also provided a detailed framework for legislatures and courts to assess the constitutionality of subsequent abortion regulations that were likely to arise. This form of guidance introduces an interesting aspect of American law. In some countries, such as the United Kingdom and New Zealand, the attorney general or a special committee must certify to the parliament that any proposed legislation is compatible with the relevant bill of rights.[12] Legislation is in effect "screened" to ensure that it complies with basic rights. The United States has no such provision. States may, if they like, legislate up to or even beyond constitutional limits, sometimes as a challenge or taunt to see how far they (or the courts) are willing to go. For example, in May 2016, the Oklahoma legislature sought to bring back the good old (bad) days by enacting legislation that criminalized abortion, including three-year prison terms for doctors who proceeded anyway. In the Oklahoma case, the Republican pro-life governor, Mary Fallin, vetoed the bill because of her certainty that it was unconstitutional. This is admirable, for when the Supreme Court provides outlines of its constitutional analyses, it is instructing lower courts and legislatures about what conduct is permissible and what is not. But what legislators do with the lesson is, to a point, up to them.

The framework in *Roe* attempted to coordinate the interests held by the two stakeholders in an abortion decision at different points in the pregnancy: the right of women to choose abortion and the interest of the state in preserving potential life. These interests waxed and waned across the chronology of pregnancy. Devising a three-stage scheme corresponding loosely to the stages of pregnancy, the Court explained how all this was to work. One factor addressed the medical risk of abortion throughout the pregnancy. During the first trimester, up to twelve weeks' gestation, the risk to a woman's health was so small that she could proceed with almost no interference from the state. Because the medical risks of pregnancy and childbirth were greater than the medical risk of abortion, the state at this early point in pregnancy had only minimal reason to intervene with regard to women's health. Statistically, abortion was the "healthier option." During the second trimester, the state's interest in maternal health increased as abortion procedures became more complicated. At this stage the state could regulate abortion so long as the regulation was "reasonably related to maternal health."[13] Finally, in the third trimester, a period corresponding to the start of fetal viability—the point at which the fetus can survive (with help) outside the womb—the state's interest in protecting what the Court called potential life became "compelling" in constitutional terms: a state interest important enough to regulate, and even ban, the newly established right to choose abortion, except where the mother's life or health was at stake.

This formulation was tidy in some respects and messy in others. It was contingent on locating viability in time (scientifically a moving target) and on the scope of "health"—for example, did the term include mental health? The decision in *Roe* also left unanswered whether husbands were stakeholders in the matter and whether the right to abortion included public funding to pay for the procedure.

By the early 1980s, the Court had answered the question of funding in the negative. Neither the states nor the federal government were required to pay for medically unnecessary abortions for poor women, even though they paid for childbirth.[14] In the 1977 case of *Maher v. Roe,* the Court explained why: a state's decision (Connecticut in this case) not to fund abortions for poor women "places no obstacles—absolute or otherwise—in the pregnant woman's path to an abortion."[15] The Court acknowledged that poverty "may make it difficult—and in some cases, perhaps impossible—for some women to have abortions," but a woman's poverty is not the doing of the state of Connecticut.[16] State funding for the medical expenses of childbirth may have made childbirth "a more attractive alternative, thereby influencing the woman's decision," but Connecticut was well within its rights to implement its "value judgment favoring childbirth over abortion" in this way.[17] In the 1980 case of *Harris v. McRae,* the Supreme Court upheld a ban on federal funding known as the Hyde Amendment. It did not follow from the right established in *Roe* that "a woman's freedom of choice carried with it a constitutional entitlement to the financial resources to avail herself" of the protected choice.[18] As in *Maher,* the Court made clear that obstacles like indigence were "not of [the State's] own creation."[19] These cases reflect the accepted proposition that the Bill of Rights primarily protects "negative liberties"—things the government can't do to you—but does not provide the means to affirmatively enjoy the rights provided in the Bill itself. As the Court explained in *Harris v. McRae,* there are limits to liberty. The government may not interfere with freedom of choice in areas like abortion, but "it does not confer an entitlement to such funds as may be necessary to realize all the advantages of that freedom."[20] One exception is the right to have an attorney provided for defendants in criminal cases; without that, the right to "due process" isn't much of a right at all. Not so for abortion.

Another case, handed down the same day as *Roe,* concerned the extent to which others could have a say in a woman's decision. Plaintiff Mary Doe challenged a Georgia statute permitting pregnant women to terminate a pregnancy so long as they had first received formal approval from a "hospital committee" made up of physicians and psychiatrists. The committees had been introduced in the pre-*Roe* days in an effort to increase access to legal abortion. The committees would provide an orderly system by which some women could get an abortion without the state having to worry that the abortion was sought frivolously. Yet over time hospitals developed reputational worries that perhaps they were providing too many abortions; there was concern that women might plead depression or suicidal thoughts and that the committees would fall for it when, in fact, those women just wanted an abortion.[21] Within a short time, the committees were granting very few petitions.[22] The question before the Court in *Doe v. Bolton* was whether this system of prior abortion approval by others survived the decision in *Roe.* The answer was no. The Supreme Court struck down the Georgia statute as intruding into a decision already reached between a woman and her own doctor; the second-guessing physicians were not entitled to a veto.

The decisions in *Roe* and *Doe* stunned the pro-life community. Their initial outrage focused on what was considered the Court's abandonment of the fetus. In her study of post-*Roe* abortion politics, historian Mary Ziegler states that "as most leading abortion opponents saw it, the Court erred in leaving the unborn without the protection they deserved."[23] Early political efforts sought to restore that protection by amending the Constitution to add a Human Life Amendment, which would effectively overturn *Roe* by establishing that prenatal life was equal to born life, so that abortion was constitutionally a murder.[24] Because these efforts went nowhere, by the 1980s pro-life advocates shifted tactics as they sought to wrest back control over abortion not by criminalizing it but by medicalizing it.[25] *Roe* had acknowledged the state's interest in women's health. The task now was to establish its contours.

Two cases from the 1980s provide a good sense of where things stood during the period between *Roe* and *Casey*. The first is *Akron v. Akron Center for Reproductive Health, Inc.*[26] In February 1978, the city of Akron, Ohio, enacted a comprehensive abortion ordinance requiring that pregnant women receive pictures and descriptions of fetuses at two-week chronological intervals as part of the informed consent procedure. In addition, all second-trimester abortions were to take place in hospitals, not clinics, and the attending physician had to personally tell the patient that "the unborn child is a human life from the moment of conception."[27] Abortion providers challenged the ordinance on the ground that these provisions had nothing to do with maternal health.[28]

The Supreme Court agreed. No matter how objective the mandated description of fetal characteristics at two-week intervals might be, it is "plainly . . . not medical information . . . and it may serve only to confuse and punish the patient, and to heighten her anxiety, contrary to accepted medical practice."[29] Noting that the American College of Gynecology and the American Public Health Association no longer recommended a hospital for second trimester abortions (as they had ten years earlier), the Court found that Akron's hospitals-only provision "imposed a heavy, and unnecessary, burden on women's access to a relatively inexpensive, otherwise accessible, and safe abortion procedure."[30] The required statements about human life and the moment of conception were inconsistent with the holding in *Roe* that "a State may not adopt one theory of when life begins to justify its regulation of abortion."[31] Finally, the Court dismissed the "dubious" statement that abortion is "a major surgical procedure" with many complications was in fact a "'parade of horribles' intended to suggest that abortion is a particularly dangerous procedure" when by medical standards it was not.[32] In overturning the entire Akron ordinance, the Court drew a clear line between medical and nonmedical information. It was also attentive to the psychological consequences for women at the receiving end of misleading information: confusion, anxiety, guilt.

Three years later in *Thornburgh v. American College of Obstetricians & Gynecologists,* the Supreme Court similarly struck down Pennsylvania's Abortion Control Act. In addition to Akron-like regulations, the Abortion Control Act required that women had to be informed about available public assistance as well as whatever financial support a woman could seek from the father. These financial disclosures were made part of the medical informed consent process. Again, the Court found that such disclosures were but "poorly disguised elements of discouragement for the abortion decision" and therefore not within the state's authority to enact.[33] As in *Akron*, the Court considered the possible, almost malicious effect of the recitations on certain categories of pregnant women: "a victim of rape should not have to hear gratuitous advice that an unidentified perpetrator is liable for support if she continues the pregnancy to term."[34] Because such information was not medical in character, it "advance[d] no legitimate state interest."[35] In striking down the mandatory physician recitation of all possible medical risks, the Court concluded that the very purpose of the Pennsylvania act was suspect: "[that] the Commonwealth does not, and surely would not, compel similar disclosure of every possible peril of necessary surgery or of simple vaccination, reveals the anti-abortion character of the statute, and its real purpose."[36] Total disclosure intruded on best medical practices and a physician's responsibility to his patient in all her particularity.[37] Finally, the Supreme Court did not hesitate to expose the pictures of fetal development for what they so clearly were: "nothing less than an outright attempt to wedge the Commonwealth's message discouraging abortion into the privacy of the informed-consent dialogue between the woman and her physician."[38]

And so, in the 1980s, the majority of the Supreme Court followed both the letter and the spirit of *Roe* with regard to what kind of information properly pertained to the medical aspects of abortion. It had little patience for the pretextual use of mandated disclosures to persuade or scare women away from abortion. Determinations about informed consent protocols for the procedure itself, such as the second-trimester hospital requirement, were matters for the medical profession and not the legislature.

Regime Change

In the twenty years following *Roe*, six justices who had voted to decriminalize abortion (Burger, Douglas, Brennan, Stewart, Marshall, and Powell) left the Court. They were replaced by Justices Stevens, Souter, O'Connor, Thomas, and Kennedy, appointed by Presidents Reagan, Ford, and George W. Bush. Only *Roe*'s author, Justice Blackmun, and two *Roe* dissenters—Rehnquist (now chief justice) and Justice White—were still serving.[39] The times were clearly changing, and advocates from both sides anticipated that the 1989 case of *Webster v. Reproductive Health Services* might ring the death knell for *Roe*.[40] But although in

Webster the Supreme Court upheld all the state's regulations, including a required disclosure that life begins at conception, it declined the larger invitation to overturn *Roe*.

The showdown for that came three years later in *Planned Parenthood of Southeastern Pennsylvania v. Casey*.[41] The new Pennsylvania Abortion Control Act contained versions of the same regulations struck down in *Akron* and *Thornburgh*: disclosures on fetal development, paternal support obligations, and state financial aid, as well as a spousal notification requirement. Pro-life advocates regarded *Casey* as the long-awaited occasion for the Court to overrule *Roe* outright. Yet despite pleas to do so from Pennsylvania and from the Solicitor General of the United States, the Court refused to do so. In a joint decision written by Justices O'Connor, Souter, and Kennedy, the Justices explained that however they might have voted had they been on the Court in 1973, fidelity to the rule of law and the principle of *stare decisis* required that *Roe's* "essential holding" be upheld.[42] Under *stare decisis*, courts consider themselves bound to follow earlier decisions on the same matter except in a very limited set of circumstances, and the Court determined that between 1973 and 1992 no such circumstances had arisen with regard to abortion. On the contrary, the abortion right had become so established that its reversal was imprudent as a jurisprudential matter. "An entire generation has come of age" relying on the reproductive liberties set out in *Roe*.[43] Protesting perhaps a bit too much, the Court stressed that it was not reneging on *Roe*, stating that "[it is] imperative to adhere to the essence of *Roe's* original decision, and we do so today" and "the woman's right to terminate her pregnancy before viability is . . . a component of liberty we cannot renounce."[44]

But although the opening pages of *Casey* affirmed *Roe's* "essential holding," the remainder of the decision took large bites out of the rest of *Roe*. In a broad housecleaning sweep, *Casey* began by discarding the graduated trimester framework in which abortions could be chosen freely in the first trimester, regulated to protect maternal health in the second, and prohibited in the third unless the woman's life or health was at risk. Certainly there was nothing legally sacrosanct about trimesters; they served as a clunky but workable way to align constitutional doctrine within the schema of a developing pregnancy. Yet abandoning trimesters meant some other marker for measuring the strength of the state's interest in prenatal life had to be set. The Court announced that *Roe* had undervalued the state's interest in potential unborn life, an interest which *Casey* now fixed at the moment of conception. States were now within their rights to persuade pregnant women against abortion from the start. While once considered impermissible because nonmedical, "[appeals in the form of] rules and regulations designed to encourage [the pregnant woman] to know that there are philosophic and social arguments of great weight . . . in favor of continuing the pregnancy to full term" were now constitutionally acceptable and from the "earliest stages" of pregnancy.[45] Protecting unborn life was not the only justification for these new regulations. Women themselves needed protection from the emotional aftermath of aborting without understanding fully what this would mean for the fetus. Thus measures designed to ensure truly informed consent "will not be invalidated as long as their purpose is to persuade the woman to choose childbirth over abortion."[46]

Persuading women not to abort now fell within an expanded notion of maternal health to include mental and emotional well-being. Being instructed about the gestational age of the fetus and the details of the abortion procedure helps "to ensure that a woman apprehend the full consequences of her decision" and so "furthers the legitimate purpose of reducing the risk that a woman may elect an abortion, only to discover later, with devastating psychological consequences, that her decision was not fully informed."[47] So long as the information provided by the state was truthful and not misleading, requiring its dissemination was all right. Throwing the weight of the state against the abortion right was no longer derided as being "under the guise of informed consent" in the language of *Thornburgh;* it *was* informed consent.[48] To the extent *Akron* and *Thornburgh* had found constitutional violations in such things as informing women about the fetus's gestational age or about the comparative health and psychological risks between abortion and childbirth (abortion declared the riskier), "those cases go too far . . . and are overruled."[49] The only chronological marker that mattered now was viability, after which the states could ban abortion unless necessary to protect the woman's life or health.

Where did all this leave a woman's right to choose? Were there any constitutional limits on how a state could regulate before viability? Did the same standards used with other constitutional deprivations apply in the case of abortion? In such areas as free speech, for example, where the right at stake is also deemed "fundamental," the government must show it has a "compelling state interest"—something close to a crucial interest—before the state can significantly interfere with the exercise of the right. Indeed, this was the standard established in *Roe v. Wade*.[50] But in *Casey,* the Supreme Court rolled out a new test for assessing the constitutionality of abortion regulation: measures that sought to "express profound respect for the life of the unborn" by persuading women not to abort through a variety of interventions were all right so long as they did not create an "undue burden" on the right to choose.[51]

How were courts to determine whether a particular regulation created an undue burden? The Court in *Casey* gave something of a functional reply. A regulation creates an undue burden when it has "the purpose or effect of placing a substantial obstacle in the path of a woman seeking an abortion of a nonviable fetus."[52] How big an obstacle is "substantial"? The Court provided little by way of guidelines except to apply the new standard to the provisions of the statute before it.[53] In something close to thumbs up / thumbs down methodology, it held that all provisions of the Abortion Control Act were fine, except one. Neither cooling-off periods nor visual disclosures nor parental consent for minors amounted to a substantial obstacle for pregnant women and girls in Pennsylvania. Only the requirement that wives must notify their husbands went too far. Taking note of domestic violence as background social fact, the Court accepted evidence that a woman seeking an abortion against her husband's wishes might well be bullied or physically prevented by him from proceeding with her plan. This alone—a wife being blocked at the door by an angry husband—was held to be a substantial obstacle. (The same logic did not apply to a pregnant teen with an angry parent.)

Federal courts of appeals have found that certain other regulatory restrictions unduly burdened a woman's right, but these decisions are binding only in the particular Circuit. Mandatory ultrasound was struck down by the Fourth Circuit (covering Maryland, Virginia, West Virginia, and the Carolinas) and upheld in the Fifth (covering Texas, Louisiana, and Mississippi). This sort of zip code jurisprudence indicated the need for greater guidance from the Supreme Court on what constituted an undue burden or a substantial obstacle.

Roe v. Wade is often regarded as the touchstone of U.S. abortion law, in part because the pro-life movement has made overturning or at least overcoming the case central to its end game. Yet the right to terminate a pregnancy as first announced in *Roe* had been significantly diminished. *Planned Parenthood v. Casey* expanded the scope of the state's interest in embryonic and fetal life and endorsed a model of informed consent that swapped out medical considerations for moral ones. *Casey* endorsed a particular relationship between woman and fetus, one in which, the Court had no doubt, "most women considering an abortion would deem the impact on the fetus relevant, if not dispositive, to the decision."[54] For many women, this is simply untrue.

At present, much abortion regulation is premised on the proposition that pregnant women decide about abortion too quickly and that if only they were more informed, they would change their minds. The "more" is a bundled set of propositions: that human life begins at conception, that women who abort will suffer for the rest of their lives, and that women must grasp all of this before they can consent to an abortion. This has led to mandatory physician scripts, compulsory ultrasound and heartbeat auscultation, and cooling-off periods of up to seventy-two hours. Lately states have become bolder, banning abortions on detection of a heartbeat and for the purpose of fetal sex selection. Co-opting anti-discrimination principles as a technique for opposing abortion has caught on among pro-life legislators who have since banned abortions chosen on the basis of race, sex, national origin, ancestry, and color.[55] Casting women as killers not simply of vulnerable fetuses but of vulnerable minority fetuses is a clever move. It is unlikely that these statutes are constitutional under *Roe* or *Casey*, but until the matter is settled they will siphon off pro-choice energies, for even the preposterous must be challenged.

Thickening Undue Burden

In *Whole Woman's Health v. Hellerstedt,* Texas abortion providers challenged two provisions in a piece of Texas legislation known as H.B. (House Bill) 2. The first required all abortion providers to have admitting privileges at a hospital not more than thirty miles from where the physician practiced. The second required all abortion clinics to be licensed as "ambulatory surgical centers," along the lines of a field hospital. The providers argued that complying with H.B. 2 would put many of them out of business. Some would be unable to get admitting privileges at a hospital within thirty miles (or anywhere); others could not afford to rebuild their physical plant to satisfy the demands of an ambulatory surgical center (post-operative recovery suite, corridors wide enough to accommodate gurneys, an increased nurse-to-patient ratio). Indeed, during the period when the admitting privileges portion of H.B. 2 was in effect, the number of licensed clinics in Texas dropped from forty to twenty. Evidence at trial showed that enforcement of the ambulatory surgical center provision would reduce that number to around ten statewide.

The legal question posed by the case was whether clinic closures resulting from H.B. 2 created an undue burden on Texas women seeking an abortion. Did H.B. 2 have "the purpose or effect" of making abortion so hard to get that the legislation diminished the right to choose established in *Roe* and reaffirmed in *Casey*? Those were the substantive issues before the Court. Another more economical way to state what was at stake in *Whole Woman's Health* is the question of whether *Planned Parenthood v. Casey* stood for anything in terms of upholding the right established in *Roe*. Or were there really no limits on what states out to create "abortion-free zones" could do as a means to the legislative end of decreasing abortion? If nothing short of bullying one's wife was the only thing that counted as an undue burden then the right established in *Roe* had a very small circumference indeed. The landscape took on a pre-*Roe* hue, with abortions available in some states and barely available in others, wealthy women traveling again, and poor women just making do. This was the general picture as the eight-person Roberts Court took up H.B. 2 in the summer of 2016.[56]

The decision in *Whole Woman's Health* put state legislatures on notice that there are constitutional limits to abortion regulation after all. In a fact-saturated 5–3 decision, Justice Breyer explained that neither the admitting privileges nor the ambulatory surgical center requirement could be justified as advancing the state's interest in women's health. Abortion was such a safe medical procedure that it required neither an operating theater nor hospital admitting privileges for the doctors. Indeed, the Court explained that under existing hospital protocols abortion providers were unlikely to receive admitting privileges, in part because privileges are generally awarded to doctors in fields in which hospital care is often required. Not so for abortion.

With regard to the ambulatory surgical center provision, the Court relied on uncontested trial evidence that abortions do not require the sort of precautions occasioned by an operation. Abortion patients do not undergo anesthetization, and there is no penetration of the woman's skin necessitating the hyper-sterile environment of an operating theater. The Court approved the district court's conclusion that "many of the building standards [required by H.B. 2] have such a tangential relationship to patient safety in the context of abortion as to be nearly arbitrary."[57] The Court balanced H.B. 2's near nonexistent medical benefits against the significant burdens that the legislation placed on women's access to abortion in Texas: longer travel times, more time away from home, increased costs for child care, and the greater risk of being found out put in play by the lengthier process. Because the burdens so outweighed the benefits, the Court concluded that H.B. 2 unquestionably created a substantial obstacle in the path of women seeking abortion.

The Court made two additional points that seal the place of *Whole Woman's Health* on the map of abortion jurisprudence. First, the decision clarified how a court is to decide what the true facts (one just called "the facts") about a particular regulation actually are. Rather than accept the puffery and political prose found in legislative preambles that set out as "legislative fact" how women suffer from abortion, the Court quoted from its decision in *Gonzales v. Carhart* that the "Court retains an independent constitutional duty to review factual findings where constitutional rights are at stake."[58] This admonition reminds lower courts not only about their duty to take the fact of facts seriously but also that the interest at stake is not just any old conduct but a constitutional right. The Court's treatment gives the abortion right qua right its due.

Second, the Court gave a textured account of how women in Texas experience the consequences of abortion regulation. In response to the state's argument that the remaining abortion facilities would be amply able to handle patients who would otherwise have gone to one of the facilities shuttered on account of H.B. 2, the Court stated that

> in the face of no threat to women's health, Texas seeks to force women to travel long distances to get abortions in crammed-to-capacity superfacilities. Patients seeking these services are less likely to get the kind of individualized attention, serious conversation, and emotional support that doctors at less taxed facilities may have offered. Health care facilities and medical professionals are not fungible commodities.[59]

The pro-life movement has long characterized abortion clinics as "mills" that run women through for profit alone. *Whole Woman's Health* explains how pro-life legislation contributes to the creation of "assembly line abortion." This puts a very human spin on what clinic closures mean to an individual patient.

Abortion Rewards and Punishment

By the 1980s, pro-life advocates had adopted an incrementalist strategy designed to narrow *Roe*'s holding by expanding the state's protective interest to the well-being of women as well as to that of the fetus. This approach received a hearty boost from the 1992 decision in *Planned Parenthood v. Casey*, which

opened the door to increasingly inventive regulations that one after another
burden women's access to abortion. The decision in *Whole Woman's Health*
provided a mid-course correction as the Supreme Court clarified that the undue
burden test was no longer an empty pass-through for whatever the states came
up with. In this way abortion's constitutional structure continues to unfold.
That structure is, however, only part of the legal story, for the issue of abortion
arises in cases not directly about abortion. These cases have produced a distinctive body of law marked by a system of rewards and punishments for decisions
about abortion.

We start with the 1998 Supreme Court case of *Miller v. Albright,* brought by
Lorelyn Miller, the daughter of a Philippine mother and an American citizen
(soldier) father, against Secretary of State Madeline Albright.[60] Miller argued
that a provision of the Immigration and Naturalization Act discriminated
against the non-marital children of citizen fathers in contrast to the non-marital
children of citizen mothers because the path to citizenship for children born
outside the United States to citizen mothers was significantly easier than that
for the children of citizen fathers. Citizen fathers had to show that they had
established legal paternity over their non-marital child before the child turned
eighteen. (Lorelyn's father had not done this in time.) In contrast, citizen mothers
simply had to show that they were themselves U.S. citizens at the time of the
child's birth, with no time limit on the application. The government contended
that the congressional purpose of this stricter provision for fathers was to
"encourage[e] the development of a healthy relationship between the citizen
parent and the child while the child was still a minor."[61] Such encouragement
was less necessary for a citizen mother who gave birth abroad because she "certainly knows of her child's existence" and typically takes custody of the child
immediately after its birth.[62] The Supreme Court agreed, holding that it is much
more likely for the child "to develop ties to its citizen mother at an early age."[63]
Deferring to this congressional purpose, a majority of the justices found that
treating citizen mothers and citizen fathers differently under these circumstances
was not impermissible discrimination based on sex.

Whether one agrees with the decision or, like dissenting Justice Ginsburg,
finds that preferring mothers reinforces gender-based stereotypes, how does
abortion fit into the story? The Supreme Court noted that even before the child
has been born, its mother had already engaged in deserving conduct: "she
must first choose to carry the pregnancy to term and reject the alternative of

abortion—an alternative that is available to many, and in reality to most, women around the world. She must then actually give birth to the child. Section 1409(c) rewards that choice and that labor by conferring citizenship on her child."[64] Putting aside the Court's nod to illegal abortions as a well-known practice worldwide ("in reality" abortion is always available), the Supreme Court's compensation to the citizen mother for not aborting is explicit and clear.

A second example of rewarding opposition to abortion arose in the application of U.S. asylum policy. In the early 1980s, Chinese couples began fleeing their government's one-child family policy, which along with financial penalties for having surplus children also included forced abortions for women and sterilizations for men.[65] Many of those fleeing arrived in the United States where they immediately applied for asylum. The problem was that while forced abortions "violate every known standard of human rights since God made Man," in the words of Representative Ileana Ros-Lehtinen, they did not easily fit into the criteria for asylum status.[66] Under the Immigration and Nationality Act, asylum is available to persons who have fled their country and who refuse to return due to persecution (or a well-founded fear of persecution) on any one of five grounds: race, religion, nationality, membership in a particular social group, or political opinion.[67] The Bureau of Immigrant Appeals (BIA) held that China's one-child policy was just that, a policy and not persecution.[68] Even if a Chinese petitioner could prove a well-founded fear of coerced abortion, it was unclear which of the five statutory bases would accommodate the fear.

In 1988, in response to the early BIA rulings, President Reagan's Attorney General Edwin Meese issued guidelines to the Immigration and Naturalization Service clarifying that the refusal of a Chinese national to abort a pregnancy could be appropriately viewed as "an act of political defiance sufficient to establish refugee status" under U.S. law.[69] When the BIA failed to follow Meese's guidelines, Congress took matters into its own hands and enacted the Illegal Immigration Reform and Immigrant Responsibility Act (IIRIRA), which "deemed" as a matter of federal law that a person fleeing forced abortion had a well-founded fear of persecution based on political opinion.[70] This time the BIA fell into step, approving Chinese petitions and even holding that a male applicant could "stand in the shoes" of his wife to establish the claim of refugee for both of them, even if she was in China.[71]

Here congressional antiabortion passions were put to the test. Following the enactment of the IIRIRA, the numbers of Chinese nationals seeking asylum on this basis shot up, easily exceeding the 1,000-person yearly cap established by IIRIRA. Most of the applicants had arrived in the United States illegally, raising concerns about incentivizing illegal entry, especially by men making the derivative claim but who might never in fact send for their wives. In addition, the U.S. State Department found "wide fabrication and fraud" in Chinese asylum cases filed under IIRIRA.[72] In 2007, the Second Circuit Court of Appeals revisited the earlier BIA interpretation of the definition of refugee and held that the text was unambiguous, thereby limiting refugee claims to petitioners alone and not to their spouses.[73] Attorney General Alberto Gonzales then issued an interim decision binding on the BIA, holding that "spouses are not entitled to the same per se refugee status [accorded] persons who have physically undergone forced abortion or sterilization procedures."[74] The sequence— reward, counter-considerations, reconsideration—shows the complication of favoring antiabortion acts when the policy is matched against other policy favorites like immigration fraud.

In the area of criminal law, seeking an abortion results in disfavored treatment, including actual confinement. In 1998, Yuriko Kawaguchi, a California resident, was arrested in Cleveland, Ohio, in connection with a scheme to buy computers with a counterfeit credit card.[75] Kawaguchi pled guilty to charges of fifth degree felony. While in jail awaiting sentencing, Kawaguchi wrote to the judge in the case, Municipal Court Judge Patricia Cleary, to say that Kawaguchi was pregnant and requesting that she be put on probation in order to have an abortion either in California or in Cleveland.[76] At a hearing, Judge Cleary asked Kawaguchi whether she was planning to put her child up for adoption in Ohio or California. Kawaguchi replied that her plan was to have an abortion. "Well, honestly, your Honor, I'm pretty much fighting time right now. . . . This was an unwanted pregnancy . . . and if I am released, I will be trying to have a procedure done."[77] Judge Cleary then sentenced Kawaguchi to six months at the Ohio Reformatory for Women, unless Kawaguchi agreed to have the baby, in which case she would be released on probation and not do any more time. Kawaguchi rejected the deal. With the help of American Civil Liberties Union attorneys (described by Judge Cleary as "a couple of old harpies"), Kawaguchi eventually received probation, although it was too late for a legal abortion in Ohio.[78] A few months later, Kawaguchi gave birth to a daughter.

In April of 2000, the Cleveland Bar Association filed a disciplinary complaint against Judge Cleary alleging that her behavior in sentencing Kawaguchi violated several canons of the Code of Judicial Conduct. These included a judge's obligations to "perform duties without bias and prejudice" and to "disqualify himself or herself when the judge's impartiality might reasonably be questioned."[79] The Ohio Board of Commissioners on Grievances and Discipline found against Cleary, by this time off the bench, and recommended that she be suspended from the practice of law for two years.

Cleary appealed but the Ohio Supreme Court upheld the Board's decision, emphasizing that "[a] judge is free to hold his or her own personal beliefs [only] so long as those attitudes, prejudices, or beliefs are not translated into action or inaction."[80] Cleary had left little doubt as to her personal beliefs. While her case was on appeal, she gave a talk at a local church discussing the Kawaguchi case: "Now, again, this 21-year-old girl. [Her attorneys are] on her day in and day out. . . . They're working on this girl and browbeating her into changing her mind or to steer her toward having an abortion. . . . And, I do believe in Satan, and I've had some of his workers in my courtroom, at least a few thoroughly evil, wicked people. So, that has reinforced not only my belief in God but my belief in Satan. I mean, that force is a real presence."[81] The Ohio Supreme Court concluded that because the deal Cleary had offered Kawaguchi "displayed partiality toward certain conduct that Cleary thought morally appropriate," Cleary had improperly exhibited partiality in sentencing "based on whether Kawaguchi acted in accordance with Cleary's personal views."[82]

This may seem an aberrant case of one judicial bad apple. It is not. There is also Mason County Probate judge Francis Bourisseau of Michigan who was censured for saying that he might grant a bypass petition if the pregnancy resulted from the rape of a white teenager by a black man.[83] In another case, immediately after taking his oath of office, Washington State Supreme Court Justice Richard Sanders left the swearing-in ceremony to join a March for Life rally on the statehouse steps where he wished the crowd well "in this celebration of human life."[84] Sanders told the crowd, "I owe my election to many of the people who are here today."[85] A reprimand of Sanders by the state Judicial Conduct Committee was reversed for lack of sufficient evidence that his speech had compromised the impartiality of the judiciary.

Besides having their sentences "fixed" in ways that might prevent them from having a legal abortion, incarcerated women, some of whom are simply awaiting trial, have experienced other forms of abortion-related punishments. Some are pregnant when they enter prison; others become pregnant through rape by prison guards. The basic question has been whether incarceration extinguishes a pregnant woman's right to decide about abortion. The background rule is that prisoners retain their constitutional rights unless the exercise of those rights is inconsistent with prisoner status (prisoners lose the right to liberty) or with legitimate penological objectives of the corrections system (prisoners lose the right to association).[86] The Eighth Circuit Court of Appeals has held that abortion is a right that survives incarceration.[87]

Yet the ability of a pregnant inmate to exercise the abortion right "varies significantly among institutions."[88] In 2005 the Missouri Department of Corrections instituted a policy barring transportation of prisoners seeking an abortion absent a threat to the woman's life or health, ostensibly to prevent the women from escaping and to reduce costs. The appellate court bought neither of these arguments. After all, inmates denied abortions were transported for purposes of prenatal care and birth with no concern about security risks or cost reduction.[89] Louisiana requires pregnant inmates to get a court order authorizing an elective abortion; the policy was upheld as advancing the state's interest in avoiding liability and saving costs.[90] Pregnant prisoners face immense practical problems in complying with these rules: the logistics of arranging funding, scheduling a procedure, getting transportation, and finding a lawyer to help get the required court order. In some cases women who obtained court orders ended up giving birth because the time for a legal abortion had dwindled away following "bureaucratic delays." The Louisiana plaintiff, Victoria W., was fifteen weeks pregnant when she first told prison personnel she wanted an abortion; she was twenty-five weeks pregnant by the time she was able to get a court order, well past the legal limit in the state.[91]

Abortion's punitive underpinnings have shown up in the imposition of criminal liability on those who facilitate a minor getting even a legal abortion. *Sherron v. State* is a 2006 Georgia case in which Charlotte Sherron learned that her thirteen-year-old daughter was pregnant by Charlotte's abusive husband.[92] The husband was convicted of statutory rape and sentenced to twenty-seven years in prison. The daughter wanted an abortion and Charlotte consented as required under state law. Charlotte herself was then arrested as an accessory to her husband's crime for helping remove the "most obvious evidence" of the rape, the fetus.[93] She was convicted and sentenced to three years in prison, and her conviction was upheld on appeal. This is, of course, nonsense: there was already solid evidence about the husband's criminal conduct, including the stepdaughter's own testimony. Rape convictions do not require a fetus. It seems that the net was out for Charlotte for her failure to protect her daughter from the husband. In the eyes of the district attorney, a reprimand in family court was too small a penalty for the mother's failure.[94] Abortion stood at the ready, available in this unhappy case to right a perceived maternal wrong.

Fetal Imagery in Law

The display of fetal imagery has also made its way into such diverse areas of law as evidence, employment, and prison regulations. In each of these seemingly non-reproductive areas, contestation over pictures of dead fetuses shows how deeply the sight of fetal death is instinctively linked to abortion throughout the culture and the law.

During the punishment phase in a capital murder trial, a Texas trial court admitted into evidence an eight-by-ten-inch color picture of a pregnant murder victim and her posthumously extracted child lying together in a casket at their wake.[95] The appellate court described the picture: "The unborn child had been removed from [the victim's] body, cleaned, and swaddled in white material, possibly a blanket. The unborn child was placed next to his mother with only his face . . . showing. The unborn child is miniature in form and his face is only a fraction of the size of his mother's hand."[96] The appellate court added a few more details, noting that the coffin had "a lining made of white textured material" and that the dead mother's "hair had been fixed with spiral curls."[97]

The jury sentenced the defendant to death. He appealed on the ground that the photograph had had a prejudicial effect on the jury. Although the state argued that any possible prejudice was outweighed by the picture's relevance in showing the defendant's "violent and vicious nature," the court held that the photograph's ability "to impress the jury in some irrational yet indelible way" was improper.[98] Too much was bundled into the eight-by-ten inches: "The unborn child in the photograph appears tiny, innocent, and vulnerable. Society's natural inclination is to protect the innocent and the vulnerable. The contents of the photograph ha[ve] an emotional impact that suggests the jury's decision be made on an emotional basis and not on the basis of the other relevant evidence introduced at trial."[99] That was, of course, its very purpose. Even the state agreed that the only reason the picture has been introduced into evidence was "to whip the jury into a death penalty frenzy."[100] The language of innocence, vulnerability, and protection resonates almost subliminally with pro-life ideology and imagery, which seeks to create a similar frenzy in defense of the fetus.

What information a jury may consider is policed by the rules of evidence: if improper evidence is admitted, a jury's verdict may be overturned. These constraints on jury deliberation stem from jurisprudential norms regarding what makes for a fair trial. This is especially important in capital cases where the consequences of irrational inferences cannot be reversed. But not all pictures of dead fetuses are excluded in criminal prosecutions. A California court admitted graphic photos of a bloody stillborn fetus in a rape prosecution; a Virginia court upheld the admission of autopsy photographs of the deceased victim's fetus as relevant to proving an element of the offense; and a Texas court upheld the admission of autopsy photographs of the victim's uterus (removed from her body), the placenta, and an eight- to nine-week-old fetus as relevant to the issue of whether the fetus was alive at the time the victim was shot.[101] But as Susan Bandes and Jessica Salerno remind us, it is not so easy to cabin the purpose for which gruesome photos are introduced: "photos are the product of choices about framing and vantage point. . . . They reflect choices about whether to include wide-angle views of the area surrounding the body, and thus whether to include or exclude other objects. These seemingly inconsequential decisions have been found to influence jurors' evaluations of evidence and testimony, often in ways that are difficult to correct once the evidence has been viewed."[102] Tort plaintiffs have also sought to introduce graphic pictures of a dead fetus "as 'your basic evidence'" in wrongful death suits, though here too some courts have recognized the power of fetal images to unfairly distort jurors' judgment.[103] A 2005 Georgia appellate court found that an admitted photo showing the peeling skin of a dead fetus had been "'emotionally provocative' and inflammatory."[104]

Fetal images have also become an issue outside courtrooms. In the early 1990s, as part of a personal vow taken in accordance with her Roman Catholic faith, Christine Wilson swore that she would wear an antiabortion button to work every day until *Roe v. Wade* was overturned.[105] The button featured a color photograph of a dead fetus. Several of Wilson's co-workers objected to the continual display of the button, not because of their position on abortion (many shared Wilson's views) but because they associated the image with personal histories of infertility or miscarriage. After several employees threatened to walk off the job, Wilson's employer offered her three options: keep the button in her cubicle, cover it at work, or wear a protest button with words but no picture. Wilson rejected all of these, was fired, and then sued her employer under Title VII on grounds of religious discrimination. In *Wilson v. U.S. West Communications,* the Eighth Circuit held for the employer. The alternatives offered to Wilson satisfied the employer's duty to accommodate her religious beliefs.[106] Our interest in the case is less in the workings of religious accommodation law than in the meanings attributed to the fetal photo. Wilson understood the picture to "acknowledge the sanctity of the unborn."[107] Others found the button less morally charged than emotionally so, not a celebration of life but a reminder of their loss. The button's meanings resulted from the complex interaction among reproductive technology, reproductive politics, and reproductive desires. Even those who don't find meaning in fetal images are aware of their nuanced meanings for others.

The workplace is only one of many physical spaces in which fetal imagery is contested. In the mid-1990s, Warden Timothy Schuetzle of North Dakota State Penitentiary instituted an "aborted fetus policy" after fights broke out among inmates in response to an inmate passing around picture postcards of mutilated fetuses.[108] It isn't clear where inmate Martin Wishnatsky got his cards although a number of pro-life organizations offer aborted fetus postcards, drop cards, business cards, and envelopes all featuring bloody in-color body parts.[109] Under the aborted fetus policy, prisoners were permitted to promote their views about abortion orally but could not possess pictures of "unborn children . . . dead through abortion."[110] As Warden Schuetzle testified, his policy banning fetal photos was based in part on the existence of "abortion-related violence in open society."[111]

Wishnatsky objected to the warden's prohibition on First Amendment grounds.[112] In *Wishnatsky v. Schuetzle,* the Eighth Circuit Court of Appeals affirmed the trial court's ruling that a prisoner's First Amendment rights may be limited by regulations reasonably related to legitimate penological interests in prison security.[113] Because the display of the images had repeatedly resulted in disorder, the warden had the authority to confiscate the cards as contraband. The outcome is not surprising. The First Amendment generally has a smaller scope in prisons, schools, and other institutional settings where keeping order is an essential aspect of the enterprise.

First Amendment claims to display fetal imagery arise in places without institutional security concerns. In 2004, a federal district court in Kentucky found that the display of a three-by-four-foot color photograph of a mutilated fetus during a well-attended street concert was not "fighting words" for purposes of free speech.[114] (Speech inciting violence, or "fighting words," is not given full protection under the First Amendment.) The Kentucky court noted that "no matter how gruesome or how objectionable [the giant photograph] may be," it remains not only protected speech but a "powerful, albeit graphic commentary on a societal debate that divides many Americans."[115] Three years later, other pro-life advocates hung a four-foot-high aborted fetus banner on a highway overpass in Minnesota. The advocates were arrested for endangering the public, but their conviction was overturned on the ground that the state had failed to prove that the banner had been particularly distracting to motorists.[116] Moreover, the court found there was nothing particularly distressing in the image, noting that "signs, of whatever type, and wherever placed, are an omnipresent feature in the life of a motorist."[117] Yet in 1993, the revocation of an artist's license to display a "larger-than-life depiction of a nude woman, a coat hanger, and a fetus" in a federal building was upheld.[118]

Broadcasters have been challenged for refusing to air graphic abortion footage within political advertising on television. In 2004, the BBC refused to broadcast the ProLife Alliance Party's authorized election broadcast on the ground that it included "aborted foetuses in a mangled and mutilated state, tiny limbs, a separated head, and the like."[119] ProLife Alliance argued that the BBC had violated its right to "impart information and ideas" under Article 10 of the European Convention on Human Rights.[120] Yet a majority of Law Lords (now the U.K. Supreme Court) found that the BBC was entitled to determine and to apply standards of "taste and decency" in refusing to broadcast the "offensive material."[121] A different result obtained in the United States with its stronger protection of speech. In 1992, a federal district court upheld a broadcaster's decision to channel a candidate's campaign advertisement, including footage of an actual abortion, to "safe harbor hours" between midnight and 6 a.m.[122] There is then a range of acceptability regarding the display of fetal imagery. It may be that motorists in Minnesota are unfazed by highway overpass banners, although we cannot know if this is because they keep their eyes on the road or because a picture of an aborted fetus has become such an ordinary sight. What we see, however, is that fetal depictions are imbued with political meaning, even without the coat hanger.

THE YEAR 2023—almost spitting distance from today—will mark half a century of legal abortion. Since *Roe v. Wade* was decided in 1973, law has engaged with abortion as a right, as a medical procedure, as an adjunct to foreign policy, as an expressive statement of belief, and as protected speech. In none of these areas has law's progression been linear or consistent; abortion is too entwined with the beliefs and politics of the citizenry and of the courts for that.

3

Abortion Privacy / Abortion Secrecy

In 1970 Jane Roe, described by the Supreme Court as "a single woman . . . residing in Dallas County, Texas," filed a suit in federal court against Henry Wade, the elected district attorney of Dallas County.[1] Henry Wade was the name of Dallas County's chief prosecutor, the man responsible for enforcing Texas's criminal abortion statute. But a quick footnote following the Court's first mention of the other party "Jane Roe" informs us only that "the name is a pseudonym."[2] This raises an interesting and little discussed aspect of the famous case: just when can a party to litigation decide not to use his or her own name but to sue under a fictitious one instead? A basic requirement of our adversarial system is that a complaint—the first document filed in any lawsuit—must name all of the parties. Not only does the defendant have a right to know who has sued him, but the press has a right to report on it to the rest of us. As the Supreme Court explained in 1975, "what transpires in the courtroom is public property."[3] Twenty years later, the Seventh Circuit Court of Appeals made clear that identifying the parties "is an important dimension of publicness. The people have a right to know who is using their courts."[4]

What then are we to make of Jane Roe? What characteristics of the plaintiff or of the case so "overwhelms the presumption of disclosure mandated by procedural custom" that anonymity trumps the cherished values of publicness and transparency?[5] Without digging too deeply into the Federal Rules of Civil Procedure, it is enough to know that cases involving abortion—along with "mental illness, personal safety [same-sex prison rape], homosexuality, transsexuality, and illegitimate or abandoned children in welfare cases"—are among the few exceptions where courts permit adults to proceed anonymously.[6] One begins to catch the flavor of the exception. "The common thread," said the federal district court in *Doe v. Rostker*, "is the presence of some social stigma or the threat of physical harm to the plaintiffs attaching to disclosure of their identities to the public record."[7]

Bringing a lawsuit under an alias is one instance of women keeping a distance between their names and the subject of abortion. But even outside courtrooms, the practice is common as a matter of everyday life. Women in the United States don't talk much about abortion as a personal experience. They don't tell their friends, except maybe a very good one who will drop them off or pick them up afterward. They don't always tell their husbands or partners. Young women don't always tell their parents, and mothers rarely tell their children. Even in "pro-choice families," the news can be unexpected and unsettling. One young woman described how after her middle-aged mother confided that she herself had had an illegal abortion while a college student in 1972, "it took a few years for the shock to wear off."[8] The daughter had thought that a right to abortion was something that "only *other* women" needed, "not *my* family and certainly not *my* mother."[9]

Many women don't tell their insurance companies. Some assume abortion isn't covered, but others pay out of pocket even when it is so that the procedure won't become part of their computerized medical records.[10] Minors, especially concerned that a bill or insurance form might be sent home and opened by a parent, find ways to come up with the cash.[11] Women with family doctors don't always tell them but travel instead to places farther away, not just to find a physician but to find a physician who doesn't know them.[12] Not always sure about their own doctor's views on abortion, some women are hesitant to jeopardize the ongoing relationship: "Even if he never showed any sign [of disapproval], I would, from that day on, be a lot more leery about how I was around him and the things that I would say. And I mean, this is the person that follows you through your pregnancy."[13] Abortion providers are regularly asked by patients if their "real" doctor will be able to tell that they've had an abortion. Even clinic waiting rooms are fraught. A high school teacher in Little Rock explained that "it makes me nervous even being in the waiting room. You don't want to know who's here, you don't want to be recognized, and you don't want to see them ever again."[14]

Of course, abortion is rarely a complete secret. Suburban teenagers seem to know the drill and help one another get to a clinic: someone gets the car; another has the covering "sleep-over."[15] Some women tell others selectively and over time: "[a girlfriend] . . . and her roommate were the only people I told, they weren't my closest friends. Even when, later, women friends told me about their abortions, I kept mine to myself. . . . My mother still doesn't know, though my daughter does. My second husband never knew, and I honestly don't know if I've ever told Joe, who's closer to me than any man has ever been."[16] Another woman described telling people on a "need to know" basis: "My lover who impregnated me, the man I lived with and later married, a friend who loaned me money, women who helped me locate a clinic, and finally, in an only-on-the-left-moment, the entire steering committee of a strike I was involved in during the course of an argument about who should get arrested—I couldn't risk civil disobedience and miss the clinic appointment."[17]

Logistical disclosures aside, most women—like those willing to challenge abortion regulations in court but only under an alias—prefer to keep their names out of it.[18] Even abortion advocacy groups have ditched the word "abortion": the National Association for the Repeal of Abortion Laws (1969) became the National Abortion Rights Action League (1973) and then the abortionless NARAL Pro Choice America (2003). Here it is worth remembering that those who provide abortion services—doctors, nurses, technicians, counselors, guards, receptionists—often wear first-name-only name tags on the job and don't always tell their families what they do or where they work.[19]

These many forms of concealment—and there are more to come—are examples of what I call abortion secrecy. The term "secrecy" seems a fair description of the deliberate nondisclosure that regularly accompanies planning or having an abortion, and it explains the often furtive behavior that marks the experience as something best hidden. There is, however, another way to describe all of this. One might say that women choose to keep their abortion intentions or histories under wraps not because these matters are *secret* but because they are *private*. Private means that certain information falls within a zone of personal control that as a cultural practice and sometimes as a matter of law is the person's alone to reveal, not because it must be hidden but because it is nobody else's business.

Exploring the differences between privacy and secrecy in the context of abortion is a way of understanding why, in general, women are hesitant to talk about and eager to distance themselves from the subject. People are generally better off—freer, more in charge, more autonomous—when they control who knows what personal information about them. My argument is that secrecy rather than privacy is often the more accurate characterization of the concealment that surrounds abortion. The distinction between these two forms of non-disclosure matters in how women experience the decision, the procedure, and its aftermath.

The distinction between privacy and secrecy has implications not only for individual women but also with regard to abortion talk, or how abortion is discussed at more public and political levels. The absence of private discussion distorts the nature of public debate, which in turn distorts the political discourse that informs legislative processes. Because people approach the public abortion debate on the basis of what they have been exposed to and have talked about, we cannot entirely sever private discussion from public politics. Consider how the dynamics of the same-sex marriage debate changed as people—elected representatives and their constituents—learned that their own children were gay. Not only did the guest list for family holiday meals expand as some of the regulars began to bring (or to reveal) their special guest as a partner, but within two generations the law recognized these partners as legal spouses.

The value of the upward progression of talk from private to public to political rests on the assumption that legislators and judges want or should want to have a sound factual basis before deciding how something should be regulated. This commitment to accuracy explains the regime of legislative and other fact-finding hearings that so occupy the present administrative state. Accurate data and reliable evidence are especially important in the context of abortion jurisprudence, where since 1992 a state's rendition of facts as laid out, say, in a statute's preamble was accepted as true. However, the Supreme Court made clear in the 2016 case of *Whole Woman's Health v. Hellerstedt* that determining the constitutionality of abortion regulation must depend on the accuracy of the relevant facts and not simply their endorsement by legislatures.[20] With this judicial shot across the bow, legislators have increased incentive to use evidence-based facts rather than aspirational ones in regulating the provision of abortion.

What women have to say about abortion—recognizing that women do not all say the same things—provides the best basis for what the experience of abortion is like: the decision making, the importance of the choice, the practical arrangements, the legal requirements, the procedure itself. In considering whether an abortion in early pregnancy is the same as the death of an infant, philosopher Bernard Williams states that "in the end, this issue can only come back to the experience of women. This is not because their experiences are the only thing that counts. It is because their experiences are the only realistic and honest guide we have to what the unique phenomenon of abortion genuinely is, as opposed to what moralists, philosophers and legislators say it is. It follows that their experience is the only realistic guide to what the deepest consequences will be of our social attitudes to abortion."[21] Without this "honest guide," facts one might want to know, rather than to surmise or imagine, are missing.

Consider the testimony of some 2,000 women who had terminated a pregnancy collected by the 2005 South Dakota Task Force on Abortion. The state legislature had charged the Task Force with answering a number of abortion-related questions, including such queries as "whether abortion is a workable method for the pregnant woman to waive her rights to a relationship with the child."[22] Perhaps not surprisingly in light of the charge, those surveyed testified almost to a woman about the overwhelming trauma and grief abortion had had on their lives; over 99 percent of them strongly believed that as a result of their experiences "abortion . . . should not be legal."[23] These are important statistics. Following feminist methodology, the Task Force claims to take women's experiences seriously. Yet the pervasive secrecy around abortion makes it difficult to evaluate the Task Force numbers against or alongside the testimony of women who did not step forward but for whom legal abortion was not traumatic and who, one imagines, were well pleased that the procedure was legal.

Abortion Privacy

As we know, in 1973 the Supreme Court in *Roe v. Wade* held that a woman's right to choose an abortion was encompassed within an existing "right of privacy." That right was pieced together from a number of constitutional provisions, each protecting people from some form of intrusion by the state. These included the Fourth Amendment's requirement of a warrant before someone's home may be searched and First Amendment protection around reading materials in one's home. Privacy was the umbrella concept under which various expressions of personal liberty and choice—marrying, raising children, using contraception—had been lodged constitutionally throughout the twentieth century. In *Roe,* the Court extended that decision-making authority to women who, in consultation with their doctor, sought an abortion. Because this form of privacy respects the personal autonomy embodied in the right to decide about important matters, it is sometimes called "decisional privacy." There is, however, another important dimension to privacy. The decision in *Roe* may have given women the right to decide, but it said very little about a woman's right to control publicity around the decision itself, once made or implemented. It is this form of privacy—"informational privacy"—that I focus on here.

Decisional privacy and informational privacy protect different interests: the first the right to make the decision, the second the right to keep the decision to yourself. Although the two concepts are distinct, they are often connected, for it is easy to see how making an abortion decision might be influenced by a woman's confidence in her ability to keep the whole thing confidential. She might, for example, be concerned about attempts by those who find out about (and oppose) her decision to prevent her from acting on it, whether through physical or emotional force or threat. The "right to choose" isn't much of a right if others can so easily prevent its exercise. In a case involving pregnant minors, Justice John Paul Stevens observed that "it is inherent in the right to make the abortion decision that the right may be exercised without public scrutiny."[24] The Supreme Court has recognized the possibility of such power plays by husbands over wives and by parents over daughters. This explains why as a matter of constitutional law, states may not condition an abortion on wives notifying or getting permission from their husbands and why special judicially supervised hearings have been established for minors who seek an abortion without involving their parents.

Beyond pressure that might literally block a pregnant woman or girl's access to abortion, "softer" forms of prevention arise when publicity before or after the procedure is part of the package. There is, for example, the very real worry of being named publicly by those opponents of abortion who stake out clinics precisely to expose the identity of women as they enter or leave, whether by posting the women's pictures online, or by sending them hateful literature in the mail, or by contacting the parents of teenagers.[25] In addition to private parties determined to "out" abortion patients, law also has the power to force, facilitate, or prevent disclosure. Permission to file a law suit as a Jane Doe is a good example of protecting privacy.

There are also more routine concerns, such as the confidentiality of public health data and medical and insurance records. In a 2004 decision quashing Attorney General John Ashcroft's subpoena seeking patient abortion records, a federal district court described the particular need for abortion nondisclosure this way: "American history discloses that the abortion decision is one of the most controversial decisions in modern life, with opprobrium ready to be visited by many upon the woman who so decides and the doctor who engages in the medical procedure. An emotionally charged decision will be rendered more so if the confidential medical records are released to the public, however redacted, for use in public litigation in which the patient is not even a party. Patients would rightly view such disclosure as a significant intrusion on their privacy."[26]

Individual decisions about abortion are thus complicated by women's awareness of the possibility of exposure by one or another means. In this way informational privacy is tucked into decisional privacy. As Justice Blackmun observed in *Thornburgh v. American College of Obstetrics and Gynecology,* "[a] woman and her physician will necessarily be more reluctant to choose an abortion if there exists a possibility that her decision and her identity will become known publicly."[27] Moreover, the threat of publicity—what the Supreme Court called "the specter of public exposure"—is not time limited but lingers and lurks over time.[28] Questions about past abortions have turned up in connection with all sorts of things, such as employment applications and political campaigns. In *Thorne v. City of El Segundo,* as part of the application process for a position with the city police department, a woman applicant was given a polygraph test asking whether she had had an abortion and with whom she had gotten pregnant.[29] On appeal a federal court found that this form of questioning had unquestionably intruded on Thorne's protected privacy interests. Yet such practices may continue casually, as job applicants do not always know if a nasty question is impermissible and even if it seems like it must be, complaining might finish off any prospect of being hired. This background fear goes for elected officials as well. On rare occasion women politicians have disclosed a past abortion: Texas senator Wendy Davis in her 2014 autobiography, U.S. congresswomen Jackie Speier and Gwen Moore on the House floor during a 2011 debate over defunding Planned Parenthood. What other personal information (affairs included) stands to derail a woman politician's campaign more quickly than abortion? In the 2003 contest for the Mississippi lieutenant governorship, the incumbent Republican Amy Tuck felt obliged to sign an affidavit swearing that she had never had an abortion in response to a challenge from Democratic opponent Barbara Blackmon. Tuck, the "right-to–life candidate," expressed her outrage at "this lowest form of vulgarity and innuendo."[30]

What Privacy Protects

Privacy scholar Alan Westin has defined privacy as the claim of individuals "to determine for themselves when, how and to what extent information about them is communicated to others."[31] This is a good start, but what is it about this information that, in contrast to all sorts of other things known about us, privileges it as a matter of privacy? Not everything one might prefer to keep to one's self—age, true hair color, or number of divorces, for example—is regarded as private so that "norms of non-intrusion" attach and the claim to privacy is respected. What exactly makes a matter private in this protected, inviolable sense, whether as a matter of law or social practice or individual expectation?

Although there are different accounts of what privacy encompasses, there is a general consensus that for information to be recognized as private, it must in the first instance be both very personal and very important to the person asserting the claim. One measure of this is taken from American tort law: is the disclosure of the information such "that a reasonable person would feel justified in feeling seriously aggrieved by it"?[32] While just how a reasonable person would feel is a matter for a jury to decide, private conduct in the areas of sex, procreation, and medical treatment usually fall within this scope. Thus the parents of triplets conceived through in vitro fertilization (IVF) could rightfully sue a television program that showed the couple at an IVF patient reunion on the ground that such exposure would offend the common decency of a reasonable person.[33] As the appellate court noted, the revelations of participating in an IVF program—"the physical problems which exist with the couple's reproductive systems or that they are incapable of performing sexually"—could indeed embarrass a reasonable person: "The plight of these unnamed plaintiffs to keep their bodily procreative secrets known only to their parents or certain close friends is of the highest importance to them."[34]

Yet not all expectations of privacy are privileged. One exception is that information may be publicly disclosed if the subject is of legitimate concern to the public, that is, if it is "newsworthy." Consider a 1995 Michigan case where antiabortion protestors argued that because abortion was an issue of legitimate concern to the public, two *Doe* plaintiffs had no privacy claim against protestors who displayed the plaintiffs' names on large placards held up for public view as the women arrived at a clinic for their scheduled abortions.[35] (The protestors were two nuns who had obtained clinic appointments records retrieved from a dumpster.) The trial court agreed with the protestors: "because abortions are so controversial in our society . . . [abortion] is unquestionably a matter of great public concern."[36] On appeal, the appellate court reversed, concluding that the disclosure of the Does' true names, implicating matters of both sexual relations and medical treatment, was something that any reasonable person would consider private.[37] As for abortion's "newsworthiness," the appellate court distinguished between two types of information: while "the abortion *issue* may be regarded as a matter of public interest, the plaintiffs' *identities* . . . were not."[38]

Other exceptions to the right to informational privacy arise in the context of criminal law. The state has a strong interest in the prosecution of criminals and in the acquisition of evidence to make the case. It was common in the nineteenth and twentieth centuries for prosecutors to subpoena abortion patients to testify against the physician who performed the illegal abortion. (This explains the practice of some physicians during the period of blindfolding their abortion patients.)[39] Husbands and boyfriends of women who had died from the illegal abortion were subpoenaed and sometimes arrested as accomplices.[40] Newspapers publicized the fact that following a raid on a Chicago abortion clinic in 1941, the police had the names of thousands of abortion patients; this information was used not only to call witnesses for trial but to keep everyone else under the threat of exposure.[41] Even when a woman died from an illegal abortion, relatives did not always want to testify in order to protect the woman's reputation and their own. "Her whole family had keenly felt the disgrace," testified one mother about her dead daughter.[42] As Sally Aldrich, who had an illegal abortion in the early 1960s, recalled after receiving a summons to testify against her doctor, "Oh my God! My face is going to be all over the Daily News, and my father's going to be commuting on the Chappaqua train, and I'll be there!"[43]

In addition to demands of the criminal law, the state has well-established demographic and public health interests in collecting certain personal information about its citizens. Starting at birth, a person's birth date, sex, race, and parents' names and marital status are recorded and become part of publicly available "vital statistics," however much a person might prefer the information—illegitimacy status, for example, or in earlier eras, race—to be kept private.[44] Importantly, "public records" generally defeat a claim to privacy with regard to the information they contain. Whether a record is public in this official sense becomes tremendously important with regard to abortion disclosure. Some public records reveal abortion-related facts, such as whether someone has made financial contributions to a pro-life or pro-choice cause or campaign or how a judge has ruled in an abortion-related case, such as those involving teenager bypass petitions.

Other public records have been used to target abortion patients, or those thought to be abortion patients. Consider state drivers' licenses, which have traditionally been considered public records: anyone could go to the Department of Motor Vehicles, provide a license plate number, and get the name of the vehicle's owner. Certain pro-life groups did just that with cars parked outside clinics or doctors' offices where abortions were performed. Iowa senator Tom Harkin testified how one of his constituents had visited an ob–gyn specialist for care during a difficult pregnancy that ended in miscarriage. Having been identified through her license plate, the woman subsequently received a "venomous letter" discussing "the guilt of having killed one's own child" and "God's curses for the shedding of innocent blood" from the pro-life organization Operation Rescue.[45] Virginia senator Charles Robb similarly reported how a constituent had visited a clinic only to find black balloons and antiabortion literature on her home doorstep a few days later. Harkin and Robb gave their testimony in support of the Drivers' Privacy Protection Act of 1994, which ended the practice of reverse-searching license plates by removing license plate data from what had previously been deemed a public and therefore an available record.

In addition to information contained in public records, claims to privacy are also compromised if an activity takes place in a public place. The idea is that a person can have no expectation of privacy when anyone on the street could see them with his own eyes. For example, being celebrated in a gay bar makes it harder for the person later to sue for invasion of privacy when the event is publicized. This happened following the attempted assassination of President Ford in 1975, when news stations reported that " 'Bill' Sipple, the ex-Marine who grabbed Sara Jane Moore's arm just as her gun was fired . . . was the center of midnight attention at the Red Lantern, a [gay] bar he favors."[46] Sipple sued for invasion of privacy and lost.

To some degree, expectations of privacy on the street may depend on one's zip code. In *Chico Feminist Women's Health Center v. Scully,* the health center sought to bar protestors from standing at the entrance of its parking lot. The clinic argued that because the town of Chico was so small, protestors would be able to identify abortion patients as they entered and call out to them by name. Maybe so, but the court didn't buy the invasion of privacy argument, noting that the plaintiffs, "having chosen to live in the environment of a small city . . . cannot expect the courts . . . to guarantee them the kind of anonymity they might find in a 'large metropolitan community' such as New York City."[47] (The protestors had already been enjoined from further publicizing the names of patients they identified.)

There is also no claim to privacy when a person makes information publicly available, say by a self-post on a social media page; publicizing a fact oneself is said to "waive" the right to privacy.[48] Consider the public declaration of 300 prominent French women in 1971 that each had terminated a pregnancy in defiance of the French criminal code. They were followed in 1972 by fifty-three well-known women in the United States—Gloria Steinem, Billie Jean King, and Lillian Hellman among them—who outed themselves in the debut issue of *Ms.* magazine. In each case the disclosures were voluntary; publicity and its consequences were the very point of the plan. But although sidewalks may be spaces to which expectations of privacy do not attach, Congress and several state legislatures have offered abortion patients a measure of privacy by requiring a distance be maintained between protestors and patients. Eight feet is common or in Massachusetts twenty-five feet if ordered by the police.[49] These Freedom of Access to Clinic Entrances acts are meant to protect patients from harassment and the threat of violence from antiabortion activists.[50]

Relinquishing one's privacy rights has become a regular feature of daily life in the United States. Commercial data collection may easily uncover private reproductive matters. For example, the mega-store Target uses "predictive analyses" based on a customer's prior purchases to figure out what she is likely to buy in the future. One example that made headlines—"How Target Figured out a Girl Was Pregnant before Her Father Did"—involved Target's assessment that a teenage customer was probably pregnant; home pregnancy tests, scent-free items, and certain vitamins are three of the twenty-five data points used to detect pregnancy.[51] Target then sent coupons for diapers and cribs to the teenager's home address, to the puzzlement and fury of her dad.[52] After the coupons arrived, the father demanded an apology from Target, accusing them of encouraging his daughter to get pregnant. (He subsequently apologized: "It turns out there's been some activities in my house I haven't been completely aware of."[53]) It is unclear what Target's data points for ending a pregnancy are, but surely they have some. The metadata collected from cell phones—the time, date, duration, and location of calls—are easily minable for abortion-related data. In testifying before a committee of the European Parliament, journalist Glenn Greenwald used abortion patients as exactly the kind of identification that metadata makes possible.[54] Smartphone users give carriers permission to track their location. Accordingly, there is now direct antiabortion marketing via smartphones to abortion patients waiting in clinics. RealOptions, a California network of pro-life crisis pregnancy centers, ping women's GPS-enabled phones using a technique called "mobile geofencing" to warn "abortion-minded women" that it is not too late to change their minds.[55]

Yet even in the face of widespread data culling, coupon sending, and GPS surveillance, there remains an established notion of a "right to be left alone," which people expect as part of their social due. This expectation is maintained through a combination of social customs, professional practices, and law. Yes, the press may have First Amendment rights to report on the newsworthy among us, but the rest of us enjoy a degree of security over who can publicize what about us.[56] Sissela Bok has called this conception of privacy "control over access to what one takes . . . to be one's personal domain."[57] As stated in the principles of American tort law: "Every individual has some phases of his life and his activities and some facts about himself that he does not expose to the public eye, but keeps entirely to himself and at most reveals only to his family or to close personal friends."[58]

To be sure, not everyone keeps all phases of life close to the vest. As a culture we have become both hugely confessional and massively indiscreet. But even amidst the casual exhibitionism of Americans today, not quite everything has become the stuff of reality prime time. Some things are still regarded as private, and when such privacy is violated, different forms of recourse become available. Some are socially imposed, such as the diminished reputation of the gossiper within his community. (In colonial New England, gossiping was denounced from the pulpit as usurping the right of God alone to judge people.[59]) There are also market mechanisms for deterring offensive disclosures, such as PayPal withdrawing its services from commercial mug shot websites that post arrest mug shots and take them down for a price ("We looked at the activity and found it repugnant").[60] Other protection results from voluntary restraints, as when news media refuse to publish the names of rape victims as a matter of professional ethics, even though the woman's name is part of the public trial record.[61]

Still other remedies of particular interest to us here are legal in character. When privacy is invaded by private citizens or private entities—a neighbor publicly accuses another of being a thief (or an abortionist); a newspaper runs a story naming a woman as having had an affair (or an abortion)—the subject of the story can sue for money damages using such traditional common law torts as defamation, the invasion of privacy, or the intentional infliction of emotional distress.[62]

Thus in *Glover v. The Herald Company,* the *St. Louis Globe-Democrat* published a story that Mrs. Delores Glover, a city alderwoman, stated in a public meeting about regulating city abortion clinics that she herself had had two

abortions. The article was mistaken; another alderwoman had made the remarks. (To make things more confusing, the other alderwoman said she meant
"miscarriages" when she said "abortions.") When Mrs. Glover read the article,
she became "upset to such a degree that she required sedation" and for two
weeks received anonymous obscene telephone calls and hate mail from readers
of the paper.[63] She brought a claim in defamation for the publication of a false
injurious statement, but the case was thrown out. The problem was that the
law lowers the threshold for what the press can get wrong when the subject of
a story is, like Mrs. Glover, a public figure. To win, Glover would have had to
show that the newspaper was not simply negligent but had acted recklessly or
with malice in publishing the erroneous story.[64] *Glover* and other defamation
abortion cases reveal that although plaintiffs sometimes lose (filing a claim too
late or not meeting the heightened test for public figures), courts accept without
the need for proof that an allegation of abortion is defamatory. They take "judicial notice" of abortion as information that falls within the reasonable expectation of personal privacy.[65]

When a protected privacy interest is violated not by a private actor (the
neighbor, the newspaper) but by the state, then in addition to the possibility
of monetary damages, courts may also declare the particular practice unconstitutional and bar it across the board. We see this in tussles over the confidentiality
of abortion records. In the 1986 case of *Thornburgh v. American College of Obstetricians & Gynecologists,* the Supreme Court struck down a Pennsylvania
statute requiring physicians to officially report every abortion performed after
the first trimester, along with the patient's age, race, marital status, number of
prior pregnancies, date of her last menstrual period, method of payment, her
city and state of residence, and whether the procedure was an emergency. Not
surprisingly, the Court found that the nature and amount of this information
was "so detailed that identification is likely."[66]

However, not all informational record keeping is considered a substantial
threat to an abortion patient's privacy. To protect the informational privacy
of pregnant minors who attend bypass hearings seeking a judge's permission
to consent to an abortion, a 2000 Arizona statute provided that "members of
the public" could not "inspect, obtain copies of or otherwise have access to"
any record of bypass proceedings.[67] However, Arizona defined the word
"public" to exclude "judges, clerks, administrators, professionals or other persons employed by or working under the supervision of the court or employees
of other public agencies who are authorized by state or federal rule or law to

inspect and copy closed court records."[68] Planned Parenthood of Arizona argued that these exceptions were so broad as to swallow up whatever protection denying access to the members of the public had originally promised. Conceding that the Arizona exceptions were broader than those in other states, the Ninth Circuit Court of Appeals held that the language of the statute alone neither violated a minor's statutory right to anonymity nor her "privacy interest in avoiding disclosure of sensitive personal information."[69] The pregnant minor's rights were sufficiently protected because the release of bypass records remained within the discretion only of the courts and not of administrative personnel who might seek access.[70]

Elected state officials have on occasion sought to acquire abortion records outside the bounds of existing legislation. An aggressive example is Kansas state attorney general Phil Kline, who in the early 2000s tried to obtain confidential abortion records of minors from a private Wichita clinic by linking abortions performed at the clinic to crime. Kline's theory was that by virtue of their pregnancies, the minors had had sexual intercourse with *someone;* their medical records were therefore evidence in child abuse prosecutions Kline intended to bring against those persons whose identities would emerge during the course of interviews with the minors.[71] Kline subpoenaed not only the clinic's records but anonymous public health data on abortions performed within a particular period and the registration book from a motel near the clinic to see if he could cross-reference out-of-town patients with out-of-town guests. The clinic brought suit to block the subpoena, and the case traveled back and forth on remand and appeal in the courts for some six years.[72] In the end, Kline's legal theory collapsed: the Kansas legislature passed a new law clarifying that sexual activity of a minor did not in itself and without proof of harm constitute reportable child abuse. Nonetheless, it took six years of hard-fought legal and political activity to sort the matter out, during which time once-pregnant teenagers were in limbo about the security of their names and records. The law may be one thing, its application another. How statutes are enforced depends on the perspective, zealousness, and creativity of those who administer the law. The Kansas Kline example makes clear that privacy can be so stretched as to erode both common law and legislatively intended protections.

From time to time Congress has enacted special laws to protect privacy interests about which there are particular concerns; following the hearings on Judge Robert Bork to the Supreme Court, Congress enacted the Video Privacy Protection Act of 1988 to protect the privacy of a person's video rental records.

Patients' medical records now receive greater protection under the Health Insurance Portability and Accountability Act of 1996. We have already seen the Drivers' Privacy Protection Act of 1994, enacted in part to prevent fellow citizens from tracking down abortion patients through their license plates. These many forms of privacy protection and remedies—some compensating the person for unwanted exposure, others enjoining laws that insufficiently protect privacy—show how much privacy is valued as a matter of law and how seriously its invasions are taken.

The Stronger Shield of Secrecy

In her study of the emergence of privacy in eighteenth-century novels, Patricia Spacks observes that privacy developed from a general notion of being left alone into "a condensation of ideas about autonomy," which Spacks describes as "an inner uncoerced realm."[73] In this way privacy pertains to autonomy—the control that a person has over her self-presentation—and to dignity. A person is not properly respected if the personal contents of her life become the plaything of others' curiosity. Philosopher Ferdinand Schoeman phrases it somewhat differently, explaining that "privacy provides the context for personal objectives being respected";[74] it protects "[a] private sphere of valuation."[75] One develops one's own values from the repertoire of values offered up by society and tries them out or on, to see if they fit. This is sometimes a tentative process, undertaken with hesitation but made possible by the background security of control over what can be known by others. Thus privacy makes possible a framing of the self over time: "An individual's ability to reveal or hide information is crucial to [an] individual's ability to shape the social world in her immediate vicinity."[76] Moreover, as Spacks insists, it is the *voluntariness* associated with privacy that distinguishes it from "less desirable forms of seclusion, such as loneliness, alienation, ostracism, and isolation."[77] There is something empowering about exercising privacy as an aspect of choice and self-definition. This is what explains privacy's "self-evident desirability."[78]

If privacy embodies a self-evident desirability, secrecy is a more ominous proposition, more in line with the less desirable forms of seclusion. Secrecy suggests that it is best to keep a matter to yourself not simply because, all things considered, you prefer to do so as a matter of exploration or self-definition, but from the concern that if you do not, harm will follow. In her book *Secrets,* Sissela Bok focuses on harm to explain why revealing the secrets of others is morally wrong. It is not just that the secret concerns "matters legitimately considered private" but that the revelation will "hurt the individual talked about."[79] The pervasive silence around abortion is more a matter of secrecy than privacy in just this way: it anticipates the harm to individual women that is reasonably understood to accompany disclosure.

To be sure, abortion privacy and abortion secrecy have certain goals and techniques in common. Both concern the "subjective dimension of social life," and both reflect the desire to control publicity over a particular matter. This explains why the two concepts are often blurred in ordinary conversation. There is no suggestion of anything clandestine when the answer to the question "Are you having a boy or a girl?" is "That's my little secret." Yet while privacy and secrecy may overlap in purpose, in method, and in ordinary conversation, the two are not the same, and it is the difference in motivation for nondisclosure under one regime or the other that matters for thinking about abortion talk. Privacy is valued for what it provides to those who choose it: a decision taken for privacy is credited as reflecting a person's will; it is an exercise of autonomy. There may be reasons to keep quiet just as there may be good reasons to speak, but however things are sized up, a decision for privacy means that the person herself has done the sizing. She alone chooses to divulge or not and for whatever set of reasons she finds appealing or convincing.

By contrast, the decision to keep a matter secret in the context of abortion is often a response to the threat or prospect of harm, whether harassment, stigmatization, or fear of violence. Under such circumstances, the exercise of agency has to work alongside the fact of apprehension. To be sure, fixing the exact motive for nondisclosure in any one instance may not be entirely neat. Nonetheless, in the context of abortion, a decision for secrecy suggests the presence of more fearful concerns about disclosure that a decision for privacy as such does not. The pressure to conceal an abortion, or to conceal even thinking about an abortion, may not rise to the level of duress in the strict legal sense of the word—an unlawful threat that deprives a person of her free will, leaving her with no reasonable alternative.[80] Rather, a set of social pressures pushes the motivation for abortion nondisclosure from the preference for privacy into a perceived need for secrecy.

I am not claiming that privacy is always good and secrecy always bad. In the not-so-distant past, claims to privacy were used to shield practices of family violence from outside scrutiny; the home was the man's castle and so on. Nor am I claiming that all commitments to secrecy are motivated by fear. One may be obligated to keep information secret as a matter of private contract (trade secrets) or statute (state secrets) or professional ethics (client or pastoral secrets). There are also voluntary secrecy pacts—think of Romeo and Juliet (and the Friar)—and entire secret societies where, as sociologist Georg Simmel has explained, secrecy operates to engender trust among group members.[81] Indeed, depending on the circumstances, secrecy may have an array of positive benefits. Secret keeping is sometimes regarded as a measure of character, as when in *Sense and Sensibility* Elinor Dashwood receives an unbidden secret from Miss Lucy Steele ("I certainly did not seek your confidence, but you do me no more than justice in imagining that I may be depended on. Your secret is safe with me").[82] For others, like Oscar Wilde, secrecy adds a delicious tension to ordinary life: "The commonest thing is delightful if only one hides it."[83] What matters is that we recognize and appreciate the important substantive difference between these two modes of concealment when the subject is abortion. Abortion concealment in contemporary society aligns not with privacy but with secrecy. That secrecy is a much darker, more psychologically taxing, and socially corrosive phenomenon than privacy.[84]

What occasions the call for this more disturbing form of concealment? That is, why do people want things kept secret? One answer is for the same reasons they want to keep them private, except more securely so. The greater need for secrecy reflects a greater degree of apprehension. As Sissela Bok has observed, secrecy operates as an "additional shield in case the protections of privacy should fail."[85] Historian Deborah Cohen describes secrecy as "privacy's indispensable handmaiden."[86] And what occasions the need for shields and handmaidens is the perceived disaster that revelation is understood to produce.

Consider, by way of another analogy, the decision to acknowledge one's sexual orientation at a time when announced homosexuality was grounds for dismissal from work, the loss of custody of one's children, and arrest on morals charges. Until recently, these were all lawful responses by police, by school boards, and by courts. There were also (and still are) unlawful responses, such as blackmail, intimidation, and violence. It isn't hard to see why when being openly gay was regarded as illegal, immoral, and disgusting—and with the advent of AIDS, homicidal—a closet, preferably locked, was a safer place. But locating closets within the domain of privacy doesn't really capture the nature of "closetedness," a form of concealment that is both furtive and debilitating as the fear of exposure looms over daily life. As Eve Sedgwick wrote in 1990, "even an out gay person deals daily with interlocutors about whom she doesn't know whether they know or not [and] . . . whether, if they did know, the knowledge would seem very important . . . there are remarkably few of even the most openly gay people who are not deliberately in the closet with someone personally or economically or institutionally important to them."[87] Under such conditions, it is not hard to see how "secrecy . . . degrade[s] privacy."[88]

Something quite similar now exists with regard to abortion which, like homosexuality, has a legacy of illegality, with its lingering shadow of disapproval. Abortion doctors are not physicians but "abortionists," a term drenched in the disrepute of pre-*Roe* abortion practices; the preferred title now appears to be "abortion provider" or "provider" in part to avoid the connotation even of "abortion doctor." Recall Dr. Meyers's tale from Edgar Lee Masters's *Spoon River Anthology:*

> *I was healthy, happy, in comfortable fortune,*
> *Blest with a congenial mate, my children raised,*
> *All wedded, doing well in the world.*
> *And then one night, Minerva, the poetess,*
> *Came to me in her trouble, crying.*
> *I tried to help her out—she died—*
> *They indicted me, the newspapers disgraced me,*
> *My wife perished of a broken heart.*
> *And pneumonia finished me.* [89]

The shadow of disapproval draws from other regular (and reasonable) abortion-related practices of deception. For some women getting an abortion involves lying (about where one is going and why) and subterfuge (organizing days and nights away from home when up against a mandated waiting period and the nearest clinic is hundreds of miles away). Disrepute also explains why the loss of pregnancy through abortion is sometimes passed off as a miscarriage. Indeed, some women choose a medical abortion over a surgical one precisely because the process mimics the more acceptable miscarriage. As the husband of one miscarrying woman commented, "It's acceptable to talk about miscarriage; a person doesn't look like a killer."[90]

The word abortion keeps bad company. In *People v. Weaver,* a state police investigator attached a GPS device to the underside of Weaver's van without getting a warrant for what New York's highest court held was indeed a search.[91] The interesting part of the case for us is the court's description of the sorts of "indisputably private" activities that might be retrieved from the GPS's transmitter: "trips to the psychiatrist, the plastic surgeon, *the abortion clinic,* the AIDS treatment center, the strip club, the criminal defense attorney, the by-the-hour motel, the union meeting, the mosque, synagogue or church, the gay bar and on and on."[92] In the judicial imagination, abortion is up there with no-tell motels, AIDS clinics, and shrink appointments.

Information about a prior abortion is still taken as proof of bad—even murderous—character. In civil, criminal, and family law custody cases, evidence of a prior abortion has been admitted in court to show that a woman litigant is undeserving, untrustworthy, or unmotherly and that she should not prevail. In *Garcia v. Providence Medical Center,* for example, Mrs. Garcia brought a malpractice action against a hospital seeking damages for emotional distress following the death of her infant son while in its care. The trial court permitted the hospital to present evidence that Mrs. Garcia had had three abortions in the years prior to her son's birth.[93] At the trial's end, the judge ruled against Mrs. Garcia. She appealed on the ground that evidence of her prior abortions should have been excluded. The Washington State Court of Appeals agreed with Mrs. Garcia, observing that the hospital's claim rested on the implicit assumption "that if a woman has voluntarily consented to an abortion, she is less affected by the pain of the loss of a child than a woman who never voluntarily terminated a pregnancy."[94] This the appellate court refused to accept, ordering a new trial to be conducted without the abortion evidence that had been used to rebut evidence about Mrs. Garcia's good character.[95]

The *Garcia* case follows the logic of a 1919 Oregon case where abortion evidence was admitted in court to tarnish the reputation of a father who had paid for his married daughter's abortion. The husband had sued his father-in-law for alienation of the daughter's affection, and evidence about the payment came up in the context of the father helping his daughter. Even though abortion was illegal at the time, the Oregon court held for the father, excluding the evidence on the grounds that it only served to "debase and degrade" him. Indeed, no other evidence "could have been offered which was more likely to inflame and prejudice the minds of the jury against [him]."[96] Yet there is no hard-and-fast rule about the use of prior abortion evidence in civil cases. In a 2002 Georgia suit by a son for the wrongful death of his mother, the trial court rejected evidence of his mother's prior abortions as irrelevant to the issue of her life expectancy. However, the same court clarified that such evidence could come in to rebut statements that the "decedent was a good mother or a good person or wanted to work with children."[97]

Past abortions also come up in criminal cases. As a Florida district court of appeals stated in 2010, "the cases tell us—as if we needed to be told—that 'abortion is one of the most inflammatory issues of our time,' and more importantly, that one who takes or even approves of this course is very adversely regarded by many in our society."[98] In that case, the defendant had been sentenced to twenty-five years for the aggravated manslaughter of her thirteen-month-old child, who had died from malnutrition. The state sought to introduce evidence at trial that when the defendant first learned she was pregnant, she had considered abortion. The appellate court upheld the trial court's exclusion of the evidence, noting that "it is apparently thought that a person who considers abortion is more likely to have killed the child not aborted."[99] The appellate court was particularly concerned because the issue of exactly how the child had died "presented close questions," making any discussion of abortion "all the more deleterious to the mother's chance at a fair trial."[100]

Nonetheless, in case after case parties attempt to bring in past abortion evidence to show that a woman defendant is probably more culpable or that a woman witness is less likely to tell the truth. In *Collman v. State*, Collman was on trial for murdering his girlfriend's three-year-old son. He sought to impeach (cast doubt on) the testimony of his girlfriend, who testified she had loved staying home with her son, by introducing evidence of a prior abortion. In this case, the trial court ruled that the value of the evidence was " 'overwhelmingly outweighed' by the danger of unfair prejudice, confusing the issues, and misleading the jury."[101]

Similarly, in *Billett v. State*, convicted murderer Daniel Billett appealed his conviction on the ground that the trial court had not permitted him to cross-examine the state's key witness with regard to her prior abortions. Billett claimed that his disapproval of those abortions (he condemned her to "burn in hell") prejudiced her against him, making her testimony unreliable.[102] The court held that the witness's bias could be established through other evidence (like their breakup) so that it was unnecessary to bring in prejudicial abortion evidence to make the point.[103] In a 1979 Michigan case, *People v. Morris,* the defendant appealed her murder conviction on the grounds that prior abortion evidence had improperly influenced the jury's verdict. The trial court had ruled before the jury was seated that evidence of the prior abortions was admissible (as relevant to her sanity). Knowing this, the defense counsel felt obliged to question all prospective jurors about their attitudes toward abortion before seating them. During that process a prospective juror stated that if chosen, she would "'go into trial with the attitude that [the defendant had] already committed a murder' by virtue of her abortions."[104] The juror was seated over the objection of the defense counsel. On appeal, the court found the evidence was clearly more prejudicial than probative and a new trial was ordered.

Abortion also comes up in custody cases, sometimes with a vengeance. The idea seems to be that something profound about a woman's character as a mother is revealed by the fact of a prior abortion. In a 2013 knock-down custody fight, a New York family court judge permitted the wife to be interrogated in open court about an abortion she had after the couple split up, as part of the husband's proof that she was an unfit mother. (The abortion had turned up in the wife's subpoenaed medical records.) The husband's attorney argued that because the wife was Catholic, the abortion called her credibility into question, and the judge admitted the evidence. The husband claimed that the abortion and not the marriage had caused the wife's stressed-out behavior; in a particularly pernicious catch-22, the attorney argued that either the wife was "traumatized by the abortion . . . or worse, she wasn't traumatized by it."[105]

But evidence about a mother's prior abortion is not always admitted in custody cases. The modern rule, as stated in a 2011 South Carolina case, is that "a parent's personal, moral behavior" may be considered only when it directly or indirectly affects the child's welfare.[106] In that case the family law judge had admitted evidence of the thirty-five-year-old mother's abortion after a brief relationship with a nineteen-year-old. Said the judge in awarding custody of the child to the wife's ex-husband, "being with a 19 year old. . . . That's irresponsible. And then having an abortion. That's irresponsible. I am concerned about the environment."[107] (When questioned about the abortion, the mother testified that a second child would detract from her time with her existing child, who had been diagnosed with autism, and that she didn't want the "boyfriend" involved in her family's life.) The appellate court found no evidence of any detrimental impact on the child and remanded the case for reconsideration without the abortion evidence.

The circumstances of an abortion decision mean different things to different judges. The judge in a 2004 New York case admitted evidence regarding the wife's prior abortion and, having "considered [her] unstable lifestyle and the circumstances surrounding [her] decision to have an abortion, including the incidents of domestic violence between [her] and the purported father of that unborn child," awarded custody to the ex-husband.[108] In the days of a fault-based divorce, a party could not both engage in bad behavior (abortion in the days of illegality) *and* receive a divorce on the theory that "crime should not pay." Historian Leslie Reagan quotes a judge in 1915: "A woman who would destroy life in that manner is not fit for decent society. It is the duty of any healthy married woman to bear children. Divorce denied."[109]

These cases show that the admission of abortion evidence is never "harmless error" in a social sense, even when it is excluded from any retrial. The first trial had already made public (in her immediate circle and in law books forever) the information that the woman litigant wished to keep private. This protracted threat to women's reputations, their peace of mind, and their legal status—guilty or innocent, custodial or non-custodial, honest witness or liar—is some of what is at stake with abortion disclosure in the area of family law. Privacy is all very nice, but for such a robust concept it proves disturbingly porous in practical ways.

The fragility of privacy protections suggests to some that secrecy may be the better way to go. A well-kept abortion secret provides its keeper with a degree of solace and security: the information remains safe. No one knows. Yet the comfort often has a tentative quality, accompanied as it often is by fear of leaks or slippage or just bad luck. Depending on a sizeable list of variables—the reliability of formal safeguards, the trustworthiness of those who know, the efforts of antiabortion campaigners to publicize patient identity—the possibility of exposure hovers over women's lives, even while in other respects their post-abortion lives would seem to have moved on. As a matter of prudence, abortion secrecy seems a more secure strategy than counting on a right to privacy for protection.

This might sound as though I am building a case for secrecy if one cares about women's general well-being. But no. I am not detailing the harms of disclosure in order to make a normative argument for secrecy over privacy. Nothing would be better by my lights than to relocate abortion from the darker realm of secrecy to the more voluntaristic domain of privacy where women could talk or remain silent as they please but for reasons other than a well-founded fear of harm. I am not out to secure abortion secrecy so much as to reveal it, as part of a descriptive move to demonstrate how abortion silence works.

As what is "secret" morphs into what seems "natural," secrecy can begin to appear so normal as to lose its characterization as secret. This is true for other reproductive events that quietly mark women's lives, such as menstruation, miscarriage, and menopause. Because abortion isn't discussed or discussable at private levels, it seems as if it isn't exactly happening, or at least it isn't happening to anyone you know or care about. Any more intimate connection to abortion is confounded by the reticence of women to speak up and by a failure of imagination (or a reluctance to imagine) by those around them. Just as some people (Supreme Court Justice Lewis Powell in 1986) thought they had never met a gay person, and other people think they have never met a woman who has placed a child for adoption, abortion too comes to seem like a remote phenomenon, something that doesn't happen in our family, at least not until that breakthrough conversation when all the reasons for not talking about abortion crumble and revelation and release are possible. And though not true across all families, it is worth considering whether the sister or aunt who reveals an abortion will be regarded so very differently by her family and others than she was before the revelation.

And so we arrive at the possibility of abortion revelation. Abortion secrecy harms women by distorting their public lives—lives lived in public space—and their private talk as both the burden of keeping a secret and its unbidden disclosure are ongoing sources of stress and anxiety. It also distorts the quality of lawmaking by omitting from public consideration whatever information would emerge if abortion were not a discrediting closeted matter. Revelation (even at the level of conversations within a family) offers relief on both fronts. Things improve when secrecy's corrosive power gives way to the option of privacy. As David Bowie's character says in *The Man Who Fell to Earth,* "My life isn't secret, Mr. Farnsworth, but it is private."[110] Public discussion is improved by the introduction of new information that is released, which in turn trickles up and into political deliberation as well. And just how does abortion revelation or disclosure come about? Family secrets, or some of them, have different ways and reasons for emerging over time: the burden of secrecy becomes too great; the reason for secrecy dissolves; the conviction about not telling comes to feel like a relic; everyone knows the secret anyway. But in addition to what might seem like incidental slippage, are there more structural processes by which forbidden subjects become normalized?

Certain deep secrets of the past have been relinquished, and while they may not map directly onto our own, much of what could once not be discussed has moved into more open public space. Victorians in nineteenth-century England did not discuss the mixed-race youth brought back from India looking quite like the master; there were also the "bachelor uncle" and the lunatic child.[111] Over the course of the twentieth century, Americans have had their own list of secrets: our own bachelor uncles, mixed-race genealogies, and memberships in the Communist Party. How each of these became liberated focuses our attention on the relation between secret keeping and social and legal change.

Aspects of one's reproductive life are precisely the sort of information that is a woman's alone to reveal, share, or tuck away; this is the essence of privacy. In contrast, secrecy registers as more desperate and more necessary. In thinking through the relation between privacy and secrecy in the context of abortion, there is still room for argument about where to locate the boundary between the two forms of nondisclosure and how the costs to women of one or the other should be measured against its benefits. But wherever that line may eventually be drawn, it is no good for women to feel empowered by exercising privacy rights when secrecy masquerades as privacy.

4

The Eye of the Storm

On August 29, 2005, as Hurricane Katrina approached the Gulf Coast of the United States, the National Oceanic and Atmospheric Administration (NOAA) captured the ferocity of the storm's progress in a series of memorable color satellite pictures. The threatening hurricane appears as a dense swirling mass with a small eye at its center, the swirl thinning out into a curling tail. Think perhaps of a fat tadpole or a pronounced paisley.

Others saw a different design. On August 30, a group called Columbia Christians for Life (CCL) sent out a press release to its members containing the NOAA picture of Katrina bearing down on the coast. The accompanying text stated that the picture "looks like a 6-week unborn human child as it comes ashore the Gulf Coast. . . . The image of the hurricane above with its eye already ashore at 12:32 PM Monday, August 29 looks like a fetus (unborn human baby) facing to the left (west) in the womb, in the early weeks of gestation (approx. 6 weeks). Even the orange color of the image is reminiscent of a commonly used pro-life picture of early prenatal development. . . . This hurricane looks like an unborn human child."[1] According to the CCL this was no coincidence: there was a direct relation between the storm's prenatal manifestation and the destruction wrought upon New Orleans. As the email explained, "Louisiana has 10 child-murder-by-abortion centers—FIVE are in New Orleans." It concluded with an imperative: "God's message: REPENT AMERICA!"[2]

In some respects, the image of a vengeful, God-sent fetus taking aim at sinful New Orleans is a familiar story. For most of human history, disasters of all sorts—pestilence, dam bursts, AIDS—have been interpreted as divine retribution for one or another human failing.[3] Such calamities are often accompanied by visual imagery—Satan's face visible in the dark smoke arising from the fallen World Trade Center, for example, as a divine (or demonic) signature.

There are, of course, more scientific explanations about why disasters happen and why, when they do, the face of God or the devil seems so regularly to appear. Humans are programmed to construct faces from abstract designs. This hardwired instinct explains why people are able to see the man in the moon or, as is reported every now and then, the face of the Virgin Mary in a highway underpass.[4] There are, however, no data to suggest that humans are similarly programmed to see a fetus; that visualization is not (yet) part of the evolutionary design. Even so, the fetal shape is now readily recognizable. Fetal images turn up in high school biology texts, as cookie cutters, on postage stamps, in *Star Trek* scripts, and in challah dough.[5] In contrast to the extraordinary spectral sightings that accompany disasters, seeing a fetus is no longer itself ephemeral or extraordinary. People of all sorts—no longer just sonographers or abortion activists but graphic designers, cartoonists, and advertisers—engage with fetal imagery in one form or another as a matter of course.

Yet the Katrina fetus brought something new to the table. For while claims are made in good faith about what fetuses are like, ferocity is not usually on the list. To be sure, fetuses can be annoying, as when they disrupt a pregnant woman's sleep by kicking, but we don't usually attribute that to mean-spiritedness or retaliation. Fetuses are regarded as gentle, endearing, even friendly presences who, we are sometimes told by cheerful sonographers, "wave" or "smile" to those of us peering in via ultrasound. Yet in twenty-first-century America, even well-mannered fetuses are a force to be reckoned with. Over the last fifty years, the fetus has nestled itself meaningfully not only into the bosom of many Americans but into the heart of our politics as well. Of course the "fetus," even as a collective noun, hasn't nestled itself into anything; it is not capable of such external self-direction. Others act on its behalf, or sometimes on their own behalves, using fetal images and imagined or projected fetal interests to accomplish a particular end. Recall the clever 1991 Volvo advertisement featuring a full-page sonogram of a fetus with the simple tagline at the bottom "Is Something Inside Telling You to Buy a Volvo?"[6] As anthropologist Janelle Taylor observed, "Not long ago, a fetus tried to sell me a car—or should I say, a car tried to sell me a fetus."[7]

Yet despite its lack of actual agency, even with regard to its own growth, the fetus is an important cultural player and one that spends increasingly little time on the bench. In addition to commercial interests (or in the Volvo ad, a trifecta of commercial, fetal, and maternal interests), the fetus has become actively involved across a range of endeavors—religious, scientific, artistic, medical, literary, political, and, of course, procreative. Each form of engagement between citizens and fetuses, real or representational, further imbricates the fetus into the everyday life of twenty-first-century America. Many Americans have been socialized, or perhaps indoctrinated, into accepting fetal interests as part of what concerned citizens and legislators think about. Bartenders refuse to serve alcohol to pregnant women and fellow patrons feel free to chastise those who do take a sip. State legislatures roll out bills by the bushel in the name of fetal well-being every year.[8] As political scientist Rosalind Petchesky observed years ago, "the curled-up profile, with its enlarged head and finlike arms . . . has become so familiar that not even most feminists question its authenticity (as opposed to its relevance)."[9] In light of all this acculturation, I shall talk about "the fetus" as though it were an independent actor with decisional capabilities and preferences, recognizing that a fetus or embryo (or its images or representations) does not in fact decide anything.

Evaluating the fetus as a player is a challenging task. It requires some preliminary agreement about just who or what we are talking about, for no one fetus stands in for the group; in legal terms there is no "named plaintiff" for the class. Indeed, in a legal sense, there cannot be. In a suit seeking to ban federal funding for stem cell research, a federal district court refused to permit "would-be plaintiff Mary Doe, *ex utero* embryo" to represent a class of 20,000 other *ex utero* embryos being "held" (not "stored") cryonically in laboratories.[10] The district court explained that in order for Mary Doe to be a litigant, as a minor under eighteen, she would have to be represented by a guardian. Yet the Federal Rules of Civil Procedure permit the appointment of guardians only for persons, and "the Supreme Court has made clear that the word 'person,' as used in the Fourteenth Amendment, does not include the unborn."[11]

But although the Constitution tells us what a fetus is not, we need something more positive to work with. It seems sensible to start with the definition of fetus found in standard medical texts. There it is generally agreed from an embryological stance that human life begins with the conceptus or "product of conception," which, over time and absent miscarriage, develops from single-cell zygote to morula to blastocyst to embryo to fetus.[12] The move from embryo to fetus is "arbitrarily designated by most embryologists to begin 8 weeks after fertilization"; the fetus at this point is about four centimeters in length (1.6 inches).[13] During this "official" fetal period the biological structures formed during the embryonic period develop and mature; age during this stage is usually measured by the crown–rump measurement, or sitting height.[14] By twenty-eight weeks, the fetus is considered viable or able to survive outside the womb (with supporting medical interventions). At forty weeks, it is ready to be born.

Medical terminology provides definitions and benchmarks for biological stages of prenatal development, but it does not tell us what the word "fetus" means in other contexts. Surely there are other ways to describe or conceptualize a fetus than by its "crown–rump" measurement. South Dakota, for example, defines "fetus" in its abortion statutes as "the biological offspring, including the implanted embryo or unborn child, of human parents."[15] The definition starts the clock at implantation or what was once called pregnancy. (Other states use fertilization as the marker.) South Dakota's definition moves us as a matter of law from medical into social realms by locating the fetus within the framework of lineage. It is the biological child of human parents, a status acquired from the moment the blastocyst cozies up to the uterine lining. This kinship point appears again in the statute's official finding that "there is an existing relationship between a pregnant women and her unborn child during the entire period of gestation."[16]

To be sure, defining fetus as an "offspring" in a civil statute does not convert abortion into murder, as causing the death of more conventional (born) offspring would be. *Roe v. Wade* settled that in 1973. Yet as a matter of symbolic and social description, the South Dakota legislation announces that abortion destroys offspring; terminating a pregnancy is *like* killing one's child. This is as close as South Dakota can legally come to declaring a position contrary to *Roe v. Wade*.[17] Other states define all prenatal life as "human beings" in their abortion statutes. This does not mean that embryonic human beings, however human from the perspective of species, are "beings" or "persons" in the same sense that born human beings are persons. Unlike infants, fetuses cannot inherit property or be adopted. They are not counted as persons in the census and certainly not for purposes of traveling in high-occupancy vehicle lanes, as one pregnant driver found out when protesting her ticket.[18]

Nonetheless, there are certain entrenched positions regarding fetal meanings. Philosopher Ronald Dworkin summarizes the "standard view" of what each side in the debate says it believes: "One side thinks the human fetus is already a moral subject, an unborn child from the moment of conception. The other side thinks that a just conceived fetus is merely a collection of cells, no more a child than a just fertilized chicken egg is a chicken or an acorn is an oak."[19] What both sides *really* believe, says Dworkin, is that all forms of human life have innate value and are in this sense sacred.[20] Dworkin's 1993 argument about the intrinsic value of human life—a secular conception of sacredness— may indeed capture what concerns everyone about abortion. But it is less his substantive argument that gives pause than his view about what people really think. The problem is not tone, even though no one is ever thrilled to be told what they "really" think. Instead, Dworkin is wrong (or perhaps only out-dated) about the "really." Fetal meanings are on the move. The citizens of South Dakota have inscribed into their law the statement that abortion terminates "the life of a whole, separate, unique, living human being."[21]

The aim here is not to pin down an objective definition of what a "fetus" is but to consider what "fetus"—as word, entity, concept—has come to mean, and to connect the variety of meanings to the variety of ends these meanings serve. The approach may liberate us from what religious scholars Vanessa Sasson and Jane Law have called "the hijack[ing]" of the fetus by two dominant modes in contemporary Western culture—the political and the medical.[22] One con-sequence of this hijacking has been to reduce the imaginative potential of the fetus "to function as a symbol of greater and more complex human emotions, dilemmas, and aspirations."[23]

Historian of science Nick Hopwood observes that to chart the rise of em-bryo images or to "question their power, we need to recover past meanings too."[24] Fetuses in early religious texts offer ancient examples of the imaginative fetal potential. Readers may be familiar with John the Baptist who, when in his mother Elizabeth's womb, "lept for joy" in recognition of Jesus's unborn presence as Elizabeth greeted Mary after the Annunciation.[25] There are famous Jewish fetuses who in rabbinic narratives from the ninth-century CE studied the Torah in utero, fasted on Yom Kippur, and sang after crossing the Red Sea.[26] The Buddha too had a long and detailed fetal life, living in a fabulous sealed palace inside his mother and exiting through her side so as not to have to deal with her blood and other messy fluids.[27] These are some of the stories that were told.

In each of these accounts, the fetal activity was connected to thick (or thick-ening) norms and struggles in the non-fetal realm. The "leaping child" of the Bible became important when a rivalry later arose between the separate followers of John and of Jesus regarding which of them was meant to be the Messiah.[28] The Gospel of Luke uses the figures of the unborn John and Jesus to establish Jesus as superior not only in the womb but going forward. John's physical tal-

The Visitation, detail from a tapestry antepedium (hanging altar cloth) of silk, wool, and linen, Strassburg, circa 1410. As the pregnant Mary and her pregnant cousin Elizabeth greet one another, the unborn Jesus blesses his cousin in utero, John the Baptist, who, having jumped for joy upon first encountering Jesus, now kneels before him.

ents (the jumping) were for the purpose of preparing for Jesus, not preempting him.[29] In their turn, ninth-century rabbis constructed the fetus Jacob as Jewish to identify him with Israel in contrast to his brother Esau, who was aligned with Rome.[30] The rabbinical project rendered fetuses not only as Jewish but also as extraordinary.[31] Locating Jewishness in the womb—knowledgeable fetuses conforming to particular practices of worship—was a piece of a spiritual political project of the time. Images of unborn patriarchs, prophets, and messiahs do heavy lifting for the writers of Luke and the rabbinic narratives by establishing boundaries and hierarchies within religious traditions.

The adaptability of the fetus to such varied political purposes is impressive and highly relevant to our own time. The modern fetus—its body, its image, its potential—serves as an opaque, if not quite a blank slate upon which current preoccupations can be inscribed.

The Visible Personable Fetus

Although school children today may well be able to recognize (if not sketch) a fetus, widespread familiarity with fetal appearance has a rather short historical pedigree.[32] To be sure, there have always been miscarriages, some of which took visible form. Yet this did not always produce familiarity with prenatal appearance. Historically miscarriages were commonly understood as the shedding of blood, not the end of a pregnancy. There are several explanations for this. Miscarrying women were often unaware that they were pregnant so there was no expectation of anything to see. In addition, early miscarried embryos were unlikely to be recognized as such; the embryo is typically enclosed by membranes which have to be peeled away to see the actual entity. Moreover, until the eighth week of pregnancy the prenatal form looks quite reptilian (what else explains the tail?) so that the expulsion was often regarded not as a failed pregnancy but as a "monstrous birth."[33] (Well into the twentieth century, conjoined twins and other malformed newborns, like the thalidomide babies of the 1960s, were still called monsters in medical textbooks and research monographs.[34]) In contrast to the early modern period, miscarrying women in the United States today often know they are pregnant long before they feel pregnant; they are also more sophisticated about their bodies and know what to look for. As medical abortion becomes more common, more women will complete their abortions at home and thus be increasingly exposed to the sight of an early embryo. Even now it is not so strange for family members to have seen a miscarried embryo or a fetus. President George W. Bush recounted just this experience when as a teenager he drove his mother to the hospital following a miscarriage.[35]

Even though the form of miscarried embryos and early fetuses was known to medical people, including midwives, the fetus in utero was imagined quite differently. Early thirteenth-century medical illustrations were consistent in their depictions of fetuses as well-developed miniature men (always men) energetically engaged in fitness regimes—stretching, jumping, running—within free-standing balloon-shaped containers.[36] The early homunculi pictured in woodcuts and drawings reflected the scientific theory of preformation that posited the fetus as fully formed from the start, requiring only time to grow.[37] People could of course see that women gave birth to babies and not mini-adults, and over time additional anatomical details—the umbilical cord, placental tissue—were added to medical illustrations.[38] Nonetheless, the basic schema of a self-sufficient fetus remained in place for centuries. Women's bodies had "left the building" centuries before ultrasound images obscured fetal connection to the woman.[39]

By the 1700s, the fetus had become more baby-like in appearance in medical drawings and in the life-size wax models now used in obstetric training.[40] Historian Karen Newman points out that many of the eighteenth-century wax fetuses resembled Baby Jesus in the crèche: chubby cheeks, curly hair, cherubic. The wax women into which the model fetuses fit (by lifting off a detachable abdomen) were not at all Mary-like but often presented as reclining odalisques, sometimes wearing pearls, "their hair unbound, fanning out around the face in almost sensual abandon."[41]

By the late nineteenth century, more intricate three-dimensional wax models of embryos across species had replaced two-dimensional illustrations as the basic research tool in the developing field of embryology.[42] These models were used not only for research and medical education but for public education as well. (Some exhibits had separate viewing hours for men and women due to the delicate but inevitable relation of fetuses to sexual intercourse.[43]) In 1893, the famous Ziegler wax models from Germany won the top prize at the World's Columbian Fair in Chicago, the models of developing human embryos displayed matter-of-factly alongside embryonic starfish, beetles, trout, and chicks.[44]

By the early twentieth century, wax models had given way to actual fetuses preserved in bottles. A "graduated set of human embryos" was a popular attraction at the 1933 Chicago World's Fair.[45] There is, however, a clear distinction

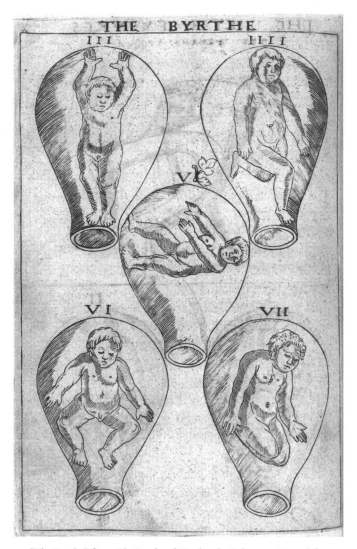

"The Byrthe" from *The Byrthe of Mankynde, Otherwyse Named the Woman's Book* by Eugene Rösslin, London, 1545. These sprightly figures in their pear-shaped containers were intended to acquaint midwives with various fetal presentations at birth. Originally published in Germany as *Rosegarden for Pregnant Women and Midwives*, the book sold well into the eighteenth century as ordinary men and women were fascinated by these early glimpses into the womb.

between the bottled fetuses of the lab or sideshow and the familiar fetus of today. The sideshow fetuses were "presented as curiosities or specimens, not as people or babies."[46] There was no claim that these earlier fetuses were themselves self-evident proof of fetal personhood or of "life" more generally: the specimens were preserved fetal remains. Yet these displays were not regarded as disrespectful or sacrilegious, as they might be today. Viewing them was understood as part education and part entertainment, perhaps like the traveling exhibits of skinned and plastinated corpses from China on display these days.[47]

Historically, the event that brought the fetus to life was quickening, fetal movement felt by the mother. After quickening, the fact of pregnancy was no longer in doubt: the woman was "with child"; she was expecting a baby.[48] Quickening was important legally and socially. To prevent the innocent unborn from dying unbaptized, pregnant women charged with capital crimes in early modern Europe were spared execution (at least until after the birth) by "pleading the belly"; a third of all women sentenced to death in the late seventeenth century entered the plea. It was crucial to the plea's success that quickening be proved, for before quickening there was no child, no innocent soul, and so no need for a reprieve. When proof was in doubt, quickening committees or "juries of matrons" were convened to evaluate the alleged pregnancy.[49] Quickening changed social relationships as well. Only then did "a child [come] into the family, the community, and the church, with the attendant care, responsibility, and commitment that are involved" with each.[50] The reality of pregnancy was marked not by sight or sound (the primitive stethoscope) but by bodily sensations felt by the mother. Seeing a living fetus in utero was, at least until the mid-twentieth century, beyond imagine.

The first wide-scale public look took place in 1965 when *Life* magazine published Swedish photographer Lennart Nilsson's beguiling color photographs of the fetus in utero.[51] As described by German historian Barbara Duden, "the unfinished child look[ed] like an astronaut in its transparent bubble, a bluish-pink figure with protruding veins sucking its thumb, the vaguely human face with closed eyes covered by a tissue veil."[52] That all but one of the *Life* fetuses were aborted or miscarried remains an ironic aspect of the now-iconic images.[53] The fetuses brought to the world by *Life* were dead, although they didn't look dead and weren't meant to be thought of as dead. Hedging on the promise of the accompanying text that these were "human embryos in their natural state," they had been surgically removed, possible only because abortion was legal in Nilsson's home country of Sweden.[54] The fetal corpses were cleaned up (no visible blood) and isolated from their natural environment (no sign of a woman or her body), then backlit and suspended in special fluid to achieve a luminous floating quality.[55] Comparisons between *Life*'s encapsulated fetus and astronauts were common, even before *2001: A Space Odyssey*, with its mesmerizing fetal conclusion, appeared in 1968.[56] Consider Nilsson's space-age description of the blastocyst as resembling a lunar module.[57]

Rosalind Petchesky observed years ago that beginning in the 1980s, pro-life strategists sought to make "fetal personhood a self-fulfilling prophecy by making the fetus a public presence . . . [in] a visually oriented culture."[58] The strategy has succeeded, in part because fetal presence, while always packing political resonance, doesn't always *appear* political: the fetus hangs around quite naturally framed on desks and embossed on magnets and shower invitations. As Lauren Berlant notes, "when the fetus became available to photography . . . it came to occupy a new scale of existence, often taking up an entire frame like a portrait."[59] Sonograms are now used to create bespoke fetal sculptures for use, as the advertising touts, at "gender and reveal" parties or as an "artistic sculpture for your display cabinet."[60] Commercial ultrasound studios advise women when during their pregnancies to schedule a photo shoot in order to get "the cutest facial images."[61] Special frames are sold with side-by-side openings so the fetal shot can be juxtaposed with that of the born baby in the same pose.

Although the routinization of ultrasound may have made the ultrasound images slightly less miraculous (except to the parents), the trade-off between awe and familiarity was not a bad deal for pro-life advocates. Almost everyone has seen and probably admired snapshots of someone's fetus, as happily expectant parents share "baby's first picture" with the rest of us.[62] We are, states Duden, "overwhelmed with fetuses."[63] But as Anne Higonnet explains, the fetuses we look at in ultrasounds, we see as children; the scan has replaced the cradle in marking the advent of childhood.[64]

A mix of reinforcing practices and beliefs, all concretized by fetal imagery, has led to a recognition of the fetus as a child, not only in the bumper-sticker sense ("I'm a Child, not a Choice!") but as a participating member of the family. Within weeks of conception, many fetuses have a known sex, a name, a page on social media.[65] Thus in wanted pregnancies, social birth—the incorporation of a child into its family—often precedes biological birth. To be sure, "social birth" is not a legal category or status, yet it has tremendous force, inaugurating the fetus into the world of sociality in which playdates, alumni onesies, and college savings accounts heave into view.

Recognizing (or remembering) that fetuses are sometimes regarded as children in this intimate familial sense provides a means of understanding the pro-life claim about personhood. That glimpse is not a concession to the pro-life position but appreciates that seeing embryos or fetuses as persons is not incomprehensible. Even those who do not regard an ultrasound image as proof of personhood understand that it functions as such for others. That the imprint of fetal imagery has been constructed through a forty-year interaction of reproductive technology, commercial entrepreneurship, reproductive politics, and personal desires may not matter at this point. Yet the evolution of the personable human fetus means that fetal meanings are neither fixed nor under the controlling grip of any one movement.

Fetal Roles and Attributes

Fetal presence expanded greatly under George W. Bush's presidency in a period officially designated by both White House and Vatican as a "culture of life."[66] Because lawmakers could no longer wholly protect a fetus from its mother, they legislated to save it from harm at the hands of felons through the Unborn Victims of Violence Act of 2004 and at the hands of doctors through such enactments as the Born-Alive Infants Protection Act of 2002, the Partial Birth Abortion Act, and the Unborn Child Pain Awareness Act of 2005.[67] And harm from its mother had not been put entirely out of reach by *Roe v. Wade;* women could still be prosecuted for delivering drugs to their fetuses intravenously or for performing a self-abortion.

Since 1995, hundreds of enactments on behalf of the unborn have been introduced at the federal level.[68] Fetuses were covered under a federal health care scheme through legislation that defined "child" for purposes of a federally funded state insurance program to include "an individual under the age of 19 including the period from conception to birth."[69] (This form of health care was once called "prenatal" care.) In 2003 a House Concurrent Resolution condemning attacks on U.S. citizens by Palestinian terrorists noted that "at least 38 United States citizens, including one unborn child, have been murdered by Palestinian terrorists."[70] It was as though someone had run a global "search and replace" for the word "pregnant" in all federal regulations and wherever the word was found, "unborn child" was substituted in. The more legislation mentions and protects the unborn—whether as child, victim, insured, pain sufferer, or person—the more established the position of fetuses becomes.

The fetus now participates actively throughout the culture in a variety of ways. Fetuses are consumers, with gift registries set up in their parents' names. They are medical patients with their own conditions and treatment teams.[71] They star in film comedies and even get speaking parts, as in the *Look Who's Talking* franchise. In literature too the fetus has found a voice. Kate Atkinson's 1997 novel *Behind the Scenes at the Museum* opens with a declaration from its knowing fetal narrator: "I exist! I am conceived to the chimes of midnight on the clock on the mantelpiece in the room across the hall. . . . I'm begun on the first stroke and finished on the last when my father rolls off my mother and is plunged into a dreamless sleep, thanks to the five pints of John Smith's Best Bitter he has drunk in the Punch Bowl with his friends."[72] Atkinson's unborn narrator pays homage to a much earlier fetal memoir, *The Life and Opinions of Tristram Shandy*. Tristram's conception was also horological in nature. As Tristram reports, "I was begot in the night, betwixt the first Sunday and the first Monday in the month of March, in the year of our Lord one thousand seven hundred and eighteen. I am positive I was."[73] (Tristram knows the exact timing because just at the crucial moment, Mrs. Shandy interrupted her husband to ask whether he had remembered to wind the family clock.)[74] These two cheeky fictional fetuses have spanned a long literary stage.

They have since been joined by the resourceful narrator of Ian McEwan's 2016 *Nutshell*, with the opening lines, "So here I am, upside down in a woman."[75] This fetus hears all from inside his mother, including what sounds like a murder plot by his mother and her lover, the uncle of our fetus. (I cannot say more about the intended victim.) The narrator has strong preferences; he enjoys sharing a glass of wine with his mother "decanted through a healthy placenta" and hates the racket when the lovers have sex.[76] He is quite concerned about the skullduggery around him which he not only describes but influences.

A less literary fetal role is that of a client. For despite a federal district court holding that a fetus could not be a named plaintiff in a class-action suit, state courts have taken a somewhat different view of the matter.[77] In Alabama, judges have long assigned lawyers to represent a pregnant minor's fetus in judicial bypass hearings. State court rules authorize the appointment of a guardian (a "guardian ad litem") in any proceeding concerning the welfare of a child, and certain judges have determined that the fetus is a child.[78] In consequence, pregnant minors have been cross-examined by their fetus's appointed counsel with such questions as "you say that you are aware that God instructed you not to kill your own baby, but want to do it anyway?"[79]

Counsel's question introduces one of the fetus's most prominent roles: that of victim. Earlier pro-life imagery often focused on images of aborted or about-to-be-aborted fetuses, as in the 1985 pro-life film *The Silent Scream,* which purported to show an abortion from a living fetus's perspective.[80] The viewer watches, to the strains of organ chords, as the abortionist's tools come closer and closer until the living fetus appears to open its mouth in the famous "silent scream." Lauren Berlant sharpens the fetus's plight by characterizing the particular brutality of the aggressor and the distinctive fragility of the target: "the pro-life movement has composed a magical and horrifying spectacle of amazing vulnerability: the unprotected person, the citizen without a country or a future, the fetus unjustly imprisoned in its mother's hostile gulag."[81] Berlant notes that the film "fuse[s] the anerotic sentimental structure of the infomercial and the docudrama with the pornotropic fantasies of a snuff film."[82]

Sympathy for fetal victims also pops up in strange corners of the literary canon. Recall Morris Zapp, the middle aged Berkeley-ish professor in David Lodge's 1975 book *Changing Places.* En route to England, Zapp notices that he is the only male passenger on his entire charter flight. The penny drops as he realizes that the ticket he bought from one of his students—no wonder it was half-price!—was for a pre-*Roe* abortion package tour from San Francisco to London, where abortion was legal.[83] Zapp had always been a liberal sort of guy, signing petitions for abortion law reform and so on. "But it is a different matter to find oneself trapped in an airplane with a hundred and fifty-five women actually drawing the wages of sin. The thought of their one hundred and fifty-five doomed stowaways sends cold shivers roller-coasting down his curved spine."[84]

In all of this, the fetus is importantly a body. Just when a fetus begins to look like a body depends in part on the viewer's knowledge of fetal development or on the desire to see a human form. Yet at some point in pregnancy, an entity of sufficient solidity emerges. Here is another strand of the tangled knot. Professor Zapp didn't actually see any fetuses or even any pregnancies. Yet he is able to imagine them, and sympathetically so, as passengers with no need for a return ticket.

This imagining extends even to unimplanted embryonic life, and here we return to Hurricane Katrina. In the dramatic opening of Robert George and Christopher Tollefsen's book *Embryo: A Defense of Human Life,* the authors describe how little Noah Benton Markham was nearly drowned in Katrina's flood waters.[85] Trapped in a flooded hospital, we are told how Noah, "one of the *youngest* residents of New Orleans to be saved from Katrina," was saved due to the heroic efforts of ten emergency responders who maneuvered flat-bottom boats to reach him just in the nick of time.[86] It turns out that at the time of his rescue, Noah was an embryo floating along with 1,400 other frozen embryos in a canister of liquid nitrogen. The authors conclude that "if those officers had never made it to Noah's hospital . . . there can be little doubt that the toll of Katrina would have been fourteen hundred human beings higher than it already was."[87] I myself have doubts about calculating Katrina's death toll this way. I think frozen embryos and not little children would have been lost had the canister gone under (which is not to say frozen embryos have no intrinsic value or may not be due respect). Yet the example gives substance to the claim that the rights and interests of embryos are "equal in importance to those of any other member of the moral community."[88] It also highlights the implications of the position. Emergency responders were in short supply during Katrina. Noah Benton was saved; patients at Memorial Center were not.[89]

Fetal bodies go beyond providing evidence (to some) about the existence of "life." They also produce meaning as corpses. Dead bodies, argues political scientist Katherine Verdery, are a "site of political profit."[90] Verdery's focus is post-socialist Eastern Europe where in the early 1990s, some bodies, such as that of Imre Nagy of Hungary, were dug up and reburied publicly with great ceremony, while the bodies of others (even those in statuary form) were pulled down and destroyed. Verdery explains that their materiality has "symbolic efficacy."[91] Dead bodies not only evoke profound feelings toward the sacred but, because they speak only through those who claim the right to speak for them, they can be usefully ventriloquized.[92]

In this way, dead bodies can create politics by turning the death of an ordinary person into a political site, as when a crowd is fired upon and corpses are retrieved, counted, and publicly mourned.[93] During the 2016 State of the Union address, Mrs. Obama sat beside an empty chair to honor the victims of gun violence. (In response, presidential candidate Senator Ted Cruz tweeted that in his presidency, the chair would be empty to honor the millions of dead abortion victims.[94]) We care how dead bodies (or at least the dead bodies we care about) are treated, handled, and disposed of. Outrage ensues when an American body is dragged through the streets of Mogadishu or when a crematorium substitutes the ashes (or even the body) of a beloved with those of someone else.[95]

Verdery's insights into the political life of dead bodies map onto the politics of abortion in the United States. Indeed, the visible fetal body has made abortion politics possible. We can see this by comparing abortion with miscarriage. Few consider miscarriage to be a political subject.[96] Miscarriage is not regarded as an issue that might be alleviated by public policies nor as a politically significant form of prenatal death. It appears natural, in contrast to abortion's deliberate quality, and miscarriage has a lack of materiality; some early miscarriages manifest as a heavy period. Abortion's materiality was highlighted in the 2015 uproar over allegations that Planned Parenthood was selling fetal remains to researchers. The claim was disproved but it illuminates the ongoing concern over the treatment of fetal remains. When abortion was illegal, accounts of the procedure by unskilled abortionists often included the disregard with which the conceptus was thrown into a pail or sluiced away.

States have attempted to dignify the treatment of fetal remains statutorily. In 1979 Louisiana enacted legislation requiring that following an abortion, the "remains of the child" were to be "decently interred or cremated within a reasonable time after death."[97] Challenged in court, a federal district court in Louisiana struck down the provision as a violation of *Roe*, noting that *Roe* held that the "word 'person' as used in the Fourteenth Amendment does not include the unborn."[98] Asking a woman if she wants burial or cremation for her aborted fetus "equates abortion with the taking of a human life," and this creates a psychological burden on aborting women that impermissibly chills their right to choose.[99] The Louisiana case was decided before the decision in *Planned Parenthood of Southeastern Pennsylvania v. Casey*, which greatly expanded the state's ability to persuade women against abortion. Several states (Indiana, Arkansas, Georgia) enacted post-*Casey* statutes along the lines of the earlier Louisiana law and required that as part of the informed consent procedure women must be told that they have the right to determine the final disposition of the aborted fetal remains.[100] Texas has gone a step further. In November 2016, the Texas Health and Human Services Commission approved new rules requiring all fetal remains (abortions and miscarriages) to be buried or cremated.[101]

Dead fetal bodies also serve as evidence of abortion practices. The discovery of nearly one hundred bottled fetuses in the basement of Mount Holyoke's Biology Department in 1997 brought to light the regular use of fetal specimens as objects of study in the field of embryology earlier in that century.[102] That the specimen bottles included mason jars and pickle jars provides insight into how the fetuses were obtained; like anatomists working in Europe, the Mount Holyoke faculty relied on friendly obstetricians and on alumni working in medical offices to obtain what was then considered the waste discarded from

miscarriage and abortions.[103] At the time, the fetuses—"unremarkable biological specimens much like skeletons or stuffed birds"—were considered entirely
suitable for undergraduate education.[104] Yet fetal bodies may reveal criminal
patterns of conduct. In 2010, over 2,000 fetal corpses were found in the morgue
of a Buddhist temple in Bangkok.[105] The discovery illuminated the flourishing
practice of illegal abortion clinics in Thailand, where abortion is a crime. The
clinics had been sending the aborted conceptuses to the temple morgue for cremation (for which a temple employee received a secret fee). Once the bodies were
discovered, reports of hauntings by disrespected fetal spirits began to spread.
Apologetic local citizens came to the temple with gifts of milk and bananas in
order to "nourish their spirits in the afterlife."[106] Things then took a curious
turn. After deciding that the spirits had been appeased, worshippers began to
regard them as harbingers of good luck, especially with regard to the lottery.[107]
Temple monks had to "[call] on superstitious lottery punters to stop gathering
at the temple to seek numbers from the foetuses."[108] Not only in the United
States are fetal meanings fluid.

Different fetal body parts take on special meaning at different points in
time. Lynn Morgan explains that the visible tail of the human embryo (which
lasts only about two weeks) came as a great shock when revealed to the American public in the early twentieth century. There was concern that babies might
be born with tails, and in any event, tails around the time of the Scopes trial
were a little too close for comfort.[109] Morgan observes that the significance of
the stir was "not in the tail per se nor even in the embryo qua embryo, but in
how people coaxed those bits of flesh to mirror their social worlds"; embryo
tails were "a focal point for debates over civilization, science, barbarism, secu-
larism, atheism, and faith."[110]

If tails told the story in the 1920s, by the 1990s the focus had shifted to fetal
feet, popular as pro-life lapel pins.[111] Their attraction was their similarity to the
feet of a born baby, especially in contrast to the ten-week fetal head, or to the
whole embryo, which Celeste Condit describes as "a wretched [looking] creature" with its "ungainly face and head, off-balance and poorly formed."[112]
Other body parts have taken a special place in antiabortion argument. As part
of informed consent procedures, a number of states have introduced fetal heartbeat legislation, which requires doctors to offer their patients the opportunity
to listen to the heartbeat before deciding on abortion. Hearts must also be
pointed out in the physician scripts that accompany mandatory ultrasounds
in some states. Other more subtle parts have proven evocative. In the 2007

movie *Juno,* fifteen-year-old pregnant Juno was stopped in her abortion tracks upon hearing from the lone sidewalk protestor that Juno's fetus might have fingernails. "Really? Fingernails?" When Juno tells her parents she is pregnant, she explains that "I don't know anything about [the baby] yet. I only know it has fingernails, allegedly."[113]

One final manifestation of the fetal body is the "bump." Demi Moore's 1991 *Vogue* cover may have started the trend of seeing the fetus under the skin. There is a cultural backstory to bump visibility. Until the early twentieth century, confinement—not exposure—marked the social status of pregnancy. When pregnant women slowly began to appear in public, their condition was camouflaged by all-encompassing maternity cloaks. These developed into the infantilizing ruffles and oversized pinafores of the *I Love Lucy* era.[114]

The acceptability of public pregnancy was brought about in part by law. By the 1970s, visibly pregnant women could no longer be fired from their jobs, as had long been the case for public school teachers.[115] School districts had expressed concern that the physical manifestation of pregnancy led in the imaginations of school children to pregnancy's origins in sexual intercourse.

Maternity camouflage has now been overtaken by spandex and cling. This development should come as no surprise. If we now look inside a woman via ultrasound to see a fetus, it is hardly more intrusive to look at the fetus from the outside. Reporters and paparazzi have special "bump beats," and the new vocabulary has migrated downward from celebrity bumps to the regular among us.[116] Consider *Bump It Up: Transform Your Pregnancy into the Ultimate Style Statement.*[117] Historical attitudes toward looking at pregnancy have been upended: "once a transgressive revelation of a woman's sacred and shameful carnality, the pictorial display of pregnancy is now an eroticized norm in American public culture."[118] The question remains whether bump displays mark the restoration of women's authority over their pregnant bodies or not.

The Tactile Fetal Form

In October 2013, a series of fourteen monumental sculptures were dramatically unveiled to the amplified sound of a beating heart outside the new Sidra Medical and Research Center in Doha, Qatar. The installation, which chronicles the process of gestation from conception to birth, was created by "controversial British bad boy" sculptor Damien Hirst.[119] *The Miraculous Journey,* as the series is called, starts with a sixteen-foot early embryo, posed upright on a spiny

The dramatic nighttime unveiling of Damian Hirst's *The Miraculous Journey*. The reptilian figure on the left depicts a fetus at approximately seven to eight weeks.

tail with squat amphibian head, and ends twelve sculptures later with a forty-six-foot free-standing scowling newborn, left leg raised Godzilla-style as though ready to stomp out small villages.

The work was commissioned by Sheikha al Mayassa Hamad bin Khalifa al-Thani, chairwoman of the Qatar Museums Authority, who proudly called it an "audacious work of art."[120] Her description seems right at several levels: the size and heft of the sculptures ("216 tons worth of bronze babies," according to one critic[121]); its wide visibility, not only from the windows of the medical center but from both a major motorway and the desert; and the subject matter—massive spliced wombs revealing developmentally graduated fetuses. All this in a conservative Islamic country where unclothed bodies, let alone reproductive body parts, are rarely shown in public.

Hirst's forty-six-foot newborn, profiled against the Sidra Medical and Research Center in Doha, Qatar.

How these fetal sculptures register with patients at the medical center or with other Qataris is not known. Al-Thani commissioned the work to transform "this city of gleaming skyscrapers and sandy beaches into a center for arts and culture," noting that "whether the public likes it or not, it's important to have an ongoing conversation."[122] The installation has been enthusiastically endorsed by pro-life groups worldwide. The Independent Catholic News called it "art in service of truth" (though the gestational "truth" of *The Miraculous Journey* is hardly to scale).[123] A spokesman for the British Society for Protection of Unborn Children praised Qatar's authorities for "their eye-catching public initiation," noting that "educating the public about the wonderful reality of human development . . . is a vital means of saving unborn children."[124] Hirst's own goals for the project were to "instill in the viewer a sense of awe and wonder at this extraordinary human process" and to expand "a cross-cultural dialogue between the UK and Qatar."[125] The array of giant fetuses thus serves a medley of purposes: artistic provocation, educational display, pro-life celebration, awe-inducing spectacle, cultural gesture toward modernity, and bilateral goodwill.

This is an impressive list for an impressive set of sculptures. But Hirst's fetuses do not stand alone. Four additional sculptural examples expand our sense of the meanings produced by the tactile fetus. They are Mesoamerican sandstone fetuses, nineteenth-century wax models (and one marble fetus) from Switzerland, pro-life fetal models or dolls in the United States, and Japanese Jizō statues. This array of sculpted fetuses is intriguing when considering the place of fetuses in art generally. Putting aside medieval depictions of the Christ child fully formed inside Mary and a twenty-first-century student exhibit claiming to be made of the artist's own abortion blood (it wasn't), fetuses have not often been the subject (and certainly not the medium) of art.[126] Fetuses did appear as a motif in late nineteenth-century French graphic art. Bottled fetuses on shelves show up in political cartoons, their fancy parents too obsessed with material satisfactions to be bothered with children. The cartoons also feature rich, fat abortionists—"Le Monstre des monstres" in one cartoon, "Docteur Forceps" in another.[127] Fetuses also appear in paintings by Edvard Munch and in drawings by Aubrey Beardsley, including a face-off between a woman and a grumpy-looking fetus reading a book called *Incipit Vita Nova* ("New Life Begins").[128] There is also a drawing by Frida Kahlo in which a naked Kahlo sheds giant tears, a small dead fetus in her abdomen tethered to a large fetus sitting at her feet.[129] More recently, British artist Tracey Emin has depicted a miscarriage or abortion in her monoprint *Terribly Wrong 1997,* but as a general matter there are few painterly instances of embryos or fetuses.[130]

This is less so with sculptural representations, where the characteristics of the medium—plasticity, three-dimensionality, durability—may offer a broader range of meanings and uses than two-dimensional representations. Sculptures are often more accessible on account of the possibility of placement in public space. Huge sculptures like Hirst's may induce awe by their scale alone as they are meant to do; smaller pieces offer more intimate tactile connection.

It turns out that Hirst's monumental fetuses are not the first such sculptures to engage viewers. Art historian Carolyn Tate has studied a fetal puzzle from ancient Mesoamerica: giant stone figures, "the earliest accurate images of the fetus yet recognized in any artistic tradition."[131] Carved by the Olmec peoples of Southern Mexico between 900 and 400 BCE, the massive statues—six-foot representations of human embryos at about six to eight weeks gestation—were rediscovered in situ in La Venta by modern investigators in 1925.[132] Tate hypoth-

Aubrey Beardsley, *Incipit Vita Nova*. Pen, pencil, and black ink on brown paper. 8×7.75 inches, circa 1893. A scowling fetus reads a self-affirming inscription as a sultry Madonna figure looks on.

esizes that because many miscarriages (even today) occur at exactly this stage of pregnancy, the Olmecs would have been familiar with the appearance of human embryos. Indeed, each Olmec sculpture appears to have been modeled on a particular embryo and depicted so naturalistically—wide-set lidless eyes, flattened noses, and an accurate head-to-body ratio of about 1:3—that an investigative panel of neonatologists was able to "pinpoint which week of gestation most of the sculptures portrayed."[133] In general they stand ex utero on deeply flexed legs with arms crossed over the chest, the very positions that fetal limbs often take in utero.

These massive fetus sculptures posed "a formidable interpretive challenge."[134] Because the Olmec were pre-literate, there are no written texts to explain the

A ten-inch Olmec fetus sculpture carved from stone between 900 and 600 BCE wears a Mesoamerican ballgame helmet like the colossal fetus sculptures at La Venta, an important archaeological site of Olmec civilization.

origins or purposes of the figures at La Venta. But there are clues. The fetuses were commonly adorned with the iconography of maize, a kernel or sprout etched onto the top of their not yet knitted fontanels, for example. A few wear snug rugby-style headgear typically worn by players in a complicated Meso-american celestial ball game that told a regeneration story: losers in the game were killed but, like crops, came back.[135] Connecting the maize iconography with the physical placement of the statues at the ancient ritual site at La Venta, Tate concludes that the statues were something like "seminal human-maize being[s]," which, when set amidst womb caves, ball game imagery, and burial sites were part of a "processional visual narrative" of a Mesoamerican creation story.[136] In this "sophisticated conceptualization of creation and regeneration," the Olmec identified similarities between embryos in the womb and planted seeds.[137] It was into this larger creation story that the fetuses fit, not as "deities but as seed spirits . . . the 'original seeds of the human race.' "[138]

Some 2,500 years later, fetus sculptures became crucial to a different origin story: scientific inquiry into the earliest forms of human life as taken up in the emerging discipline of embryology. In the mid-to-late nineteenth century, two-dimensional drawings of embryos gave way to three-dimensional wax models. The models became the gold standard for scientific inquiry into the question of how embryos across species transform physiologically from one stage to the next.[139] The models replaced the need for the dissection of corpses by medical students, a disfavored practice because of its association with grave robbing and buying the bodies of the poor.[140]

The founder of modern embryology was a Swiss anatomist, William His, who in 1865 invented the microtome, a special knife that could cut through embryo specimens to produce extraordinarily thin slices or sections that made the field technically possible.[141] The sections were placed on microscope slides, the images projected onto screens, copied by hand, and the enlarged drawings then modeled in wax.[142] The wax sections were layered to create a model showing the interior structure of embryos at the earliest stages of life. The result was that "a tiny uncertainty became a solid object that an anatomist could clasp."[143]

In addition to the wax models, His occasioned one additional sculpture that further increases the meanings of the fetal subject. This was a commemorative marble bust of His himself, likely commissioned by his colleagues for His's seventieth birthday. Nick Hopwood points out that the bust is in fact a "double portrait," in that His is holding one of his own embryo models.[144] The marble fetus was copied from a specific wax model that His had made years earlier from an embryo found in a blood clot brought to him by a midwife. Like other anatomists of the period, His depended on doctors and midwives for their raw materials. Indeed, he designated each wax model by the initials of the donating doctor; the initials of cooperative midwives and miscarrying women went unrecorded.[145]

Few scientists today would choose to be memorialized holding an embryo or fetus; most of the collections of fetal specimens so painstakingly assembled during embryology's twentieth-century peak have since been warehoused, dismantled, or destroyed.[146] Hopwood offers several takes on the meaning of the bust in its period. The first is disciplinary. The contemplative pose of the professional man with the "accessories" of his work had become commonplace in commemorative portraits in order to "signal identities":[147] botanists contemplated plants, chemists molecules, and so on. Thus although an embryo was something new, its purpose was not. It raised embryology to a bust-worthy discipline as part of a "campaign for institutional recognition."[148] The second take clarifies the personal significance of the model to His, who for some time kept the bust in his study among family portraits and other memorabilia. Certainly an ultrasound scan today finds a natural home among family photographs, but for His the embryo models were "intellectual offspring, not relatives."[149]

Finally, because the sculptor Carl Seffner was himself a renowned artist, the His bust was twice shown in public exhibits of Seffner's work. The bust therefore operated as art, as personal memorabilia, and as disciplinary signal all at the same time. Is such a multiplicity of meaning possible with fetal imagery today?

In 2010, as part of a campaign "to put God back into the schools," a group of religious high school students called "The Relentless" organized the distribution of 2,500 small rubber fetus dolls at two high schools in Roswell, New Mexico.[150] As other students entered the school, each was offered one of the two-inch dolls with a card explaining that it was the actual size and weight of a "12 week old baby" (or, as the Tenth Circuit Court of Appeals later clarified, the size and weight of "a fetus at 12 weeks gestation"[151]). The card quoted a passage from the Psalms ("For you formed my inward parts; You knew me in my mother's womb") and provided contact information for the Chaves County Pregnancy Resource Center, a pro-life counseling center that does not provide or refer abortion services.[152]

The doll distribution became a federal matter after school administrators decided "to shut [the whole thing] down" following "doll-related disruptions" at both high schools.[153] Students had torn the dolls' heads off and used them as projectiles and pencil erasers. Dolls were used to plug up toilets; some were doused in hand sanitizer and set alight. "One or more male students removed the dolls' heads, inverted the bodies to make them resemble penises, and hung them on the outside of their pants' zippers."[154] The Relentless argued in court that the shutdown violated their rights to equal protection (other student groups had been permitted to hand out valentines) and to free speech and free exercise: distributing dolls was not merely a constitutional right but their Christian duty.

The federal appeals court ruled on summary judgment (without a trial) in favor of the school district on the technical ground that the students had failed to get approval for the distribution ahead of time, as required under school rules. But it is less the constitutional posture of the case that interests us than how the little dolls were used. To The Relentless, the dolls stood in for the unborn child. To others it seems they signified nothing more than just another destructible piece of plastic. The dolls also triggered more political meanings; the Tenth Circuit noted that students "engaged in name-calling and insults over the topic of abortion."[155] And the conversion of fetuses to penises was distinctly transgressive, a sort of campy form of defiance.

Two three-inch Precious Ones, leaning against a briefcase. The facial features of these soft sculptures are somewhat undefined, befitting a twelve-week-old fetus.

The dolls distributed in Roswell are sold under the name "Precious One" by Heritage House, a pro-life merchandise retailer. They come in three skin tones (described in the catalog as white, brown, and Spanish), plain or wrapped in little blankets, and are sold at discount in bulk. But for their tiny size (and the blankets), Precious Ones bear remarkable resemblance to the Olmec sculptures in La Venta. The Heritage House sales copy states that the dolls' "beautiful detail, softness and weight can really move hearts and change minds!"[156] They are recommended as gifts and for use outside abortion clinics, at schools, and in crisis pregnancy centers. In 2014, the dolls created a ruckus among fairgoers at the North Dakota State Fair, as seen in the headlines from pro-life and pro-choice reportage: "Abortion Advocates Go Nuts over Pro-Lifers Distributing Fetal Models" and "Worst State Fair Ever Has Squishy Fetus Toys for Unsuspecting Kids."[157]

Another more detailed fetus model, One Tiny Life, is similarly marketed as a pro-life figurine for $25 plus shipping, although free to "certified pro-life organizations."[158] The doll's legs are crossed at the ankles and buyers can choose legs up to expose the genitals or legs more modestly down in a gender neutral position. The creator of One Tiny Life explains her purpose: "My deepest desire is that a Mom who was considering the abortion option would hold one of these tiny babies and change her mind."[159] Sculpture theory explains how holding the doll might work toward that end. In his work on small Neolithic figurines, art historian Doug Bailey explains that although we don't definitively know what the ancient figurines were—toys? votives? fertility fetishes? mini-deities?—thinking about them as handheld objects may inform our understanding of how they functioned.[160] (And handheld they were; many have rounded bottoms and, like Precious Ones, cannot stand up.) Bailey notes that people gain "subtle empowerment" from miniaturized works.[161] Holding a miniature anthropomorphic form like the Neolithic figures may have increased the holder's sense of power. When the figure looks like a tiny baby, holding may also trigger a desire to protect. Thus both scale and tactility increase the doll's power over us through its very vulnerability.

Precious One and One Tiny Life are meant to prevent abortion through a woman's physical connection to a figurine that fits in the palm of the hand. But sculpture is also invoked after an abortion, as we see in the Japanese practice of *mizuko kuyo,* a rite (*kuyo*) for an aborted fetus (*mizuko* or "water child," a sort of in-between life) that developed in the mid-1970s.[162] Around that time independent religious sects improvised a ritual for women who had terminated a pregnancy and who wanted to offer amends to the spirit of the aborted child. This was done by purchasing a small stone statue of the Japanese deity Jizō, the protector of children and fetal spirits, and placing it in a special temple statue garden. William LaFleur explains that the statue represents both the soul of the *mizuko,* to whom the parents offer apologies, and Jizō, to whom the parents appeal to guide their aborted fetus through the otherworld of dead souls.[163] The bald Jizō wears the robe of a Buddhist monk, but the statues, lined up row upon row, are often dressed in bright sometimes hand-knit baby clothes and surrounded by toys and colorful pinwheels brought by their ancestors, giving the gardens the cheerful look of an over-decorated child care center.

For women who practice *mizuko kuyo*—and most Japanese women do not—formal apologies are usually offered annually, sometimes by a paid temple priest in a sort of perpetual care arrangement. Unlike the statues and models we have looked at from Qatar, Mexico, Europe, and New Mexico, the Jizō statues are not representations of the fetus itself but of its spirit as expressed in the body of its protector. Unlike His's wax models, the statues exist in the realm of spiritual belief, not scientific inquiry, and unlike the plastic fetal dolls, they convey

A statue of Jizō, representing the spirits of aborted and miscarried fetuses, wearing a red knit cap and little cloak at the Buddhist Zōjō-ji Temple in Tokyo.

no antiabortion agenda. Abortion was legalized in Japan in 1948 and has been an accepted reproductive practice since.[164]

Certainly, this ritual resonates culturally in Japan. Because the fetus children died before their parents, they have in a sense become their parents' ancestors, and giving offerings to ancestors is a traditional feature of Buddhism, though few of the sects offering *mizuko kuyo* are themselves Buddhist. Similar practices

are also found in Taiwan, Korea, and Vietnam, countries with their own traditions of ancestor worship.[165] Some argue that *mizuko kuyo*—the statue, the
package of prayer services—is at core a commercial enterprise, concocted by
start-up or financially failing religious sects to generate an income stream.[166]
Others suggest that the ritual offers a formal public mechanism for acknowledging the aborted child's existence.[167] In this regard *mizuko kuyo* shares much in
common with the Missing Angel statutes that provide birth certificates to stillborn babies as official recognition that a particular child existed and was born.[168]

Fetal sculptures demonstrate the power and plasticity of meaning in the fetal
form over time. When some 2,000 years from now our own sculptures are
unearthed—whether Hirst's bronze uteruses perched on poles in a Middle
Eastern desert or boxes of resin mini-fetuses scattered around North America—
they too, like the Olmec fetuses of La Venta, are likely to present a "formidable
interpretive challenge" to the anthropologists, art historians, theologians, and
political scientists of the future.[169] They are a challenge even today, as three di-
mensional fetuses join other artifacts in the material culture of abortion.

Threatening Fetuses

The notion of a vengeful fetus operating at hurricane strength is arresting. The
standard story is that fetuses are at constant risk of having harm done to them,
not the other way around. But while the modern fetus is generally understood
as a peaceful, vulnerable presence, a more menacing set of fetuses does not conform to the usual profiles in innocence. Threatening fetuses, like Asian carp,
have already infiltrated protected space, and it is worth considering how this
rougher fetus got in and what it's about.

One of the most belligerent literary fetuses is the unborn Ben in Doris Lessing's 1988 novel, *The Fifth Child*.[170] Harriett, already the mother of four perfect
children, is now pregnant with her fifth, and this time things are different. Early
in the pregnancy, the fetal Ben begins to batter Harriet in the womb; she imagines hooves and claws and feels the fetus "trying to tear its way out of her
stomach."[171] She manages the pain only by taking tranquilizers: "If a dose of
some sedative kept the enemy—so she now thought of this savage thing inside
of her—quiet for an hour, then she made the most of the time, and slept."[172]
By the seventh month, Harriet "silently addressed the being crouching in her
womb: 'Now you shut up or I'll take another pill.' It seemed to her that it lis-
tened and understood."[173] After Ben's birth, he continues his aggressions, even

as a baby picking off his weaker relatives, strangling the family dog, a broken arm here, a bruised grandmother there.

Lessing continued the boy's story in a sad and terrifying sequel, *Ben in the World*.[174] But it is Ben as malevolent fetus that interests us here. Critics have suggested variously that *The Fifth Child* is about maternal pride, urban decay, suburban complacency, thalidomide, and eugenics.[175] This may all be so. But what is important for our purposes is that a tough-guy fetus can plausibly mean all these things and that this meaning-laden fetus became a vivid, even magnetic literary presence.

Ben was belligerent because that was his nature. In this way, he is something like the satanic fetus in *Rosemary's Baby*.[176] It isn't their fetal status that makes them bad but their DNA. In contrast, other fetuses menace precisely because they are fetuses. We saw this in the Japanese practice of *mizuko kuyo*, where women offer gifts, apologies, and ritual obeisance to appease the spirits of aborted fetuses. Recognizing that practices called "rituals" can pop up in Japan rather quickly, what occasioned this one? The answer seems twofold. The first is a combined effort by entrepreneurial "new-new" Japanese religions and the tabloid press. Tabloids and teen magazines ran luridly illustrated stories of wrathful fetuses attacking young women in their beds and threatening them with a long list of middle-age maladies: chronic hip pain, nasal congestion, cancer, and bedwetting.[177] The headlines accompanying the articles tell the tale: "Do You Know the Horror of the Mizuko Spirits?,"[178] "Fetuses Unable to Receive Ritual Cry out in Sorrow!,"[179] and, from the magazine *Young Lady*, an interview story called "The Mizukuyo Spirit Attack Which Suddenly Assaulted Me."[180] Clever photographic manipulations made the spirits—called *tatari*—appear especially ferocious. Ultrasound images of well-developed fetuses were enlarged relative to the screaming women, thus visually "increas[ing] the sense of the fetus's power."[181] In addition, the illustrators flipped the ultrasound images from the usual fetus-on-its-back position to the giant fetal head on top, so that the *tatari* looked like giant barrage balloons looming above their prey. Helen Hardacre has detailed the connections between the tabloids, temples, and travel agencies that made *mizuko kuyo* not only desirable but convenient; temples were sometimes specially located at the intersections of major highways on bus routes.[182]

Yet Hardacre and others acknowledge that women not targeted by *Young Lady* magazine also practiced *mizuko kuyo*. These women had ended pregnancies in the 1930s and 1940s. Their participation, it is suggested, was not in response to fear but out of unsettled feelings regarding abortions performed decades earlier.[183] Interestingly, this takes place against a legal and social back-ground that for many reasons—postwar fears of deformed children, the unavail-ability of the pill, Buddhist views on death and reincarnation—accepts abortion as a reasonable response to unwanted pregnancy.

In considering the *tatari* as fetal scaremongers, we should ask what it is that these spirits want. Each *tatari* wants recognition for itself from its progenitor. *Mizuko kuyo* is not a collective action movement. Indeed, it is emphatically apolitical. There is no accompanying call for abortion's criminalization or reg-ulatory curtailment, as fetal commemorative cemeteries in the United States are meant to convey.[184] The wrong committed is not the abortion itself but the failure to respect the fetal spirit afterward. Thus *mizuko kuyo* is not a front for pro-life activism, nor does it induce pro-life sentiments in the women who practice it. The fetus simply but adamantly wants to be cared for in the after-life as it awaits rebirth.

Although the United States has no such tradition, we have a fair few fetal spirits of our own. In her 1990 novel *The Witching Hour,* Anne Rice offers up an inventory of fetus-themed horror movies. The character Michael, distraught after his girlfriend's abortion and her decision to leave him, observes something that seems to go unmentioned by everyone else. This is the "uncanny resem-blance" of the cinematic monsters of this time to "the children being aborted every day in the nation's clinics":

> Take Ridley Scott's *Alien* for instance, where the little monster is born right out of the chest of a man, a squealing fetus who then retains its curious shape, even as it grows large, gorging itself upon human victims. And what about *Eraserhead*, where the ghastly fetal offspring born to the doomed couple cries continuously. Why, at one point it seemed to him there were too many horror films with fetuses in them to make a count. There was *The Kindred* and *Ghou-lies* and *Leviathan* and those writhing clones being born like fe-tuses out of the pods in *Invasion of the Body Snatchers.*
>
> God only knew how many more fetus horror movies there were . . .
>
> What must this mean, Michael tried to figure out. Not that we suffer guilt for what we do, for we believe it is morally right to control the birth of our young, but that we have uneasy dreams of all those little beings washed, unborn, into eternity? Or was it mere

fear of the beings themselves who want to claim us—eternally free
adolescents—and make us parents. Fetuses from Hell![185]

Perhaps, and certainly there is one rather well-known fetus from hell.
In *Rosemary's Baby,* as some readers may remember, wide-eyed Rosemary is
drugged, raped, and impregnated by Satan, all with the collusion of her actor
husband, who traded his wife's uterus for a good part in a play. The movie follows the travails of Rosemary's pregnancy during which she withers as the fetus
grows. Only after its birth does Rosemary understand what has happened;
nonetheless she agrees to mother her satanic offspring. The audience never sees
Rosemary's baby, although her scream "What have you done to its eyes!" ends
the film with a chill. In another movie on the *Witching Hour* list, *Alien,* the chills
start when the now gestated alien pulsates its way out of the human space trav-
eler's abdomen. The image sticks in the brain.

Yet things change. What was once a disturbing moment of horror has become in some ways a playful pregnancy trope. Google Images quickly reveals
a bevy of pregnant Halloween revelers wearing t-shirts through which little,
sometimes bloody, fetal arms have burst forth holding their own candy containers, ready for trick-or-treat. (One woman expecting twins had two candy
buckets reaching out.) The women themselves are having fun: they have poured
fake blood around the protruding arms; they have posted the pictures online.
It seems that they are sporting with—perhaps owning—their inner alien. The
erupting alien has merged with Rosemary's baby, also claimed by its mother,
and it's now all in good fun. This is something new.

Putting aside fetuses from hell, even fetuses without satanic DNA or cinematic credentials may threaten a pregnant woman. This was certainly true
historically, when pregnancy itself was an ever-present threat to women's lives.
Pregnant women rightly feared death or physical ruin through childbirth.
Historian Sally McMillan notes that this specter of death or debilitation as a
result of childbirth forced white antebellum Southern women to think repeatedly in childbirth "on the state of their souls."[186] There was also the dread, spoken
quietly among communities of women in the early American Republic, about
what another living child itself would mean. Nancy Cott quotes Millicent
Liebhunt who, upon learning in 1832 that she was pregnant for the fifth time,
wrote: "Yes, even now the frail foetus within me is the abode of an immortal
spirit, and this has caused thoughts of discontent. I would it were not thus. I love
my liberty, my ease, my comfort and do not willingly endure the inconvenience

and suffering of pregnancy and childbirth."[187] The burdens were greater were the child itself damaged during birth or otherwise born infirm.

Fetal disability returns us to the trope of monsters. While medical texts no longer describe conjoined twins as "double monsters," as was the case in the mid-twentieth century, the last half century has seen the return of other "monsters." The drug thalidomide used for insomnia and morning sickness in pregnant women in the 1960s produced thousands of babies with foreshortened or missing limbs and other physical deformities. Husbands abandoned wives ("If you bring that monster home, I leave"); a Belgian couple killed their infant (and were acquitted); and a doctor reported a "basic murderous attitude" toward deformed infants among his staff.[188] The rubella epidemic of the early 1960s in the United States followed close upon thalidomide, from which American women had been spared thanks to the prudence of Dr. Frances Oldham Kelsey of the Food and Drug Administration.[189] Pregnant women were terrified, and because the damage from rubella—blindness, retardation—was widely known, there was a softening in views toward abortion as hospital committees granted the petitions of rubella-exposed women more readily than those of other women.[190] Environmental causes of birth abnormalities, like the Zika virus, provide another instance in which pregnancies are laden with fear and the burdens of motherhood are greater than usual.

Nowadays, at least in the United States, childbirth is generally quite safe. Thus women's concerns are less about actual death than about the cessation of their social, familial, or occupational lives. Expectant women today, especially those with children, are more aligned with Millicent Liebhunt, who felt that a fifth pregnancy would sink her. In the United Kingdom, where a woman must always give reasons for her decision to terminate, the Abortion Act of 1967 provides that one acceptable reason is that "the continuance of the pregnancy would involve risk, greater than if the pregnancy were terminated, of injury to the physical or mental health of the pregnant woman or any existing children of her family."[191] The calculus acknowledges the consequence of another child to the well-being of existing children, as well as for the woman herself. The burden of raising a disabled child, another express ground, is similarly premised on the threat to existing family arrangements of an additional child.[192]

In the United States, at present, no reasons need be formally given as a condition to consent. Nonetheless, aborting women in the United States tell a like story of fear and despair at the prospect of not being able to care properly for existing or prospective children and about their own lives coming to a sudden halt. One woman looked back on an earlier abortion: "Kevin's view was that we would drop out of school and we would [marry and] go live with his parents and he would work at the Owens Corning glass factory [and] I would stay home with his mother and take care of the baby. This was his plan, and it sends shudders up my spine still to think of it."[193]

FETAL IMAGERY HAS BEEN USED imaginatively and purposefully over time. In mapping fetal imagery on a chronological spectrum, Karen Newman describes how the fetus was seen (and drawn and described) in relation to reigning philosophical and political orientations:

> In the sixteenth century in relation to Aristotelian and Galenic notions of generation . . . ; in the seventeenth century in relation to the Cartesian *cogito* with its important links both to Renaissance perspective and to developing [Enlightenment] notions of subjectivity . . . ; in the eighteenth century in relation to political economy, an evolving public sphere, and the production of a rights-bearing subject; in the nineteenth century in relation to a positivist biologism; in the late twentieth century in relation to the proliferation of rights claims, particularly feminism, the "technologization" of representation and reproduction, and changing notions of what constitutes "life."[194]

The twenty-first century is too young for fetal meanings to be announced with much assurance, although it seems clear that fetal representations are always part of a political discussion, whether about state building or modernization or rights or vocabulary and the meaning of "person."

As Newman's analysis makes clear, the creation and reception of fetal imagery draw from the particularities of a specific culture at a specific moment in a specific place. So although we learn that fetal images are honored and even revered at many points in time, the fact of reverence does not tell us whether the fetal image is revered as deity, as perfect research tool, or as an icon of life.[195] The reception of the same fetal imagery is rarely constant. Two-inch fetal dolls are precious to some and sources of irreverence to others.

Fetal imagery can prompt different responses even within the same person. Pro-choice women may scoff at "I'm a Child, Not a Choice" placards and at

French sculptor Alexandre Nicolas creates highly detailed fetal figures taken primarily from pop culture. He then suspends the figures in fourteen-inch blocks of synthetic crystal so that the figures appear to float in space. *From left to right, top row:* Grendizer, Batman (Dark Knight), Batman (traditional); *bottom row:* The Thing, Catwoman, Captain America.

the same time feel excitement looking at the scan of an expected grandchild. This is not inconsistency but rather an awareness of context: wanted versus unwanted pregnancies; placards versus family photos; the political use of the image versus the personal. We live in the contradictions that visual technology has brought.

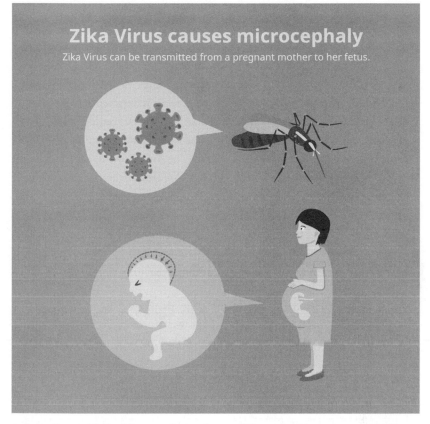

A design for a public health poster during the 2016 Zika epidemic, warning women about the risks of acquiring the Zika virus during pregnancy. The halo-like hatch marks around the fetus's head indicate the smaller skull size of a fetus with microcephaly, a common consequence of the Zika infection.

Looking at fetal images over time also reveals resonances among periods that prompts a second look, not so much at the earlier imagery as at our own at present. Thirteenth-century woodcuts of fetuses doing calisthenics in their free-standing womb jars are amusing and quaint. What were the artists thinking? They knew that women gave birth to babies, not homunculi. Yet today's fetuses offer something awfully close to preformation. Modern fetuses are less physically talented, but they too are engaged in all sorts of activity. They become offspring from the moment of conception, listen to Mozart in utero, and go trick-or-treating carrying their own buckets.

We are indeed awash with fetuses in the first decades of the twenty-first century. But in comparison to earlier times, there is a greater sense of playfulness among sculptors, authors, cartoonists, and advocacy groups toward the image. Some of this is cutesy in nature: Santa hats or Easter bunny ears imposed on ultrasound images to include fetuses more fully in the holiday fun. But other engagements are more outré: superhero fetal sculptures encased in plexiglass cubes and a parade of online and cinematic fetal zombies and aliens.[196]

Graphic design websites now offer an array of fetal logos and up-to-the-minute clip art, such as instant Zika warnings in 2016 showing a microcephalic fetus in its mother's womb.[197] Thus despite a general agreement that pro-life advocates have held the rhetorical advantage—unborn child, "partial birth abortion," and so on—the fetus may no longer be wholly owned and operated by those who oppose legal abortion. Certainly some uses are distasteful (fetal porn), but some are inventive (sci-fi; digital modeling), some therapeutic *(mizuko kuyo),* and some in the service of public health.

One consequence of the capaciousness of current fetal meanings may be to reduce the formerly unassailable position of the fetus as the pro-life poster child. The playfulness with which the fetus can be approached, modeled, appreciated, and transformed disrupts the pro-life grip on what fetal imagery means. Some of the disruption is disconcerting (fetal doll heads as penises?) though we can't be sure if the little doll was ever sacred to a bunch of high school cutups. Still, the disruption wouldn't be quite so disruptive if it were not responding to or set alongside a more glorified, more official notion of how a fetus doll should be treated. An analogy is found in the current phenomenon of "Hell Houses," sin-themed haunted houses set up by evangelical Christian groups around Halloween. (Abortion is one of the five featured sins.) As performance theorist Ann Pellegrini explains, the idea is not to "scare the bejeezus out of you . . . [but] *to scare you to Jesus.*"[198] The complication is that some of the performances of sin and its wages are so powerful that their meaning to the audience cannot be wholly controlled by pastoral intent. Pellegrini describes the poignant death of a gay man from AIDS in one of the recommended sketches. Might this tableau prompt empathy, Pellegrini asks, rather than the intended lesson of revulsion or fear? So too with the novel twists on fetal iconography. Just what is a teen who keeps a poster of superhero fetuses on his or her wall doing? It's unclear but it seems a far cry from Precious Ones.

5

Facing Your Fetus

On September 27, 1964, David Legg was driving south on Bluegrass Road in Sacramento, California. At just the same time, four-year-old Erin Dillon was crossing Bluegrass Road and was struck and killed by Legg's car. Erin's mother, Margery Dillon, had been sitting on her front porch watching Erin cross and saw the whole thing.[1]

When Margery later filed a lawsuit against Legg for the emotional shock and physical pain she suffered on account of witnessing her daughter's death, Sacramento County Superior Court Judge Robert Cole threw her case right out. Under existing California law, for a bystander like Mrs. Dillon to recover damages from a negligent driver, she must not simply have witnessed injury to someone else but must have feared for her own safety. This rule—affirmed by the California Supreme Court just three years earlier—applied even when the victim was a close relative.[2]

Mrs. Dillon appealed the dismissal of her case to that same Supreme Court. Her opening brief set the stage: "Could anyone be so callous, so naïve, so devoid of human experience not to understand the anguish that would result when a mother not only watches a car crush her infant, but in addition is subjected to the sight of the lifeless remains of someone small and dear lying in the middle of the street?"[3] The court held that she could indeed proceed with her suit against David Legg. To do otherwise, wrote Justice Tobriner, would "frustrat[e] . . . the natural justice upon which the mother's claim rests."[4]

In reaching its decision, the court relied on a number of assumptions about maternal love and maternal duty. Fear of fraudulent claims in bystander cases—the standard reason for denying bystander recovery—was overcome by the certainty that a mother who sees her child killed will suffer physically. from shock. Concern about expanding the scope of a driver's duty to any number of unknown persons who might be standing around was answered by strong presumptions about maternal presence: "Surely the negligent driver who causes the death of a young child may reasonably expect that the mother will not be far distant."[5] Justice Tobriner concluded the opinion by characterizing the harm Margery Dillon had experienced as "the most egregious case of them all: the mother's emotional trauma at the witnessed death of her child."[6]

In 2007 the state of Alabama passed the Women's Right to Know Act. Among the things that the legislature decided pregnant women in Alabama would want to know before consenting to an abortion is what their own embryo or fetus looks like. To accomplish this, the act requires that any physician performing an abortion must first "perform an ultrasound on the unborn child" and must ask the woman if she would like to see the image.[7] She is, in effect, asked by law to witness her child soon before its death. At the end of the procedure, she must complete a form acknowledging either that she looked at the image of her unborn child or that she was "offered the opportunity and rejected it."[8]

Ten states have enacted similar legislation, and North Carolina and Texas have added a bit more. In those states, during the actual scanning physicians must display the monitor so that the patient can see it and must describe to her out loud what appears on the screen in detail and in real time. (The North Carolina provision is called the Display of Real Time View Requirement.) The display and the description are to include "the presence, location, and dimensions of the unborn child within the uterus and the number of unborn children depicted," as well as "external members and internal organs, if present and viewable."[9] Nine more states provide that any doctor who for other reasons performs an ultrasound in connection with an abortion—usually in order to date or locate the pregnancy—must inform the woman that she too has the right to view the image.[10] Because doctors now frequently use ultrasound in this way, almost all women seeking an abortion in these states will be informed about their "right to view."[11] Their decision to look or not must be obtained in writing and, somewhat ominously, the writing kept in the woman's medical files for periods ranging from three (Arkansas) to seven (Texas) years.[12] Starting in 2016, North Carolina additionally required doctors to send the ultrasound scan for any abortion performed after sixteen weeks of pregnancy to the state department of Health and Human Services. This is to enable the state to make its own determination whether the doctor is performing an abortion beyond the legal limit of twenty weeks.[13]

Like the California Supreme Court's decision in *Dillon v. Legg,* Women's Right to Know Acts, as they are generally called across the states, draw upon a deep reserve of sentiment about what mothers are like and what causes them harm. Both the common law rule of *Dillon* and Women's Right to Know Acts are concerned with maternal loss at seeing or imagining the death of one's child. Also called mandatory ultrasound statutes, the acts take a particular view of the relationship between pregnant women and the embryo or fetus, starting with the supposition that there *is* a familial relationship between the two. Some of this is signaled linguistically: the fetus is described as an unborn child; the ultrasound is performed not on the woman but on the unborn child; a mother who declines to look has "rejected" the opportunity to see her unborn child.

The premise of the ultrasound project against abortion is that a woman who sees her baby's image on a screen will be less likely to abort. The requirement of looking or even being invited to look is meant to produce a confrontation, whether actual or notional, between the pregnant woman and her fetus, and once the woman faces up to her fetus (or at least its real-time image), she will change her mind and cancel the abortion. The fetal image is meant to foreshadow the impending loss by making the fetus as real a baby as technology now permits. (To be sure, the confrontation is one-sided; the fetus does not actually stare back, even though one can find repeat-loop "Hi, Mom!" fetal images waving online.) To the extent that the law accepts that there is no greater maternal harm than to see one's child killed, mandatory ultrasound offers pregnant women something like a sneak preview. While *Dillon v. Legg* was an action by a bereaved mother against a careless driver, mandatory ultrasound statutes put the mother in the driver's seat, and the egregiousness of the action is no one's fault but her own.

Mandatory ultrasound—its appeal, its success, its perniciousness—results from a fortuitous combination of imagery (the scan), imagination (what one thinks one sees), and ideology (background beliefs that inform what and how one sees). To understand just how this reproductive trifecta comes about requires looking further into the nature and power of imaging and photography and at the transformation of ultrasound from a medical to a social practice. Ultrasound scans are not technically photographs, yet they are commonly read and treated as if they were: framed, displayed, and cherished as representations of the real thing.

Over the last few decades, developing alongside ever-improving fetal imagery, there has been a highly successful campaign focusing not only on what the fetus looks like but also on how it feels, what it likes, and what it wants us to do on its behalf. The identification of fetal needs means that maternal duties now begin in utero and every year the list grows longer. Fetal preferences, at least in the United States, now include classical music, organic food, and conversation.[14] Indeed, pregnant women can "homeschool" their fetuses by creating what one how-to book calls a "prenatal classroom."[15]

Putting maternal sanity to the side, perhaps this is all to the good. Certainly in the case of wanted pregnancies, parents and others may be well pleased to imagine the fetus getting smarter, enjoying itself, and being protected from secondhand smoke. For not all of what we imagine is imaginary. Prenatal care is not a hoax. If seeing one's baby on an ultrasound screen concretizes the pregnancy so that the likelihood of taking vitamins or giving up margaritas is enhanced, then public health and public imagination seem to have felicitously joined up through the medium of ultrasound.

Mandatory ultrasound, however, is not aimed at women who intend to keep their pregnancies and who might therefore benefit from early investment in fetal health. It is for women who seek an abortion; that intention triggers the requirement. The official explanation is that ultrasound improves the quality of informed consent. In its Statement of Findings and Purpose—a sort of statutory preamble to the Woman's Right to Know Act—the Alabama legislature explains at some length that "the decision to abort is an important, and often a stressful one, and it is desirable and imperative that it be made with full knowledge of its nature and consequences. The medical, emotional, and psychological consequences of an abortion are serious and can be lasting or life threatening. . . . It is [therefore] the purpose of this chapter to ensure that every woman considering an abortion receives complete information on the procedure, risks, and her alternatives."[16] The ultrasound scan is now part of what counts as complete information. But this feint toward informed consent is just that. Women know that abortion terminates pregnancy and that some form of life—whether a human life with full human attributes or something more inchoate—is extinguished by virtue of the procedure. Most women know what a fetus looks like or could quickly learn by looking at the materials that a good number of states provide to abortion patients through pamphlets or websites. What exactly is gained by replacing an accurate drawing or a generic photo with an image of a particular fetus that is the woman's very own?

Whatever one's thoughts about abortion, something about mandatory ultrasound seems intuitively unsavory, a use of state power that is both excessively intrusive and too transparently manipulative. Mandatory ultrasound takes abortion regulation up a notch. But still there is a challenge to be answered. What is so bad about the requirement if it makes pregnant women think harder about a decision as significant as abortion? That question is complicated by the fact that abortion is not only a medical procedure for which consent is required, it is also a right. Might mandatory ultrasound statutes—like the spousal notification requirements struck down in *Planned Parenthood of Southeastern Pennsylvania v. Casey*—unduly burden a woman's right to choose abortion?

So far two federal appellate courts have considered the constitutionality of these statutes and reached opposite conclusions. Interestingly, in both cases, the right at issue was that of the doctor to free expression and not that of the pregnant woman to decide about abortion. In 2012, the Fifth Circuit Court of Appeals upheld Texas's Women's Right to Know Act, noting that although requiring doctors to display and describe the patient's sonogram to her is a "direct and powerful" way of delivering information, the "show and tell" did not amount to "compelled" speech and was not unconstitutional under the First Amendment.[17] In contrast, two years later the Fourth Circuit Court of Appeals struck down North Carolina's Real-Time View Requirement, holding that the requirement "explicitly promotes a pro-life message by demanding the provision of facts [to the patient] that all fall on one side of the abortion debate"; this, said the court, "impose[s] an extraordinary burden" on the doctor's expressive rights in violation of the First Amendment.[18]

Acknowledging the importance of doctors' rights in the matter, I concentrate here on mandatory ultrasound as a constraint on *women's* rights and interests. What values, constitutional or otherwise, does mandatory ultrasound kick to the curb? For even if mandatory ultrasound is found to be constitutional by some courts, lawmakers may still want to take account of moral or policy objections to the legislation and vote against or repeal it. In particular, should the law be asking a pregnant woman not only to look at something—the coerced use of the fetal image—but also to cooperate in the production of the very thing to be seen—coerced production? Put another way, should women be made to offer up the content of their bodies in the form of an image for inspection before the law permits them to end a pregnancy? Are there limits on the state's ability to produce a decision from the gut?

In *On Photography,* Susan Sontag notes that photography has "alter[ed] and enlarge[d] our notions of what is worth looking at and what we have a right to observe."[19] While that is surely right descriptively, Sontag's observation does not answer the question of who gets to decide what is worth looking at—the viewer, the subject, or the state. There is no question that the state can require aspects of seeing as a condition to obtaining particular state benefits. It can, for example, demand proof that a person can actually see and see properly before being issued a driver's license. The state can require that would-be drivers watch gory films on highway fatalities to emphasize the solemn responsibilities that attach to driving. But the state's interest in what the citizenry must see is not always a matter of public safety. Politics also plays a role, as when the state decides that certain images—flag-draped coffins of soldiers killed in Iraq, for example—should not be taken or seen, but that other images, such as the ultrasound scans of pregnant women, must be.[20] In this way, mandatory ultrasound statutes are part of a political project of abortion persuasion, one last move in the state's refusal to take "no" for an answer.

Anthropologists of visual practices explain that to understand the meanings that people assign to an image, one must examine the circumstances of the image's production and also of its consumption or use.[21] These circumstances include the "intention[s] of the maker, the conditions of reception, and the needs and capacities of the viewer."[22] We already have some sense of the legislative intentions with regard to mandatory ultrasound, but I want now to look more closely at the conditions of reception—the context and conditions of pregnant women undergoing a scan, beginning with the mechanics.

Looking at Sound Waves

Ultrasound is a form of sonar ("sound navigation and ranging"). Originally developed to detect icebergs and submarines in the early twentieth century, it works by transmitting high-frequency sound waves through a body of water. The waves bounce off submerged structures and are converted to electrical impulses that are processed to form an image displayed on a screen. It is, as one scholar has observed, a form of "seeing through sound."[23] By the 1950s, ultrasound had moved from military and industrial uses to medical ones as researchers began to explore its potential for imaging structures (dense tissue or bone) within the human body.[24] The breakthrough for obstetric care came in 1958 when Scottish doctor Ian Donald produced a crude image of a fetal head while experimenting with ultrasound as a way to differentiate among abdominal tumors.[25] In these early days, the technology itself severely limited what could be seen. Images consisted of two-dimensional black and white lines that looked more like disturbances on the Richter scale than anything anatomical. Yet even these crude images were medically important: they refined doctors' assessments of gestational age and they ruled out (or in) the possibility of twins and the need for increased monitoring at a much earlier stage of pregnancy.[26]

The 1960s and 1970s brought significant developments in the delivery of ultrasound services. The quality of the technology improved as new "gray scale scanning" produced three-dimensional images in graduated shades of gray, permitting diagnoses of formerly undetectable fetal conditions and impairments. This led to an enormous decrease in perinatal mortality, not because most of the diagnosable conditions could be treated but because some women took the opportunity to terminate their pregnancies.[27] In addition, as the use of ultrasound became more commonplace, the methods of obtaining measurements, such as the relation of cranium size to age, became standardized. This meant that doctors themselves no longer needed to conduct the scans; trained sonographers could do the job.[28] This led to the now familiar practice of technicians typically mediating between the woman and the image on the screen, at least in the first instance.

Around this same time, the use of ultrasound expanded from diagnostic purposes to psychological ones. An early and much-cited 1983 study (of two patients!) in the *New England Journal of Medicine* heralded the possibility of ultrasound for maternal–infant bonding before quickening.[29] Seeing the image of one's own fetus might just "work upon the viewer an emotional transformation, which would in turn inspire the desired behavior."[30] The desired behavior was not simply enlisting pregnant women in prenatal care but possibly "influenc[ing] the resolution of any ambivalence toward the pregnancy itself in favor of the fetus."[31] In an uncanny bit of musing, the authors posed the question of whether ultrasound could become "a weapon in the moral struggle" over abortion.[32] Perhaps, they concluded, "a new stage of human existence, 'prenatality,' previously only mirrored in poets' and mothers' dreams about the fetus, will be as real to our descendants as childhood is to us."[33]

Of course the story of how looking into "prenatality" came about is not entirely poetical. Part of the story is economic. Early marketing of the technology by manufacturers, first to hospitals and then expanding to private obstetricians, emphasized ultrasound's ability to please pregnant clients by offering them an earlier intimacy with their baby.[34] (This became possible only after the introduction of the abdominal scanning wand; early machines sent sound waves through a huge tub of water that was suspended above the patient.[35]) The aesthetic design of the machines evolved to combine high-tech authority with friendlier consumer sensibilities, such as lighter colors, softer edges, and a swivel monitor so that the patient herself could be in on the action.[36]

Today almost all pregnant women in the United States receive at least one ultrasound examination as part of their routine obstetric care and many now have several. The procedure has become so routinized that specific informed consent is often dispensed with, the scan treated more along the lines of giving a urine sample.[37] This helps explain why many women "approach scans not as a procedure that may reveal anomalies, but as a harmless routine procedure that allows them to see their baby and confirm that all is well."[38] There are also commercial keepsake video packages marketed by specialized ultrasound studios: "Imagine the thrill of glimpsing into your unborn baby's world as you observe real-time 4D images of your baby stretching, yawning and moving about in the womb."[39]

Obstetric ultrasound reflects what Sontag describes as "an aesthetic consumerism to which everyone is now addicted"—the need to have reality confirmed and experience enhanced by photography.[40] The "virtually unlimited authority" of images has replaced experience as the means of knowing something for sure.[41] Ultrasound has been "incorporated into the script of pregnancy as itself a fact of life": it is the moment when modern mothers meet their baby.[42] Quickening as an announcement of arrival now seems pokey and old-fashioned—of course there's a baby in there; we saw it weeks ago!

If ultrasound scans are now the first snapshots in baby's first book or blog, it is important to understand the processes by which this all feels so natural. The impact of being offered a look is intensified by the distinctive role of photography in the family context or what anthropologist Mary Bouquet has dubbed "the family photographic condition."[43] Photographs, as "the only material traces of an irrecoverable past," derive their power and their important cultural role from their embeddedness in the fundamental rites of family life.[44] By creating a shared, visible record, family photographs help constitute the family. The ultrasound scan has inserted itself onto page one of the new baby's album, replacing the nursery shots of newborns in little knit caps.

For those unfamiliar with the process of obstetric ultrasound, anthropologist Lisa Mitchell offers a description of scanning as commonly performed on patients with wanted pregnancies:

> The sonographer asks the woman to lie down on a table, then squirts her belly with a cool blue gel, moves a device over her ab-

domen, and taps at a keyboard. Suddenly, a greyish blur appears on a luminescent screen. Customarily during this ritual, the couple smile, laugh, and point at the screen, even though they often do not recognize anything in the blur. The sonographer taps at the keyboard again and looks closely at the grey-and-white blur. She measures parts of it and calculates its age, weight, and expected date of delivery. She observes the couple closely to see if they like the blur and show signs of "bonding" with it. The couple also look closely at the sonographer, anxious in case she finds something wrong with the blur. Sometimes, when the blur seems really pleasing, the sonographer talks to it, strokes it, and congratulates the couple. After about fifteen minutes, the blur is turned off, and the gel wiped away, and the couple are given a copy of the grayish blur to take home.[45]

But as scholars of technology remind us, "visibility is not transparency."[46] The images on the screen are incomplete; parts of the larger picture—the mother's body—are not seen. In addition, without some serious guidance by a knowledgeable technician or physician, the viewer might not know exactly what she is looking at. Images in the early stages of pregnancy are not always recognizable as that of a baby, or even a human. As one unsentimental mother confessed after the technician had announced the presence of the baby on the monitor, what she saw was not a baby but rather something "suggestive of the human," something "with its oversize head and flipperlike appendages, closer to the amphibious."[47] But most happily pregnant women seem able to dismiss amphibious thoughts and identify a creature that is not only human (or human-ish) but that is theirs.

If we think of ultrasound viewing as a form of "assisted seeing," it is the sonographer who often helps parents transform the grainy splotches on the monitor into their baby. "She told me what it was, then I could see it. When [the technician] said, 'That's the head,' I looked for a head."[48] Parents then mimetically educate grandparents and friends: "That's an arm; there's the rump." The transformation is accomplished through techniques which, though unnecessary for diagnostic purposes, have become embedded in the social experience. During the scan sonographers may impart personality to the fetus; it is "shy" if obscured on the monitor or "a good baby" if easily visible; fetal movements are similarly described as "clowning around" or "waving." The advent of 4-D ultrasound images has added to the fetus's ability to perform. As noted British obstetrician Stuart Campbell suggestively stated in 2005, "At 12 weeks we can see it bouncing off the uterine wall and making a stepping motion that seems to anticipate the first real steps it will take a year or so after birth."[49] (Campbell's comments were made in support of changing U.K. law to ban all abortions after eighteen weeks.) Physical descriptions of the baby are filtered through a "cultural sieve, as [sonographers] select out those parts which they believe are most appealing and reassuring for women—the beating heart, the skull and brain . . . the hands and feet, [and] especially the fingers and toes," details now incorporated into Real Time View Requirements.[50] These practices—the sonographer's vocabulary, deciphering skills, selections of parts, manner, and enthusiasm—are the more authoritative because of the "presumed status of the interpreter as a medical specialist."[51]

At the same time, anthropologist Janelle Taylor points out that there is nothing inevitable about the prevailing manner of ultrasound screening; nothing requires a screening to be a family occasion or a guided tour that concludes with a souvenir snapshot to take home. As Taylor states, the experience might be quite different if it "were a little more like an EKG and a little less like a visit to the hospital nursery."[52] But current practices are not a matter of happenstance. There are also occupational explanations. The field of obstetric sonography—in contrast, say, to X-ray imaging or MRIs—tends to attract people interested in interpersonal as well as technological job satisfaction.[53] Obstetric sonographers find connection with their pregnant patients an important feature of their work. There are also self-identified pro-life training and certification programs, such as "Windows to the Womb," which instruct technicians on how to personify the fetus through such techniques as urging the woman to give it a name.[54] Over the last several years sonographers have started to discuss the ethics of influencing ultrasound patients about a pregnancy decision.[55] One widely held view is that sonographers should never attempt to counsel a patient: as technicians their professional training is limited, and they have no information about a patient's medical or personal circumstances.[56] Concerns within the field about the ethics of counseling were frequently linked to questions about the professional status of sonography: is it an occupation or more like a profession?[57]

All of this works to produce a form of screening in which the fetus is indeed ready for its close-up. Women who undergo ultrasound are more likely to call the fetus a baby and perceive their baby as being "more vivacious, more familiar, stronger and more beautiful," "more real" and "more there."[58] In cases of wanted pregnancies, the screening functions along the line of a fetal coming-out party in which the doctor affirms that the pregnancy is fine and the process of connecting with one's fetus begins. And while much of the data is anecdotal, some women say that they could never thereafter have an abortion.

Yet connection and joy are not universal responses to undergoing ultrasound, even for women who were, at least in the first instance, happy to be pregnant. Some pregnancies become unwelcome precisely because an ultrasound scan reveals some troubling fetal anomaly or characteristic. For mothers who learn during the screening that their baby is not as they had hoped—sometimes because the chatty sonographer goes suddenly still—the procedure becomes a more complicated phenomenon.[59] With some revealed conditions—heart defects, for example—there is the possibility of treatment. But couples who receive a negative diagnostic outcome—microcephaly, for example—are often faced with the decision of whether to continue the pregnancy. And depending on a range of factors—the nature and severity of the diagnosis, religious or philosophical beliefs, past reproductive history, and what physicians advise—a decision is reached.[60] Taylor identifies this as the "prenatal paradox" of ultrasound: the technology simultaneously promises reassurance that all is well and provides an assurance that if things are not, in most cases there is time to do something about it.[61] Some women, aware in particular cases that the screening may produce an unfavorable diagnosis, attenuate their emotional connection to the fetus until the results of further testing are known. The self-protective phenomenon of a "tentative pregnancy" makes sense, although for some couples, an ultrasound image preceding an abortion may later become a source of solace, tangible proof that both the pregnancy and the baby were real.[62]

And what is the significance of the ultrasound process for women whose pregnancies are unwanted from the start, not because of the particulars of this pregnancy but because of pregnancy itself? It is against the background of unwanted pregnancies that we explore the question of whether mandated ultrasound under the Women's Right to Know Acts is really all that bad. Its purpose may be transparent, but is it so bad that it is bad law? The answer emerges from the mechanisms by which mandatory ultrasound works or is plausibly believed to work upon pregnant women.

Facing up to Your Fetus

Even if one does not believe that life begins at conception—as the law of several states insists it does—deciding whether to have an abortion or a baby is often an occasion for reflection.[63] As the Supreme Court observed in *Casey*, abortion is "fraught with consequences . . . for the woman who must live with the implications of her decision" one way or the other.[64] Mandatory ultrasound not only slows down the decision-making process but adds something new to think about. While some women may be wondering why the heck they have to do this when their mind was already made up, legislatures hope that most women will think harder about the entity the image represents and the reality of its impending death. To be sure, no one pries the woman's eyes open until she glimpses the image, although in 2007 South Carolina gave it a try until the state attorney general decided that forcing a woman to look was a form of physical coercion and was probably unconstitutional.[65] The bill was amended to remove the compulsory viewing. Nonetheless, the question put to the woman cannot be avoided: do you want to see the image of your unborn child? Until struck down in 2014, North Carolina's "real-time display and description" required abortion providers to "display and describe to every single patient, even those who go so far as to cover their eyes and block their ears to prevent receipt of the information."[66]

Pro-life organizations have long recognized what anthropologist Faye Ginsburg describes as the "conversion power" of fetal imagery. This is the belief that the visible fetus reveals a certain truth and, as with the revelation of other truths, there is then "only one path to follow."[67] Certainly some women may be deeply moved by seeing their own ultrasound. We are often awestruck when we first see something that could not have been seen before, whether the first pictures of Earth from space or *Life* magazine's first fetus in utero.[68] Some may even be "awestruck" in a religious sense. Religion has always strained to see the unseen, whether through pictorial representations or through sacred architecture. In this way, a woman seeing or being offered the sight of her own unseen fetus for the first time is guided into something like a religious or sacred moment.[69] On this account, the ultrasound requirement seems less an appeal to reason than an attempt to overpower it.

One objection to mandatory ultrasound is that alerting women to the gravity of an abortion decision is unnecessary. They already know. Abortion has been a matter of intense public debate and disruption for some forty years, and most women—most everyone—cannot help but be aware of moral claims on all sides that now attach to the issue. These claims are made not only through public discourse—campaign rhetoric, online sites, billboards, sermons, talk radio—but also through the many constraints now imposed on abortion access and provision. There must be something highly suspect about a medical procedure that is excluded from public funding, unavailable in 87 percent of counties, and whose facilities, providers, and patients are subject to unprecedented levels and modes of regulation (not to mention protests, picketing, and other forms of private disapproval). Polls show that opposition to abortion on moral grounds has been increasing, perhaps especially among younger women, and it is reasonable to think that the increased moral status of the fetus has something to do with this. *Glamour* magazine observed in a 2005 piece, "The Mysterious Disappearance of Young Pro-Choice Women," that "today's twenty-somethings . . . [have] never lived through the sordid conditions of back-alley abortions, the deaths from botched procedures, the desperation of a woman trapped by her own changing body. It's ancient history to them, and about as compelling."[70]

Pro-life advocates say they are only asking that women directly confront the object of their action before agreeing to abort it. Without doing so, the argument goes, it is impossible to make an informed decision. Something of an analogy is found in adoption. In most states a pregnant woman cannot legally consent to the adoption of her child before the child is born. Legislators have decided that some experience of one's infant, if only childbirth itself, is necessary to grasp the profound nature of what is at stake in the decision to separate from one's baby. On this account, an ultrasound is as close as a woman can come to an interaction with her child before knowingly deciding to abort. The scan stands in for a born child. The statutes ask women before declining motherhood to step up and face their fetus first.

Ultrasound is meant to establish that the fetus is not just "potential life," to use the U.S. Supreme Court's phrase in *Roe v. Wade,* but is "life" itself.[71] The scan seeks to inform a woman not about fetal life in general but about the reality of her fetus: the one right there on the monitor. That fetus is not just a life, it is a relative; not a brochure fetus but the woman's own son or daughter. This is who she must confront, either by looking it squarely in the eye (although the eyes are closed) or by signing a paper saying she has refused to do so. Although couched in the protective terms of informed consent, these statutes are unabashedly meant to transform the embryo from an abstraction to a baby in the eyes of the potentially aborting mother. The victim of her decision is no longer faceless. Unlike bombardiers who more easily drop their payload on unknown victims, ultrasound removes the anonymity of the hit.

Here it is useful to keep in mind the properties of visual images that give them such force in our cognitive schemes. One is the relation between the image of a thing and the thing itself. This leads to a second property of image making: the acquisition of something as information rather than experience.[72] The scan blends science with affection or tenderness: presented as though it were information pure and simple, the fetal image also has the cultural force of a portrait, betokening the presence of the entity depicted. Ultrasound masterfully connects the viewer to the image, not only because the woman may choose to look at it, but because whether she does or not, she already knows what the image represents. The social significance of the image helps determine its significance for the individual woman. Preexisting cultural familiarity with the public fetus and its general status as an independent being makes affinity with one's own fetus a natural next step. The woman knows even before she lies down on the table what the image stands for, and it is against this imprint that she will have to proceed with her abortion.

To be sure, many doctors now administer ultrasound routinely before an abortion even without legal dictate. Why then object to requiring as a matter of law what is already accepted as a matter of good medical practice? Important distinctions between medical ultrasound and mandatory ultrasound suggest a set of answers. When done in preparation for an abortion, the primary purpose of the scan is diagnostic; it gives the most accurate information about the date and location of the pregnancy. In this way, medical ultrasound enables the physician to choose the most appropriate medical course for the patient. In contrast, mandatory ultrasound is not a medical prerequisite to performing an abortion but rather a legal prerequisite to consent. Unlike a medical scan, which provides medical information to the doctor, the mandated scan is meant to provide nonmedical information to the patient. The requirement assumes that a woman who consents to abortion without the invitation to look cannot have fully understood the significance of what she is doing. Alabama elaborates its suspicion of the genuineness of consent or prior reflection: "Most abortions are performed in clinics devoted solely to providing abortions and family planning services. . . . In most instances, the woman's only actual contact with the physician occurs simultaneously with the abortion procedure, with little opportunity to receive counseling concerning her decision."[73] In one case an

Alabama judge described abortion physicians as people interested in only one thing, "getting this young lady's money."[74]

Mandatory ultrasound replaces a suspect source (doctors) with a better informant: the fetus itself. This counteracts the patient's presumed reliance on information from a physician who is necessarily (from the legislative point of view) pro-choice: what more to say than that he or she performs abortions? In contrast, the sonogram itself has no point of view; it is a static image offered up as an objective datum incapable of bias. This was the view of the Fifth Circuit Court of Appeals in its 2012 decision upholding Texas's ultrasound statute on the ground that an ultrasound scan is simply (and permissibly) a "truthful, nonmisleading, and relevant disclosure."[75]

This is to ignore all we know about how viewers read images. Photographs are always imbued with contextual meaning. Consider an example from criminal procedure. The faces of possible assailants offered to victims in a police photo array (a lineup with pictures) are often read as connoting guilt; why would the person otherwise be included in the array?[76] (Fetuses on the other hand have a presumption of innocence.) Legislative claims about the objectivity of a sonogram are necessarily incomplete. They fail to account for preexisting public and personal familiarity with and affection for fetal imagery, for coaching by the sonographer, and for the cultural significance of having an ultrasound in the first place.

A second difference between medical and mandated scans concerns the viewing. When an ultrasound is done as part of the prep work for an abortion, the woman may ask or be asked if she wants to look at the monitor. In contrast, the very point of the mandated scan is to remove the question. Doctors must offer a look and document the woman's decision.[77] The woman must be told she has the *right* to look. She is not told she has a constitutional right to an abortion, but to the extent she is at all thinking about rights at this fraught moment, the abortion right is apparently being matched against something so important that it too is called a right, the right to be persuaded against exercising the right you came in with.

The mechanism of "merely offering" fetal imagery counts on the imaginative capacity of a woman to know what has been offered and whether to look or not. To be sure, depending on the stage of her pregnancy, there may not be much to see at all; early ultrasounds reveal only the gestational sac, which appears as a tiny oval.[78] The absence of anything very much to look at is especially pointed in the context of medical abortion, which takes place no later than nine weeks into pregnancy.[79] Where there is something to see, the image on the monitor is a massively magnified version of the actual size of the conceptus, and in this sense, it is misleading.

The social significance of obstetric ultrasound is crucial in comprehending the power and the perversity of the mandatory requirement.[80] In wanted pregnancies, it is not just happily anticipated participation in the procedure but the excitement that precedes the scanning and the display after. As one woman, four months pregnant, explained about showing her ultrasound picture to friends and coworkers, "I wouldn't be a good mommy if I didn't."[81] Here lies the force of cultural practice. Mandatory ultrasound statutes require women with unwanted pregnancies to participate physically and culturally in what has become a rite of full-term pregnancy. By virtue of having the screening at all, women are scooped into the social category of pregnant women, however brief they intend that status to be.

This phenomenological wallop is not lost on those who oppose legal abortion. At the early stages of pregnancy—when the great majority of abortions are performed—women rarely look pregnant. Many do not feel pregnant. This enables women who are ambivalent or unsure about the pregnancy to deliberate with a degree of privacy and control over who knows. They proceed within an emotional framework of their own construction.

But mandatory ultrasound disrupts a woman's control over her pregnancy, at least as far as the organization of her own attitudes is concerned. While an ultrasound screening is not quite like lining up with the kids at Kinder-Photo, once her fetus has had its picture taken, the woman has embarked on the social experience of motherhood. The purpose of the ultrasound is to do everything possible to shift the woman's thoughts, her experience, and her expectations from someone who has decided not to remain pregnant into the position of an ordinary mother-to-be. Once a woman is transformed or at least beckoned into maternity, a formidable set of expectations are imposed and sometimes assumed. By requiring her to go through the very procedure she would happily go through if she wanted a baby, she is shepherded into the maternal fold, even if within a few hours or days she intends to stand down from those ranks.

Coerced Use and Coerced Production

It is not only the coerced production of the fetal image but its coercive use that further discredits the practice of mandatory ultrasound. Mandatory ultrasound works in the realm of persuasion. But certain choices that people make about the structure and content of their lives are and ought to be regarded as protected choices that are not subject to all forms of what the law considers mere persuasion. For it is not only the decision that is protected but the route one takes to arrive at the decision as well. Requiring ultrasound as a matter of law violates the space properly accorded such decisions and burdens an abortion decision with coercion regarding both the use and the production of the scan. Understanding the requirement this way helps explain the unease that kicks in upon learning there is such a thing as "mandatory ultrasound."

It is generally accepted that in a liberal democracy certain decisions about how a person organizes his or her life reside within the special competence and authority of the person making the decision. These decisions encompass a range of deeply personal, often self-defining preferences and commitments. Whether to marry, who to vote for, and what religion to practice are the kinds of decisions that people are entitled to make for themselves. People use contraception, vote in a primary, refuse to swear an oath on a Bible. In the United States, these decisions are often framed in constitutional terms: rights of privacy, religious association, personal liberty, and so on. Since 1973, the decision whether to end a pregnancy has been a similar sort of protected decision, one characterized by the Supreme Court in *Planned Parenthood of Southeastern Pennsylvania v. Casey* as involving nothing less than a woman's choice about her "destiny."

Interfering with the deliberate (or meandering) path a woman takes to decide about an unwanted pregnancy is more than a nudge. Consider by analogy the example of religion. The state protects religious freedom and it also protects the right of people to come to their religious convictions in their own way. Imagine, however, that before you could decline to swear on a Bible in court, the state required that you first read a monograph on the compatibility of religion and patriotism, hear the Sermon on the Mount, or look at Fra Angelico's *Annunciation*. However intellectually or spiritually profitable any of the three may be, the proposal seems preposterous as a precondition to religious exercise. How one comes to a choice about religion is as intimate and important and ought to be as inviolate as the exercise of the choice itself (swearing or not swearing on the Bible). Arguments about religious toleration have often focused on exactly this point. Even if it is accepted that coercion is unlikely to produce sincere religious belief, at certain historical moments the opponents of toleration tried to do so indirectly, for example, by compelling not belief itself but attendance at religious services. John Locke, in his famous

Letter on Toleration, showed that coercion was powerless to produce genuine faith.[82] Yet in his *Second Letter on Toleration,* Locke argued that the means of arriving at one's faith were to be given as much protection as a person's basic decision to follow a particular creed: "No way whatsoever that I shall walk in, against the Dictates of my Conscience will ever bring me to the Mansions of the Blessed."[83]

In the religious case, it seems clear that the constitutional protection of free exercise extends to the means by which people decide what religion to practice or whether to practice a religion at all. Schools cannot require religious education on the grounds of informing believers' choice. Nonbelievers cannot be made to attend religious services so they can see for themselves just what they are missing. The path to belief is understood as an integral part of one's faith, and there is no question of withholding constitutional protection just because the exercise of religion itself is not directly under attack.

The analogy to religion helps show how close mandatory ultrasound laws come to an assault on the basic right to abortion. It is important then to see why protecting choice involves protecting a woman's control over the process by which she reaches her decision. In both cases, the same values of autonomy—control over the shape and content of one's life—that underpin the protection of the ultimate decision are crucially in play with regard to a person's chosen path to that decision. Philosophically, it makes no sense to protect one and not the other. Respect for individual autonomy requires protection of both.

There are, of course, better or worse ways of coming to a decision. We might, for example, disapprove of a woman throwing dice to decide about an abortion. But if a choice is protected because of the profound significance it bears to the meaning of a person's life, then the part of life devoted to the choosing—the thinking it through—has got to be protected as well. Adults may arrive at certain decisions, including whether to have a child, having negotiated their own path to get there without intercession from unborn offspring or from God or from legislatures doing God's work.

Unlike informational brochures on the stages of fetal development, mandatory ultrasound statutes require the woman to participate in the physical production of information that she is then urged to consider. But there is something unjust in using a woman's innards to make the state's case against abortion. Diagnostically, ultrasound, in contrast say to amniocentesis, may be admired for its noninvasiveness: no cutting, no punctures, no blood. Nonetheless, when stripped of its glossy meet-the-baby production values, an ultrasound screening is an intimate, sometimes raw invasion of a woman's bodily privacy.

Federal district court Judge Catherine Eagles has described typical screening procedures as performed in accordance with North Carolina's Real Time View Requirement: "During this ultrasound procedure, the patient must lie on an examination table where she either (i) exposes the lower portion of her abdomen, or (ii) is naked from the waist down, covered only by a drape. Depending on the stage of pregnancy, the provider (i) inserts an ultrasound probe into the patient's vagina, or (ii) places an ultrasound probe on her abdomen. The provider must display the images produced from the ultrasound 'so that the pregnant woman may view them.'"[84] And while all this is going on, the doctor must provide a detailed medical description of whatever shows up on the monitor.[85] In the context of criminal law, there are limits on the state's right to secure evidence from inside a defendant's body. As Justice Felix Frankfurter explained in *Rochin v. California,* where the suspect's stomach was pumped in a search for illegal drugs, "it would be a stultification of the responsibility which the course of constitutional history has cast upon this Court to hold that in order to convict a man the police cannot extract by force what is in his mind but can extract what is in his stomach."[86] Something like that is going on here. Historically, prosecutors used the bodies of abortion patients as evidence in criminal prosecutions of abortionists.[87] In a 1950 case, *State v. Stanko,* the Chicago police apprehended a woman as she left midwife-abortionist Stanko's apartment and brought her to a physician's office, where the woman was given pelvic examinations that produced evidence of abortion, later admitted at trial to secure Stanko's guilt.[88] Of course, neither performing nor receiving an abortion is now criminal activity, though there is always the tinge.

The case regarding coercion becomes clearer in those states—Virginia, North Carolina, Oklahoma—that initially specified the use of a vaginal transducer rather than an abdominal wand if it would "display the embryo or fetus more clearly."[89] (In a *Doonesbury* comic strip, the doctor, required to do a vaginal ultrasound, announces to his patient, "With [this] shaming wand . . . I thee rape.")[90] The North Carolina legislature insisted a vaginal probe (on the order of a large vibrator) was meant only to provide more information, not to make things more horrible. Public outcry over vaginal ultrasound—hard to describe as anything other than penetration under the color of state law—caused the statutes to be amended and the word "vaginal" removed. However, the requirement remains that the physician use whichever method will show the image "more clearly."[91] Whether legislators find it outrageous, irrelevant, or justifiable for the state to order vaginal examinations for women seeking abortion is unclear; perhaps the thought is that a vaginal probe is nothing new for someone who is pregnant. Even putting aside the vaginal probe, which, as one law student put it, is "not nothing," scanning is physically and psychologically intrusive. It underscores for women that what they are about to do is wrong— so wrong in fact that the law can require them not only to be lectured but to be examined bodily. It is hard not to understand mandatory ultrasound as a mechanism of humiliation.

The official explanation behind Women's Right to Know Acts is that they are the best shot at bringing women to their senses so that they will not later suffer the trauma alleged to follow an abortion, though from another perspective, one could argue that mandatory ultrasound inverts the chronology of trauma by ensuring it precedes any abortion. Some forms of punishment by regulation are more subtle than others. How bad is it really to inform pregnant women that if they decide to have their baby, they don't have to keep it since the state offers full adoption services? Whether that sort of information is intended to help or intended to haunt is subject to debate. But mandatory ultrasound takes the state's punitive intentions to clever lengths. Requiring a woman to produce her body and its contents, even under the guise of informed consent, goes beyond the indignities even of our criminal justice system. And pregnant women are not criminals.

As a form of persuasion, an ultrasound image operates less like a brochure than like a sidewalk protestor. As Justice Scalia explained, the sidewalk protestor is hoping "to forge, in the last moments before another of her sex is to have an abortion, a bond of concern and intimacy that might enable her to persuade the woman to change her mind and heart."[92] This is precisely the aspiration for mandatory ultrasound. The appeal is powerful as the proffered bond of intimacy comes from the tiny (though magnified) victim himself. Maybe the appeal causes some women to change their minds, although there are only anecdotal stories to support this. In contrast, a Canadian study found that not one patient who chose to look following an invitation, not under the compulsion of law, changed her mind.[93] In any event, requiring a woman to cough up an image of her own fetus is not the stuff of informed consent.

Fetal images mean different things to different people: "For some parents, the ability to see fetal parts . . . may demonstrate that the fetus . . . has the potential for or actually possesses distinctive human consciousness and person-hood."[94] To some, the ultrasound image represents life itself; to others, it shows a form of developing life, what one pregnant columnist called an "entity in the act of becoming."[95] To still others, a sonogram may be more like an X-ray, a technological depiction of one aspect of interior physical self, the condition once understood as pregnancy. These alternative understandings of a scan may illuminate what Justice O'Connor identified in *Casey* as "the right to define one's own concept of existence."[96] But as Justice O'Connor stated, "beliefs about these matters could not define the attributes of personhood were they formed under compulsion of the State."[97] In deciding whether to end a pregnancy, women may choose to engage with their pregnant bodies and those bodies' vibrant contents on their own terms. The problem is not the fact of confronta-tion but rather its imposition.

Women come to their own views about pregnancy and abortion by drawing on a variety of faculties, senses, and intelligences. It is up to each of them to decide how to evaluate what is at stake. Mandatory ultrasound commandeers the decisional process by insisting that women take a particular view of fetal ex-istence. That insistence stems not from any innate truth about what an ultra-sound image reveals but from what the visual politics of abortion has taught us to see. French sociologist Bruno Latour has suggested that science and politics have always been intertwined, as "groups of people argue with one another using paper, signs, prints and diagrams."[98] The recorded echoes that comprise a sono-gram are a form of argumentation, one that has been put to use in the public debate over abortion, as groups of people continue to argue with one another.

Yet the fight is not quite a fair one, for mandatory ultrasound relocates the argument from the realm of private persuasion to that of legal requirement. All women must comply, disrobe, and listen. Moreover, a woman's decision whether to have an abortion or a baby is unlikely to be a matter of politics or law for her. Deploying the image of her own fetus to argue against her is ha-rassment masquerading as information. It confuses coercion with consent and public debate with this ever so personal and protected choice.

6

"You Had Body, You Died"

Among the various traditions that accompany family gatherings—weddings, vacations, and so on—a familiar ritual plays out at the moment someone tries to organize a group photo. As everyone begins to take their places, there is one person who stays put. Cheerfully urged to "get in!" the person remains outside the frame, mumbling, "No, I couldn't; I'm not in the family." These professions of reluctance are followed by encouragement from some (and stony silence from others), and the new girlfriend is pulled into the picture. At least for that moment, she becomes a member of the family, and everyone says cheese.

Just as family photos mark who is in the family when the picture was taken, they also remind us at later points in time who is not. Things may not have worked out with the reluctant girlfriend and her temporary inclusion was, in the end, just that. Her status becomes known or knowable only over time. Some of those pictured in a group photograph may have died or otherwise departed—an ex-husband, for example. In school settings, absences are formally recorded: the names of children missing on the day the class picture is taken appear in an inset under the heading "not pictured." Family photographs rarely include such notations; it is up to family members to keep their own membership records.

Traditionally, looking at family photographs has offered a record only of the past. Certainly the photos may intimate the future—the promise inherent in wedding photos, for example—but the idea of a "record" of the future makes little sense. The future might be imagined, but unlike the past, it cannot itself be pasted in an album or downloaded onto a DVD. This is no longer the case. There has been a sonic breakthrough in the chronological boundaries of the visual family. The first page in many baby albums is reserved for the prenatal scan. In time that image will be followed by zillions of additional photos, though not in every instance. Some pregnancies end in miscarriage or stillbirth, and in such cases the prenatal image may become a treasured memento mori.

Other pregnancies end voluntarily, and that circumstance poses a new question: What does a woman see when she looks at an ultrasound scan of an embryo or fetus she intends to abort? What might such an image mean to her? Even without the force of law, some pregnant women choose to look at a scan before an abortion, and they do so for all sorts of reasons. Some look out of curiosity to see what, if anything, is there. Others look more purposefully, not just to see but to confront the image, some to gather information, others to test their resolve, still others to prove to third parties they have taken the situation seriously. In judicial bypass cases, for example, some courts look favorably upon pregnant girls who have "stepped up" and looked at their scan before making their decision.[1] Lawyers who represent petitioning minors routinely recommend that their client look at the ultrasound scan to strengthen the evidentiary case for her maturity.[2] Still other women look at their ultrasound scans with fond excitement because at the time the scan was taken, they had no thought of abortion. Only some later event—the results of prenatal testing, the disinterest of a partner—caused them to reconsider the pregnancy. And as we know, in a fair number of states, women undergo ultrasounds because they have to. Some look and others do not.

How might the ultrasound scan of an aborted fetus register in the long term? Does it stick memorably in the brain? Does the once-pregnant woman impose a silent "not pictured" caption on family group photos for years to come or is the subject of the scan more like the reluctant girlfriend who might have become part of the family but whose existence is now hard to remember and over time slips away?

As a culture, we put great faith in the authority of sight: eye-witness accounts are favored over secondhand hearsay; modern social theorists write about "the hegemony of the visual."[3] Visuality is not the only way meaning is figured, but pre-abortion scans and descriptions of fetuses are meant to imprint an image and are worth our closer attention. Recall that the state of North Carolina now collects pre-abortion ultrasound scans from pregnancies over sixteen weeks. Here, however, my focus is on the significance of looking in the personal realm, not the governmental.

What then do women see? The question is complicated first by technological distortions. Ultrasound images are not literal versions of what lies within:

the image on the monitor is supersized; color is washed out to gray or sepia; and in early pregnancies, there isn't much to look at.[4] In addition, a person's description of what she has seen may not always be the best account of what was there. There are familiar explanations for this: poor vision, atmospherics, mis-identification, and so on.[5] There is also the matter of sight's subjectivity—the fact that people sometimes see what they expect, want, or are encouraged to see.

There are a number of tricks and tropes involved in displaying an ultrasound: cultural familiarity with fetal imagery, the significance of ultrasound as a social experience, and certain properties of photography itself.[6] We are prepped for the experience, not only because we have seen scans before but because we know how we are expected to respond.

Yet our approving sounds and smiles are something more than good pre-natal etiquette. Most of us know which response file to pull up when shown an early ultrasound scan. We do not say, "Hey, nice sac!" but focus instead on the semi-discernible shape in the center. We know that we are being asked to look at something regarded less as a something than a someone.

For some women, having an ultrasound may transform even early pregnancy into motherhood. That, however, is not the only plausible response. Much may depend on the nature of the pregnancy—planned or accidental, voluntary or involuntary, wanted or unwanted. Much may depend as well on the circum-stances of the abortion: an early first-term abortion, an abortion after prenatal testing or selective reduction, an abortion following testing when an anomaly is detected only later in pregnancy, as with the Zika virus. In short, looking at scans of to-be-aborted fetuses—or even looking directly at their actual bodies, their mass—is a more varied and nuanced proposition than abortion oppo-nents may have considered.

Scan as Portrait

Ultrasound scans can be squarely located within the genre of the family photo-graph. Art historian Anne Higonnet notes that in the United States the "nar-rative of the album" typically begins prenatally.[7] Showing off an ultrasound has become a routine reproductive practice, whether an old-fashioned wallet photo (if anyone still carries these) or the images that fly past on smartphones. Taking and displaying pictures of one's children, even the prenatal ones, is an essential part of American parenting, particularly American mothering. As Susan Sontag said in 1977: "Not to take pictures of one's children, particularly when they are small, is a sign of parental indifference."[8] Ask any second child. Gestation jump-starts the "family photographic condition."[9]

Law capitalizes on the scan's status as a family photo. It is, after all, the image's relational attributes that give mandatory ultrasound its bite. Were it not for the imaginative visual connection between the viewer and subject, representations of generic fetuses as the means of educating pregnant women would do as well. But an ultrasound scan is not a picture of any fetus; it represents the viewer's flesh and blood. Displays from four-dimensional ultrasounds are offered in "real time," so that when the woman moves, the image moves, and the connection between the two seems all the more palpable. In his meditation on how photographs acquire meaning (he was thinking of a picture of his mother), Roland Barthes described "a sort of umbilical cord link[ing] the body of the photographed thing to my gaze."[10] Barthes's metaphor becomes a bit strange when an actual umbilical cord (invisible in most scans) links the photographed thing not only to the woman's gaze but to her body. This is a family photo, fortissimo.

Nevertheless, in the context of abortion, ultrasound images are not just any family photograph; they are family photographs relating to extinction. What is being extinguished, on the legislative account, is the woman's unborn child. The fetal scan exists in relation to the impending demise of the thing represented.[11] To the extent the fetal scan is presented or received as the picture of a child (or a thing), it is a picture of a child or thing that will no longer exist. The impending disappearance is part of what conveys meaning for the woman making the decision. It is meant to operate at a visceral level as a forecast of the death of this particular photographic subject. Other photographs, often from wartime, similarly present the viewer with a look at imminent death. Consider the pictures taken (and secretly saved by the photographer Nhem En) of prisoners in Cambodia's Tuol Sleng Prison before their execution by the Khmer Rouge in the 1970s. Looking at these photos—some of prisoners with children—is always deeply distressing. One is aware of the impending loss even now. Ultrasound images are meant to create a visual construction of loss for women awaiting an abortion.

Although pregnant women are not yet mothers, there is an increasing cultural confidence in ascribing feelings to pregnant women as though they were. Consider Justice Anthony Kennedy's observation in *Gonzales v. Carhart*, the 2007 case upholding the federal Partial Birth Abortion Act's ban on the late-term abortion procedure called intact dilation and extraction. Writing for

the Court, Justice Kennedy stated that "respect for human life finds an ultimate expression in the bond of love the mother has for her child. . . . While
we find no reliable data to measure the phenomenon, it seems unexceptional
to conclude that some women come to regret their choice to abort the infant
life they once created and sustained."[12] These few lines offer up a series of
mother-focused propositions as though they were simple matters of fact: the
proposition that abortion destroys *infant* life, that the woman herself *created*
that life (missing the joint and sometimes non-consensual nature of conception), and that respect for human life is supremely encapsulated in maternal
love. All of this leads the Court to conclude that once women understand what
this form of abortion does to the fetus (kills it), at least some women will immediately or over time "come to regret" their decision. The sheer possibility of
that regret justifies the total ban on a procedure that a woman and her doctor
might otherwise choose. Other regulations such as required disclosures regarding fetal development, appearance, and heartbeat similarly proceed on the
view that women need to confront the physical substance of pregnancy—the
fetus—through their own sensory abilities in order to avoid later regret. In *Gonzales v. Carhart,* the Court decided that it is better for everyone to ban the whole
thing rather than to force a confrontation through disclosure ahead of time.

Without accepting Justice Kennedy's observation tout court, let's consider
what a woman might have regret (or other feelings) about ending. Depending
on the woman, that thing may be a human life or a pregnancy; it may be an unborn child or an embryo; a conceptus (though women themselves rarely use
that clinical phrase); or the thing that will ruin her life. In contrast, in France,
the early product of conception is often described as "an egg" *(l'oeuf)*.[13] However it is conceptualized, after an abortion it will no longer exist and this brings
us to the relationship between absence and loss.

To have an abortion means that the pregnancy is over and one will not have
a baby six or seven months hence. Abortion also puts an end to the anticipa-
tion of a future baby and all that is imagined to come with it: womanly fulfill-
ment, social recognition, the perfect baby who will love you forever, a partner's
commitment, and so on.[14] With all these possibilities gone, a woman might
well feel that something has been lost. (I put aside for now what may have been
gained.) Yet loss is different from regret. Regret implies that one would have
made a different decision at the time if only one had known (something). In
contrast, loss rues not the decision but one or another aspect of its consequences. One experiences loss when one focuses specifically on the costs of a

decision, costs that have been weighed against benefits or against the avoidance of even greater costs. Even if one thinks the decision is justified—even if one has no regrets about the decision—the costs that it involved don't cease to be costs, and they may well be experienced as a form of loss. Feelings of loss are sometimes constructed, built up almost architecturally from layer upon layer of meaning regarding pregnancy, adulthood, maternity, and so on. These layers of meaning are intensified by the visual significance of the fetus.

It is important to acknowledge that for those who oppose legal abortion, an ultrasound scan depicts not loss but life. Fetal imagery unveils the truth that to kill the living thing represented by the image is murder. On this account, fetal imagery is not a harbinger of loss; it is a visual siren meant to sound the alarm for the very purpose of *avoiding* loss or any other perilous consequence of abortion. Some women, like those interviewed by the South Dakota Task Force on Abortion, may experience terrible loss.[15] There has been considerable reluctance on the part of those who support legal abortion to say anything negative about the experience. Pro-choice advocates have been concerned—and not unreasonably—that the slightest mention of loss gets worryingly close to regret (or worse, remorse) and will be celebrated as an authentic moment of true confession. Important aspects of abortion have therefore gone un- or underspoken within the choice community as a matter of strategy. The fear of reinforcing those who would recriminalize abortion has chilled expression, not in the constitutional sense, but as a matter of normal, desirable human expression and discourse.

But loss and regret are two different things. Some women who decide to terminate a pregnancy might wish that their circumstances were otherwise. They may wish they had an income, a partner, a healthy fetus, support, medical insurance, and so on. They have, however, assessed their circumstances and made a decision. But whatever the circumstances, women might subsequently feel loss, though whether for the fetus or for the pregnancy or for all that either may stand for, we cannot know. The crucial point here is that acknowledging the possibility of loss is neither prediction nor endorsement; it is simply recognition.

While some women may experience some form of loss in connection with an abortion, we should keep in mind that the experience is not necessarily catastrophic. Loss is a consequence of most decision making: some roads are not taken, and others feel the tread. In a society where people regularly make significant personal choices for themselves, any decisions will have consequences, costs as well as benefits. Commercial law (the law of buying and selling things) uses the concept of "lost opportunities" for deals one didn't do by virtue of deciding to do something else. When the chosen deal fizzles, the disappointed party may try to get damages for "lost opportunities"—the money one would have made had the deal you put to the side been chosen, but the general rule is that you made a choice and in that sense took a risk. That is a consequence of the right to make the choice in the first place. The concept of loss may be the analogue to Justice Kennedy's statement that it is unexceptional that some women who abort late in their pregnancy will feel regret. However, unlike Kennedy's view that the choice should be closed down, the possibility of loss as I am using the term does not trigger a moral or a legal claim against abortion. Instead it seeks to open a wider space in which to discuss how women may experience aspects of abortion. Of course women (and their partners) may respond to these losses differently, some matter-of-factly, others not. For some, any pregnancy loss is experienced as a form of death; a Canadian father described his wife's repeated but unsuccessful attempts at fertility treatment as "twenty-four funerals."[16] In each, the fact of loss is accepted and, when revealed, sympathy sometimes appropriately extended.

Looking at Loss

Is there a relationship between women's experience with fetal imagery, understood as a form of family photograph, and the construction of loss in abortion? Certainly much has been written about women's engagement with the excitement and charm of fetal imagery. As a way of deepening our thinking about how seeing an aborted or about-to-be-aborted fetus signifies, I want to consider pre-abortion ultrasound scans alongside other photographs that embrace the meaning of children's deaths. Two once well-known photographic traditions from the nineteenth century, each engaged with parental loss, are post-mortem photography and spirit photography. The first refers to the custom of bereaved relatives—our interest is in parents—commissioning a formal photograph to be taken after a child's death in order to have a visual remembrance of its face and form. The second practice, spirit photography, was a curious combination of séance and photo shoot. Grieving relatives would hire professional spirit photographers to capture the deceased's spirit on a photographic plate. The resulting photo was taken as proof by the surviving kin that the deceased's spirit had been present in the room trying to make contact with them. While both post-mortem and spirit photos focused mainly on adults, pictures of dead children (or their spirits) were also taken and treasured by those who commissioned them.

Both of these practices seem a bit odd to modern sensibilities, either morbid (post-mortem photographs) or preposterous (spirit photographs). Yet the creepiness fades as familiarity with the genre not only normalizes but endears the images. Gertrude Stein had it just right: "A picture may seem extraordinarily strange to you and after some time not only does it not seem strange but it is impossible to find what there was in it that was strange."[17] And as Jay Ruby insists, the meanings given to photographs cannot be grasped from the picture alone; they require an understanding of the conditions of reception as well as the needs of the viewer. With this admonition in mind, we should be open to the various ways in which these earlier practices of seeing and finding meaning may not be so far removed from the uses to which prenatal images in the context of modern pregnancy loss, including abortion, are now put. The comparison may be disquieting.

I know that linking the word *abortion* with *children, loss,* or *death* is risky business. The analogy between abortion and childhood death could be taken, ungenerously, as an acknowledgment that abortion kills children. That is not the argument here. Reflecting on the various ways in which loss is experienced is not incompatible with respecting a woman's underlying decision to abort. It is not incompatible at a personal level, and it certainly does not answer the question of how abortion should be regulated at law. Even from a pro-choice point of view, we should understand what it is like for a woman to choose abortion and what it is like for her to hold to that choice with an image of her fetus in her mind's eye.

The curators of a 2004 exhibit *Photography and the Occult* explained that spirit photography—the belief that the spirit of the dead could be captured on film or plates—tells us about "a specific use of photography during a particular period, about the expectations and disappointments it generated, and its impact on attitudes."[18] Like any other photographic genre or taste, spirit photography also tells us "about human nature, its relationship to technology, its valorizing strategies, its hopes and beliefs."[19] A similar inventory may help us understand the impulses of our own period with regard to the use and the reception of fetal imagery. Over time the visual representations of the fetus have been put to all kinds of purposes—scientific, theological, educational, artistic, entertainment—as fetal imagery showed up in science labs, sideshows, and museums. Only recently, however, has the image come to signal a child as morally significant and as scientifically real as a born child.

But let us turn to the mid-nineteenth century where the most successful photographic subjects were stationary: landscapes, still lifes, anything that didn't move.[20] Within twenty years of photography's invention, the Civil War expanded the realm of stillness as photographers took to the field to record the deadly aftermath of battle. Commenting on the exhibit *The Dead of Antietam* on display in 1862 at Matthew Brady's New York portrait gallery, a *New York Times* editorial observed: "If [Mr. Brady] has not brought bodies and laid them in our dooryards and along the streets, he has done something very like it."[21]

In much the same way, post-mortem photographs of children brought the living child's face and form back to their parents. Photographs of these smaller bodies were also "laid in dooryards," placed ceremonially on mantels. Sitting for one's picture in mid-century America was wildly popular; picture taking was still something special. Photography had not yet been "democratized": the equipment was bulky, professional skill was needed to develop the plates, and not everyone could afford the fee. Thus picture taking was more often reserved for special occasions—a young woman on her betrothal, a worker with the tools of his trade, and in the 1860s, "with death an unignorable reality," young men upon their enlistments.[22]

For all these reasons, the likelihood of possessing an image of a loved one taken during life was far from certain. This was especially true for children. Not only was there less likely to have been a sufficiently celebratory moment for a photograph, but the nature of childhood made them bad photographic subjects. Early sitters had to remain perfectly still for a minute or so—often with their heads held stiffly in place by a neck brace—in order for the plate to develop clearly.[23] As photographer Edward Wilson advised in a widely distributed instructional pamphlet, "[Children] are subjects that make lovely pictures, but they are often difficult to secure. [If the photograph] is not satisfactory the first or second time it is not apt to be so all *that* day, and it is best to bring them again."[24] Against the background of high rates of childhood mortality, commercial studios reminded parents of the need for a photograph—"the ruddy cheek and loved features upon which you are now fondly gazing, ere tomorrow may be pallid in death"—and a picture taken soon after death was often the only way to secure the child's likeness.[25]

In this regard, post-mortem photographs of children followed the earlier tradition of painted posthumous portraiture.[26] Until the late nineteenth century, the death of infants and small children was an ordinary feature of family life. Beginning in the seventeenth century, dead children were memorialized in poems, mourned in letters and diaries, and their likenesses reproduced in sculpture and painting.[27] Early representations typically presented the child as clearly dead: eyes closed, bound in coffin or cradle, and sometimes accompanied by the iconography of early death, such as weeping willows and cut flowers.[28] But as children's posthumous portraiture moved from Europe to North America, the genre took an interesting turn. Grieving parents were "no longer satisfied" with the traditional presentation of the cold child on its bier; they wanted to see their child as he or she had been in life.[29] Beginning in the 1830s, portraits portrayed dead children as alive: elegantly dressed, eyes open looking at the viewer, and often posed against a familiar setting. (It is now thought that many portraits of children were in fact painted posthumously.)[30]

No longer meant only to memorialize the child, these poignant yet less somber paintings served as artifacts of consolation, intended to comfort the bereaved. They hung in homes, sometimes behind velvet curtains, sometimes with special viewings on the anniversary of the child's death.[31] Colonial artist Shepherd Alonzo Mount, who painted a charming portrait of his niece Camille within a week of her death, noted that the child's family would sit before it "in raptures" for an hour at a time; "next to the dear babe herself—it is now the idol of the family."[32] Indeed, there were also group portraits of families looking at the posthumous portrait of a deceased child.[33]

While posthumous portraiture was largely reserved for wealthier families, the arrival of the daguerreotype in the early 1850s expanded the availability of this form of visual consolation to middle and working classes.[34] They too experienced the "emotional longings that underlay the desire for such remembrances of the dead."[35] Like the professional painters before them, commercial daguerreotypists and photographers advertised their services by emphasizing the fragility of life. There was no time to waste; relatives were urged to "Secure the Shadow, Ere the Substance Fade."[36]

Because most children died at home, that is where they were photographed, sometimes even as they were dying.[37] As in the nineteenth-century painted portraits, the children are prettily dressed, sometimes in their coffins, but also in such lifelike poses as sitting in a chair, resting on a sofa, or sleeping in their parents' arms.[38] These photographs were dearly held memento mori, and parents paid—often ten times the price of a live studio portrait—to have their child's image captured and preserved in this way. However disquieting the pictures may initially strike us today, at the time, commissioning images of children who had just died was an accepted ritual of consolation.[39] It was part

An elegantly dressed mother holds her lifeless child. Quarter-plate ambrotype, circa 1857. Encased in an ornate brass and velvet frame, the image has been hand-tinted to give their faces some color and perhaps to cover the signs of the baby's fatal illness.

of a mid-nineteenth-century American culture that "encouraged . . . conspicuous methods of burial and commemoration."[40] The format of little portraits produced particular intimacy: the images were very small (2 ¾" by 3 ¼") and were housed in brass protective cases that had a "jewel-like intimacy."[41] To see the picture, one held the case in one's hand and brought it to the eye, sometimes unlatching the cover for a clearer view. The very manner of looking, then, created physical closeness between parent and the child's image.

Because nineteenth-century parents regularly posed with their dead child, they also saw themselves. In this way, they appeared both as parents and as mourners, each a socially significant role, especially for mothers.[42] Toward the end of the century, as *cartes-de-visite* and cabinet cards—photographic images developed on paper—began to replace daguerreotypes and tintypes, practices of looking changed as well. The new technology was not only cheaper, but a single plate produced twelve images, which could be cut apart and mailed to distant relatives. As images on paper began to circulate, traditional photograph albums replaced the tiny metal case as the means of protection and display.

The introduction in 1905 of the Kodak Brownie—portable, cheap, and easy to use—turned picture taking into a popular amateur activity. Parents were more likely to have a photograph or snapshot of their child taken during its life and these, not staged photographs of the child's corpse, became the cherished remembrance upon death.[43] Attitudes and conduct around death itself were also changing. During the nineteenth century, death was part of family and social life: people died and were laid out at home; families strolled in public cemeteries; the bereaved wore special clothes to signal their loss.[44] But as death moved out of the house and into hospitals and funeral parlors, photographing the dead began to seem both old-fashioned and in slightly bad taste.[45] Post-mortem photographs were viewed as less a ritual of consolation than a sign of pathological grief—evidence of the inability to achieve "closure," in the startling vocabulary that now determines the proper shelf life of grief.[46] Twentieth-century people may not have grieved less, but they displayed it less publicly, as even armbands—that quiet public announcement of bereavement—and post-mortem photography fell into disuse.[47] One important exception was the well-known Harlem studio photographer James Van Der Zee who continued the post-mortem tradition, superimposing choirs of angels around the crib. As Van Der Zee said of a portrait of a father holding his dead child, "If it wasn't for the picture, the mother [still hospitalized] wouldn't have seen the child for the last time."[48] But most families purged inherited family albums of post-mortem photographs, now viewed as "appalling," so that by the late twentieth century, post-mortem photographs had become a form of collectible exotica.[49]

In the last few decades, however, formal post-mortem photography has returned among a particular group of mourners: the parents of stillborn babies. Well into the twentieth century, stillbirth was regarded as an unfortunate, even embarrassing event that was unaccompanied by ritual or even much discussion. Parents limped along in their sorrow. An Irish mother recalled a stillbirth in the 1940s: "You never named it or nothing. The man that looked after the graves just came and took it and buried it and there was a wee plot in the graveyard."[50]

But much has changed. Stillbirth is increasingly treated with the solemnity and ceremony that attends any other childhood death. Because there has been very little life to commemorate, stillborn parents have created rituals with what they have: the baby's footprints, snips of hair, and scraps from the fetal heart-beat monitor and the stillborn birth certificate are collected in special "memory boxes."[51] Parents are now regularly asked if they want to spend time with their infant, say farewell, and take photographs.[52] Organizations of volunteer photographers such as Now I Lay Me Down to Sleep explain that "for families overcome by grief and pain, the idea of photographing their baby may not immediately occur to them. The soft, gentle heirloom photographs of these beautiful babies are an important part of the healing process. They allow families to honor and cherish their babies, and share the spirits of their lives."[53] Carefully lit portraits sensitive to the baby's often distressed physical condition have replaced (or at least supplemented) the clinical photographs taken by morgue technicians as pathology specimens.[54] As in nineteenth-century post-mortem photographs, the stillborn infant is dressed and posed, sometimes in its parents' arms, and the photographs are displayed on mantels as well as on Facebook, YouTube, and special stillbirth memorial websites, such as Our Angel Babies.[55]

To be sure, not all parents want or are prepared to publicly post photographs of this kind. Novelist Elizabeth McCracken explains her husband's decision to decline a post-mortem photograph of their stillborn son: "He was afraid we'd make a fetish of it, and he was right. The photo would not have been of our child, just his body."[56] But for those who want them, post-mortem portraits may provide both solace and a record of social identity for parent and for child.[57]

To further understand looking at the dead in photographs, we turn now to spirit photographs. These were images taken by photographers able and quite willing to "exploit the resemblance between the effects of photographic superimpositions and the ghostly imagery in the collective imagination of the time."[58] Beginning in the 1860s, in New York, London, and Paris, relatives desperate for contact with a deceased loved one engaged these photographers to communicate (in a fashion) with the dead. If everything in the darkened room went well (rapping was a good sign), *two* persons would appear on the developed plate—the solid living sitter and the deceased in more translucent form. Such photos were produced and gratefully accepted as visual proof of the spirit's presence and desire for contact.

In an 1863 article on photography, Oliver Wendell Holmes offered a biting description of how this worked: "Mrs. Brown, for instance, has lost her infant, and wishes to have its spirit-portrait taken with her own. A special sitting is granted, and a special fee is paid. In due time the photograph is ready and, sure enough, there is the misty image of an infant in the background. . . . Whether the original of the image was a month or a year old, whether it belonged to Mrs. Brown or Mrs. Jones or Mrs. Robinson, King Solomon . . . would be puzzled to guess. But it is enough for the poor mother, whose eyes are blinded with tears, that she sees a print of drapery like an infant's dress, and a rounded something, like a foggy dumpling, which will stand for a face; she accepts the spirit-portrait as a revelation from the world of shadows."[59] Where the photographer had obtained an existing photograph of the deceased, the person's actual image did appear, as in a photograph taken by the famous New York spirit photographer William Mumler of the widowed Mary Lincoln with a ghostly Abe behind her, his hands (or someone's hands) resting on her shoulders. There is also the picture of Mrs. French and her handsome young son returned from the grave and standing behind her right elbow.[60] We see how the meaning of the image is tightly tied to the needs of the viewer.

Victorians on both sides of the Atlantic were deeply interested in apparitions and spirits, interests that derived from scientific developments as well as from the dictates of spiritualism. Here is a straightforward account of spirit photography written by a twentieth-century spiritualist, Tom Patterson, the general secretary of the International Spiritualist Federation. "We who are Spiritualists have an unshakable belief that man is more than a physical body. We believe that his spirit part survives the condition which is medically known as death. We know that under certain conditions the spirit of man after death, can and actually does communicate with the living. . . . Those who are gifted with the faculty to receive spirit messages are known as mediums. The gift takes many forms and the production of spirit photographs is one of them."[61] Thrilling new technologies such as X-rays, electricity, and telegraphy showed that forces, signals, and messages could be "sent invisibly over vast distances."[62] Why should the dead not also cross such boundaries?

In addition to what viewers believed was possible to see, there is also the matter of what people wanted to see. And so we come to grief, where the

In this widely circulated *carte-de-visite,* the widowed Mary Todd Lincoln
sits with President Abraham Lincoln's spirit behind her, his (or
someone's) hands on her shoulders. The image was taken in 1872 by
American's best-known spirit photographer, William Mumler. Mrs. Lincoln,
an ardent Spiritualist, had held séances at the White House to make
contact with the Lincolns' son, Willie.

Portrait of Mrs. French and the spirit of her son, taken by William
Mumler at his Boston studio around 1870.

desire for continued connection with the dead may be most acutely felt, even today. In the latter part of the nineteenth century, spirit photography served as "a reaching out of the living to the dead, and metaphorically of the dead toward the living."[63] The photograph showed that the deceased had the living relative in mind and was looking out for her. As one newcomer to spiritualism explained, "it is only recently that I have learned that our loved ones are neither dead nor indifferent to the welfare of those left behind. I believe she [Addie, her dead cousin] has given me this [photograph] to comfort me and I prize it very highly."[64] The need for "reaching out" was particularly acute when entire communities were engulfed in death. Hence the increase in spiritualism in the United States following the Civil War and its resurgence following the First World War.[65] Arthur Conan Doyle and Rudyard Kipling were among those who sought consolation in spiritualism in order to communicate with their lost sons.

It may be difficult, as modern onlookers, to understand how rational people could find comfort in this form of consolation.[66] But our initial skepticism may be too demanding: when one has actually seen something—we can all make out Mrs. French's little boy—the process of how it was done may matter less than that it is there. It is not that the bereaved thought their relatives were not dead: rather, they thought that they were present. That the image might be blurry was not so important. As art historian Martyn Jolly observes: "When a client chose to believe that the dead lived and were struggling to transmit news of their continued existence back from the other side; and when, in the mysterious alchemical cave of the darkroom, that client saw before their very eyes a face emerge to join their own face on a photographic plate; and when they decided, perhaps even after some initial trepidation, to let themselves be flooded with the absolute conviction that they recognized the face as a lost loved one; then a certain photographic truth was revealed. Not a forensic truth, but an affective truth."[67] An affective photographic truth.

During the period when spirit photography was in full swing, not all spirits and ghosts who turned up on photographic plates were relatives from the other side. There was a simultaneous recreational use of double exposure as photography studios and publishers produced "entire series of ethereal ghosts, angels, and fairies for the amusement of the public."[68] Consumers were aware of both practices. Thus within the same period, imagery accommodates what may seem contradictory aims. Yet the two uses—hilarity and consolation— were not so much incompatible as discrete in purpose. And we see in this versatility an intimation of the multiple ways—the flexible ways—in which modern people are able to look at the image of an embryo or fetus at different points in time.

These same factors—the "situatedness" of human nature, human needs, and human knowledge—are at work not only when a connection to a loved one has been ended but also when connection is sought through the creation of a relationship. That is, while grief may enable a glimpse of a lost life, the desire for contact with a new life works similarly, allowing some to see those who are not quite here. A modern variation of spirit photography is the prenatal, sometimes preconception, visualization of children. Linda Layne explains that many women begin to construct fetal personhood "from the moment they do a home pregnancy test": "each cup of coffee or glass of wine abstained from . . . adds to the 'realness' of the baby growing within."[69] There is great receptivity in wanted pregnancies to see what the pregnancy test announces is already there. Some readers may have experienced a version of this with their own early ultrasounds. Once the technician explains key features (the head), it is not so hard to point them out to others. Conjuring a baby sometimes even precedes conception. As one woman explained while undergoing in vitro fertilization: "Before transfer, they give you a Polaroid of your embryo. . . . You look at this greenish picture of a few dividing cells, and you will that photo to assume life, you will that photo to become your baby."[70] Barbara Duden writes that "when I do not get my menstrual period, I wait a week. . . . Seeing the result [of my pregnancy test], I conjure up a fetus, and with it, the abstraction of 'life.'"[71] And again, Rayna Rapp notes that pregnant women awaiting prenatal diagnosis "often describe amniotic fluid in terms of the child, substantialized, acorn to oak, in the fluid itself: . . . The doctor told me the fluid looked good, so I know the baby looks good."[72]

Visualizing pregnancy now appears to be not only a practice but a technique. In *Healing Visualizations: Creating Health through Imagery*, Dr. Gerald Epstein offers an exercise called the Fertile Garden. "Close your eyes. . . . [S]ee yourself going into a beautiful garden. Find there a tree and a stream of flowing water. Bathe in the water, allowing it to enter and to clean all the ova. . . . Then call your mate into the garden to join you under the tree. Lie down with him, holding hands. See the blue light forming a dome over you. . . . Afterward, go out of the garden together holding hands, cradling a child between you. Then open your eyes."[73] Audio recordings, such as *Visualizing Pregnancy*, are available on Amazon.[74] Another site advises women to talk not only to their bodies but also to the unconceived child. It offers the example of Emily, who "used a simple guided visualization exercise in which she explored and conversed with her ovaries, tubes, and uterus. While communicating in this open-hearted manner with her body, Emily discovered and healed the block that had prevented her from having this little boy being who was hovering just above her shoulder."[75]

Yet women's attitudes regarding prenatal life are not fixed or universal. Anthropologist Linda Layne had six miscarriages over a ten-year period in the 1990s. She explains that "during each of my pregnancies I thought of myself as 'with child' and I have been changed by the grief I felt each time I lost a 'baby'; unlike many members of pregnancy-loss support groups, however, I did not name them, and do not think of them as 'members of my family.' At times, in fact, I had the sense that they were not separate individuals, but more like a Trobriand Island spirit baby, a single spirit who kept trying to enter the world."[76] Layne's description may carry its own disciplinary flavor; most of us don't know about reproductive practices in the Trobriand Islands. Nevertheless, we quickly understand the idea and recognize the varied ways that women are able to picture children born and not born.

Sometimes, however, there are disturbances in the field and "seeing expectantly" is abruptly put on hold. This happens when a pregnancy does not go as planned—for example, when a prenatal diagnostic test such as ultrasound or amniocentesis has produced an unwelcome result (a "positive diagnosis").[77] For women undergoing routine ultrasound, such information often comes as a surprise; most understand the scan to be about "confirming that everything [is] all right" rather than looking for something wrong.[78] Yet for mothers who learn during screening that their baby is not as they had hoped, ultrasound becomes a more complicated phenomenon.[79] The wantedness of the pregnancy may suddenly be put at issue, as, depending on the diagnosis, the woman "must make conscious the fears, fantasies, and phobias she has about mothering a disabled child."[80]

Twenty years ago Barbara Katz Rothman introduced the concept of the "tentative pregnancy" to describe the emotional distancing that attenuates a woman from her fetus while the results of genetic testing are awaited and absorbed.[81] In this way, ultrasound produces what Janelle Taylor has called the "prenatal paradox": the technology occasions early prenatal bonding at the same time that it produces the very information that makes bonding a risky or more costly move.[82]

The tentativeness can take several forms: a reluctance to wear maternity clothes, keeping the pregnancy a secret, even a delay in feeling fetal movement.[83]

Such distancing is perhaps a modern version of Philippe Ariès's historical parental indifference theory, the proposition that at periods of high childhood mortality, parents invested less in offspring because they were in general unlikely to survive. Ariès, among others, argued that parents did not grieve children's deaths. "People could not allow themselves to become too attached to something that was regarded as a probable loss."[84] Yet the historical record seems clear that at least some parents were not at all indifferent and deeply mourned their children's deaths.[85]

All this complicates the visualization involved in ultrasound connected to prenatal diagnoses. A process supposed to intimate the presence of a fetus or child suddenly portends the opposite. And confusion rather than decisiveness may attend the unwelcome news.[86] For many women, "viewing the fetus on ultrasound had made coping with the loss more difficult."[87] Nothing is certain. Ultrasound is sometimes determinative in deciding to continue a pregnancy. One woman who had considered terminating when Down syndrome was first suspected changed her mind after ultrasound. The technician told her, "Look. . . . It's (the fetus) saying, 'Hi, Mom, I'm okay.'" She explained that "I made up my mind that whatever they told me. . . . I couldn't do away with it. That if this is what God's blessing me with, then I'm having it."[88]

For some couples who experience unhappy reproductive outcomes—whether stillbirth, miscarriage, or voluntary termination following unfavorable diagnosis—the earlier ultrasound may become a source of solace, comforting proof that the pregnancy was real. In all these ways, the meaning of the ultrasound may not be fixed. As one parent recalled, "the other ultrasound where the doctor said the aorta was burst and the baby's chest was being crushed. I used to think that was gruesome, but now I think about it and it goes to show that there was a child, a person, even though dead, who once lived."[89]

The Whole Fetal Body

Our discussion so far has considered an array of images—images of embryos, of fetuses, and of children long dead—as a way of thinking about how imagery acquires meaning in abortion. We now explore three instances where women look not only at an embryonic or fetal image before an abortion but at its actual mass or body afterward. The first two instances involve early first trimester abortions; the third concerns abortions that occur later in pregnancy, after the fetus has taken fuller shape and size.

In 2007, two Canadian obstetricians decided to investigate whether seeing the actual products of conception—the aborted conceptus—made the experience of abortion emotionally harder for their patients.[90] The doctors were concerned that exposure to antiabortion fetal imagery—often featuring pictures of well-developed, second trimester fetuses—might upset patients, even though most abortions (65.8 percent in the United States) take place within eight weeks when the fetus is much less developed.[91] Nonetheless, due to even the possibility of patient distress, the protocol was that abortion clinic staff did not show either ultrasound scans or the products of conception to patients.

To test this out, the staff designed a study. All women presenting for an abortion at two Vancouver clinics over a yearlong period were asked if they would like to view the ultrasound and the products of conception (the actual results or content of the abortion). Specifically, the women were asked: "The doctor will check the pregnancy to check the tissue after the abortion to make sure it is complete; would you like to see it too?"[92] Of the 508 women who were asked, 152 or 28.7 percent said yes. Immediately following their abortion, a doctor or nurse showed them the products of conception, floating in water in a glass dish usually after being washed. While in the recovery room, patients filled out a questionnaire asking whether viewing the products of conception made the experience emotionally harder or not.

Eighty-three percent of the women who filled out the questionnaire reported that it did not, and their written comments provide texture to the reply. Some found relief in what they saw: "I'm glad I chose to look"; "I thought it would be much worse"; "It was smaller than I thought"; "It actually made me feel better emotionally, because it was so small."[93] Others found some relief: "Seeing the tissue helped—it was almost a relief because it didn't look like anything"; "not as bad as I expected, but it was still difficult."[94] Other comments were candid, if not wholly explanatory: "It was gross"; "Thanks for the option"; "It was very interesting"; "[I am] going to take a good sleep and forget about it."[95]

Clinic doctors, nurses, and counselors were also interviewed. All were positive, although each of the eight who did the actual showing said they initially felt uncomfortable displaying parts with the "higher gestations"; stated one nurse, "When the pregnancy is further along and there are fetal parts . . . I double check with the woman that she knows she will see recognizable parts and that it will be in pieces."[96] There were no significant differences in age, ethnicity, or gestational age between those women who found that viewing did not make things emotionally harder and those who did. The only demographic characteristic that seemed to matter was that patients who were mothers already found that viewing made things harder, though it is interesting that they still chose to look.

The researchers' conclusions are modest. The study confirmed their hunch that viewing products of conception does not necessarily make things harder and might provide some relief, at least in a supportive clinic where the looking is entirely voluntary and the abortions occur at a relatively early gestational age. As a result of the Canadian research, the two clinics now offer all abortion patients the option to look at the fetus before and after an abortion.[97] What at first sounds like an odd and gruesome question to ask an abortion patient turns out not to be. This is not to say that the looking has no meaning; indeed, it appears to have many meanings, most of them salutary, to those who choose to look. The experience might well be different in a less supportive political environment. In March 2012, Arizona legislator Teri Proud of Tucson expressed support for legislation that would require women to witness an abortion being performed on someone else before they could legally consent to their own.[98] No such legislation was introduced, though the suggestion made a stir.

With the small but telling Canadian case study before us, we now turn to more complicated and far rarer instances of looking at a post-abortion fetal body. In *Gonzales v. Carhart,* the U.S. Supreme Court upheld the Partial Birth Abortion Act, which banned a second trimester abortion procedure known as intact dilation and extraction (intact D&E). The procedure involves collapsing or emptying the fetal head while it is still in the birth canal so that the fetal body can be pulled out (extracted) in one piece (intact). This distinguishes intact D&E from standard D&E in which the fetus is disarticulated in utero and removed in pieces.

The two procedures are further distinguished by their status under the law. In 2000 the Supreme Court held in the case of *Stenberg v. Carhart* that Nebraska's ban on standard D&E was unconstitutional because it failed to include an exception for maternal health, as required under *Roe* and affirmed in *Casey.*[99] In contrast, in *Gonzales v. Carhart* the Court upheld a federal ban on intact D&E even without the health exception. Although Justice Kennedy found both procedures to be "laden with the power to devalue human life," he and a majority of the Court regarded the intact procedure as truly barbaric.[100] The Justice quoted from a detailed description presented during congressional hearings on the Partial Birth Abortion Act: "Then the doctor stuck the scissors in the back of his head, and the baby's arms jerked out, like a startle reaction, like a flinch, like a baby does when he thinks he is going to fall. The doctor opened up the scissors, stuck a high-powered suction tube into the opening, and sucked the baby's brains out. Now the baby went completely limp."[101] The Court declared that it was entitled to take Congress at its word that intact D&E was "disturbingly similar to the killing of a newborn infant."[102] No pictures could improve upon the graphicness of this description.

In *Carhart,* the Supreme Court seemed to accept the health-related explanations of the defendant physicians as to why they sometimes preferred to perform intact D&E. In contrast to standard D&E, the intact procedure does not require the repeated "passes" through the uterus necessary to remove bony fetal fragments, a process that risks perforating the uterus. In addition, the intact method is a quicker procedure; it reduces the risk that fetal parts might remain in the uterus; and it is safer for women with certain medical conditions or with fetuses with certain anomalies.[103] Nonetheless, despite its medical benefits in some cases, the Court held that the Partial Birth Abortion Act did not constitute an undue burden because it was not the only available late-term abortion procedure. Patients could still obtain standard D&E abortions, so there was no "substantial obstacle" for women seeking a second trimester abortion. Because there was an alternative, Congress was justified in barring intact D&E to further "its legitimate interests . . . to promote respect for life, including life of the unborn."[104] Moreover, the Court found that banning intact D&E upheld congressional concern about the reputation of the medical community and about the moral uplift of the society itself: "Implicitly approving such a brutal and inhumane procedure by choosing not to prohibit it will further coarsen society to the humanity of not only newborns, but all vulnerable and innocent human life, making it increasingly difficult to protect such life."[105]

In its decision, the Court put primary stress on the particular harm of intact D&E for women. Noting that in order to spare the feelings of their patients, doctors might not explain to them in detail just what the procedure involved, the Court stated that "it is self-evident that a mother who comes to regret her choice to abort must struggle with grief more anguished and sorrow more profound when she learns, only after the event, what she once did not know: that she allowed a doctor to pierce the skull and vacuum the fast-developing brain of her unborn child, a child assuming the human form."[106] Usually when legislators think women must know more before they can properly consent to an abortion, they mandate more detailed disclosures, like "real time viewing" requirements. In this case no amount of disclosure can cure the innate brutality of the methods used to secure that the fetus is dead before it is removed from the woman's body. Because doctors might not tell their patients graphically enough about the skull, the vacuum, the pick, and the potassium chloride, patients will be unable to consent knowingly.

Yet in all the Court's discussion of butchery something important has been missed. Sometimes intact D&E is preferred by the patient herself. This is precisely because the intact process produces what Justice Kennedy found an unthinkable preference: an entire fetal body and not a set of disarticulated parts. A close reading of the depositions in the case reveals that for women with wanted pregnancies now facing an abortion late in pregnancy, the possibility of seeing, holding, and bidding goodbye to their baby was crucially important. One abortion provider explained that over 95 percent of his patients "who must give up their pregnancies in the second trimester 'really, really, really wanted to have a baby.' "[107] And so, as Dr. Amos Grunebaum testified, "many women request that the fetus be preserved as intact as possible for a proper burial or so full testing can be done to learn why the pregnancy failed."[108] Some women prefer to have the body in order to have the fetus baptized.[109] Another doctor testifying under an alias provided more detail:

> If the patient wants to see the fetus, [the nursing staff] will prepare [it] to make it look as untraumatized as possible. They have little gowns that they dress the fetus in. They wrap it very gently in a blanket. They sometimes have a little bonnet that they put over the head. If it's an anencephalic fetus, which means the top of the head is completely missing, they'll put a bonnet on it and put a little bit of tissue paper or something to kind of shape—make it look less abnormal. And then they present this to the patient and generally her husband as well. And the patients are sometimes satisfied with that, and sometimes they completely undress the fetus, and look at it, and touch it, and cry, and say good-bye. And after they have had enough time with the fetus, then it's taken away to the pathologist.[110]

Not every patient wants to greet and hold her fetus, but many do. "With an intact fetus, the family may hold their baby and have time to say good-bye as part of the grieving process. Reconstituting the fetal head with a jellied substance can restore fetal anatomy."[111] Dr. Doe tells us that parents "sometimes imagine that their fetus is going to look terrible. And even when the fetus does look terrible to the average person, when they actually see it, it's not as bad as they imagined. And so it's helpful for them to be able to see the fetus and to hold it. Some of them kiss it."[112] As one mother recalled, they "wrapped her up . . . and she didn't look so deformed, she just looked beautiful."[113] One pa-tient, a conservative Christian who opposed abortion until her own unborn twins were diagnosed with severe disabilities, explained that "I didn't know much about abortion before all of this. . . . But . . . it makes so much sense: If you can give a grieving mother a baby to hold afterward, you give her a more healing way to end a wanted pregnancy."[114]

PHOTOGRAPHS OF THE DEAD and graphic descriptions of death itself produce different affective truths. In the case of intentional conception and wanted pregnancy, the desire for the presence of someone not entirely here creates meaning in the image, as when women who want a baby are able to look at a blurry ultrasound scan, a Petri dish, or even amniotic fluid and see their child. There is, however, no official affective truth or meaning; as the Supreme Court stated in *Roe*, it is up to each person individually to decide when protected human life begins. Thus some of what passes for official—Justice Kennedy's views about what women know about abortion and what they can bear to know—is wrong.

Poets Anne Sexton, Gwendolyn Brooks, and Lucille Clifton have written about abortion from the mother's perspective.[115] Theirs are not easy pieces and don't stint on the fact of death: Anne Sexton's thrice-stated refrain in "The Abor-tion" is "Somebody who should have been born is gone."[116] Nor do the poems stint on responsibility or on the possibility of continued connection with the fetus. In "The Lost Baby Poem," Lucille Clifton writes, "you would have been born into winter / in the year of the disconnected gas / and no car . . . if you were here I could tell you these / and some other things."[117] In a powerful, illumi-nating essay, literary critic Barbara Johnson observes that each of these poets uses the rhetorical device of apostrophe, that is, "the direct address of an ab-sent, dead, or inanimate being by a first-person speaker."[118] Addressing the fetus directly, states Johnson, animates it or, perhaps more accurately, reanimates it. And "what happens when the lyric speaker assumes responsibility for pro-ducing the death in the first place, but without being sure of the precise degree of human animation that existed in the entity killed? What is the debate over abortion about, indeed, if not the questions of when, precisely, a being assumed a human form?"[119] The poems do not answer the question, although the use of apostrophe enables mothers to address their children and so to "keep from finishing with the act of killing them."[120] Women take responsibility for their decisions, which is not to say they take it hard or easy either way. Philosopher Karen Houle apprehends her experience this way: "I have two biological children. I also do not have at least two biological children."[121]

Let us return to the question of how a woman might conceptualize an aborted fetus. Gwendolyn Brooks provides one answer. In the last stanza of her poem on abortion, "The Mother," Brooks writes

> *oh, what shall I say, how is the truth to be said?*
> *You were born, you had body, you died.*[122]

Hers is one way to express what she lost and what she did. Yet as powerfully blunt as Brooks's summation may be, we know there is more than one way for women to comprehend the loss or absence of an aborted fetus.

7

Sending Pregnant Teenagers
to Court

What does it take for an unmarried girl under age eighteen to get an abortion in the United States today? Putting aside such practical problems as finding a doctor, the cash, and someone to take her, what does the law have to say about minors and abortion? Thirty-nine states have answered the question by enacting special "parental involvement" laws. These provide that before a pregnant minor can legally consent to an abortion, she must do one of two things. She must either notify or get consent from her parents, or in the alternative, she can leave her parents out and petition a judge for permission to consent on her own.[1] Because petitioning "bypasses" parents, the hearings are often called "judicial bypass hearings." How these hearings work in fact tells us a great deal about how, in the case of pregnant teenagers, legal process has been put to use in the campaign against abortion.

This peculiar arrangement—parents or petition—is the result of a constitutional compromise announced by the Supreme Court in the 1979 case of *Bellotti v. Baird*.[2] The question before the Court was the constitutionality of a Massachusetts statute that required both parents to consent to their daughter's abortion and both parents to be notified if she went to court without their consent. The Supreme Court's starting points were *Roe v. Wade*, where the Court held that a constitutional right of privacy was "broad enough to encompass a woman's decision whether or not to terminate her pregnancy," and *Doe v. Bolton*, which made clear that no one could override a woman's decision.[3] But did the language of *Roe* and *Doe* regarding *women's* decisions include "little women" as well? Could Massachusetts constrict the rights of a pregnant minor by inserting her parents into the process and still comply with the Supreme Court's rulings in the abortion cases?

The answer emerged from a predictable collision between abortion jurisprudence and parental rights. The Supreme Court has long upheld the authority of parents to make decisions on behalf of their children, even in areas of life about which teenage children might well have an opinion, like who they hang out with or whether to have a baby. Yet as the Court explained in *Bellotti,* the decisional superiority of parents results from the sum of several parts: that minors (in general) do not make sound decisions; that parents (in general) will decide wisely on their children's behalf; and that wise or not, parents have a constitutionally protected liberty interest in raising their children as they see fit.[4] At the same time, however, the Supreme Court recognized in 1967 that the Constitution, or parts of it, applies to minors. In providing a right to counsel for juvenile offenders, the Court clearly stated that "whatever may be their precise impact, neither the Fourteenth Amendment nor the Bill of Rights is for adults alone."[5]

The tension between pregnant girls as juvenile rights bearers and pregnant girls as their parents' daughters was squarely joined in the context of abortion, and in *Bellotti* the Supreme Court did indeed work out the "precise impact" of *Roe* for girls. Acknowledging that "there are few situations in which denying a minor the right to make an important decision will have consequences so grave and indelible," the Court held that as with pregnant women, no one—not parent, not boyfriend, not anyone—may have an absolute veto over a pregnant girl's abortion decision.[6] Nonetheless, taking account of children's "peculiar vulnerability," their "inability to make critical decisions," and the importance of parents in child rearing, the Court held that states could require parental consent so long as there was some other way for a minor to proceed without it.[7] The Court acknowledged that pregnant teens, especially those living at home, were vulnerable to parental efforts to obstruct their access to abortion. To avoid the possibility of a de facto veto, the Supreme Court concluded that a satisfactory alternative was for the minor to go directly to court and plead her case there. This arrangement was understood to harmonize the parents' right to control with the minor's right to choose. In effect, *Bellotti* extends *Roe* to minors more or less—less, in fact, because the judge has the authority to deny her request and so prevent her access to an abortion.[8]

And so each year thousands of pregnant teenagers learn, whether by searching online, calling a clinic, or through teenage word of mouth, that if they want an abortion they must first have either a note from home or an order from court. There are no exact data on how many girls take Door Number 1, parents. Minors who choose the court door must participate in a hearing where the judge decides, based on the evidence presented, whether the minor is mature and informed enough to decide about abortion. If the judge finds she is, he must grant the petition, which she then takes to the clinic. If the judge finds she is not mature enough, the petition must be denied. Because that result was so head-shakingly odd, the Court in *Bellotti* insisted on one last step: if a judge denies a petition, he must decide whether, putting the minor's immaturity aside, it would nonetheless be in her best interests to let her consent to the abortion she seeks.

How do minors fare in these hearings? Because the hearings are closed and confidential, the only information about how things go comes from the appellate record, those cases that are appealed after a denial by a trial judge. Since the bypass scheme was first introduced in the late 1970s, petitions have been denied on the following grounds. An Alabama judge held that because sex education was taught in the public high school, the minor's "action[s] in becoming pregnant . . . [are] indicative that she has not acted in a mature and well informed manner."[9] Another Alabama minor was declared immature because "seeing the difficulties encountered by friends who have become pregnant, [she] got 'herself into the same situation.'"[10] The trial judge denied her petition, stating that it was "not an act of maturity on [the minor's] part to put the burden of the death of this child upon the conscience of the Court."[11] A Mississippi court denied the bypass petition of a college-bound seventeen-year-old who, having recently lost her own mother to cancer, testified that she would not be able to give up a baby for adoption, on the ground that the petitioner was "simply afraid of the responsibility of motherhood."[12] An Ohio judge denied the petition of a minor—a minor who was days away from her eighteenth birthday, taking college preparatory classes, and working to save for college—because the pregnancy alone demonstrated immaturity.[13] A Texas trial court turned down the petition of a seventeen-year-old who had researched abortion and its alternatives, had consulted with several counselors (including her home economics teacher and three formerly pregnant teenagers), and had chosen to look at her ultrasound scan in order to confront her decision directly, on the grounds that "she did not understand the intrinsic benefits of keeping the child or of adoption."[14]

In the early bypass cases, some judges denied petitions with no explanation. This happened in a 1987 case where the petitioner was a month away from her eighteenth birthday, lived by herself, held down a full-time job, and was studying for her general equivalency diploma. She was on good terms with her mother but decided not to discuss the abortion question with her because "her step-father . . . would cause 'a bunch of problems' for her mother."[15] The trial judge denied her petition. In reversing the ruling, a frustrated appellate court noted that "we can safely say, having considered the record, that, should this minor not meet the criteria for 'maturity' under the statute, it is difficult to imagine one who would."[16] The cases remind one of the old Southern literacy tests designed to keep black citizens from registering to vote. As a fifty-seven-year-old farmer, who tried unsuccessfully to register in 1954 and 1961 before finally giving up, told an interviewer, he "had done his best and does not think that he could do any better."[17] In none of the abortion cases above did the trial court decide after declaring the minor immature that terminating the pregnancy was still in her best interest.

Although some of these cases were reversed on appeal, not all denials are reversed or even appealed. Thus, as with most low-level criminal cases, "for all practical purposes, the lower courts of first instance are also courts of last resort."[18] The result is that some girls tell their parents and hope for the best, some travel to more congenial counties or states, some risk illegal or self abortion, and the rest, we assume, become mothers.

Denials of bypass petitions in which judges declare well-informed young women immature for the purpose of defeating their intention to abort are deeply disturbing and excite our sense of injustice. The decisions appear to be deliberate misapplications of the legal standards by judges who disapprove of abortion, or of the minor, or perhaps both. But although these unprincipled denials rightfully rile us up, they also serve to divert our attention away from an aspect of the bypass process that is just as troubling and far more pervasive. That is the set of harms inflicted on young women whose petitions are approved and who by that measure might be considered bypass success stories. Over the last twenty-five years, legislatures and courts have clarified the meanings of "maturity" and "well-informed" so that fewer judges are able to disregard the factual record without being reversed on appeal. The result is that in most states, nearly every bypass petition is granted.[19]

This raises a basic question about parental involvement statutes. If bypass hearings are here to stay—as the Supreme Court grumpily assured us in *Planned Parenthood of Southeastern Pennsylvania v. Casey* is constitutionally the case—and if almost all petitions are granted, where is the harm?[20] Sending girls to court may seem a highly legalistic response to the problem of unwanted teen pregnancy, but polling data suggest that most Americans agree that parents should know about an underage daughter's abortion, even if most Americans are unaware of the actual system now in place.[21] If a minor is able to negotiate her way through the process, terminate her pregnancy, and move on with life, the statutory scheme may be annoying but is there more to it than that? Parents can know the law is formally on their side, other citizens can take satisfaction that this is not an "abortion on demand" state, and in the end, girls can consent to the abortion they seek.

The argument here is that the very requirement of participation in the hearings is troubling regardless of the outcome in a particular instance. The problem is the use of legal process to inflict a series of harms and humiliations on pregnant minors seeking to end an unwanted pregnancy, even if they are eventually permitted to do so. Some of the harms imposed are immediate: the risks of medical delay and public exposure that result from participation in any sort of legal process. Other harms, more subtle and perhaps more searing, result from what transpires not on the way to court but during the hearings themselves. Certainly some judges interrogate rather than question and hector rather than assess, but the core problem is not a matter of judicial style. The heart of the matter is the very nature of the bypass inquiry. The hearings require young women to testify before strangers regarding the most private matters in a teenager's life: the fact of sexual intercourse, the predicament of pregnancy, and the structure or disarray of home life that cause petitioners to decide against involving their parents. Such revelations are intensely difficult for teenage girls, as they would be for adults who, at least since the pre-*Doe* days of hospital abortion committees, have been spared the public display of their private accounting.[22]

What does the law mean to accomplish through the formal interrogation of pregnant minors in court? State legislatures set out their official purposes in "Legislative Findings" that accompany parental involvement statutes. Alaska's is typical. It states the purposes as "protecting minors against their own immaturity; fostering the family structure and preserving it as a stable social unit; protecting the rights of parents to rear children who are members of their household; and protecting the health of minor women."[23] But although the Legislative Findings are couched in the language of family togetherness and child protection, the statutes are also concerned with achieving a set of political goals aimed at thwarting abortion and punishing young women who decide to go ahead anyway. As four justices of the Alabama Supreme Court stated, "it seems clear that the [Alabama] legislature intended, in adopting the Parental Consent Statute, to preserve the life of the unborn, and that it deliberately was doing what it could within the constraints of the Federal Constitution, as interpreted by the Supreme Court of the United States, to accomplish that purpose."[24]

Preserving the life of the unborn is achieved through a clever pincer move with parents (who are all presumed to oppose their daughter's abortion) on one side and judges on the other. For while "your parents or a hearing" are presented as statutory alternatives, in practice the two are not offered up as equal choices. As one Texas Supreme Court justice candidly explained, "once a minor becomes aware of what she must go through to obtain a judicial bypass, she will choose for herself to involve her parents."[25] If the bypass experience is known to be an ordeal, girls will turn to their parents, who, it is assumed, will either refuse to consent (in the consent states) or will talk the girl out of it (in notification states).

And an ordeal they are. Bypass hearings have come to operate as a form of punishment for a reproductive decision that since 1973 has been subject to no other form of state sanction. As the Texas Justice made clear, the severity of bypass hearings is not incidental to the process but an integral part of it. This is a curious historical inversion. When abortion was a crime, the extralegal punishment for women was being pushed into the unsavory and dangerous world of illegal abortions. Now that abortion is legal, the punishment (for minors at any rate) is embedded in the lawful hearings that young women must engage with in trial courts around the country.

Bypass hearings should concern us not only because of individual indignities but because of a more systemic issue: the misuse of the legal process to harass pregnant minors. Under our system of justice, law is supposed to be a source of dignity. Yet there is something intuitively unseemly about funneling pregnant girls to court. Part of the unseemliness is that for most of these girls, the hearings are their first introduction to law. As sociologist Malcolm Feeley observed with regard to the treatment of small-time criminal defendants in pretrial hearings, "whatever majesty there is in the law may depend heavily on these encounters"; this is where many people "form impressions of the American system of criminal justice."[26] Of course, bypass hearings are not criminal proceedings—the petitioning minor appears unopposed in a civil action—but the hearings often seem as if they were, particularly to minors, once the "favorites of law" because of their vulnerability. It is as though if abortion can't be made illegal, it can still be made to *feel* illegal. Minors may be declared immature, but they are not dumb. As one Massachusetts teen stated, "I'm only 16, and usually at this age, you know, you don't see people going to court for good things."[27]

The feel of criminality comes about not only because the hearings take place in a courtroom with its many trappings of authority—the judge, the court reporter, the paneling, the robe—but through the mechanism of humiliation inherent in the process. Bypass hearings require detailed disclosures on deeply private aspects of intimate life and personal ethics. Judges have asked petitioning minors whether they understood that abortion is murder, whether they would kill their own three-year-old child, and whether they would change their mind if they knew their baby would go to a loving adoptive family or if they were given $2,000.[28] These questions are considerable intrusions on privacy, which philosopher Avishai Margalit has described as "in itself a paradigmatic act of humiliation."[29] The assaultive nature of such questions can also be seen as a dignitarian harm. As the Supreme Court stated in *Planned Parenthood v. Casey,* a decision about abortion involves "the most intimate and personal choices a person may make in a lifetime, choices central to personal dignity and autonomy."[30] And this is not just any hearing but that of a litigant seeking to exercise her constitutional rights.

In thinking about how the hearings work on teenagers, it is helpful to distinguish between embarrassment and humiliation. To reveal or confide facts about a pregnancy to a sister, friend, or counselor might be embarrassing. The sex or the relationship may have been a big mistake; one should have known better, been more careful or less trusting. But these same confidences register quite differently when their revelation is not a private matter but is instead compelled in court. These are the very subjects—sex, secrecy, mistakes—that are so very interesting when they take the form of gossip and when they are about someone else. Bypass testimony requires something like gossiping about oneself. The judge, even in a closed courtroom, represents the state. For minors, this is less a private hearing than a recitation before a powerful public official of the law.

Besides, humiliation does not depend on the presence of an audience. Consider a corporal punishment case from the European Court of Human Rights. In *Tyrer v. United Kingdom,* the Court had to decide whether the "birching" (three strokes with a cane) of a fifteen-year-old boy by the local constable was degrading treatment under Article 3 of the European Convention on Human

Rights, which protects "a person's dignity and physical integrity."[31] The local authorities had argued that the birching was not degrading, in part because, like a bypass hearing, it took place in private and because the boy's name was not published. In rejecting their argument, the Court observed: "Publicity may be a relevant factor in assessing whether a punishment is 'degrading' . . . but the Court does not consider that absence of publicity will necessarily prevent a given punishment from falling into that category: *it may well suffice that the victim is humiliated in his own eyes, even if not in the eyes of others*."[32] That only the judge and a few others—court reporter, attorney—are present at a bypass hearing does little to diminish the magnitude of the minor's humiliation.

It is useful to consider bypass hearings as a type or genre of legal proceeding that like other genres has "select characteristics" and "shared grammatical rules."[33] Hearings are not trials where adversaries oppose one another under the supervision of a judge. They are a less formal tribunal in which the petitioner, with the assistance of her appointed lawyer, requests relief not from any other party—the minor is the only party—but from a judge. Looking at bypass hearings as a genre—comparing them with other hearings where the content and tone of the petitioner's presentation has been crucial to the outcome—casts important light on how the process conveys meaning to its participants and to a wider political audience.

Bypass Basics

In providing girls with a scheme that accommodates the basic holding in *Roe v. Wade* that a decision about abortion was the woman's alone, the Supreme Court in *Bellotti* took a realistic view of the situation for minors and concluded that two specific aspects of the process had constitutional significance: anonymity and speed.[34] Without anonymity, a minor might be found out by her parents and blocked from going to court or clinic: the de facto veto.[35] Without a speedy resolution of the petition, she might be timed out of a safe or legal abortion so that the right in *Roe* becomes illusory.[36]

To comply with the requirement of anonymity, states have put a number of measures in place. Petitions are identified by the girl's initials or by Jane Doe or anonymous aliases. To avoid parents answering the home phone only to find the clerk of the court on the other end, many states now permit petitioners to designate how and where they want to be notified about dates and rulings; Texas's online instructions remind girls that they can leave their cell phone or email as the contact method.[37] In 2016 the Texas legislature made clear, however, that there were limits to technology in the bypass setting. Minors could not appear using "videoconferencing, telephone conferencing, or other remote electronic means," but had to go before the judge in person.[38]

The hearings themselves are closed to the public, although petitioners may bring a relative or friend for support. The content of the hearings is confidential, with one important exception: because judges are required to report child abuse, they must report any instance of rape or incest that comes their way to the local Department of Social Services. It is crucial for bypass minors to know this before they are asked in court about the circumstances of the pregnancy, only to have the entire child welfare system descend on them and their family. Thus a few states, such as North Carolina, require that bypass petitioners be specifically informed before a hearing begins about the rape exception to confidentiality.[39]

Despite these safeguards, physical participation in the bypass process puts minors at risk of exposure. Online forms and filing, available in some states, are a huge help to minors with access to computers, who can avoid at least one additional trip downtown. Yet in the main, the logistics of traveling to court, getting the forms, returning for the hearing, and waiting around outside the courtroom involve hours of public face time.[40] Fellow citizens in court to pay a parking fine or take out a hunting license may well wonder what Jane is doing at the courthouse in the middle of a school day. Bypass petitioners have bumped into classmates attending their own juvenile court hearings, and parents have received anonymous letters from neighbors who saw their daughter in court.[41] To avoid such run-ins and to facilitate getting a court order in the same vicinity as the clinic that was to perform the procedure, Texas had permitted minors to file a petition in any county in the state. But in 2015, Texas had amended the statute to require minors to file only in their county of residence.[42] There are two exceptions: if the minor's parent is the presiding judge of the county or if the county has fewer than 10,000 people, she may use a contiguous county or the one in which the abortion will take place.[43]

In addition to being spotted in person, either inadvertently or by avid court watchers, the nondisclosure of minors' identities has also been put at risk through the ethically charged problem of what I call "revelation through appeal." In these cases the minor is not seen but is instead described, and not by members of the public but by appellate judges ruling on the appeal of a denied petition. The problem comes about when an appellate opinion—which in almost every instance becomes part of a publicly available record—incorporates so much factual information from the transcript of the hearing that despite her Jane Doe alias, the petitioner's identity is susceptible to discovery, particularly in a small community. The practice was the subject of ferocious debate among the justices of the Texas Supreme Court in 2000 when Justice Enoch challenged Justice Hecht for his "routine practice of revealing to the public 'in complete detail' the minor's testimony . . . for no apparent jurisprudential purpose."[44] Enoch observed that in a series of decisions, Hecht had written separately from the main opinion in order to "publish chapter and verse the minor's confidential testimony. It would appear that Justice Hecht intends nothing more than to punish, as best he personally can, minors for seeking a judicial bypass. Although the law promises them confidentiality, he promises them notoriety."[45]

It is important to remember just what is at stake in abortion notoriety. It is not only that a minor's parents may prevent her from proceeding if they find out, but as Judge Richard Posner noted in refusing to release even the redacted medical records of late-term abortion patients, "skillful 'Googlers'" might be able to "put two and two together, 'out' the . . . women, and thereby expose them to threats, humiliation, and obloquy."[46] Part of the "two and two" for minors is the fact of pregnancy and the sex that brought it about. Gossip about these subjects is always interesting and has long been a basis of reputational injury.[47] Consider the fourteen-year-old pregnant minor in foster care, who testified too honestly that one reason she wanted an abortion was because "her continued pregnancy and delivery of a child would affect her image with boys, who were bound to find out about it."[48] (She also stated that "she wished to continue her education and make something of herself," but her petition was denied and the denial upheld on appeal.[49])

For minors living at home, pregnancy is proof that the girl is not the trustworthy kind of daughter her parents thought she was. As one Ohio Juvenile Court judge stated about bypass petitioners, "they are here because they don't want their parents to know that they are less than perfect."[50] Once a pregnancy is revealed, neighbors, friends, and church members will know that she has had sex, that she was not smart or careful about it, and that no boy has stepped forward to make things right. Historian Cornelia Dayton uncovered near identical concerns regarding abortions by unmarried women in colonial New England. In pursuing why in 1742, nineteen-year-old Sarah Grosvenor would have undergone a secret abortion even though prior to quickening abortion was legal, Dayton found that abortion was regarded as blameworthy not in itself but because it was intended "to hide a prior sin, sex outside of marriage."[51] As Dayton explains: "Reading the depositions, it is nearly impossible to disentangle the players' attitudes toward abortion itself from their expressions of censure or anxiety over failed courtship, illegitimacy, and the dangers posed for a young woman by secret abortion."[52] Although the physical dangers of abortion encountered in the eighteenth century are no longer present, Dayton's account otherwise rings true today.

The second constitutionally significant feature of the hearings is the requirement of speed, or what the Supreme Court has called "sufficient expedition to provide an effective opportunity."[53] To accomplish this, bypass petitions receive priority on court calendars and there are prescribed maximum periods for the judge's decision to be handed down. In Mississippi, it is no more than seventy-two hours after a petition is filed; in North Carolina, no more than seven days.[54] A judge's failure to rule within the specified time (the so-called pocket veto) results in a default judgment in favor of the minor.[55] Such "deemed granted" provisions are tremendously important in counties where judges might prefer to miss the deadline in passive protest against abortion. The state of Texas had a "deemed granted" provision, but as part of an overhaul of the statute in 2015, the provision was removed.[56]

The issue of timing is particularly acute because we are dealing with teenagers, who tend to acknowledge their pregnancies later than adults. While we understand the mix of causes—irregular periods, denial, and the magical hope for blood of some kind—delay puts added pressure on bypass timetables as a more developed pregnancy pushes up against legal limits and against more complicated (though still safe) medical procedures. In states like Ohio that grant maximum periods for trial court and appellate decisions, the time a petition is filed until the final ruling "can consume up to three weeks of a young woman's pregnancy."[57] The passage of time raises an arresting point. Requiring a woman or girl to remain pregnant for three additional weeks after she has made the decision to terminate imposes a disturbing psychological burden as well.[58] There is a punitive air in some of this: after the Alabama Supreme Court gave a trial judge twelve additional days to hold a second hearing, a concurring justice soberly noted that "the mind-set of the trial court apparent from the record forebodes that a remand will not yield a different judgment. . . . All the while the time for a safe abortion will be ticking by."[59]

Although the legal process does not begin until the minor files her petition with the clerk of the local court, time also ticks by as minors figure out just how to engage the legal process. The bypass process is not taught in civics classes or sex education, where it might sensibly find a home. Many girls find out that parents or judges have to be involved only when they call a clinic.

There are also procedural hurdles. In her detailed study of the reception of bypass petitions in local courts, political scientist Helena Silverstein found that assistance from court personnel was a curious combination of inept, morally tinged, and nonexistent: "40 percent of Alabama courts, just over 45 percent of Tennessee courts, and a whopping 73 percent of Pennsylvania courts proved inadequately acquainted with their responsibilities."[60] Minors therefore turn to brochures or online materials provided by the state or by private agencies, such as the Women's Law Project in Pennsylvania, Jane's Due Process in Texas, and regional Planned Parenthood affiliates.[61] These provide answers to frequently asked teenage questions regarding such matters as costs (none), confidentiality (mostly assured), and the provision of a lawyer (appointed).

The importance of timing is not lost on minors. A Texas teen who could have avoided a hearing by waiting just a few weeks until her eighteenth birthday endured a bypass hearing so that she could secure an abortion at the earliest moment.[62] Yet money worries also deter minors from acting. The hearings are free but the abortion is not. As the Women's Law Project in Philadelphia counsels pregnant teens: "Do not delay calling for an appointment just because you haven't raised the full fee."[63]

Proving Her Case

The bypass judge's task is to determine if the minor standing before him is sufficiently mature and well informed. How is he to make this determination? The Supreme Court noted in *Bellotti* that maturity is "difficult to define, let alone determine" and that the "peculiar nature of the abortion decision requires . . . case-by-case evaluations."[64] Yet to provide some consistency across cases, many states have established "maturity guidelines." The Pennsylvania statute, for example, provides that "the court shall hear evidence relating to the emotional development, maturity, intellect and understanding of the pregnant woman, the fact and duration of her pregnancy, the nature, possible consequences and alternatives to abortion, and any other evidence the court may find useful," the last phrase opening the door to just about anything.[65] In Texas, the Supreme Court focused on the process by which a decision is reached: the evidence must demonstrate that the minor's "decision is not the product of impulse, but is based upon the careful consideration of the various options open to her."[66] The right answers are placing the child for adoption, knowing what benefits an unwed mother is entitled to, and understanding that the father of the child incurs a support obligation.

Despite the articulation of standards by appellate courts and legislatures, there is great variation in their application. In explaining the discrepancies in bypass outcomes by county, one Ohio judge noted simply: "My view of maturity is not someone else's view of maturity." An Ohio bypass attorney put it slightly differently: "We're starved for standards because everyone thinks they have the answer."[67] And a Kansas judge has cautioned a little humility, urging that "the examining court must weigh [the minor's] situation not against the ideal but against a standard of basic understanding of her situation, her choices, and her options."[68]

As to whether a minor is "sufficiently well informed"—the second factual prong—the Texas criteria are typical. The minor must show that she has learned about medical risks from a health care professional, that she understands those risks, knows there are alternatives to abortion, and is aware of its emotional and psychological implications.[69] Looking at ultrasound images has been taken as evidence of the minor's recognition of what is literally at stake. In some communities there may be few health care professionals to confide in, and petitions have been denied because the information though correct was not obtained from the right source.[70] Moreover, in applying the standards, judges are sometimes distracted by other considerations. In a 2001 Alabama case, the minor, when asked about the specifics of the medical procedures, testified that "I understand they have a local anesthetic which they'll give you anesthesia. They also have this oral medicine that you can take. When you take that, it numbs the bottom half of your body. And they would go in with an aspirator which is like a vacuum or sucking machine. And they go in there around the uterus wall and they just suck it out. That is what they [three different nurses at different clinics] told me."[71] Not bad. Still, the judge declared the minor to be insufficiently informed, stating that "you know, these people [the physicians] are interested in one thing it appears to me and this is getting this young lady's money. . . . This is a beautiful young girl with a bright future and she does not need to have a butcher get a hold of her."[72]

One reason petitions are denied is that the petitioner is found not to have met her "burden of proof." In every legal action, one party or the other is assigned the burden—the responsibility—to sufficiently prove the elements necessary to prevail. In bypass cases, these are the minor's maturity and that she is sufficiently well informed. Because the minor is the only party in a bypass hearing, she necessarily has the burden of proof. But just how convinced must the judge be?[73] Because the preponderance of evidence test (the trier of fact is 51 percent convinced) is typically used in civil cases, most states apply it in the civil context of bypass hearings. However, a number of other states—Nebraska and Arizona, joined by Texas in 2015—have chosen to use the higher clear and convincing standard. The argument is that the tougher standard "avoid[s] making judicial bypass a mere pass-through proceeding," which the Arizona Court of Appeals characterized as "a proceeding that encroaches on a parent's ability to exercise [traditional authority]" over a child.[74] The Arizona court noted that granting a petition too easily would have "irreversible consequences" for the minor.[75] Of course, denying the petition also has irreversible consequences—the baby—that through her petition the minor is specifically seeking to avoid. The general point is that judicial and legislative views about minors and abortions sometimes flavor the procedural rules, making it easier for petitions to be turned down.

The Constraints of Genre

Genre-meister Alistair Fowler has explained that "every genre has a unique repertoire, from which its representatives select characteristics."[76] The repertoire of the novel, for example, includes such features as length, setting, character types, and character names. Such conventions help us understand what sort of novel we are reading, its dynamics and its possibilities. Discrete characteristics similarly illuminate legal genres such as trials, inquests, and our subject here, hearings. There are, of course, many kinds of hearings—parole hearings, sentencing hearings, custody hearings—yet they share representative characteristics: procedural informality, looser evidentiary rules, a colloquy between petitioner and decision maker, and the special role played by the petitioner's testimony.

As a subset of the larger category, abortion bypass hearings fine-tune these features further. The primary actors are the minor, her lawyer, and the judge; a court reporter is also present, and the minor can bring a friend or relative. Alabama has added an additional player: judges in that state may appoint a lawyer for the fetus, and some judges regularly do so.[77] The stage for these three (or four) participants is an empty courtroom, properly though eerily cleared

to protect the petitioner's identity. These general features of a hearing—
informality, plea, discretionary decision maker—then combine with the distinctive aspects of the bypass process—the plaintiff's anonymity, her age, the origins
of her plea in a constitutional right—to create a distinct form of hearing that
nonetheless shares characteristics and grammatical rules with others.

In her study of sixteenth-century French letters of remission or "pardon
tales," historian Natalie Zemon Davis explains that these were written letters
sent to the king from wrongdoers convicted of capital offenses who sought
through their letter the king's mercy from execution.[78] In describing the narrative structure of pardon tales, Davis describes the pleas as "a mixed genre: a
judicial supplication to persuade the king and courts, an historical account of
one's past actions, and a story."[79] Written in the third person, the letters attempted to build narrative coherence by showing that the offender's wrongful
behavior was both understandable under the circumstances and uncharac-
teristic.[80] And although sometimes embellished by royal notaries and by
lawyers, it was important that the primary voice of the letter remain that of
the supplicant. This not only made the supporting facts sound more authentic
and believable but also captured the personal expression of remorse that was a
necessary element of the plea.

Bypass hearings give us judges, not kings, but the task of those seeking
relief is similar. Like supplicants trying to persuade the king, minors must
organize the circumstances of their predicament into a compelling, convincing
narrative. Because the bypass hearings are a live colloquy in court, the minor's
presentation is likely to be less polished than the written pardon tale, which
not uncommonly saw several drafts. The immediacy of the oral bypass testimony puts increased pressure on whatever limited preparation time there is between the petitioner and her attorney. A lawyer from a well-staffed jurisdiction
described the process: "We have enough pro bono attorneys ready to drop everything so that the clerk's office can find one of us to get down there, spend fifteen minutes with the client to prepare for the hearing, get to the hearing, and
get the order."[81] In that time, the bypass petitioner must pull together a picture
of herself that accounts for her past actions (the sex and resulting pregnancy)
and despite the rights-based nature of the plea, before some judges the minor
must also gesture toward remorse.

This is no easy task, for the bypass petitioner must explain how a girl who
stands before the court pregnant and unmarried is mature enough to decide
about abortion—an act that for some judges is worse than what she has already

done. The best she can do is to rely on a set of social conventions to prove her good character: a part-time job, above-average grades, activities in school, plans for college, a savings account. These are the vocabulary of the genre. (This too is complicated in that the minor must argue in a delicate alternative: first, she is mature, but if that fails, that she is so hapless that it is in her best interest to have an abortion.) And there is an added complication. The bypass petitioner is not simply seeking the passive forgiveness of a pardon. Rather, she is asking the court for permission to take additional positive action. Some judges, particularly in Alabama, regard this as implicating them in the abortion and so make clear to girls when they do grant a petition that they have been required to do so under the law (because the girl has proven her maturity) but that this does not mean she has to go out and get an abortion. Two judges regularly conditioned their approval of the petition on the minor first visiting the pro-life organization Save-a-Life.[82]

The minor's performative task is made the harder by features of the bypass process which make her appear an unreliable sort of girl from the start. By virtue of her petition, the court knows she has had sex and is "in trouble." The very word "bypass" suggests an end run around something (her parents) and explains why some attorneys representing minors prefer to call the hearings "waivers." The procedural requirement of anonymity—although intended for her benefit—further contributes to the aura of furtiveness. The minor has literally snuck into court in order not to be seen, and she uses an alias in order not to be known. In the eyes of some, she is sneaking around the traditional rules of parental control and, more to the point, she is trying to sneak around the very wages of sin. There is irony amidst all this sneakiness, for these are not the girls who typically turn up in court for misconduct. As one Ohio judge commented, "the common denominator is that they are intelligent and have a lot on the ball."[83] But for their pregnancies and their intention to abort, these are the "good girls."

As part of this structure of stealth, the cases reveal a pervasive dismissiveness of minors' reasons for not involving parents. Minors' concerns about being beaten or thrown out of the house (as was one petitioner's older sister when she got pregnant) or about parental well-being (a depressed mother or the abusive stepfather who would "cause 'a bunch of problems' for her mother" if the mother consented) were all discounted as exaggerations and excuses for not wanting to get in trouble.[84] In this regard, little has changed since the 1960s and 1970s. Historian Johanna Schoen quotes a minor's explanation of why she

couldn't tell her parents about her pregnancy: "it was like hell in the family."[85]
Putting families aside, two features of the time made the problem of unwanted
pregnancy more difficult even in those few states where abortion was legal under
certain circumstances. The age of majority was twenty-one so that young women
as well as teenagers were unable to proceed without parental consent, and pregnancy often meant immediate dismissal from high school or college.[86]

Of course pregnant minors today don't want to get in trouble at home, and
some may overestimate the severity of their parents' reactions. On the other
hand, many may well have the pulse of their domestic situations and be able
to gauge the emotional fallout of the sex / pregnancy / abortion bomb that they
have decided not to throw into the midst of the family. The judicial suspicion
that minors are exaggerating fears about being thrown out, say, seems particularly stingy given that the Supreme Court in *Planned Parenthood v. Casey* took
quite seriously the "justifiable fears of physical abuse" against wives if their husbands learn of planned abortions.[87]

Another difficulty concerns the quality of a minor's testimony. In deciding
whether a bypass petitioner is mature, trial judges are entitled to "draw inferences
from the minor's composure, analytic ability, appearance, thoughtfulness, tone
of voice, expressions, and her ability to articulate her reasoning and conclusions."[88] Courtrooms are fairly intimidating settings, even for adults who are
not testifying about the details of their sex life and unwanted pregnancy. Statements by judges who hear bypass cases, by advocates who accompany petitioners,
and by minors themselves leave no doubt that the experience is one of anxiety
and dread.[89] A Minnesota judge described the level of apprehension of petitioners
as worse than that of women seeking orders of protection for domestic violence.[90]
The judge noted that "you see all the typical things that you would see with somebody under incredible amounts of stress, answering monosyllabically, tone of
voice, tenor of voice, shaky, wringing of hands, you know, one young lady had
her—her hands were turning blue and it was warm in my office."[91] Minors report
a feeling of terror that they will say something wrong and lose their case, and this
in a state where nearly every petition was granted. As one petitioner fretted "what
about the 1%? I could be the 1% . . . and I was nervous."[92]

Stammering and other inadequacies of speech such as slang or blurting are
regularly counted against petitioners. When asked if she understood the risks
involved in abortion, a thirteen-year-old petitioner answered, "well, I hear you
have bad cramps or you may get something up inside you that could cause
risks"; when asked about childbirth, she replied that she "wouldn't be able to

go through with that."[93] The court concluded that the minor was "unable to communicate . . . a sufficient understanding of the medical procedure involved, the associated risks, or of any alternatives to abortion."[94] Yet even explanations from more articulate minors have been discounted. An Alabama minor answered the risk question by stating: "You could have an infection if you don't take care of yourself afterwards. Sterilization if the instruments they use are not properly cleaned. You could have bleeding because you bleed after you've had the abortion. You have bleeding internally and externally. You could have— what was the other one they told me—death, the main one, I guess. But they said that's always a factor."[95] Her petition was denied because she had not spoken personally to the physician who was to perform the abortion, as required by the statute. There are many ways to catch a petitioner out.

In some instances the minor's discomfort has been intensified by the conduct of the judge. In a 2008 Florida case, the judge denied the petition, telling the minor that "you know your mother and father, especially your mother, are going to know that you are pregnant. And if she sees you, she will know. Major things happen to your body when you get pregnant, even if you have an abortion."[96] The denial was upheld on appeal, although a dissenting judge observed that "the [trial] judge's improper and openly argumentative personal assertions likely would have intimidated most adults—indeed, most attorneys. It is not difficult to imagine the chilling effect that his behavior had on this young woman's ability to elaborate on her situation."[97]

The fact is that bypass petitioners are teenagers and many of them talk like teenagers. In presenting her reasons for seeking an abortion, a Texas petitioner testified that "if I really put the cards out on the table and look through them, I—I—having a baby right now would probably stop 75 percent of what I want to do . . . I know—I'm—like I said, I'm very busy. I have a lot of high goals, and having a baby would stop me from having them."[98] "Very busy" isn't the best way to express why you would rather finish your education than have a baby, and perhaps stammering sounds tentative. However, the minor's testimony seems honest and natural. Babies do interfere with "high goals." Yet the Texas Supreme Court upheld the trial court's ruling that "a minor who was reluctant to carry her child to term because, at least in part, she was 'very busy' was not mature enough to make the [abortion] decision without parental guidance."[99] In another verbal misstep, an Ohio minor stated in response to questioning that she was both "planning to get on birth control" and that she was never going to have sex again.[100] Her petition was denied because the internal inconsistencies of her remarks called her credibility into question. Well, maybe, but it is not hard to see how such contradictions (no sex but more contraception) come about when honesty and the flustered desire to give the right answer bump into one another in court.

Some might argue that whatever respect is the proper measure for the treatment of adults before the law, its application is less necessary when applied to minors. Minors are, after all, still children, unformed, still subject to the control and discipline of others. John Locke writes that children "are not born in this full state of equality, though they are born to it"; in this sense they are only "destined for dignity."[101] Certainly parents may punish, chide, and shame their children without taking the child's dignity or respect into consideration. But bypass judges stand in a different relation than parents to the children before them. As Robert Ferguson has noted, judges enjoy unprecedented authority in a democracy: "[We] set judges apart."[102] They are supposed to represent the state, though some judges have gotten confused on the point. In denying the petition of a Florida minor, the trial court judge stated: "Miss, I know this seems like the most terrible thing in the world. And, I will tell you, as I indicated, [I am] a father of two daughters, and I want you to know that I am Catholic. And, I have always told my daughters, whatever it is, you can discuss it with me. . . . I'm not telling you that you can or cannot terminate that pregnancy. I just think, in your best interest, where you are going to have to go through with it with your parents, it would be best for you to notify your parents. And, I am sure they love you."[103] Another noted that he "has four children of his own and once was a seventeen year old himself";[104] another couched her denial of the petition with "let me just say, I'm very concerned about this young lady's welfare. Like counsel, I'm a mother."[105] This blending of parental and judicial roles is particularly maddening in a hearing that is meant to be an express alternative to parental involvement.

Gender necessarily plays a role in the tribulations of bypass petitioners, as it has for other women who have had to provide a narrative in court. Natalie Davis reports that very few sixteenth-century pardon seekers were women. This was because the range of explanatory settings that could excuse a wrongful behavior—drinking too much on a festival day, taking umbrage at an insult—was much smaller for a woman. Killing to protect one's sexual honor was an acceptable ground upon which a woman might ask for mercy but not much else. Davis also notes that because subjection was an everyday feature of women's lives, "being on their knees in humble supplication" was a less impressive gesture than when displayed by a man.[106] But the absence of women pardon seekers was also a function of substantive law: the capital crimes most associated with women were witchcraft and infanticide, and neither was pardonable.[107] By the sixteenth century, the death of an unbaptized infant following a concealed pregnancy was evidence of sexual sin punishable by death. Both family morality and royal majesty were better served by giving such a woman the justice she deserved.

The same problems that vexed women supplicants centuries ago operate in the bypass setting. How to position oneself as worthy of judicial sympathy when the underlying act was sexual, secret, and (sometimes) consensual? How to make the error of one's ways seem aberrational when the hearing is proof of ongoing stealth? And how to overcome the view in the eyes of some bypass judges that despite its legality, abortion and infanticide are one and the same and that each is simply "too wicked for the king's pardon"?[108]

One possibility is to convey a sense of remorse. Remorse is understood as an aspect of rehabilitation and thus an indication of maturity. Depending on the judge, the successful petitioner's story may include not only her grade point average but some indication of why she deserves to have her petition granted. This requires an appropriate shading of the tale, one that gestures toward contrition for the mess she has gotten herself into and from which she now asks the court's help to escape. Like a defendant before a sentencing judge or an inmate before a parole board, she must present a version of herself that matches a set of expectations about what a remorseful defendant, a reformed parolee, or a contrite pregnant teenager looks like. As a popular jailhouse manual tells parolees, "[board] members will consider whether you understand why the crime happened, whether you feel any remorse for the crime, and what you would do differently in the future."[109] Allocution before sentencing, where the convicted defendant gets to speak directly to the judge, works much the same way. The Third Circuit has described allocution as "the opportunity [for the court] to evaluate the total person who stands at the bar of justice: to note the physical appearance and demeanor; the tone, temper and rhythm of speech; the facial expressions, the hands, the revealing look into the eyes. In sum, [the absence of allocution] deprives the judge of those impressions gleaned through the senses in any personal confrontation in which one attempts to assess the credibility or to evaluate the true moral fiber of another."[110]

Talking to clergy or otherwise reflecting on one's religion is sometimes regarded as revealing of moral fiber, and some advocates urge their clients to consider doing so before the hearing and to report, at the hearing, that they have done this.[111] A minor's appreciation of the "moral and religious dilemma presented by her decision" is a factor courts have regularly taken into account, though the answers may not always please.[112] In a 2000 Texas case, the minor testified that "she understood that many women experience guilt after an abortion" but that "all of her choices would involve guilt, [and] that she felt most comfortable with the decision to have an abortion."[113]

The mid-twentieth century provides an analogy in the form of a hearing that has now disappeared from law's horizon: divorce hearings in the days of fault-based divorce. Before the enactment of no-fault divorce in the 1970s, a plaintiff could get a divorce only by proving specific statutory grounds of marital misconduct; adultery, desertion, insanity, and various degrees of cruelty were typical.[114] Unhappily married couples who had not misbehaved in these ways (and had no desire to do so) were in a pinch. The solution, usually suggested by legal counsel, was to manufacture a different sort of misconduct: collusion, or an agreement between them to lie in order to get their divorce. Coached by counsel, one spouse would testify that the other had engaged in one of the accepted fault-based behaviors. Although collusion itself was a bar to divorce, the practice was rampant, as litigants recited by rote that their spouse had been cold and indifferent or had treated them cruelly in what one scholar called the "melancholy and perfunctory litany of uncontested divorce, recited daily in the courtrooms through the state."[115] Over time, the widespread practice of dissembling under oath became too much for the legal system to countenance. No-fault divorce was introduced with the expectation that it would "put an end to the dissimulation, hypocrisy—and even outright perjury—which is engendered by the present system."[116]

Bypass petitioners want an abortion and they can describe, if sometimes in teen speak, how the pregnancy came about, why they don't want a baby now, and why they want to proceed without involving a parent. There is little to lie about, unless they are reluctant to reveal the circumstances of nonconsensual sex. Nonetheless, a minor's testimony is sometimes treated like the ritualistic recitations of fault-based divorce hearings. One disgruntled Texas judge stated, "Doe's evidence that she is mature and sufficiently well informed is very limited, consisting almost entirely of monosyllabic answers to conclusory questions posed by her counsel."[117] In affirming the denial of a bypass petition, a Florida court similarly observed that when "her counsel asked Ms. Doe if she had considered all the alternatives to terminating her pregnancy . . . the monosyllabic

her (or abortion's) morality. To be sure, not all judges who personally oppose abortion behave in ways that call into question the impartiality of the judiciary. Consider this statement by an Ohio judge: "It's really tough. I'm as Roman Catholic as you can get and I follow the church's teachings. But where these cases come before the court, I must follow the law. Whether I agree with [a girl's] decision is another matter."[127]

But not all judges are able to subordinate their personal convictions, and opposition to teenage abortion takes many forms. These include appointing counsel for the fetus and letting that counsel cross-examine the petitioning minor.[128] Other techniques involve establishing a higher than usual burden of proof or denying a girl's petitions on extra-statutory grounds, such as requiring her to be "extraordinarily mature," or on extramedical grounds, such as declaring the pregnancy too developed, undisputed medical evidence to the contrary.[129] Judges have questioned petitioners as though the only measure of a petitioner's maturity is a decision not to abort so that the hearing becomes an official opportunity for the judge to remonstrate against abortion's legality. Judges have equated abortion to murder and the death penalty: "This is a capital case. It involves the question whether [the minor's] unborn child should live or die."[130] In that case the judge damned the petitioner to hell, noting that "she said that she does not believe that abortion is wrong, so, apparently, in spite of her church attendance, there won't be spiritual consequences, *at least for the present.*"[131]

Occasionally a judge goes too far. In 1992, Michigan trial judge Francis Bourisseau stated in a news interview that while he rarely grants bypass petitions, he might do so in the case of a white girl raped by a black man.[132] In affirming his censure, the Michigan Supreme Court held that Bourisseau's remarks were "clearly prejudicial to the administration of justice": the judge's conduct "called into question the impartiality of the judiciary, and exposed the judicial system to contempt and ridicule."[133] The case is now used as a textbook example of "bias toward litigants." But let us look at Judge Bourisseau's remarks more closely. In the full interview, the judge had stated that he didn't want to have "blood on his hands" for participating in permitting abortions at all.[134] Bourisseau's racialized rape example was simply an exception to his general policy of denying all bypass petitions, and that conduct—day-to-day denials because the judge thinks abortion is murder—went relatively undiscussed and uncensored.

In addition to religious or moral opposition to abortion, concerns about reelection influence judicial behavior. Some 87 percent of all state and local judges now run for their office, and abortion has become a prominent campaign issue.[135] Judicial candidates have advertised themselves as being pro-life during an election and have publicly celebrated the fact thereafter. Bypass hearings come in for special attention because of the judiciary's intimate involvement in the process. Thus the official 2006 platform of the Texas Republican Party called for the "electoral defeat of all judges who through raw judicial activism seek to nullify the Parental Consent Law by wantonly granting bypasses to minor girls seeking abortion."[136] And while the thought has long been that nonpartisan judicial elections would increase judicial independence, freeing candidates from association with party platforms, new data suggest that nonpartisan elections encourage judges to run on their character. How better to prove one's judicial character than by taking a stand on such radioactive issues as abortion?[137] Television ads against an incumbent judge claimed that "[in Judge] Janet Stumbo's opinion . . . there's no criminal liability for killing an unborn child."[138] Without challenging the free speech rights of judicial candidates, the exercise of judicial speech with regard to abortion provides another reason why bypass hearings should be abandoned as the means of supervising teenage abortion decisions.

Judges have used different techniques to avoid any association with the issue of abortion. Some have fought to keep their own names off their bypass decisions when the decisions are filed. This was unsuccessful in Ohio, where an industrious local reporter sought to obtain statewide information on bypass decisions. The Ohio Supreme Court made clear that so long as neither the minor's name nor her identity was revealed in the decision (as was already required by law), there was an obligation under the Ohio Constitution's "open court" provision (Article I, § 16) to release the decisions.[139] Judges in Texas, on the other hand, have succeeded in keeping their names off the decisions.[140] Other judges refuse to hear bypass petitions at all. A few formally recuse themselves, but others simply have their clerks turn petitioners away ("We don't do that in this county").[141] In one urban jurisdiction, only three judges out of a pool of sixty will hear bypass cases; in another, lawyers have experienced "up to five recusals before [the petition] lands on someone who will take it."[142]

This practice—a form of forum exclusion—appears effective. In counties where judges shun bypass cases, few petitions are filed. Pregnant minors have little time to waste and so have learned to file in jurisdictions where they are more likely to be heard (and where there is also a medical clinic should they prevail). In Ohio, for example, girls from around the state—and it is a big state—tend to file in Cleveland, Akron, or Youngstown. They do not file in Geauga County, where no bypass cases were filed over a two-year period. When asked why, the education chairman of the Geauga County Right to Life answered that "maybe it's because it's more of a Christian place. We don't have any abortionaries here. We don't have any killing centers. And a lot of girls who are going to kill their babies don't want anyone to see them."[143] Refusing to hear petitions may deter local filings, but it does not prevent teen abortions; it simply relocates them and increases the costs to the minors.

This informal system of forum deprivation is deeply problematic as young women scramble to find a court where they can be heard. They understand abortion's disfavored status long before they get to court, but denying young women a legal forum takes things up a notch. It tells them that their claim falls outside the requirements of justice and that the problem of how to gain access to the courts is theirs alone to solve. The result is more than inconvenience, delay, and expense (though it is surely those). It is also an affront to the self-worth that participation in the legal process can bestow. Professor Frank Michelman has explained that formal legal process is "an important means through which persons are entitled to get, or are given assurance of having, whatever we are pleased to regard as rightfully theirs."[144] It is part of one's due as a citizen, part of one's dignity.[145] Minors are not guaranteed that every petition will be granted, but they are entitled to have their petitions accepted and their evidence evaluated fairly. This is the core of the legal process and the unpredictability brought about by outright exclusion upends this deeply rooted norm. We have already seen examples of mean-spiritedness in the bypass context, but we should not lose sight of the arbitrariness of it all.

The Constitution's promise of due process is woefully thin when no process is available. The Supreme Court considered a similar problem in the early 1970s. Gladys Boddie, an indigent resident of Connecticut, couldn't afford the sixty-dollar divorce filing fee. She argued that because she couldn't get into court at all, and because a judicial declaration was the only way one could get divorced, she was being denied due process of law itself.[146] The Supreme Court agreed, holding that at a minimum, due process requires that "persons forced to settle their claims of right and duty through the judicial process must be given a meaningful opportunity to be heard."[147] For pregnant minors who don't want to involve parents, the bypass hearing is their only recourse to the right established in *Roe*. As the Court stated in *Boddie v. Connecticut,* at the point where a "judicial proceeding becomes the only effective means of resolving the dispute at hand," the "denial of a defendant's full access to that process raises grave problems for its legitimacy."[148] Bypass hearings are a curious species of dispute (between daughters and parents, with the latter unaware that this is going on) but the Supreme Court's concerns in *Boddie* get close to why denying girls a bypass forum is not good for girls and not good for law.

Limits of Law

Are there limits to what a pregnant girl should be asked to do in exchange for exercising her rights under *Roe*? Perhaps the intimate information squeezed out of minors at bypass hearings does help the court evaluate their maturity. Perhaps it isn't really all that humiliating. No doubt teenagers experience some things as humiliating that are not so for others (the existence of parents, for example). But teenagers can be humiliated even if there is no universal agreement about the definition. Justice Ruth Bader Ginsburg has suggested that gender might have something to do with detecting (and experiencing) humiliation. During the oral argument in a case involving the strip search of a middle schooler, several Supreme Court Justices mused that the search of the girl's underpants in the principal's office didn't seem all that different from having to undress for gym class. Justice Ginsburg later observed that "they have never been a 13-year-old girl. It's a very sensitive age for a girl. I didn't think that my colleagues, some of them, quite understood."[149]

But the situations we are considering are surely humiliating for young girls if anything is. Bypass hearings concern matters that are not only private but perhaps disturbing, involving secrets about their bodies, their relationships, their religious beliefs. In response to questions from judges or from their own attorneys, young women have had to explain that they were impregnated by their own fathers, had a prior abortion, had intercourse with more than one man, and experienced family violence (against them or against their mothers).[150] Girls have testified about depression and self-cutting following the death of a mother (displaying the scars to the court), broken condoms, discord between parents, and parental opposition to the prospect of an interracial child.[151] The concern is not whether these facts were accepted as grounds for maturity (they weren't) but rather that they had to be given at all. As an experienced Texas bypass attorney explained: "These cases are hard on everyone. . . . You must ask a 17-year old why her family is dysfunctional. Odds are her boyfriend dumped her when he found out she was pregnant, and she is having the biggest crisis of her life. Now she has to go to court and tell a bunch of strangers about it. It's heartbreaking stuff."[152]

Here we circle back to my working hypothesis that bypass hearings operate as a form of punishment. The hearings cause great distress to vulnerable young women already experiencing the predicaments of unwanted pregnancy in circumstances of perceived isolation from their families. Unhappily pregnant girls learn that if they won't talk to their parents, they must file papers, talk to a lawyer, and testify in court, each time reviewing with strangers details of their home lives, sex lives, and contraceptive failures. This is the price young women are expected to pay for having sex and for seeking an abortion, and for doing both without owning up to their parents. As the presiding judge of an Ohio juvenile court told a minor's attorney after denying the petition of his college-bound client, she had just not had enough "hard knocks."[153] Some parents also sometimes regard bypass participation as the proper price for ending a pregnancy; bypass lawyers report that some parents refuse to consent, even knowing that their daughter is likely to succeed at the hearing: "You have to go through judicial bypass. This is your responsibility, not mine."[154]

It is not enough to say that some people think that subjecting young women to all this is what they deserve or that it is a small price for them to pay. In the birching case before the European Court of Human Rights mentioned earlier, the United Kingdom argued that this form of punishment was not "degrading punishment" under the European Convention on Human Rights because the practice "did not outrage public opinion."[155] The European Court of Human Rights rejected this argument, noting that "even assuming that local public opinion can have an incidence on the interpretation of the concept of 'degrading punishment,'" the lack of outrage does not mean the public finds that birching is not degrading: "it might well be that one of the reasons why [the public] view the penalty as an effective deterrent is precisely the element of degradation which it involves."[156] Unlike birching, bypass hearings are not technically punishment; we are not a signatory to the Convention, and "degrading treatment" is not a basis for constitutional review in the United States. However, as parents, as citizens, as once-pregnant persons possibly faced with a similar decision, we should think harder about how the parental involvement process operates in the lives of young women.

The enactment of parental involvement schemes is the more dispiriting because nothing about it is constitutionally compelled. The Supreme Court focused on judicial hearings in *Bellotti* because that was the Massachusetts statute before the Court. But as the Court made clear in a much overlooked footnote, "much can be said for employing procedures and a forum less formal than those associated with a court of general jurisdiction."[157] States choosing to require parental consent could certainly "delegate the alternative procedure to a juvenile court or an administrative agency or officer."[158]

A few states have done just that. Delaware has widened the scope of those to whom a minor might turn: notice of the abortion can be given to a grandparent or a licensed mental health professional. As in Maine, that person is required to inform the minor about alternatives to abortion and must also agree in writing that waiving parental consent is in the minor's best interests.[159] Similarly concerned that an adult be involved in the matter, Maine authorizes minors to get consent from a parent or from another adult family member or, in the absence of such consent, to receive guidance from designated counselors— clergy, nurses, or psychologists.[160] The counselors must provide the minor with information not only about abortion but also about adoption, pregnancy, and state benefits for child rearing.[161] Counseling as a means of informing women about abortion alternatives exists outside the United States. Germany, for example, requires that all women must go to a counseling service of their choice, where they will be informed that under the German basic law human life begins at conception. The counselor provides information, but she does not evaluate the quality of the woman's consent and cannot countermand a woman's decision. After receiving counseling the pregnant woman may do as she likes.[162] It is hard to imagine such a scheme working well in the United States, where even the moral views of county court clerks handing out marriage licenses come so powerfully into play.

Nonetheless, these more capacious mechanisms for non-judicial adult involvement in a minor's abortion decision make much better sense than a judicial hearing. Teenagers are often connected to a broader network of support than their immediate families, and the law should take advantage of those connections. Because most states insist on parental consent only, actual families with whom minors live—foster parents, legal guardians, adult siblings, grandmother—are ineligible to receive notification or to give consent on their minor's behalf.[163] Other parents may be present but in the United States illegally and afraid to sign any official paper, especially ones in Louisiana and elsewhere that require notarization.[164] Importantly, a parent's refusal to consent does not always signal disagreement with the daughter's plan to abort. An Alabama mother testified at her daughter's hearing that she would take her daughter to the clinic and care for her during any recovery but that her religious beliefs prevented her from consenting to her daughter's abortion. The trial court denied the petition because no parent had consented.[165] The pleas of a grandmother to approve her orphaned granddaughter's petition were similarly disregarded. And Georgia threw a particularly vicious wrench into the process by prosecuting a mother who had consented to her daughter's abortion as part of the bypass procedure on the ground that by securing the abortion, she had helped dispose of the incriminating evidence against her daughter's rapist.[166] The mother's conviction was upheld on appeal.

Offering minors an array of trusted sources is likely to produce a more involved intervention than the haphazard, often reluctant participation of a judge who has no stake in the particular minor, doesn't know her actual name, and is unlikely ever to see her again. Relaxing the age requirement is another sensible adjustment. Delaware exempts minors over the age of sixteen, and West Virginia defines a minor for bypass purposes as "any person under eighteen years who has not graduated from high school."[167] In all states minors may receive contraception and treatment of sexually transmitted diseases without parental notice or consent, and in many they may consent to sexual intercourse with one another. It seems reasonable to coordinate the age of consent for abortion with that for other sexually related decisions. And then there are those states that have enacted no parental involvement statutes at all. They rely instead on doctors to determine whether the patient has given informed consent, content that, as for every other medical matter, doctors are capable of and invested in doing so with the greatest care.

For people outside the United States, the bypass system comes as something of a shock, a very American and legalistic approach to a common though sometimes momentous predicament. Yet the fact that the bypass scheme seems so counter-productive to encouraging intra-familial conversation, or that it seems just plain mean, and suggests that the law's premises, purpose, or implementation are worth another look.

A version of a "second look" at another procedure of supplication arose in the context of the French letters of remission in the mid-sixteenth century. It seems that the king was ratifying almost all the letters, restoring to every supplicant "his good name and reputations and goods."[168] This led to concerns that the pardons were being granted to the well connected as much as to the truly deserving. Yet the practice continued because the letters served an important institutional purpose with regard to state-building: "The habit of language insisted upon in the letters of remission and the roles in which supplicants were required to present themselves were among the civilizing mechanisms of the early modern French state, reminding people subjectively of the locus of power."[169]

This led to a "double reputation" for pardons: "simultaneously believed in as a needed mechanism for social peace and reintegration, and scoffed at as a sham."[170] Bypass hearings are not shams, but many are demeaning, harsh, and punitive. They are an attempt to remind girls where the locus of power in twenty-first-century America is located. Legislators can do this because of the partial status of minors as constitutional rights bearers. But it is not beyond our collective talents to reconcile social concern about the well-being of pregnant young women with respect for their own judgments about what is best for them when unwanted motherhood is on the line.

8

Fathers and Fetuses— What Would Men Do?

Putting aside the odd seahorse, it is the female of the species, and not the male, who bears the children. In recent years this has meant that decisions about whether to bear a child have increasingly been matters for women themselves to think through and resolve, sometimes but not necessarily with their (mostly) male partners. This is the result of advances on several fronts. The development of oral contraception has made pregnancy more preventable than in the past, both because it is medically more effective than earlier methods and because it is largely under women's control. Home pregnancy tests in their turn have made pregnancy more quickly and privately knowable.[1] Expanding conceptions of what women can do with their bodies, brains, and talents have also played a role as women have come to see motherhood less as a compulsory status—the undisputed raison d'être of female existence—than as something to be chosen, planned, and sometimes declined. In addition to these technological and cultural reasons, women's increased control over childbearing is also the result of law, as women have acquired not only the ability and inclination to control their fertility but also the right to do so through the legalization of both contraception and abortion.

This is not to say that some husbands and wives and other procreating couples do not decide together about whether to terminate a pregnancy. Couples are often of the same mind, as we see in this tender exchange of letters between Sir Edward Stanley and his wife Henrietta in 1847. Learning that Henrietta was pregnant with their tenth child, Edward writes to his "dearest love": "This your last misfortune is indeed most grievous & puts all others in the shade. . . . I only hope it is not the beginning of another flock for what to do with them I am sure I know not."[2] Henrietta replies that "[a] hot bath, a tremendous walk & a great dose have succeeded."[3] Edward answers that he hopes by her "violent proceedings" Henrietta has not done herself harm, but agrees that "[if] however you are none the worse the great result is all the better."[4]

In our own century, excepting relationships involving domestic violence, married and cohabiting women regularly discuss how to resolve an unwanted pregnancy with their partners and most women report feeling supported in their decision, whether it is to terminate or to keep the pregnancy.[5] This explains why men have become more familiar presences not only during labor and delivery but in the waiting rooms of abortion clinics as well. Consider the spousal solidarity recounted by a woman whose fetus had been diagnosed with chronic kidney disease: "When the diagnosis was confirmed, my husband and I looked at each other and knew immediately abortion was the only thing to do. Why give birth to a baby who will die? In Wisconsin, you need to sign a form that says you're aware that the fetus has a heartbeat, fingers, and toes. After I signed, my husband took the pen. They said, 'No, only the patient needs to sign,' but he said, 'I want to.'"[6]

Yet spousal preferences do not always coincide, and in such cases disagreement is typically followed by discussion, negotiation, and modes of persuasion. One mid-century modern example is found in Richard Yates's 1961 novel *Revolutionary Road* in which the husband Frank plots a metered campaign to persuade his wife Alice not to terminate her newly diagnosed and unplanned third pregnancy: "Almost from the start he had seized the initiative, and he was reasonably confident of victory. The idea he had to sell, after all, was clearly on the side of the angels. It was unselfish, mature, and (though he tried to avoid moralizing) morally unassailable. The other idea, however she might try to romanticize its bravery, was repugnant."[7] In addition to Frank's morally unassailable reasons, a baby would also derail—happily from Frank's point of view—the couple's plans to abandon leafy Connecticut and, with their two children, move to Paris to find themselves. Frank plays it cool until the moment when, up against the deadline for a safe abortion, he begins "to employ his final tactic, the dangerous last-ditch maneuver he had hoped to hold in reserve against the possibility of defeat."[8] This is the triumphal accusation that Alice's desire to abort is a pathological denial of her womanhood and that she needs to see a shrink. Frank's charges were backed up by the psychological theories of the day.[9]

That was 1961. And although Frank's arguments that abortion is a selfish, unnatural, and immoral choice have currency still today, the decision about how to proceed is now Alice's alone to make. We can understand from a bodily perspective why women are favored here. As Margarete Sandelowski observes, "the pregnant woman has a privileged relation to the fetus because she carries it in her body. . . . Because her knowledge of the fetus is embodied (corporeal and concrete), she has a tactile and kinesthetic awareness and overall sense of knowing the fetus that her male partner cannot have."[10]

The Supreme Court has followed the logic of biology in this regard. Soon after the decision in *Roe v. Wade,* the state of Missouri began testing *Roe's* limits by enacting legislation requiring doctors to have in hand the written consent of the husband before performing an abortion on the wife. The law was challenged as violating *Roe's* holding that abortion was at core a matter for the woman to decide. In the 1976 case of *Planned Parenthood v. Danforth* the Court acknowledged "the deep and proper concern and interest that a devoted and protective husband has in his wife's pregnancy and in the growth and development of the fetus she is carrying."[11] Yet that concern did not make husband and wife equals in the matter. The Court stated that "as between the two, the balance weighs in [the wife's] favor" for it is "the woman who physically bears the child and who is the more directly and immediately affected by the pregnancy."[12]

Some twenty years later in 1992, the issue of spousal involvement came up again. This time Pennsylvania's Abortion Control Act required married women merely to notify their husbands of their intent to abort, rather than get written consent. (No notification was necessary if the wife provided a signed statement that her husband had not impregnated her, that notification would "cause [the husband] or someone else to inflict bodily injury on her," or that the pregnancy resulted from spousal sexual assault already reported to the police.) Yet while observing that notification might appear a lesser intrusion on the woman's decision than obtaining spousal consent, the Supreme Court in *Planned Parenthood of Southeast Pennsylvania v. Casey* held that "the notice requirement will often be tantamount to the veto found unconstitutional in *Danforth*" and so clearly violates the holding in *Roe.*[13] Acknowledging the general social problem of spousal abuse, the Court was persuaded that some husbands, once notified about the wife's plans, might physically block or bully her from continuing with them. (In the twenty-five years since the *Casey* decision, social science studies have only strengthened this finding.)[14] In considering whether fathers had any legal interests in the fetus, the Court in *Casey* rejected the claim that a "father's interest in the fetus' welfare is equal to the mother's protected liberty, since it is an *inescapable biological fact* that the state regulation with respect to the fetus will have a far greater impact on the pregnant woman's bodily integrity than it will on the husband."[15]

Many men have views or preferences upon learning about a particular pregnancy. But whether they are delighted, opposed, or reconciled to a pregnancy they brought about, men remain, at least in a bodily sense, removed from the main event—"vicarious knowers" in Sandelowski's phrase.[16] This vicariousness may be diminishing as technologies like ultrasound now offer men a sensory stake in pregnancy earlier in time and closer in kind to that of the woman. And certainly fatherhood as a category of male endeavor has become more socially valued.[17] Fathers are now entitled to take family or parental leave when a child is born or becomes ill, and some do.[18] Nonetheless, women's physical connection to gestation and birth means that in twenty-first-century America, decisions about terminating a pregnancy are not in the end the man's to make. For many, this allocation of authority responds to an intuitive sense of fairness, and I do not argue otherwise.

I do argue that the steady focus on women's reproductive bodies as the nub of what abortion is about has costs. In tracing the development of the Supreme Court's abortion jurisprudence, Reva Siegel observes that "the physiological framework in which the Court reasons about reproductive regulation . . . obscures the gender-based judgments that may animate such regulations and the gender-based injuries they can inflict on women."[19] She calls this "reasoning from the body" and explains that it misconceives the core problem of women's reproductive situation. For the costs to women of unwanted motherhood are not just nine months of pregnancy and the messy business of birth but the social consequences of motherhood—the obligations of child raising, which, nursing aside, extend far beyond the body. *These* obligations, not childbearing, are what mark women's adult lives as different from men's, and as Siegel insists, these explain why the involuntary motherhood that results when abortion is unavailable as a matter of law is more accurately understood as a form of sex discrimination than as a denial of privacy. It is the impact on women's control of their lives, not the important but discrete impact on their bodies, that matters most.

In addition to the misdirection of legal doctrine, the focus on women's reproductive bodies has produced a ferociously maternalistic account of abortion: how it is talked about, portrayed, and regulated. The contributing factors are familiar. All women are imagined to be mothers someday; all girls are in a state of pre-motherhood. Until the latter decades of the twentieth century, a network of interlocking practices guided women big and little toward maternity, in part through women's lawful exclusion from most other areas of civic, scholarly, or commercial endeavor.[20] Motherhood was the site of women's social recognition, starting with Republican Motherhood after the American Revolution and the subsequent rise of what Ruth Bloch identified as the "moral mother," the selfless woman who put her children's interests above her own.[21] The duty and privilege of motherhood was used to explain why white women should not think too vigorously, or exercise, or vote, or work outside the home. Each of these activities was scientifically understood to put at risk "that part of [woman] which is sacred to heredity."[22] In 1873 concurring Justice Bradley explained why the Supreme Court was correct in upholding the state of Illinois's prohibition on married women practicing law: "The natural and proper timidity and delicacy which belongs to the female sex evidently unfits it for many of the occupations of civil life. The constitution of the family organization . . . indicates the domestic sphere as that which properly belongs to the domain and function of womanhood."[23] Such views about the domestic sphere have not lost all currency. News of pregnancy is still assumed by some to be a tiding of joy. Yet there is this from Lynn, a seventeen-year-old high school student: "The lady administering the pee test said, 'Congratulations, you're pregnant!' and I thought, 'Congratulations, you're an idiot!' I was in my gym clothes, obviously distraught."[24]

Abortion is the antithesis of all that women are traditionally understood to be and do. In the late twentieth century, those social expectations were met with a matching theory of female development based not on liberal conceptions of rights but on an "ethic of care" that specially marked the moral development of girls. *In a Different Voice,* Carol Gilligan's 1982 study of gendered differences in children's moral development, laid out the case. In contrast to the standard story that girls' moral development was stunted compared with that of men, Gilligan used a comparison between eleven-year-old children, Jake and Amy, to show that girls' moral development was grounded in a different value matrix. Theirs was organized around caring for others, boys' around a hierarchy of rights.[25] This redescription of women's moral capabilities felt good: women were not inferior and immature; they were instead caring to their core. *In a Different Voice* became massively influential among feminists across disciplines; we will return shortly to its application to abortion decision making.

The conceptualization of abortion as a women's issue has meant that women alone are the primary targets of efforts to shut down abortion through regulations and campaigns that are themselves saturated in maternalistic ideology of nurturance. Mandatory ultrasound statutes offer up fetal scans as a pre-birth pre-death portrait of one's child. Compulsory dissemination of adoption materials is meant to prod maternal sensibilities, the state reminding women that there is a softer, more altruistic way out. Women entering clinics are entreated not to murder their own babies. On occasion, witty, male-focused, and short-lived campaigns pop up urging, for example, male use of condoms, like the 1970s poster of a shaggy-haired pregnant young man.[26] But in the main, men who are implicated in an unwanted pregnancy are not picketed or prayed for.[27] Women carry the moral burden for everyone.

Is it possible to shake abortion loose from gender's grip? I propose to untether the subject of abortion from the anchor of motherhood by investigating what men would do if the disposition of an embryo or fetus were up to them. Taking women out of the picture opens up the subject of abortion decision making without the usual assumptions about the usual suspects shading the analysis. Might the decisions that people make about becoming parents turn out to be in some ways more generic than gendered?

This is not to deny that abortion is at core a woman's decision. The Supreme Court has already explained why men do not have a veto over her decision, either way. Yet something important is lost by considering abortion exclusively as a woman's issue, however much we agree that in the end women should make the call. How might the problem of an unwanted pregnancy be resolved when women are put to the side? What would men do if it were up to them? What factors make a pregnancy unwanted for a man? Because no man has ever had an abortion, more imaginative sources are necessary to ease us into thinking about men as abortion decision makers. Two examples, one from literature, the other from philosophy, yield clues and insights.

We begin with Mary Shelley's *Frankenstein*. Recall that after Victor Frankenstein breathes life into his creation (and things have gone rather badly around town), he strikes a bargain with the lonely monster. In exchange for the monster's promise to quit Europe forever, Frankenstein agrees to create a female monster to accompany him into exile. But the deal falls through, for after Frankenstein's "labour [on the new creature] was already considerably advanced," he pauses to "consider the effect of what [he] was doing."[28] Frankenstein ponders the possibility that "the fiendish couple" might themselves reproduce and propagate "a race of devils . . . upon the earth."[29] That proposition is too hideous to contemplate and as Frankenstein records in his diary, "with a sensation of madness on my promise of creating another like to him, and trembling with passion, I *tore to pieces the thing on which I was engaged.* The wretch saw me destroy the creature on whose future existence he depended for happiness, and with a howl of devilish despair and revenge, withdrew."[30] (There are echoes here of Supreme Court Justice Kennedy's vivid, horrified description in *Gonzales v. Carhart* of the intact dilation and extraction procedure.)

Literary critic Ellen Moers has observed that one reason *Frankenstein* registers so strongly with female readers is that "it articulates in unprecedented detail the most powerfully felt anxieties about pregnancy and parenting."[31] Certainly much has been written about Frankenstein's creation of the monster in relation to Mary Shelley's own maternal tribulations.[32] But let us for the moment accept Anne Moller's description of the novel as "first and foremost . . . about what happens when a man tries to procreate without a woman."[33] (Shelley helps us here: Frankenstein describes his work as his "confinement."[34]) His efforts are deliberate and intentional: first the monster, then the mate, then the decision to destroy the mate on eugenic grounds. *Frankenstein* is of course not science but science fiction. Still, it is useful to have before us so clear and powerful a depiction of male reproductive deliberation, and one that has intrigued for nearly 200 years.

The second imaginative example is philosopher Judith Jarvis Thompson's arresting hypothetical of the famous violinist.[35] A person (you, whether male or female) wakes up one morning to find that a world-famous violinist has been plugged in to your circulatory system by an organization of music lovers. The violinist is terribly sick and without your blood transfusing into his veins, he will die; hooked up to you, he will live. Annoying? Not to worry! The treatment he needs (your blood) is time limited; the violinist will be cured in only nine months. Analogizing to abortion, Thompson asks whether it is morally permissible to unhook the violinist now. Accepting for purposes of the argument that a fetus is a person, what does one person owe another with regard to the use of his or her body? Developing an argument from something like self-defense, Thompson suggests that so long as the blood provider has not voluntarily hooked the violinist up, nine months of bodily occupation by another may go too far. My interest here is less Thompson's conclusion than her approach to the decision. There is nothing sex-based about the blood the violinist needs:

the dilemma of whether to disconnect him could be anyone's. Thompson develops an argument about abortion that is unconnected to women's bodies—*any body* will do.

Putting aside both the literary account (however intriguing) and the philosophical one (however provocative), I am not asking what men would do if men (and not women) became pregnant. I am wary of a full-fledged gender swap for if childbearing and child rearing were magically reassigned to men, I suspect that men would simply be women, and women men, and the analysis of human behavior would likely remain the same, except women would be on top of the heap. I mean to keep men as we know them (recognizing, of course, the dangers of essentializing an entire sex). The question is: what would men do if the fate of a pregnancy or an embryo was up to them? If men's reasons for ending pregnancies turn out to resemble women's, there are implications for abortion's regulation. The concerns that so occupy lawmakers at present—convictions about women's borderline competence to understand what an abortion is or their inability to make a thoughtful decision without a cooling-off period—might seem less necessary, less fair, if men and women in fact think similarly about ending a pregnancy.

To figure out men and abortion, we need some data. We might borrow evidence from other forms of male reproductive behavior, the steps men take to ensure or to prevent progeny now or in the future. We know that many men value the reproductive potential of their genetic material: they have sperm frozen before deploying to Iraq or undergoing chemotherapy; they sell, donate, and bequeath their sperm.[36] Many protect themselves from unwanted or unintended procreation through contraceptive practices such as condoms and vasectomies, while others are nonchalant about risking pregnancy.[37] ("I left the method entirely up to her . . . whatever she wanted to use was fine with me 'cause I'm that kind of guy.")[38] Yet extrapolating from these forms of reproductive behavior takes us only so far. Neither safeguarding nor preventing conception is quite the same as destroying the products of conception; for most people, sperm do not have the same moral or emotional valence as a fetus: there isn't the entity that abortion operates upon.

There is of course polling data about men's views on abortion generally. We know, for example, that older white men who identify as evangelical have less liberal attitudes toward abortion than other men and that men's attitudes are more liberal when a pregnancy is unplanned or the woman's health is endangered.[39] Yet polling data are unconnected to any specific pregnancy and so cannot be taken as a proxy for action. The same problem arises with sociological studies, which focus either on men's retrospective views regarding the abortions of former girlfriends or their views regarding hypothetical abortion decisions with a present partner.[40] From these we learn that cohabiting men generally support whatever their partner wants to do and, perhaps not surprisingly, that the former boyfriends of women who actually aborted report that they were unready for fatherhood and wouldn't have wanted a kid with her anyway. Still, in all of this, we are stuck in the subjunctive and learn only what men think they would do at one remove from the action.

To get closer to the decisional bone, three circumstances provide insight not into what men might do but what they have done. The first involves disputes over the disposition of cryogenically frozen embryos (sometimes called pre-embryos) where it is the male progenitor who wants them destroyed. The second example concerns commercial surrogacy contracts between men seeking a biological child and women willing not only to be impregnated with the man's sperm but who also agree to abort the pregnancy under certain circumstances. These are in effect contracts for abortion. The third circumstance involves the fortunately rare cases in which men must decide whether to withdraw care from brain-dead or comatose pregnant women, understanding that to do so ends the fetus's life as well.

There are limitations in all three examples. The frozen embryo cases, for instance, work by analogy to abortion, although the decisions are to destroy an unimplanted embryo. Moreover, and importantly, in each of these categories, only the biology of pregnancy drops out and not the social role of parenting that follows birth. Deciding whether to terminate a pregnancy might well look different if the outcome of the decision were to include the daily work of parenting—the doctor's appointments, playdates, laundry, and so on—included within what Elizabeth Emens has called "domestic admin."[41] Another difference is the highly gendered reputational consequences of declining parenthood. A divorced mother awarded only visitation rights in a custody dispute draws attention; a father hardly at all. The difference between men and women is even greater when declining parenthood takes the form of the deliberate destruction of the pregnancy. For all these reasons, men who make or are authorized to make decisions about embryos or fetuses are not situated identically to women. We can keep these differences in mind as we look at the cases of frozen embryos, surrogacy contracts, and pregnant brain death in order to illuminate, as best we can, the question of what men would do. The plan is not to establish exact equivalences but to compare male explanations with what we know about the reasons women give for choosing abortion.

Frozen Embryos

A trove of cases from across the country introduces the problem. Each case involves frozen embryos created in happier times but whose proposed implantation is now challenged by one or other progenitor after the marital relationship has collapsed. The question is whether the embryos should be destroyed or whether they should be given to the party who wants them for procreative use or donation. Deciding what to do with a frozen embryo is perhaps as close to an abortion decision as a man can get. Because there is no pregnancy, the woman's body is no longer the determinative legal factor. The biology of gender—the reproductive circumstance on which abortion jurisprudence has traditionally fastened—falls out of the picture. But although there is no pregnancy, there is still a something (or someone). Indeed, for some the destruction of a pre-embryo is not an abortion by analogy but an abortion outright. This follows directly from the position in natural law thinking and in Roman Catholic theology that considers an embryo, whether inside or outside the womb, as a human person equal in moral worth to any other fetus or born person.[42]

In the early cases, courts struggled with how to characterize pre-embryos. Were they children so that custody rules should apply? Were they property subject to the rules of marital property division? Or were they something in between? Most courts have held that whatever the characterization (most commonly that they are property), their disposition should be guided by the terms of the contract entered into between the couple and the clinic. And almost all such contracts provide that embryos cannot be implanted without the continued consent of both parties.

In the absence of a contract, the question becomes whether anyone can be forced to become a genetic parent against his or her will through the use of the embryo by the other. Following the logic of *Roe,* the answer has been no. In most jurisdictions either progenitor can block the reproductive use of jointly created embryos. Yet what I am after here is not the law of frozen embryos but the facts of the cases. What reasons do men give for wanting to destroy their frozen embryos?

One of the earliest and most factually rich sources is the 1992 Tennessee case *Davis v. Davis.*[43] Junior and Mary Sue Davis were married in 1980. After a trying six-year history of failed natural pregnancies and seven unsuccessful rounds of in vitro fertilization (IVF), Junior filed for divorce (he later testified that he had hoped the birth of a child would improve the couple's troubled marriage). During the property settlement phase of the divorce, the parties were unable to agree on the disposition of their unused frozen embryos. Mary Sue originally wanted them implanted in herself and later in the litigation proposed to give them to an infertile couple; Junior wanted them gone.

At the trial Junior explained that his position stemmed from his own miserable childhood. At age five, his parents divorced and Junior and three brothers were sent to a Lutheran home for boys. He saw his father only three times before the father died, and although his mother visited monthly, Junior testified about the "severe problems" caused by the separation from his parents.[44] The "lack of opportunity to establish a relationship with his parents" and "the absence of his father" had left him with lifelong problems.[45] The trial court summarized Junior's testimony: "Because of his own shattered and disappointing childhood . . . [Junior] strenuously objects to bringing a child into the world who would suffer the same or a similar experience without any opportunity on his part to bond with his child."[46] Junior also opposed Mary Sue's later plan to donate the embryos on the ground that he would consider any child born of his genetic material to be his child and this would create a "great psychological and emotional burden" on him.[47]

The Tennessee Supreme Court ruled in Junior's favor.[48] Applying the holding in *Roe v. Wade,* it held that no one can be forced into parenthood against his or her will. The court also took note of the implied contractual understanding between Junior and Mary Sue that the embryos were to be used only in the context of an ongoing marriage. Immediately following the judgment, Junior had the embryos destroyed.

Five years later, a divorcing New York couple, Steve and Maureen Kass, were embroiled in a similar dispute.[49] Like the Davises, the Kasses had a long and difficult history of infertility treatment—five egg retrievals and nine attempts at implantation at a cost of some $75,000. In his submissions to the court, Steve explained that although he had agreed to IVF when he and his wife were married, he "vehemently opposed" his ex-wife's attempt to bear his genetic offspring outside their marriage.[50] This, he argued, echoing Junior Davis, would constitute an "enormous emotional, psychological and financial burden."[51] Despite Maureen's promise to waive all rights to child support for the future child, Steve was still concerned about the economic consequences of being that child's biological father. As in the *Davis* case, Steve prevailed.

Financial concerns loom large in a number of the cases. In a 2000 Alabama case, Patrick and Deborah Cahill had already conceived one child through IVF; their disagreement was over the three remaining embryos.[52] Patrick claimed that ex-wife Deborah wanted another child in part to obligate him financially; as he put it, "[This] would be another way for her to suck money out of me."[53] In a 2012 case from Montana, *In re Marriage of Johnson,* the parties were battling over the division of their sizeable assets (house, cabin, dental practice, gun collection) and their nine frozen embryos.[54] David Johnson was concerned about the effect of a post-divorce child on the eventual distribution of his estate; he wanted to protect the interests of his children from a previous marriage. Mary herself had argued that any subsequent child would have an interest in David's estate. Indeed, she contended that David was refusing her the embryos specifically to avoid this financial consequence. The Montana Supreme Court sent the matter back to a lower court to sort out.

But resistance to embryo implantation is not only a matter of fiscal reckoning. As an Iowa ex-husband Arthur (Trip) Witten stated, the financial burden "pales in comparison with the psychological burden of not knowing for the rest of a person's life if people they see and meet in the future might be their own child that was formerly a frozen embryo awarded to your former spouse."[55] This "out there problem" encompasses the pain and anxiety of knowing that one's genetic child exists in the world but is unknown to you. Steve Kass objected to the possibility of "his genetic offspring walk[ing] the earth without his love and guidance."[56] A less savory version of the argument arose in a 2009 Ohio case, *Karmasu v. Karmasu,* where the ex-husband was concerned that the use of his embryos, if donated to strangers, would put him at risk for "accidental incest."[57] He was, after all, "a single male who openly has relationships with any woman at or above the age of eighteen."[58] Without addressing that particular worry, the court held that the parties had agreed at the outset that any unused embryos would be donated to infertile couples and awarded the embryos to the clinic.[59] Mr. Karmasu was not alone in wanting to have fun instead of children. In the British case of *Evans v. United Kingdom,* twenty-six-year-old Howard Johnston opposed his thirty-one-year-old ex-girlfriend's use of the couple's frozen embryos because, as he explained in an interview, he was a young man with a rising salary who wanted to "go out and enjoy himself."[60] This was his moment to "be himself and live on his own."[61] Yet the story is rarely age-appropriate hedonism alone; financial and relationship issues creep in as well. In another English case ex-husband Wayne had concerns about "a child coming after me for maintenance" and the fact that the dispute over the embryos was proving "very upsetting for my [current] girlfriend."[62]

Returning to the unhappy Cahills from Alabama, there was yet another reason why ex-husband Patrick wanted the embryos destroyed: his hatred of his former wife. As Patrick told one interviewer, "there's no way I want her having my children. I certainly don't trust her to run off with my cells," elaborating that "it's like being forced to have sex with your ex-wife and have more children with her. Would you want to do that?"[63] Similar sentiments were expressed in *Roman v. Roman,* where the husband's lawyer stated that his client simply didn't "want to bring a child into a relationship that is already divorced and so acrimonious."[64] In a 2012 Pennsylvania case, Bret Reber contended that should his ex-wife produce a child from their frozen embryos, the two would be in "constant battle" over how the child should be raised and that such impasses would "require frequent court intervention and resources to resolve custody and support issues."[65]

Alongside the specter of a miserable ongoing relationship with a former spouse is the troubling prospect of a relationship with the prospective child, should the eggs be hatched by an ex-wife.[66] Even though the child would come into being under protest, many men expected a paternal relationship would follow. In *Roman v. Roman,* the husband stated that "if my DNA does bring a child in this world, I would want to be a father in every sense of the word, as [in] financial, emotional, spiritual, soccer, little league, [and] every [thing] else in between."[67] Invoking his own childhood experiences as an adopted child, Bret Reber explained that he did not want his child to feel "that missing link that there is somebody out there . . . that they are not able to obtain or learn from."[68] Bret was further worried about the impact of the new child on the child he already had with his current partner: "[I] would have to explain . . . that there is somebody else out there."[69] The post-divorce child is understood to implicate emotional and financial relationships between the protesting parent and children of the original marriage, of a present marriage, and of future marriages or relationships, as existing regimes of blended families become even more complicated.

Contracts for Abortion

Contracts for commercial surrogacy are a second source for understanding what makes a pregnancy unwanted for a man. Let me first offer a quick review of how surrogacy contracts operate in states like California, Virginia, and Nebraska, where such contracts are legal. In "traditional" surrogacy, a woman promises that she will be artificially inseminated with the man's sperm, carry the pregnancy to term, and relinquish her parental rights in the infant once born in favor of the man, all in exchange for the man's promise to pay her a specific sum. Fees in the United States now range from about $40,000 to $170,000; some surrogacy centers, such as Growing Generation, now offer their own financing plans.[70] In "gestational surrogacy," the bargain is similar except that instead of artificial insemination, the woman is implanted with an existing embryo made up of the man's sperm and another woman's egg. While the exchange of money for insemination and gestation or implantation and gestation is the essence of the deal, subsidiary promises are also exchanged between the parties. These subsidiary promises are often quite important: the woman's promise not to have sexual intercourse with her husband at the time of the inseminations, for example, or her promise not to smoke or take recreational drugs during the pregnancy.

Our interest is in one particular promise: the woman's agreement to terminate the pregnancy if prenatal testing reveals a fetal condition that the commissioning man has specified in the contract is a ground for termination. Contracting is a standard mechanism to secure one's preferences about almost anything, and here preferences about quality control of offspring, for lack of a more congenial phrase, have become contractual rights. Identifying what conditions trigger this right adds to the list of men's reasons for desiring abortion. Contract law offers a distinct vantage point into the question of why men choose to abort on account of fetal anomaly. Married couples can decide such matters when circumstances arise; parties dealing at arm's length have to figure out their preferences ahead of time.

An early example of such a clause is found in the 1985 contract between Mary Beth Whitehead and William Stern in the well-known "Baby M" surrogacy case. In this case the New Jersey Supreme Court refused to enforce a surrogacy contract after Mrs. Whitehead kept the baby and Mr. Stern sued to get the baby back. The court held that surrogacy for pay was too close to state prohibitions on baby selling and on payments for adoption. Although the contract was declared unenforceable on general policy grounds, it is still worth looking at the details of the deal. Paragraph 13 of the Whitehead–Stern Surrogate Parenting Agreement provided that Mrs. Whitehead would "not abort the child once conceived" unless an abortion was necessary either for Whitehead's health or because "the child has been determined by [the inseminating] physician to be physiologically abnormal."[71] In the latter circumstance, Paragraph 13 stated that upon Stern's demand, Whitehead would have an abortion. (If the abortion took place after the fourth month of pregnancy, her compensation was reduced from $10,000 to $1,000.) If the abortion provision had been triggered, would a court have ordered Mrs. Whitehead to abort so that Mr. Stern would get what he bargained for? Unlikely. *Roe v. Wade* locates the core of the abortion right in women and this may be one constitutional right that cannot be waived. This explains why the trial court in *Baby M* specially held that although the surrogacy contract was generally enforceable, the abortion clause was not.[72]

Although contractual promises to abort are legally unenforceable, these provisions regularly show up as boilerplate, or standard printed terms, in surrogacy contracts. Professional journals provide family lawyers with suggested wording for abortion clauses.[73] What function do such "in terrorem clauses" serve if a court will not enforce them? One purpose is to scare the less sophisticated party into thinking that the clause *is* enforceable so that the party complies because she thinks she has to. Some contracts attempt to impose something like a moral duty on the woman to keep her promise: "The Parties recognize that the Surrogate has the constitutional right to abort or not abort the pregnancy, however, the Parties intend to conform, to the best of their ability, to the following terms of this Agreement."[74] The agreements then include terms suggesting that the woman also has a legal duty to abort: "The Surrogate waives any rights she may have to abort the pregnancy, except for medical reasons"; and "if the fetus(es) has been determined by any designated physician to be physically or psychologically abnormal, the decision to abort the pregnancy or not to abort the pregnancy shall be the sole decision of the Genetic Father and Intended Mother."[75] (The language is modified when same-sex couples commission a pregnancy.)

And commissioning men, sometimes along with their wives, have indeed demanded that surrogates abort a pregnancy. The wording of the abortion clauses is generally broad, giving the man wide discretion about the triggered diagnosis. To introduce some objective measure into the process, the clauses usually require a physician to confirm that the malady or condition specified in the contract actually exists. For example, in a 2013 case, the contract provided for abortion in case of "severe abnormality." After the fetus was diagnosed with a cleft palate, heart defects, and a brain cyst, the commissioning couple invoked the abortion provision. The couple explained that they did not want the child once born to suffer as had their other children who were born with the same conditions and spent months of their early lives in hospital.[76] When the surrogate refused to terminate the pregnancy, the couple offered her an additional $10,000 to do so.[77] (The surrogate, who did not want to keep the child herself, refused again; the child is now being raised by an adoptive family.) In another surrogacy case, upon seeing the impaired infant immediately after its birth, the commissioning man, Alexander Malahoff, announced that this simply could not be his biological son and refused to take custody. (The infant had, among other things, microcephaly and severe neuromuscular disorder.) Subsequent testing revealed that Malahoff was in fact not the biological father, who turned out to be the surrogate's husband; neither Malahoff nor the surrogate took custody of the child.[78]

Abortions have been requested in surrogacy cases where the fetus was the wrong sex (girl twins when a boy was desired; boy twins when the couple wanted a girl) and in cases involving the wrong number of fetuses (based on an oral agreement that the surrogate would abort one fetus if pregnancy resulted in twins).[79] The issue of "multiples" is now often provided for through special "selective reduction" clauses in which the surrogate agrees to reduce (abort) some embryos if "three (3) or more fetuses" result from the embryo transfer.[80]

Abortion clauses in surrogacy contracts provide insight into the kinds of fetal characteristics—whether abnormality, disability, or numerocity—that make a fetus unacceptable. They identify preferences for the kind of baby that a commissioning father is willing to raise as his own. It is impossible to know how many contractually based requests are made or how many terminations are carried out voluntarily; we know only that men try to protect themselves from the obligation of parenting a particular kind of child by bargaining for an abortion option.

At least one contract for abortion has been litigated outside the context of surrogacy. In an interesting and much overlooked Missouri decision, an unmarried adult woman (LG) informed her father (HAG) that she was pregnant and planned to stay that way.[81] HAG then informed LG he would cut her out of his will unless LG terminated her pregnancy, in which case HAG promised that he would reinstate the terms of his original will. LG thought it over, agreed, and aborted the pregnancy. Following HAG's death it turned out that he had not reinstated the terms of the first will. LG then sued her father's estate for breach of contract, seeking the amount she would have received had he kept his promise.

In defending the suit, the estate made two arguments. It first argued that there was no legal contract between father and daughter because to permit people to contract with one another for abortion violates public policy. The New Jersey Supreme Court had used public policy in striking down the surrogacy contract in *Baby M.,* and HAG's estate was hoping for a similar ruling: no liability for the broken promise because the deal was no good from the start. The estate additionally argued, somewhat ironically, that because LG had necessarily been coerced into the agreement, the contract should not be enforced under the doctrine of duress. Duress in contract law means that one can be persuaded or cajoled or convinced to make a particular promise, but the promise cannot have been extracted through oppressive or unfair pressure.

In rejecting both of these arguments, the Missouri Court of Appeals situated abortion promises in an interesting economic framework. The court rejected the proposition that a woman's promise to abort is necessarily involuntary: "Even if the . . . plaintiff was induced or persuaded to have an abortion it does not conclusively follow that the decision to have an abortion was *coerced*."[82] The court held that decisions about unwanted pregnancy often involve a cost–benefit analysis and that part of the calculation may well be financial. At least some of the costs to LG of not aborting were readily quantifiable; she loses a share of her father's estate. (Women college athletes who become pregnant during the season face a similar calculation in that they lose their scholarships if they remain pregnant.[83])

The court further held that the bargain between LG and HAG did not violate Missouri public policy. Nothing in their bargain constituted unlawful consideration. That is, because abortion is legal, a promise to abort could be an acceptable "quid" for a desired financial "quo." This conclusion was probably easier for the court to reach since LG had already terminated her pregnancy; it surely would not have required her to abort if she had been the one to change her mind. The decision offers a rare public characterization of an abortion decision as the reasonable subject of bargaining. Of course, in most cases the "bargaining" is internal to the woman herself as she balances the costs of motherhood against her present life.

What did HAG get out of the deal? One possibility, suggested by the court, is that the bargain may have facilitated "family harmony and reconciliation," which are both "naturally encouraged as a matter of public policy."[84] Or perhaps HAG wanted to avoid the social embarrassment he anticipated for himself (or for LG) in having a non-marital grandchild by this particular guy. All we can be sure about is that preventing his daughter's single motherhood by promising to restore her interest in his estate was worth it to HAG, and the court accepted that the trade was fair.

Post-Mortem Pregnancy and Other Catastrophes

Post-mortem pregnancy presents another example of male decision making which, like the facts in *L. G. v. H. A. G,* involves an existing pregnancy, except that the woman herself is no longer in a position to decide anything. Consider the case of thirty-three-year-old Marlise Munoz who, fourteen weeks pregnant with her second child, collapsed in her kitchen in Fort Worth, Texas, in 2013. She had suffered a stroke, most likely caused by a blood clot in her lung. Munoz was immediately taken to the nearby John Peter Smith Hospital and put on a ventilator, but doctors at the hospital soon declared her to be brain-dead.

Munoz's sad story introduces the circumstance of what is sometimes called "post-mortem pregnancy."[85] The term refers to a pregnant woman who is pronounced brain-dead—that is, she has suffered "irreversible cessation of all functions of the entire brain, including the brain stem."[86] She cannot be resuscitated, treated, or brought back to life; the "entire brain is destroyed just as if decapitation had occurred."[87] What then becomes of the pregnancy? Historically, the fetus would either be quickly removed by Cesarean section or die soon with its mother.[88] Now, however, it is possible for a brain-dead pregnant woman to be "maintained"—dead but her organs working through artificial support—for the purpose of incubating a nonviable fetus until it can live (with substantial support) outside the woman's body. Medical journals detail the complications of caring for the woman's body under such circumstances: the provision of nutrition and oxygen, the regulation of body temperature, electrical impulses, skin condition, and so on.[89]

But although protocols establish how to maintain a brain-dead woman's body, there is a question about who decides whether it *should* be maintained or whether, as with non-pregnant brain death, there is no further intervention. After all, doctors have an ethical duty not to provide meaningless "care" to a corpse that cannot benefit from it.[90] On some accounts, pregnancy complicates the matter by providing another patient—the fetus—who, for the moment, is still alive. Who decides which course to follow? The general rule is that the decision to withdraw life support from a brain-dead pregnant woman is made by the next of kin, unless she has formally designated someone else.[91] In the

Munoz case, Marlise's husband Erick, as next of kin, directed the hospital to withdraw the life support in accordance with his wife's wishes. Both Marlise and Erick were paramedics and in the course of their work they had discussed end-of-life issues with one another, including their mutual requests not to continue on life support in the case of brain death. Erick's decision to withdraw care from Marlise thus adds a new and important factor to the arsenal of reasons why men have terminated a pregnancy: in this case to effectuate the woman's own wishes. On this basis, some husbands have continued their wife's life support until fetal viability, and others, like Erick Munoz, have not.[92]

But it is just here that the story becomes more complicated. For when Erick asked for his wife's life support to be withdrawn, the hospital refused to do so.[93] The problem was not insufficient evidence regarding Marlise's preferences; in addition to Erick's testimony, Marlise's parents confirmed their daughter's wishes. The basis of the hospital's refusal was Section 166.049 of the Texas Health and Safety Code. This subsection of the statute on advance directives creates an exception to the general rule authorizing the withholding of medical care from a patient in "a terminal or irreversible condition."[94] Section 166.049 provides that "life-sustaining treatment" may not be withheld when a patient is pregnant.[95]

Erick Munoz sought a judicial ruling on the applicability of the subsection to Marlise's circumstances, and in a short two-paragraph decision, Tarrant County District Court Judge R. H. Wallace decided in Erick's favor.[96] Judge Wallace held that Section 166.049 did not apply to the facts of the case because Marlise was not in terminal or irreversible condition; "Mrs. Munoz is dead."[97] He then ordered the hospital in no uncertain terms "to pronounce Mrs. Munoz dead and remove . . . all 'life-sustaining' treatment from the body of Marlise Munoz."[98]

In other states the matter has been decided quite differently. The facts in a 1986 Georgia case are similar to those in *Munoz*.[99] Donna Piazzi, sixteen weeks pregnant, was declared brain-dead after falling unconscious, probably as the result of a drug overdose. When her husband asked for all life support to be withdrawn, the hospital petitioned for a court order to keep Donna's body maintained until the fetus became viable, a period of about two months. The *Piazzi* case was complicated in another way, in that another man claimed that he was the father of the fetus, and he wanted the life support continued.

The Georgia Superior Court of Richmond County decided the matter not by resolving the competing claims of the lawful husband and the possible progenitor but on the basis of the state's own interests in the fetus. Although no statute then governed the matter, the court declared that "public policy in Georgia requires the maintenance of life support systems for a brain dead mother so long as there exists a reasonable possibility that the fetus may develop and survive."[100] In a curious move, the court analogized the withholding of life support during pregnancy to an abortion, holding that whatever rights Donna might have had under *Roe* to end her pregnancy were "extinguished upon the brain death of Donna Piazzi."[101] To further thwart the efforts of Donna's husband, the court appointed a guardian to represent the best interests of the fetus in the matter. Not surprisingly, the guardian advised the court that those interests required the life support systems to be maintained.[102] Donna's body became an incubator as required under the common law of Georgia until after the baby's delivery. After the delivery, Donna was taken off life support; the baby died thirty-two hours after its birth.[103]

What would the result have been if Marlise Munoz had not been declared brain-dead but had suffered a lesser form of catastrophic neurological injury and was either in a coma or in a persistent vegetative state? The general rule is that unless the patient had already designated a specific person or signed an advance directive stating that she wanted no extraordinary measures under such circumstances, the next of kin decides whether to withdraw treatment. But as in so many other areas, pregnancy disrupts the legal protocols that would otherwise govern, such as carrying out an advanced directive or "living will," mechanisms much heralded by the medical profession and by patients as an exercise of a person's free will until the very end.

Yet more than half the states have enacted legislation denying effect to an advanced directive if the patient is pregnant.[104] Some exclusions focus on the woman: "This designation cannot be used to make a medical treatment decision to withhold or withdraw treatment from a patient who is pregnant that would result in the pregnant patient's death."[105] Others, like the Minnesota statute, offer a different objective: "In the case of a living will of a patient that the attending physician knows is pregnant, the living will must not be given effect as long as it is possible that the fetus could develop to the point of live birth with continued application of life-sustaining treatment."[106] Had Marlise Munoz been in a chronic vegetative state—alive but with no hope of recovery because of the massive damage to her brain—Erick could not have secured his wife's death with the dignity she sought even if Marlise had already executed an advanced directive.[107]

Men, Women, and Unwanted Pregnancies

In mining the frozen embryo cases, surrogacy contracts, and post-mortem pregnancies for their facts, a picture emerges of men's concerns about becoming a father. Because the circumstances that give rise to their decisions are somewhat unusual, the assembled "database" may seem relatively small, especially in contrast to the robust empirical data regarding women's reasons for terminating a pregnancy. Even so, these instances tell us some important things about fathers and fetuses and about the role of gender in abortion. So let us compare men's reasons in the three areas where men have had a say with women's reasons more generally. The comparison produces some striking findings. Perhaps most striking is the degree of overlap between the two sets of factors.

In the embryo cases, men's explanations fall into three general categories: relationship issues, children's welfare, and the interruption of one's own life or plans. Relationship issues refer to concerns about the difficulties of personal relationships imagined to follow from the birth of a new post-divorce child. In almost every frozen embryo case, a strong objection to implantation in the former wife has been the husband's dismay in contemplating ongoing contact with "that woman" by virtue of a shared genetic child. Men described the unpleasant entanglements wrought by shared custody as insurmountable. This is not surprising; the couple was already involved in contentious divorce, which in several cases arose amidst a trying period of infertility treatment that brought about the embryos in the first place.[108] Even when no embryos are involved, family law has recognized the problems generated by continuing contact between sparring exes. This is why spousal maintenance increasingly takes the form of a lump sum payment in order to avoid the monthly hit of hostility. Many states have dropped the once popular presumption of awarding joint physical custody in all contested divorces on the principle that without cooperative interaction between the parents, joint physical custody works against children's sense of stability and well-being.[109] In the embryo cases, accusations of bad faith added to existing antagonisms with allegations that the woman knew perfectly well the embryos were to be used only if the couple was still together or charges that the ex-husband was intentionally denying the ex-wife her last chance for a biological child.[110] Destroying frozen embryos operates as a preemptive strike against the travails of parenting with the wrong person.

Relationship concerns also extend to the imagined relationship—or nonrelationship—with the future child. This is something different from worries over the future child's material or emotional welfare but is a form of injury affecting the father himself: the anxiety caused by knowing the child is being raised either by the hated ex-wife or by a loving couple who may seem perfectly nice, but who really knows in this age of divorce? One way or another the child could end up being raised by a single mother. In several cases the psychological burden of this uncertainty was intensified by specters of the father's own unhappy childhood. A final relational anxiety was more existential. This is the disquieting fact of the child's mere existence, even if it is well cared for— in Steve Kass's words, the burden of knowing that his "offspring walk the earth" without his supervision or love.[111] Some men said that to avoid this they would rather step up and care for the child, even though they preferred the child had not come into being in the first place.

In a longitudinal 2013 study of 954 women (the Turn-away Study), one-third reported "partner-related reasons" as one reason they sought an abortion.[112] Forty-eight percent of the 1,209 women surveyed in the 2005 Guttmacher study linked relationship issues with not wanting to raise a child alone.[113] Sometimes the pregnancy itself produces or reveals problems with the relationship as the man moves from partner to potential father in the eyes of the woman. One twenty-three-year-old stated, "My boyfriend said things like, 'I don't have to worry about it until it pops out.' I just looked at him and couldn't imagine raising a child with him. It was an epiphany."[114] Another woman described a decision made in the context of domestic violence: "My boyfriend terrorized me. At some point, I decided it was safer to have him in my life than cut him out. But when I got pregnant, I knew right away I didn't want a lifelong connection to that person. I was right; when we later broke up, he sawed my clothes in half and poured corn syrup in my gas tank."[115] Of course, relationship issues need not involve violence to fall below the mark. Writer Joyce Maynard describes a decision made with her then husband: "Back when I had agreed to the abortion, I said it was because we didn't have the money, but the truth ran deeper, and was more ominous than that. We didn't have the love, I think."[116]

Like men, women too confront the "out there" problem: the unknown child of unknown whereabouts haunting the future. In some states the option of adoption is incorporated into informed consent procedures through the compulsory provision of information about adoption. Like the advice of pro-life counselors, such state mandated material makes clear that you don't have to become a mother: just complete the pregnancy and adoptive parents will take over. From this perspective, the situation is very win-win: only the briefest of motherhoods for the pregnant woman and a baby for the desirous couple. But the "win" chalked up for the birth mother misses two important pieces. There is the fact of pregnancy—itself a highly visible and taxing physical state—and the worry that bearing the child will make giving it up an emotional impossibility. Women fear that continuing the pregnancy will not lead to adoption at all but rather, through bonding, to unwanted, chin-up motherhood: "If I go that far, I'm attached. I cannot just give my baby away to someone."[117] Abortion operates to tie oneself to the mast of the core decision not to become a parent.

And if a woman can see her way to adoption, there is still, for some, the intolerable awareness of her child out there somewhere. This sentiment was behind early birth mother support groups, such as Concerned United Birthmothers in the 1970s, whose efforts led to the reform of adoption law by opening it up and unsealing records. But giving birth mothers the option of choosing the adopting parents, as most states now do, has not been the antidote to abortion. Women are not sure that things will really turn out all right with the nice couple, and they note that maybe the couple isn't all *that* nice; many open adoptions seem to close rather quickly once the couple has the baby.

A second reason for destroying frozen embryos given by men was concern about the future child's well-being in a more material sense. The provision contemplated was economic, emotional, and physical—"kicking the ball around," as one progenitor mentioned earlier. Present financial concerns mattered, but they were rarely the primary reason for rejecting post-divorce implantation. Men in the frozen embryo cases tended to be older and perhaps more financially stable; they were after all able to afford fertility treatment or had jobs with infertility insurance coverage. The arrival of a new child was not imagined as economically catastrophic but rather as disruptive of financial obligations to existing children, including dilution of an existing heir's expected share. Men entering surrogacy contracts are also generally well-off and less concerned about adding children than about adding certain kinds of children.

In contrast, for women, financial concerns are paramount. Seventy-three percent of the Guttmacher subjects said they could not financially afford to have a baby at present. In the Turn-away Study, 40 percent of the 954 women interviewed reported financial concerns as one of their main reasons for choosing abortion, and 6 percent stated it was their only reason: "I'm unemployed, no health insurance, and could not qualify for any government assisted aid, and even if my fiancé decided to hurry up and get married, I still wouldn't have been covered under his health insurance for [this pregnancy]."[118] Thus quite apart from prospective concerns about money, the more immediate costs of pregnancy also factor into abortion decisions. Although material provision mostly concerns money, the desire to provide for one's child is not imagined as mere basic provision. As one twenty-year-old woman put it, "I would want to give my child, like, everything in the world."[119] This sometimes includes the presence of a father: "My father was hardly around, and I was like, I'm not doing that to my child. I won't."[120]

The third category that mattered to men about potential fatherhood was disruption of life as presently lived. One expression of this was the problem of starting to parent anew at a time when one's family was considered complete. In the frozen embryo cases several men said they were absolutely done—that they were old enough to be a new child's grandfather or that they had children from a prior marriage or from a subsequent relationship. Very few of these men expressed concern about the interruption of career or education by virtue of another child. This makes sense. Men's careers are rarely disrupted or disfigured by the birth of children. Several men also mentioned their plans to have some fun as a single man, including kicking up of heels. Women rarely present their decision as the chance for more fun, though now and again a description of how much would be lost by unwanted motherhood slips in: "I still want to be free and have my youth. I don't want to have it all gone because of one experience."[121]

In contrast to male responses, three-fourths of the women in the Guttmacher study reported that their decision to abort rested in part on their assessment that a new baby would interfere with education, work, or the ability to care for dependents.[122] Although this is something of a composite reason, women are quite clear about how a new child will compromise present obligations and endeavors. Consider the spirited statement of Abigail, age twenty-eight: "From the time I was a teenager, the idea of having an abortion if pregnant was a no-brainer. I had this idea you can't let life get in the way of your plans. My friend drove me."[123] For other women, the decision is not quite so hardwired and subject to greater internal debate. Still, the dislocation or burdening of present work and future plans is a crucial reason in every account of why women choose abortion.[124] Aborting women who were already mothers—as two-thirds of women who choose abortion are—were very clear about this: "I have a 3-month-old already. If I had had that baby, he wouldn't even be one [year old by the time the baby came]."[125]

That the welfare of existing children may be put at risk by the arrival of another child is a statutory ground for choosing abortion under the U.K. Abortion Act, where women must provide one of three reasons for what would otherwise be a crime. The ground most frequently invoked is that continuing the pregnancy would harm the pregnant woman's physical or mental health or that of her existing children.[126] In the United States, no reasons need be given for why one is choosing abortion, although the welfare of existing children looms large. This concern is linked not only to a woman's finances but to her strength, energy, and patience as well. A single thirty-nine-year-old mother of two gave body to the decision: "One of my children is disabled. She don't walk or talk, and she just got out of the hospital after having some back surgery, and it takes a lot of time. . . . I could not spend as much time with my nine-year-old. . . . I can't have another baby right now."[127]

Unlike the variety of reasons given in the embryo cases, the abortion clauses in surrogacy contracts announce one particular ground for choosing abortion: fetal disability. Bargaining for the right to demand termination has a rather cold cast to it, perhaps because the criteria for termination are set out in black and white even before any fetus exists.[128] We have already seen the kinds of abnormalities that trigger the clause "severe abnormality," "physically or psychologically abnormal," or "physiologically abnormal." Here it seems the decisions of men and women are similar. Although women do not formally declare themselves ahead of time, abortion rates for fetal anomalies, particularly for disorders of the central nervous system, are high. Over 90 percent of pregnant women who receive a fetal diagnosis for Down syndrome, anencephaly, or spina bifida decide to abort.[129] Their decisions are sometimes made jointly with partners; an interview study reveals that couples use different narrative conventions (God's will, nature's way, too late to choose) to explain their decision to themselves and to their communities.[130]

In sum, it turns out that most of men's reasons for terminating a pregnancy or destroying an embryo—wrong time, wrong partner, enough kids, too tired, already committed enough—are strikingly similar to the reasons given by women for ending an unwanted pregnancy. Both sexes want to do right by the children they already have and the ones they expect in the future. Recognizing that parenthood is not just a change in parental status but a change in everything, they also want to do right by themselves. Differences seem to fall less along absolute gender lines than along such markers as situational stability, relationships, support networks, finances, and stamina.

If men's and women's reasons for terminating a pregnancy are substantially similar, what might this mean for how abortion decision making is regulated at law? Before a man destroys an embryo or unhooks his wife from life support, should he too have a forty-eight-hour waiting period, be made to look at ultrasound pictures, and listen to physician scripts about the anatomical markers of this very fetus? That seems hard to imagine. The aim is not to bring men within the jurisdiction of current abortion regulation but to help pull women out from under it. If men's decisions not to parent a particular child seem reasonable and prudent, ought not the same reasons from women similarly count as sound and acceptable? Logic (and basic equality) suggest they should.

But neither logic nor equality determines views about abortion. The problem comes down not to what the reasons are but to how they are characterized. Women who choose abortion are selfish; men who destroy frozen embryos are self-regarding. Choosing to terminate an unwanted pregnancy looks selfish even when the decision is motivated by maternal obligations to others. From certain pro-life perspectives, altruism toward existing children (or parents or partner or self) cannot trump the fact that this decision is something far more than rejecting motherhood: it is an active killing. For those who see abortion in these terms, no reason can balance the taking of an unborn life.[131]

Three additional items swirl under and around the decision-making process for women that get little play in the narratives of men. They are sex, stigma, and selfishness, and a closer look at each helps us understand why women's reasons read differently, even when those reasons are pretty much the same as men's. Take the simple matter of sex, by which I mean sexual intercourse. Abortion is never the starting point for an unwanted pregnancy but rather the consequence of two earlier matters, sexual intercourse and conception. The possibility of publicity around these two factors contributes to women's abortion decisions. In one study the revelation of sexual activity was reported by a quarter of women interviewed as a ground for their decision to abort; a third chose abortion in part to keep the pregnancy from becoming public knowledge. The predicament is not hard to understand. Absent complete concealment, pregnancy will announce itself, and once it does, sooner or later there must either be a baby or an explanation about why there is not. This explains why some women mask abortions as miscarriages. Pregnancy can be a devastating revelation. Consider the teenager whose parents believe that she is the kind of girl they raised her to be. Pregnancy is not just proof of sex (though it is surely that); it is evidence that the daughter is not the upstanding and trustworthy girl her parents thought she was. On this score, women are careful even about where they buy a home pregnancy test, concerned about casual surveillance at the checkout counter. One woman bought her test kit out of town because she didn't want to share this intimate moment in her life "with the public (or, at least with the people in the grocery store)."[132] Compare this with some of the embryo fathers who, in the midst of litigation seeking to destroy embryos, were out there giving press interviews about what active sex lives they lead and hope for.

The second point of divergence is that in neither the embryo nor the surrogacy cases was stigma mentioned by men. One explanation, at least in the embryo cases, is that there was too little to feel stigmatized about destroying; it was only an unimplanted "pre-embryo."[133] Certainly the men who include abortion clauses in surrogacy contracts do not worry about stigma; their legal actions become part of the public record and generate news coverage aplenty. What explains men's willingness to be exposed as a father who rejects a disabled child? One explanation is that fatherhood has a much weaker center of gravity than does motherhood. Child abuse aside, men are not condemned for their parenting deficiencies with the same intensity as are women. We expect less of men in terms of duty, of sacrifice, of talent. Men are not ensnared in the web of connection and caring relationalism.

In contrast, women are keenly aware of the stigmatizing nature of an abortion decision. But what a tight space a woman with an unwanted pregnancy has to maneuver in. Abortion stigma is wedged in between many other stigmas: careless, indulgent sex on one side and accusations (public and internalized) either of baby killing or of abandoning one's baby to strangers on the other. The message is inserted directly into the informed consent disclosures required in many states with no attempt at camouflage. As one doctor who testified in a successful lawsuit brought against North Carolina's mandatory ultrasound statute stated, "requiring me to describe the pictures to her if she says she does not want it sends the message that her decision is wrong or immoral or selfish and that she should reconsider."[134] One woman who chose abortion explained it this way: "Truly pro-life people should go light on the judgment, because shame motivates abortions."[135]

This leads to the question of selfishness. Why is deciding to end a pregnancy selfish when made by a woman and acceptably self-regarding when made by a man? The answer takes us back to gendered notions of maternal duty and altruism. Mothers do not harm their children. Mothers suck it up for their kids and for their fetuses.

But the idea of selfishness and altruism as moral opposites requires a closer look. Philosopher Jean Hampton has argued that not all altruism is morally acceptable.[136] Hampton is not against altruism, but she insists on evaluating it alongside other standard conceptions of morality, such as recognition of one's "own inherent worthiness."[137] Here, selflessness as an absolute virtue loses its footing. "'Altruistic' behavior is morally wrong," Hampton states, "when it prevents one from paying moral respect to oneself."[138] Morality involves self-regard in that it "demands of each of us that we take a certain kind of pride in ourselves."[139] Choosing in favor of yourself is not only a morally permissible choice but "in some circumstances the morally *required* choice."[140] The analysis echoes Judith Jarvis Thompson's conclusion that there are limits to Good Samaritanism: absent any voluntary undertaking, no one is required to "make large sacrifices to sustain the life of another who has no right to demand them."[141] Thompson says a person may choose self; Hampton's claim is that sometimes a person must choose self. Julia Ward Howe expressed the idea in a letter to her sister: "It is a blessed thing to be a mother, but there are bounds to all things, and no woman is under any obligation to sacrifice the whole of her existence to the mere act of bringing children into the world."[142]

Here we have a new knot to untie. How can Hampton's reconception of self-oriented moral decision making square with relational feminism and the ethics of care? Carol Gilligan found a way to accommodate both in her interview study of twenty-nine pregnant women trying to decide whether to end their pregnancies. By the end of the study, twenty-two women chose abortion, four had babies, two miscarried, and two couldn't decide in time to be counted. While these numbers hardly sound like feminist relationalism at work, Gilligan explains that they involve a three-stage process of getting to yes. She observed that in the first stage, the women acted on their own desires and wanted to abort (selfishness). At stage two, they reconnected to their relationally centered selves, recognized the ethic of care (goodness), and wavered on abortion. Finally, the women came to understand that their own needs are included within the ethic of care. In this way, women were able to both choose abortion and stay true to their relational selves.

Maybe. Critiquing Gilligan's three-part progression, law professors Pam Karlan and Daniel Ortiz observe that on Gilligan's own terms, "webs [seem to] give way to hierarchies and the ethic of care unravels to resemble the logic of justice."[143] Recognizing that one's own needs should be valued alongside the needs of others acknowledges the very principle—equality—that "animates the logic of justice."[144] I introduce Gilligan's abortion study not to take on (or apart) the decades-long debates among feminists regarding relational feminism.[145] Rather, I want to use Gilligan's study as one final example of the similarities between men and women as they reason their way to decisions about abortion.

In the frozen embryo and surrogacy cases, men's reasoning turned out to be quite similar to the reasons invoked by women. In Gilligan's study, women's reasoning turned out to be similar to men's, as on Karlan and Ortiz's persuasive account, the women made their decisions with the same self-regard that is usually (and blamelessly) attributed to men. The issue is not "why can't a woman be more like a man" but how men's decisions already mirror women's when it comes to choosing parenthood.

The conclusion is an important one. Not only does it complicate our relatively simplistic thinking on these matters, but it throws into question the implicit (or sometimes all-too-explicit) characterization of women's abortion decisions as hasty, uninformed, coerced, and above all self-centered. This in turn is used to justify restrictions and obstacles to women's access to the procedure. It is time to look anew and straighten out how all this reasoning is represented. Now that we are alert to how similarly both men and women step up to the problem of unwanted pregnancy, empathy and mutual understanding across gender lines become possible. Perhaps this is why couples are so often united in their decisions about abortion or childbirth. They know what they want, and what the other wants, at this point in their lives and, because there are two of them, the woman's own self-regarding reasons get legitimated through the jointness of the decision. I am hardly suggesting everyone run out and get married to increase abortion's approval ratings but rather that couples may be an underused resource for abortion disclosure in breaking down the standard story that aborting women are unnatural.

In attempting to degender abortion decisions, gender has nonetheless imposed itself on the investigation. Let us return to Richard Yates's novel *Revolutionary Road,* that sobering depiction of domestic politics in mid-twentieth-century America. Recall that Frank had mounted a masterful campaign to convince his wife April that she should not abort her pregnancy and that in the end April conceded: "the deadline [for a safe procedure] had come and gone. The debate was over, and he had won."[146] The morning after his victory, Frank, inexplicably disconcerted, goes down to the kitchen for some juice: "Only very gradually, there at the table, was he able to sort out and identify what it was that had haunted him on waking, that had threatened to make him gag on his orange juice and now prevented his enjoyment of the brilliant grass and trees and sky beyond the window. It was that he was going to have another child, and he wasn't at all sure that he wanted one."[147]

9

Normalizing Abortion

In *The Emperor of All Maladies: A Biography of Cancer,* Siddhartha Mukherjee reports how in the early 1950s, Fanny Rosenow, a breast cancer survivor and advocate, sought to post a notice in the *New York Times* for a breast cancer support group and was put through to the society editor: "When she asked about placing her announcement, a long pause followed. 'I'm sorry, Mrs. Rosenow, but the *Times* cannot publish the word *breast* or the word *cancer* in its pages.' 'Perhaps,' the editor continued, 'you could say there will be a meeting about diseases of the chest wall.' "[1] Sixty years later, on May 14, 2013, the *New York Times* published an op-ed piece by actress Angelina Jolie discussing her high statistical chance of developing breast cancer, her decision to have a prophylactic double mastectomy, and, in great detail, the particulars of the breast reconstruction surgery that followed.[2] Jolie's piece was printed above the fold and it used all the forbidden words and then some.

What transformed a euphemized notice about "diseases of the chest" into news that was at last "fit to print"? How did breast cancer move from whispered diagnosis to the subject of pink-ribboned fun runs, a public health campaign, and a basis of solidarity among women? What happened between 1950 and 2013 to liberate the words "breast" and "cancer"?

The answer surely begins with First Lady Betty Ford who in 1974 decided to come out (if not as fulsomely as Angelina Jolie) with regard to her own diagnosis and treatment. Breast cancer—indeed, any cancer—was one of many issues not much talked about in polite company, in the press, or in the political arena until later in the twentieth century. Other closeted subjects included depression, being gay, getting divorced, and, within the reproductive sphere, miscarriage or stillbirth. Yet through varying combinations of personal disclosure, collective action both social and political, and law reform, these once undiscussables are now talked about (though not by everyone) as former subjects of shame or scandal and have become normalized.

This has not been the case with abortion. In contrast to other untouchable topics, abortion has only just begun to stick its head over the parapet and we understand why: not only slings and arrows but real shots have been fired. Abortion is still a risky subject. In some communities, some families, some workplaces, and some houses of worship, the costs to a woman's reputation, her safety, her relationships, and her self-conception remain high. The dense interplay of law, culture, and politics has worked to keep the subject of abortion disreputable and low. Women's reluctance to discuss abortion openly, even amongst intimates, is understandable.

A number of distinctive factors make abortion disclosure especially fraught. Abortion concerns women's physical bodies, including their sexual bodies, matters long entrenched in secrecy. Unlike other traditional taboos whose origins are innate or accidental or just bad luck—homosexuality, miscarriage, cancer—abortion is intentional. It is not only an intentional decision but one taken for the purpose of ending fetal life, and so for some it is nothing less than a deliberate killing. The closest analogy may be HIV-positive or AIDS status, which similarly involves bodies, sex, morality, and possible harm to others. Like women who have terminated a pregnancy, people with AIDS or HIV are loath to reveal what is understood as deeply stigmatizing information about themselves. South African Court Justice Edwin Cameron describes how these factors fit together in the context of AIDS, putting sexual intercourse at the center: "The embarrassment and shame seem to stem from the fact that an intimate bodily connection that should have exchanged life-affirming joy, instead becomes a source of possible illness and death."[3] The diagnosis becomes the basis for rebuke and reproach; "knowing that others may judge us stupid, irresponsible, immoral and unclean, shames us deeply."[4] Cameron kept his own diagnosis a secret for years, disclosing it at last in order to contribute to the political project in South Africa of recognizing the disease as a disease for which research, treatment, and compassion were fitting responses. That required conversation, which in turn required disclosure: "if we can talk about it, we normalise it."[5]

It is now time to make a similar move in the United States with regard to abortion and to relocate what now passes for abortion talk to a more fitting cultural position for this common medical procedure and much-exercised right.

Even with all the care and contraception in the world, unwanted pregnancy is a constant feature of women's reproductive lives; 40 percent of pregnancies in the United States are unintended and some of these surely end in abortion. The beauty of "choice" is that there are several ways to go. Some may be committed to birth or abortion even before the stick turns pink. Others figure out what to do only after gathering information relevant to their immediate circumstances.

Normalizing abortion—recognizing it as an acceptable option to the predicament of an unwanted pregnancy—is not to trivialize the decision nor to make choosing abortion the new normal. The aim is to pry abortion loose from the confines of a paralyzing secrecy so that the possibilities can be discussed—vetted, challenged, reviewed—with others beforehand and, importantly, after. Normalizing abortion talk aligns ordinary discourse with experience. It enables women to discuss their decision making and their own experiences with greater ease and security. Talking about abortion does not circumvent deliberation or disagreement but rather opens up space so that those who want to can have the conversation.

The willingness of women and others to talk about abortion will over time make an immense difference to its legislative fate, for legislatures are where states go toe-to-toe with the abortion right. Legislatures decide that doctors must read scripts out loud to their patients who, but for this mandatory recitation, have already consented to the procedure. But legislative lawmaking depends in part on what legislators know, and that depends on how and when and with whom the issue of abortion has been discussed, and not only from a policy perspective. Private talk by women and their families improves the quality of public discussion, which in turn influences political action. This discursive progression is not magical thinking; it is political science. We have seen it in the movements for same-sex marriage, cancer research, and disability rights. Genuine discussion between those who have considered an abortion (whatever the outcome) and those who have never done so (or who, because they are men, have never had to) widens the scope of what people are able to take on board.

A culture used to linking abortion to shame and secrecy as though the connection were natural presents a significant challenge to the project of normalization. Yet a number of theories and strategies that have helped crack open other forbidden topics may also benefit abortion. Technologies new to the twenty-first century are also now in play. Rallies are not a thing of the past—sometimes a poster on a stick is just the thing—but they have been joined by the use of social media, where an idea can be tweeted or inserted into a movement rather smartly. We begin, however, with a few tactics from the twentieth century.

IN RESPONSE TO SEGREGATIONIST CLAIMS made in the mid-1950s following *Brown v. Board of Education* that racial integration in the schools would lead to greater social friction, psychologist Gordon Allport began investigating the consequences of social interaction between white citizens and black.[6] Allport concluded that under certain conditions, social contact—interaction between "regular folk" and those with a perceived stigma—reduced rather than stimulated prejudice.[7] Direct social contact disconfirmed stereotypes held by the majority group (whites) about the stigmatized minority (blacks) and lessened pre-existing racial prejudices. A necessary precondition to these experiments was that the stigmatizing characteristic was apparent. If the stigma is concealed—as when someone "passes" as white or "covers" as straight—then existing prejudices remain untouched by the interaction. In contrast, when the stigmatizing characteristic is patent, it loses its salience as something to be bothered about. The stigma ceases to define the person who bears it.

Sociologist Sarah Cowan has connected a number of important dots to reveal how Allport's social contact hypothesis operates in the area of pregnancy loss.[8] Cowan investigated which of two groups of women holding a reproductive secret—for some, a secret about miscarriage; for others, a secret about abortion—was more likely to disclose their secret to another person. Not surprisingly, women more often confided the fact of a miscarriage. Although miscarriage has long been regarded as a reproductive failure (at least for women with wanted pregnancies), its "failure" is unintentional.[9] On this calculus, abortion is unquestionably worse: it is not a happenstance, but a decision, however constrained the surrounding circumstances.

It is less the comparative disclosure rates between abortion and miscarriage that interests us here than it is the consequences of disclosure or, more to the point, of nondisclosure. Cowan builds on the proposition that secrets are revealed selectively: people tend to confide in those they think will be supportive rather than judgmental.[10] This makes sense. Secrets can be dangerous and secret keepers are rightly cautious about the personal consequences of disclosing; the circumference of revelation may widen of its own accord, as "from trusted friend to trusted friend, the secret travels along that immense chain until it reaches the ear of the one or the many whom the first person who spoke never intended it to reach."[11]

The corollary of secret keepers disclosing only to those thought to be supportive is that people considered unsupportive will not be told. In consequence, people imagined to oppose abortion are "much less likely than their pro-choice peers to hear abortion secrets and as such think they do not know any woman who has had one."[12] And just here the contact hypothesis merges with the psychology of secret keeping. If a woman or girl conceals the fact that she has had an abortion, then no matter how many church socials or book clubs she goes to, the persuasive potential of social contact is lost. Without some disclosure, the contact hypothesis hasn't got a chance. The person who thinks he doesn't know anyone who has had an abortion goes right on thinking that, and whatever conceptions he has about women who abort go unchallenged.

In contrast, as Cowan discovered in her study, "Americans who have heard abortion secrets . . . have a more accurate understanding of how common abortion is, who has them and why."[13] Following an abortion disclosure, listeners are "more likely to believe that women who have abortions are mothers and attend religious services regularly."[14] The new information is grounded in fact: 30 percent of women who have an abortion identify as Protestant and 24 percent identify as Catholic; 59 percent gave birth at least once.[15] All this suggests that even though data about motherhood and religious affiliation have long been known, it is social contact rather than the availability of statistics that may produce a difference in attitude.[16]

The intransigence in attitudes about abortion may not be entirely a matter of embedded worldviews, in sociologist Kristin Luker's classic framing.[17] Yet those worldviews may lack information about the characteristics and proximity of women who have abortions. This deficit is not because pro-life people don't get out enough, but because the contact that might provide the counterweight goes unrevealed by the abortion secret keeper. The missed opportunity leads to the political implications of secrets. As Cowan explains, "when individuals keep secrets from those who will disapprove of them, processes of social influence—on public opinion, on tolerance and behavior—are thwarted."[18]

On the brighter side, by virtue of their decision to terminate a pregnancy, a fair number of American women—over fifty million since 1973—have "themselves become social and political actors who can influence others, particularly their peers."[19] I suspect that few women who have terminated a pregnancy are likely to consider themselves as political actors. It was quite enough to make the decision, end the pregnancy, and move on with life. Yet is it not possible that some of the these women might start to think of themselves as capable of affecting the views of others by revealing on an appropriate occasion that they once had or contemplated an abortion?

In Allport's early desegregation studies, interaction between racial groups had been rare and social contact was something new. In contrast, women (including women who have terminated a pregnancy) are already well integrated at work, at school, at shops, and so forth. The problem is that unlike visible stigmatizing characteristics, "having had an abortion" is not an apparent attribute. No one knows when a woman enters a room if she has had an abortion, though of course any woman might have. Abortion is not something women seek out for the experience. It is a decision taken in response to particular circumstances, not an evident identity. In light of abortion's invisibility as a trait, something more than contact is needed, and the extra step is disclosure.

The necessity of disclosure leads to another problem. Because the risks of revelation are the woman's alone to shoulder, is it fair to put the burden of talking about abortion decisions on individual women in order to break the stranglehold of abortion secrecy?[20] To educate fellow citizens, must women follow Facebook chief operating officer Sheryl Sandberg's admonition to "lean in" by disclosing their own abortions?[21] It seems a bit much to ask women who are already "leaning in" in their own lives in all sorts of ways to take on the personal risks of disclosure "for the team." Perhaps the personal risk would seem worth it if the connection between private talk, public discussion, and political decision making were better understood.

There is also something familiar but disquieting about calls for women to disclose their abortions. Pro-life advocates have long argued that pregnant women should talk about their abortions for the purpose of seeking forgiveness. Putting "forgive" and "abortion" into a search engine turns up pages of sites, many religious, where women are invited to unburden themselves and be forgiven.[22] Does this mean that breaking silence on abortion provides an unexpected point of convergence that might be mined for solidarity? Not quite. There is a difference between discussing an abortion within a prescribed framework of moral wrongdoing and frameworks that are not so purposefully directed. Women may disclose (rather than confess) an abortion for all sorts of reasons: relief, sharing the loss, guidance to others, acknowledging the decision, commemorating the fetus (without the shrine garden), or simply externalizing the thoughts and feelings the experience has produced.

Anonymous disclosure may be a good start so long as the reality of stigma still hovers. Yet reproductive candor has benefits even now. Consider women who find themselves able to discuss a miscarriage and in so doing discover that the woman in the next cubicle has had one too. As journalists Emily Bazelon and Dahlia Lithwick discovered while discussing a proposed piece on miscarriages for *Slate,*

> we had been working together professionally through the previous year without knowing that we had each suffered miscarriages, each struggled to become pregnant again, and that we had both finally succeeded. Several heartfelt e-mails later, we decided to publish a dialogue about our shared experience. It was a difficult decision for two legal reporters to "go public" with this kind of secret. In hindsight, we think it has been one of the most important things we have done as journalists.[23]

Women post abortion experiences anonymously on sites like Exhale, which describes itself as the "after abortion talkline"—neither pro-life nor pro-choice but "pro-voice."[24] As abortion talk of this kind becomes more familiar, soliloquy may over time become colloquy. In the meantime, an intermediary step is to widen the audience for abortion disclosure through new forms and locations of outreach.

Every Sunday, the *New York Times* Styles section publishes pages of wedding announcements. Over the years the announcements, disdained by some and scoured by others, have become not only more chatty—how the couple met, what they wore at the ceremony—but also more zeitgeisty. In August 2002, the *Times* changed the name of the section from Weddings to Weddings / Celebrations and started publishing notices of same-sex "commitment ceremonies." Executive editor Howard Raines explained to the readership that the decision was based on "the newsworthiness of a growing and visible trend in society" and the significance of that trend to many *Times* readers.[25] Reassuring readers that the *Times* would continue reporting same-sex *news* with impartiality, Raines stated that "the Styles pages will treat same-sex celebrations as a discrete phenomenon meriting coverage in their own right."[26] Debates over same-sex marriage were news; the unions themselves were one of Sunday's secret pleasures.

Some ten years later in the section now called Vows, the *Times* published a near full-page announcement of the wedding of Faith Rein and Udonis Haslem, a professional basketball player with the Miami Heat. The piece detailed the couple's fourteen-year relationship—beaus, college, proposal—and included the following paragraph: "Their first challenge took place the following spring when [Faith] became pregnant. It was her junior and his senior year, and he had begun training for the NBA draft. Despite the pregnancy, she was busy with track meets and helping him complete homework. The timing was bad."[27] The article then describes, somewhat murkily, the couple's negotiations over what to do. Readers were given Faith's perspective ("Udonis appreciated that I was willing to have an abortion") and Udonis's ("I am not a huge fan of abortion, but we both had sports careers, plus we could not financially handle a baby").[28]

The Rein-Haslem wedding announcement was something new. Reactions by columnists and bloggers of all stripes followed, some congratulating the couple on their public candor, others accusing the *New York Times* of trying to normalize abortion by including it so casually among other wedding stories.[29] In this regard, everyone was right, candor and normalization being different ends of the same stick.

Although Faith and Udonis chose not to keep their secret in the family, collective or group secret keeping is a familiar phenomenon, even when the "group" is only family sized. Intimates keep secrets from one another to protect the subject of the secret (Lou Gehrig's wife concealing the diagnosis of amyotrophic lateral sclerosis from Gehrig himself), to protect a marriage (an affair), or to protect the family's reputation from the ill-judged conduct of one of its members.[30] As we have seen up to now, the goal of abortion secrecy has been to protect individual information from public scrutiny. This is why abortion plaintiffs seek "Doe" status, why transcripts in bypass hearings are sealed, and why medical records are sometimes protected against efforts to use them in litigation.[31] But the failure of family members to disclose secrets even to one another creates its own set of harms.[32]

Doris Lessing's short story "Debbie and Julie," set in 1970s London, provides a fictional example of how this can work. Julie, "a fat girl in [a] skyblue coat," has run away from home to London to hide her developing pregnancy.[33] Months later, when labor begins, Julie is left to deliver the baby by herself in a shed she had scouted out ahead of time. Having read up on the process, she had packed scissors for the cord and a clean blanket for the baby. A baby girl is born. Julie swaddles the baby and places it in a phone booth, having first alerted the emergency services to the whereabouts of an abandoned baby. Julie watches the rescue from a nearby pub window. Cold and blood-soaked, she returns home to her parents, who are overjoyed to see her. After a bath and a sandwich, Julie sits with them watching the telly, just like before. When a report of a newborn found in a phone booth comes on the screen, Julie's father breaks down (in an English sort of way), explaining that he had been worried sick that such a predicament might have been what caused Julie to flee, and says in an aside to his wife, "[I] often wonder what Jessie thinks."[34] Only then does Julie learn that her Aunt Jessie when younger and unmarried had given birth to a child but refused to give her up. Her own cousin Freda! Maybe Julie could have brought her own baby Rose home. Or might she then, like Aunt Jessie, have had to marry just anybody to put things right?

Although in Lessing's story Julie hadn't contemplated abortion, women's reproductive secrets often have much in common with one another. The scandal of Aunt Jessie's "love-child" kept Julie from imagining a larger realm of the possible. Hidden births, hidden children, hidden abortions. Disclosure is sometimes difficult, but nondisclosure has its own costs, as when secrecy hides potential solidarity or resolution. As Julie's father kept murmuring, "It can happen easy enough, can't it?"[35] That's the point about women and pregnancy.

Adoption provides another example of how family secrets move into the public realm. Until the 1970s, it was generally accepted that children were better off not knowing that they had been adopted. Freed from the knowledge of their sketchy origins, they could develop just like "natural children." The law played its part in this. Adoption records were sealed and new birth certificates were issued with the adoptive parents' names substituted in as the birth parents. Only when birth mothers and adult adopted children began to seek—demand—information about each other did the structural secrecy of adoption begin to shift. To incentivize birth mothers to choose adoption over abortion and to keep a supply of adoptable newborns coming, the law began to offer transparency as part of the deal.[36] A regime of open adoption, where birth mothers knew and sometimes chose the adopting parents, took hold, sometimes to the dissatisfaction of mothers who had surrendered a baby decades earlier, believing that their secret was protected by law.[37] Abortion law has a similar duality about secrecy. Sometimes it protects a woman's privacy—as with the Doe alias—and sometimes it encourages secrecy by regulating abortion so differently from all other medical procedures—so shamedly—that laying low becomes the prudent response.

One conundrum about abortion is that the practice remains so secretive even as we head to the half-century mark of its recognition as a right. Legalization did not translate into openness nor did it move abortion into the medical realm. It may be that social revelations like the Rein-Haslem wedding announcement prove the greater moving force. To be sure, law has contributed to the project of normalization. The right to choose abortion is an absolute good even if the regulations that fill in how the right is exercised reinforce the stigma. Those born before the 1950s know that divorce became less scandalous when the legal requirement of fault—naming it, proving it—was abandoned in the 1970s and 1980s. Even the language of "broken homes" has trailed off. Getting rid of the legal shaming mechanisms around abortion similarly stands to bring about more and better talk.

Shifts in what counts as shameful (divorce out, smoking in) also result from more organized reform efforts. After receiving her cancer diagnosis, Betty Ford decided to ignore the social delicacy that had kept Fanny Rosenow's advertisement out of print twenty years earlier. Emboldened by Ford's lead, a more comprehensive movement for breast cancer awareness emerged, with the slogan "Don't Die of Embarrassment." (A more forceful version was later introduced by AIDS activists: Silence=Death.)

An appealing representative—a respectable "face" like Mrs. Ford—is often a productive tactic in legitimating social movements. Yet what makes for a good poster child is tricky business. Critiques of the use of Betty Ford argue that "the articulation of the ideal patient as an optimistic non-confrontational figure functions to aestheticize the grimness of the breast cancer experience and the uncertainty of breast cancer research."[38] Racial disparities in breast cancer mortality rates suggest that something has fallen short somewhere.[39] From another perspective, a poster child may be regarded less as sympathetic than as pathetic. Disability rights advocates have so argued with regard to fund-raising telethons like the March of Dimes and the Muscular Dystrophy Association, which beginning in the 1950s featured crippled children bravely staggering across the stage under the weight of their heavy braces and crutches.[40] This remains a topic of debate among human rights advocates today who recognize the power of an image of a child washed ashore in Turkey or injured in Syria but who worry about objectifying their clients.

What then about abortion? Can it have a "face"? Of course, in one important respect, it already has one: the fetus. But is there anyone or any type that might transform the characterization of a woman seeking an abortion from suspect and selfish to reflective and responsible? Consider the fate of the sincerest of pro-choice poster women imaginable, Sherri Finkbine. Finkbine, not part of any political movement, was the married Catholic mother of four and Phoenix area hostess of the children's program *Romper Room*.[41] In 1962, pregnant with her fifth child, Finkbine took a drug for morning sickness that her husband had brought back from a trip to Europe. The drug contained thalidomide, which even in small or singular doses causes severe structural abnormalities in a developing fetus; thalidomide had not been approved for use in the United States.[42] Upon discovering what she had taken, Finkbine followed existing protocols and sought permission for an abortion from a hospital abortion committee on the permissible grounds of suspected fetal anomaly.[43] The committee approved her request, but before the abortion was performed, Finkbine contacted a local Phoenix paper urging it to use her story to alert other pregnant women about the dangers of the drug. The publicity that followed changed everything. Finkbine's scheduled abortion was canceled, as was her subsequent application for a visa to Japan, where abortion was legal. (She was finally able to have the procedure in Sweden.) Finkbine's would have seemed a most sympathetic case for considering when in the age of illegality a woman's decision to abort is an acceptable moral choice.

Because litigation is often part of any strategy for social change, sympathetic plaintiffs sometimes serve as representatives of the issue. In the marriage equality cases, for example, once there was an established gay rights movement, plaintiffs were carefully chosen by lawyers with an eye to the couple's good jobs, good looks, and years together.[44] Until recently, this has not worked so well for the pro-choice movement. Plaintiffs' actual identities and circumstances were often hidden behind the Doe aliases. Thin on detail and texture, she was essentially a "woman who wants an abortion"—or, more forcefully, a woman who wants to kill unborn life. The value of plaintiffs on the abortion public relations front was cast into doubt when plaintiff anonymity unraveled in two major cases. Norma McCorvey, the Jane Roe of *Roe v. Wade,* and Sandra Cano, the Mary Doe of *Doe v. Bolton,* have fiercely disavowed the pro-choice movement. McCorvey describes her role in *Roe* as "the real despicable act, the real blight on my life"; Cano regularly files amici briefs in cases seeking to overturn or to limit *Roe*.[45]

On the other hand, there are "collective poster people" who have appeared as "amici" in support of the abortion right. In 2016, "Janice MacAvoy, Janie Schulman, and Over 110 Other Women in the Legal Profession Who Have Exercised Their Constitutional Right to an Abortion" filed an amicus brief in the *Whole Woman's Health* case.[46] Three other briefs on behalf of the Whole Woman's Health clinic were filed by public officials, including Texan Wendy

Davis, as part of an "abortion voices project" that began with amici willing to sign their names in the 1986 case of *Thornburgh v. American College of Obstetricians & Gynecologists.*[47] Some of the women who signed on to these briefs have since written longer op-eds in their local papers explaining what their abortion so many years earlier has meant to them.[48] This is a very good example of abortion talk.

In addition to real women willing to speak up, slogans and control over rhetorical turf are hugely important to the success of social change. Mothers Against Drunk Driving (MADD) got nowhere under its first acronym, RID (Remove Intoxicated Drivers).[49] Abortion rhetoric, starting with the bundle of problems inherent in the word "choice," testifies to the difficulty.[50] The charge is that "choice" makes abortion a consumer issue, it smacks of individualism, and it radiates selfishness (I want what I want! It's my choice!). Pre-*Roe* rallying cries like "Abortion on Demand" and "Abortion without Apology," however forthright and energizing, were up against a pro-life campaign that had already commandeered the word "life" to its purposes and was on its way to serving up "partial birth abortion" as the loaded tag for abortions performed late in pregnancy. These phrases went a long way in casting abortion as a "non-normative practice . . . unworthy of societal approval."[51] The antiabortion riposte "I'm a *Child,* Not a Choice" quickly made its way onto fenders nationwide. "Save the Baby Humans" isn't far behind, featuring an adorable panda with its riff on environmentalism.

A more recent pro-choice slogan has been the seemingly uncontroversial proposition that abortion should be "safe, legal, and rare." Introduced by Bill Clinton during the 1990s, the phrase is perfect for (and from) a savvy pro-choice politician.[52] It lets politicians show their pro-choice bona fides while establishing that in an ideal world (think ample contraception, cooperative partners, no rape, good child care from birth, job security, paid maternity leave, and other maternalistic policies on tap) all pregnancies would be desired. As for the slogan, abortion was already legal on account of *Roe* and "safe" as a by-product of legality. It was the "rare" that took it on the chin, not from antiabortion people but from pro-choice advocates concerned about its subtext.

In a complicating critique, Tracey Weitz explains that "rare" "creates an immediate normative judgment about abortion," suggesting that there is already too much abortion going around; it ought to happen less.[53] This in turn increases the stigma for aborting women generally because maybe theirs isn't one of the good, properly rare abortions. Weitz also points out that the goal of making abortion rare justifies further restrictions on the procedure now. If only women would be more responsible and have fewer abortions, the law wouldn't have to police the situation so vigorously. In short, says Weitz, "rare" is a "linguistic trick," affirming the right to abortion on one hand while devaluing it as part of women's lives on the other.[54] As we know, abortion is not rare, for all sorts of reasons that have nothing to do with callousness about an unwanted pregnancy. During the 2016 presidential campaign, Hillary Clinton "tweaked" the mantra, leaving out the "rare."[55]

Solidarity, another common feature of successful social movements, is also hard to obtain on the issue of abortion disclosure. Having had an abortion does not constitute an identity for most women. Women do not (and have no reason to) socialize or organize on that basis. Unlike LGBTQ movements, there is little pre-existing social solidarity or other commonality to ground an experiential abortion movement. Abortion support groups are few and far between, although some, like A Heartbreaking Choice (AHC), focus on commonality of motive. AHC provides "support for those who have terminated a much wanted pregnancy."[56] The introductory pages of the book *Our Heart Breaking Choices* laud the narratives of forty-six women who aborted due to fetal anomaly: "If you question their decision, you may come to understand that these parents bravely and unselfishly entered the suffering of grief in order that their babies be spared another kind of suffering."[57] While surely important for those who have made a choice of this nature, it also suggests a hierarchy of abortion goodness. Abortion providers regularly hear from patients who are sure that everyone else in the waiting room is there for a "convenience abortion" or some other bad reason. Making other women deviant may be a way of inoculating oneself against guilt by association (or guilt full-stop), but this is not the stuff of social movement solidarity.

Still, there are some signs of solidarity, and many are located online. Like-minded people today find one another less often in response to posted or printed notices—think of Mrs. Rosenow—than from blogs, social media, tweets, and other modes of online interaction. The like-mindedness that anchors the solidarity need not focus solely on reproductive practices but on other centers of interest, such as—get ready—knitting. Beth Ann Pentney describes several online communities of feminist knitters who knit for social and political causes. These include not only Knitters Without Borders but Knit4Choice, which sought to publicize the abortion right when it came under special attack with the "Culture of Life" motif of the George W. Bush presidency. Their 2005 project was called "Wombs on Washington." The goal was to knit wombs from an online pattern and then deposit them en masse on the steps of the Supreme Court. The aspiration was that "by seeing the vast differences among our representative [knitted] wombs, laid out before the Supreme Court building, our elected and appointed officials will remember that every woman is an individual with unique needs and circumstances, and [is] capable of making personal decisions without government interference."[58] The project failed in part (wombs were knit but not delivered to the Court), but it sparked a year of productive online debate about political strategies for abortion.

A more recent and bolder approach is something called #ShoutYourAbortion. The "something" is the directive to women who have had an abortion to say so out loud and, better yet, to say it loudly. The idea came about in 2015 when a Chicago woman, Amelia Bonow, furious at congressional efforts to defund Planned Parenthood, posted an announcement on her Facebook page: "Hi guys! Like a year ago I had an abortion at Planned Parenthood on Madison Avenue and remember this experience with a near inexpressible level of gratitude . . . I have a good heart and having an abortion made me happy in a totally unqualified way. Why wouldn't I be happy that I was not forced to become a mother?"[59] Bonow's whole-hearted gratitude is on occasion echoed by others. Gloria Steinem dedicated her 2015 autobiography to the London physician who sixty years earlier had referred Steinem for an abortion in violation of the criminal statute then in effect. The physician asked Steinem in return to promise that she would make what she wanted of her life. As she recounts in the dedication, "I've done the best I could with my life. This book is for you."[60]

Bonow's friend, writer Lindy West, tweeted Bonow's post under "Don't Whisper, #ShoutYourAbortion," and voila! a movement with attitude was born.[61] #ShoutYourAbortion isn't looking for a poster woman. Rather, every woman who "shouts" by posting or tweeting accepts that abortion isn't and ought not to be shameful. The message is optimistic and confident: "However glacially society evolves, it is evolving in the right direction. Abortion is common. Abortion is happening. . . . Abortion is a thing you can say out loud."[62]

Because tweeting is open to anyone with a smartphone or laptop and a good Internet connection—which is not everyone—responses took shapes of all sorts. Former Republican presidential candidate Michele Bachmann wrote that "#ShoutYourAbortion gives a new meaning to macabre."[63] Other pro-life supporters made their own hashtags, like #unplannedparenthood and #praytoendabortion. More to the original point was the post of Ruby Sinreich, who had terminated a pregnancy several years back but realized that "I was carrying around some residual shame."[64] Sinreich noted, "you see a hashtag and it connects you to this whole community, so you see you're part of this larger thing."[65] There are other outlets for expression: 1 in 3, Tell Your Story, Silent No More, Share Your Abortion Story Writing Workshop, and "I Had an Abortion" t-shirts.[66] From a technological perspective, hashtag activism is not your mother's activism nor Mrs. Rosenow's. With regard to abortion, a second difference is women's readiness to speak out. Some women who terminate pregnancy do so and are willing to say so without anguish.[67] This is not to say that their abortion decisions are made on a whim. Why when abortion is legal must discussing it be done in corners? #ShoutYourAbortion rejects the very idea of abortion secrecy.

Of course, the secretness around the actual practice of abortion is a strange sort of secret indeed. Abortion providers advertise openly in the Yellow Pages under the heading "Abortion Services." Clinics are identifiable, sometimes by the "women's health" in their name, sometimes by the protestors on the sidewalks. Patients' cars are daily parked in clinic parking lots. In addition to all this visual evidence, the law keeps reminding citizens of what's going on. The current avalanche of abortion regulation is more than an expressive gesture on the part of lawmakers. The statutes, rules, and regulations are meant to operate upon real women as they sit out the forty-eight-hour waiting period in some motel or come in for their pre-consent ultrasound or are informed that all fetal remains must be buried or cremated. Legislators, employers, and parents may not know about a particular abortion, but pretty much everyone knows that pregnant women and girls in general are having abortions. In this way, abortion is an open secret: the procedure out there, regularly sought and received, but individually unclaimed. Women who abort are like former Defense Secretary Rumsfeld's "known unknowns." That is part of what makes them dangerous.

The openness of abortion as secret is seen in vocabulary now and in the past. In colonial Massachusetts, abortion was known as "taking the trade"— "trade" the term both for goods and for abortifacients.[68] Cordelia Dayton explains that young people who used the phrase "had no need to explain to one another the meaning of 'taking the trade.'"[69] Today the ordinariness of abortion is found in immigrant communities throughout the United States on the open shelves of botanicas, or traditional Latino apothecaries, which sell special herbal teas—hierba de ruda, or just plain ruda—meant to bring on a woman's missing period, thereby avoiding the twin stigmas of unwanted pregnancy and abortion.[70] As in colonial times, today's herbal abortifacients are not always safe and are often ineffective.[71] They pose legal risks as well. Women who have used herbal teas late in pregnancy have been arrested for the crime of self-abortion in cases where a viable fetus has been born dead.[72] Even so, the easy availability of these drugs and the ordinary mode of their use is about as open as a secret can be.

Open secrets have social value. They let a disfavored practice go on without anyone having to acknowledge or condone it. Consider the use of maternity homes in pre-*Roe* mid-twentieth-century America.[73] High school girls or, more commonly, white high school girls, since few homes would take pregnant black teenagers, would disappear for a semester—off to care for an aunt in a distant state or some such—and return the following fall, no longer a member of the honor society. Abortion providers and clinics similarly manage the problem so that other physicians and hospitals don't have to. That is a measure of clinics' utility as well as their isolation.

Related to the peculiarities of open secrets is a phenomenon known as "preference falsification." In studying how news of popular uprisings around the world is reported—the fall of the Shah, the end of Communism, the Arab Spring—economist Timur Kuran observed a curious pattern. This was the reception of such news as a great surprise: "sudden," "unexpected," or in the words of Radio Free Europe in reporting the fall of the Berlin Wall in 1989, "our jaws cannot drop any lower."[74] Kuran argues that this "surprise factor" is the result of citizens believing one thing in private and saying (falsifying) another in public. The revolution may seem a surprise, says Kuran, because "preference falsification concealed the opposition developing under the surface."[75] This kind of double tracking "distorts human knowledge, and hides political possibilities."[76]

The same phenomenon is at work with regard to abortion nondisclosure. Members of the medical community may ostracize the local gynecologist who performs abortions, but will help a daughter go out of state; citizens contribute to the campaigns of pro-life candidates while remaining loyal and even sympathetic to a friend who terminated a pregnancy back in the day. Such opposing positions might seem confused or hypocritical, or they might more accurately be understood as instances of preference falsification. The public view responds to the exigencies of professional and social life. And the two positions are not completely inconsistent. The under-the-radar view responds to a different, perhaps more intimate or personal set of reflections. Because the causes of abortion nondisclosure are more nuanced than the direct repression of an authoritarian political regime, the "overthrow" of abortion silence may not take the form of an outright uprising. The current regime of shame and secrecy may not topple so much as fade away.

This is not to say that the entire nation is secretly pro-choice. Many are vocally opposed; others are steadfast but hold their peace. Normalizing abortion talk does not answer the question of how any particular woman should resolve her unwanted pregnancy. It simply reframes abortion's status from presumptive moral outrage to that of a simple medical procedure that a person might elect when parenthood seems impossible or is not desired, perhaps like the 500,000 vasectomies chosen by men each year in the United States.

Medical and communication technologies have also become part of the story. For pregnancies under ten weeks, medical abortion has simplified the procedure from a physical intervention to pill swallowing; telemedicine has increased access by transcending distances. Each of these has given women more control. Each operates to make abortion more like a regular trip to the doctor. Yet a cartoonish cat-and-mouse situation has developed as legislatures are primed to pounce on the new technologies by restricting or banning their use but only as applied to abortion. The potential of technologies to improve patient care is thwarted by such legislative smackdowns.

We see this with regard to medical abortion, sometimes called "the abortion pill" or, more accurately, "the two pills." Pill One is mifepristone. Taken (ingested) in the doctor's office, it starts the process by thinning the uterine lining. One to two days later, in a place of her choosing, the patient takes Pill Two, misoprostol, which produces the cramping that expels the pregnancy. Two weeks after that she returns to the clinic for an ultrasound or blood test to confirm that the pregnancy is completely over.

Why would a woman choose one procedure—medical or surgical—over the other? One factor is timing. Medical abortion is available only up to the tenth week of pregnancy; after that, surgical abortion using a manual aspirator is the only option. A second factor is privacy. From one perspective, medical abortion offers more privacy in that aside from swallowing Pill One at a clinic, the process itself unfolds in the comfort of home or some other supportive place. There are no waiting rooms, no picketers, no staff to interact with. Yet for women whose pregnancy must remain a secret, surgical abortion has certain advantages. The whole thing takes about four hours (the procedure itself takes fifteen minutes), one leaves the clinic no longer pregnant, and no one is the wiser. Some women prefer medical abortion because the body does all the work and it seems more natural. In addition, the days of cramping can be passed off as a difficult period. In short, the choice of procedures responds in great part to the woman's social needs. That these considerations are often still in play shows how normalizing abortion will remove the demands of secrecy and intrigue that so often play a part in the calculus.

But now comes the legislative rub. In order to increase the number of abortion providers, especially in rural areas, some states authorize medical professionals other than physicians to dispense the two pills. In contrast, several pro-life legislatures have now banned non-physician practitioners—registered nurses, licensed midwives, physician assistants—from dispensing abortifacients on the ground that the nurse would therefore be performing an abortion. The savvy and sophisticated Americans United For Life distributes model legislation kits for states considering similar bans as part of its "Proven Strategies for a Pro-Life America" campaign.[77]

There has been more pouncing in the area of telemedicine. The term has been defined as "a method of practicing medicine in which the physician is at one geographical location, the patient is at a different geographical location, and the two communicate through a secure electrical audio-visual connection that complies with the privacy requirements of the Health Insurance Portability and Accountability Act (HIPAA)."[78] Although advertisements often highlight dramatic intercontinental uses of the technology, telemedicine is at work much closer to home and in the relatively mundane (medically speaking) area of abortion. In 2008 Planned Parenthood of the Heartland (PPH) began using telemedicine for medical abortions, particularly in more rural areas of Iowa where PPH clinics did not have a doctor regularly on the premises.[79]

This is how it works. A clinic nurse in, say, the Council Bluffs Clinic describes the two-pill process to the patient, takes her medical history and consent, answers questions, and orders lab work. The patient has an ultrasound to establish that the pregnancy is under ten weeks. (No other physical examination is necessary under the standards of care approved by the American Congress of Obstetrics and Gynecology.[80]) The labwork, scan, and medical history are sent electronically to the physician in a larger PPH clinic in Iowa City or Des Moines, and the patient schedules a return appointment at the local clinic. When the patient returns, the nurse reaffirms her consent, reviews what to expect, and emphasizes the importance of the later follow-up visit. The patient then sits down in a private conference room across from a TV monitor, with a glass of water and something resembling a small hotel safe nearby. When the physician appears on the monitor, she asks the patient to explain in her own words what is going to happen and whether the patient has any questions saved for the doctor herself. Once the doctor is satisfied that everything is in order, she presses a button at her desk in Iowa City that pops open the safe in the clinic, and a drawer with two vials of medicine slides out. In a slightly Alice in Wonderland moment, the doctor instructs the patient to take a pill out of the vial with a blue marking on top (the mifepristone) and swallow it. The patient takes the second vial (the misoprostol) home with her, the pills to be downed within twenty-four to forty-eight hours. The nurse reminds the patient about the return visit, and with a "Come back, good luck, and take care" the appointment is over and the abortion process has begun.[81] That is the step by step. Columnist Lindy West summarized her experience of medical abortion this way: "Almost exactly five years ago, in September 2010, I took one pill, and then another, and lay in my bed for a night and a day, and then I wasn't pregnant any more. It was a fairly smooth experience, distressing only because my relationship was bad and I had no money."[82]

Telemedicine for medical abortion benefits patients in its efficiency regarding time and travel—no need to travel to Des Moines so a doctor can hand the patient a tablet—and with regard to proximity to home once the process starts. Because cramping can begin after taking the first pill alone, it is more comfortable for the woman to be in a place where she can rest rather than in a bus or car en route, especially when the trip is long. Iowa patients who have experienced medical abortion via computer hookup report great overall satisfaction with the process, although some said they missed face-to-face contact with the physician.

Yet despite earlier praise given to telemedicine in general by the Iowa Board of Medicine—increased access to health care, cost savings, expanded use of specialists—in 2013 the Board issued a rule providing that henceforth a physician had to be physically present with the woman "at the time the abortion-inducing drug is provided."[83] (Other states, like Arkansas, are even more specific and require that "the woman and the physician both be present in the same room when the drugs are administered.")[84] So much for technology.

In 2015 the telemedicine ban was struck down by the Iowa Supreme Court for placing a substantial obstacle in the path of women seeking to terminate a pregnancy.[85] Foreshadowing the rationale of *Whole Woman's Health,* the Iowa

Supreme Court held that because increasing the distance to a provider compromised women's physical well-being at no medical benefit to the patient, it was an undue burden and could not stand. There is something more than a glimmer of hope that the standard for assessing whether an abortion regulation is constitutional will now have real content and real bite.

Another force at work in rethinking attitudes toward abortion is what I shall call "current events." I don't mean the term in the seventh-grade sense but rather to include the unexpected vagaries of modern life that sometimes cause people to reconsider a position they thought they had already figured out. Many who believe that protected human life begins at conception believe this through thick or thin; some would add opposition to the death penalty as an extension of the same principle. Others might not hold the view as absolutely. During the German measles epidemic of the early 1960s, for example, pregnant women across faiths ended pregnancies in the face of anticipated birth defects. Leslie Reagan describes a group of Catholic women in San Francisco who formed Catholic Mothers for Merciful Abortion.[86] In response to the epidemic, and aware of the thalidomide births in Europe around the same time, California enacted the Therapeutic Abortion Act. It provided that if two doctors sought permission on behalf of their patient from a five-member abortion committee, the patient could have an abortion if they unanimously agreed that continuing the pregnancy would gravely impair her physical or mental health. To twenty-first-century eyes, this may not seem like much of a right. Nonetheless, the state had at least authorized a form of legal abortion.

In 2016 a Zika epidemic broke out in Central and South America, posing similar questions about law, disability, politics, and abortion. Although the virus hit heaviest in South America, by October 2016 at least 4,000 people in the United States were infected, some from mosquitoes abroad or within the United States, others from sex with a Zika-infected partner. The Zika virus is also acquired by an embryo or fetus as it crosses the placental barrier from an infected mother. In October 2016, the Centers for Disease Control and Prevention (CDC) reported 878 cases of pregnant women in the United States who had tested positive for the infection. (There were also twenty-three cases of Zika-infected infants born with birth defects and five reported cases of pregnancy loss—including miscarriage, stillbirths, and terminations—all with fetal birth defects.) The consequences for the developing fetus who contracts the virus in utero are a cumulative set of significant birth defects for which there are no cures. These include intellectual and physical disability, hearing and vision impairment, difficulty swallowing, and seizures.[87] Most people are now familiar with the appearance of these microcephalic babies with their unusually small heads that slope downward from the mid-skull.

The CDC advises women who are pregnant or thinking about becoming pregnant not to travel to active Zika zones and not to have sex of any kind with someone who has done so for six months. Pregnant women who already have the virus are advised to seek a fetal medical diagnosis both during pregnancy and after birth. Yet some women may not want to continue their pregnancies at all under these fraught circumstances. The decision for women with wanted pregnancies has two particular complications. Not all Zika-infected women will transmit the virus to their fetuses, and diagnosing the virus in utero cannot at present be definitively done until around the twentieth week of pregnancy.

However a woman may resolve the issue for herself, the law in several states has already settled the matter for her. Texas prohibits abortions after twenty weeks as a general matter for all terminations. Because microcephaly cannot be diagnosed until around twenty weeks, pregnant women with Zika may be timed out of legal abortion in Texas or they might have to play the odds before twenty weeks by terminating a pregnancy they would, with more information, keep.

Timing is but the first problem. In order to prevent "prenatal discrimination," Indiana and North Dakota ban abortions sought on the basis of fetal disability. Babies born with microcephaly will almost certainly be disabled. Their distinctive heads are small because the brain has not grown as it should have; this explains the massive birth defects many will endure. Yet should a pregnant woman in North Dakota disclose her Zika-based reason to her physician, the abortion may not proceed. Doctors who go ahead out of compassion, conscience, or professional judgment are subject to fines and jail time.

It seems likely that statutes requiring reasons will sooner or later be struck down as unconstitutional; a federal judge has already blocked the Indiana ban while a challenge to the statute is litigated.[88] These bans were not enacted with Zika in mind but rather to emphasize as a matter of red state rectitude the ruthlessness of women willing to destroy unborn lives on the grounds of disability or other grounds that would constitute discrimination if the state were doing it and if we were not talking about abortion. By using the word "discrimination," antiabortion advocates invoke classic equal protection analysis: two groups who are "similarly situated" being treated differently. But born persons, or what are usually called persons, are not similarly situated with embryos. The Supreme Court has stuck to its guns that with regard to terminating a pregnancy, deciding when human life begins is up to the woman (even though states may permissibly persuade her toward childbirth). Bans on abortion "discrimination" have certain publicity value but they don't hold up legally. Women do not have to give reasons when consenting to abortion.

Even before getting to bans on abortion for "wrong reasons," current regulations are already quite harsh for pregnant women carrying the Zika virus. Like all other women seeking an abortion under the regulatory regimes in a fair number of states, Zika-infected women will be asked if they want to see the ultrasound image of their "unborn child." They too must listen to the doctor describe the size of the fetal head. They too must wait up to seventy-two hours after they consent in order to "cool off" and sit with their decision, as though it was made on a whim. The point is not that there should be special rules for Zika cases. Rather, Zika-related pregnancies reveal the cost to all women of these intrusive and unnecessary requirements.

The guidance provided by the Supreme Court to lower courts and to legislatures in the 2016 *Whole Woman's Health* decision may in time curb legislative antiabortion creativity. A few states have already acted on the decision. Within weeks of the June decision, the Alabama attorney general decided to withdraw its appeal of a district court decision invalidating Alabama's admitting privileges law, stating that "while I disagree with the high court's decision, there is no good faith argument that Alabama's law remains constitutional in light of the Supreme Court ruling."[89] In October 2016, the Virginia Board of Medical Appeals rescinded that state's requirement that existing abortion clinics comply with standards for ambulatory surgical centers.[90] And, referring to Missouri's admitting privileges and ambulatory surgical center requirements, a spokesperson for the state attorney general said that the decision in *Whole Woman's Health* "calls into serious question the constitutionality of certain Missouri laws."[91] These states have taken seriously Justice Breyer's admonition that choosing an abortion is a fundamental right and that states must take notice of this in devising regulations that appear burdensome.

On the other hand, there is Texas, which within two weeks of *Whole Woman's Health* announced a new regulation requiring that all fetal remains, whether from an abortion or a miscarriage, must be either buried or cremated.[92] In both content and timing the regulation was a defiant finger in the Supreme Court's eye. Moreover, these new regulations were not enacted by the Texas legislature but came into being through the rule-making procedure of the Texas Health and Human Services Commission, an administrative agency that draws less public attention than the statehouse. Texas is not the only state using administrative procedures to burden abortion with proposals that have already been declared unconstitutional. In September 2016, the South Carolina Department of Health and Environmental Control (DHEC) proposed regulations requiring the written consent of a woman's husband before she can have an abortion.[93] This issue was put to rest in 1992 in *Planned Parenthood of Southeastern Pennsylvania v. Casey*. That particular regulation may not survive the rule-making process, but in general the DHEC must first receive public comments and debate the matter further. As part of its standards for licensing abortion clinics, the DHEC also proposed that abortion providers must report all sexually transmitted diseases of a patient to the county health department and report all fetal death, including abortion, to the bureau of vital statistics.[94] Journalist Andy Brack states that DHEC "seems to have been co-opted into making significant changes to how abortions are done in South Carolina under the cover of stealth, hoping people wouldn't figure it out."[95] But sometimes they do. After a ruckus in the press South Carolina withdrew the spousal consent requirement, stating that it had been submitted "in error."[96] Nevertheless, the pattern is repeating in Kansas and other states.

Attempted end-runs aside, *Whole Woman's Health* is a grand decision not only for its substantive content but for its tone. Indeed, the decision is an exercise in the normalization of abortion. This is partly because its matter-of-fact description of abortion as a medical procedure follows the gore-filled description provided by Justice Kennedy in *Gonzales v. Carhart*.[97] To be sure, *Carhart* dealt with a challenge to a complete ban on late-term abortions; perhaps some greater discussion of the procedure was appropriate. As Professors Michael Dorf and Sherry Colb observed with regard to the material quoted by Justice Kennedy, "only a psychopath could read that description without viscerally reacting with sympathy for the fetus."[98]

But *Whole Woman's Health* is not about fetuses. It is about how far a state can go before it has placed a substantial obstacle in a pregnant woman's way as she attempts to exercise the right to terminate a pregnancy. It is about the quality of medical care for pregnant women. Its tone is matter-of-fact as evidence about the costs to women of clinic closures (significant) are weighed against the benefits to women of the admitting privileges and ambulatory surgical center requirements (none).

Aspects of the actual procedure are presented not in the evocative moral terms of *Gonzales v. Carhart* but straightforwardly as they relate to the undue burden standard. Even the vagina gets a (very boring) shout-out. When explaining why there is no need for a hyper-sterile environment to prevent infection, the Supreme Court observed that in contrast to procedures where doctors must cut into the skin, "abortions typically involve either the administration of medicines or procedures performed through the natural opening of the birth canal, which is itself not sterile."[99] *Whole Women's Health* focused on abortion patients as worthy of respect and able to make the decision by themselves. Were the Texas restrictions to stand, patients seeking abortion services would be "less likely to get the kind of individualized attention, serious conversation, and emotional support that doctors at less taxed facilities may have offered."[100] As with any other doctor's appointment, being taken seriously and treated well is part of patient care. The Supreme Court did not query why the patients are aborting or whether the Court should worry about how patients would feel if they later learned that the product of conception (the same unborn child as in *Carhart*, though less fully formed) was suctioned out of their uterus through a plastic straw called a cannula. Instead the Court explained why Texas cannot make patient care worse for women seeking abortions in the name of unproven claims about how it is making things better.

❦

Let us return to mid-twentieth-century Connecticut and the goings-on of the Wheeler family from Richard Yates's *Revolutionary Road*. We last left Frank as he sought to savor his victory over Alice, who had at long last agreed not to have an abortion, signaling for Frank the return to domestic sanity and home life as it was meant to be.

But Frank pondering his victory was not the end of the story. Although the time for a safe abortion had passed, Alice remained quietly determined. One weekday afternoon, Alice asks her neighbor if she would mind watching the kids for a bit, as Alice is tired and would like to nap. Alone in her house, Alice gets things ready:

> In the kitchen she took down her largest stewing pot, filled it with water and set it on the stove to boil. From storage cartons in the cellar she got out the other necessary pieces of equipment: the tongs that had once been used for sterilizing formula bottles, and the blue drugstore box containing the two parts of the syringe, rubber bulb and long plastic nozzle. She dropped these things in the stewing pot, that was just beginning to steam.

By the time she'd made the other preparations, putting a
fresh supply of towels in the bathroom, writing down the number
of the hospital and propping it by the telephone, the water was
boiling nicely. It was wobbling the lid of the pot and causing the
syringe to nudge and rumble against its sides.[101]

Having sterilized her equipment, Alice proceeds with the abortion. Later that
day, she dies in a hospital of septic shock. Immediately approached by real estate agents, Frank puts the house on Revolutionary Road on the market, and
despite the unhappy death of the previous owner, it sells.

One might read this grim ending as a cautionary tale: head's up everyone,
when abortion is unavailable whether by law or circumstances, determined
women will find a way. But this we know already, except of course for the unhappily pregnant women who give up and have the baby, or for women elsewhere who like Alice die trying not to. More telling is the way Alice goes about
her plan. The pot has come to the proper boil, the towels newly laundered, the
emergency numbers posted in useful view. These details remind us how domes-
tically responsible Alice has always been: the formula bottles; her stewing pot.
Alice's character, her way of doing things, holds steady as she proceeds with
something else she's decided she has to do. For women do not change who they
are by virtue of deciding to end a pregnancy. This assurance cuts very close to the
essence of the abortion right. In *Roe v. Wade,* the Supreme Court acknowledged
that whether to terminate is up to the pregnant woman: she is best placed to
know what is right for her. That is, the woman who decides on an abortion is at
core the same person she was up to that moment. The woman Frank trusted to
raise their first two children is the same woman the law vests with authority to
decide about the third. Deciding to have an abortion is not acting "out of character." The pro-choice slogan "Trust Texas Women" says it all. We can trust Texas
women (and women of the other forty-nine states) because everyone has trusted
them (and with so much) up to this point.

Abortion silence has deep roots in patterns of social and private life, in etiquette, in religious commitments, in the demands that a steeply gendered
culture makes on women's self-conceptions. As abortion becomes less stigmatized,
as it will in time, it will come to be regarded like other medical decisions—
thoughtfully taken and exercised without a gauntlet of picketers on the pave-
ment or hard looks at home. For now, there doesn't have to be a full-on revolution, just a bit more openness and generosity.

NOTES

ACKNOWLEDGMENTS

ILLUSTRATION CREDITS

INDEX

Notes

Chapter 1   ABOUT ABORTION

1. Ewen MacAskill, "Doonesbury Abortion Cartoon Dropped by U.S. Newspapers," *Guardian,* March 12, 2012, p. 21. The cartoons are available at http://gawker.com/5892879/here-are-all-the-controversial-doonesbury-abortion-strips-your-local-papers-not-running. See also Michael Cavna, "The 'Doonesbury' Interview: Garry Trudeau Says to Ignore Abortion-Law Debate Would Have Been 'Comedy Malpractice,'" *Washington Post,* March 9, 2012, http://www.washingtonpost.com/blogs/comic-riffs/post/the-doonesbury-interview-garry-trudeau-says-to-ignore-abortion-debate-would-have-been-comedy-malpractice/2012/03/09/gIQAjTHyiR_blog.html#pagebreak.

2. Caitlin Dewey, "GoFundMe, the Site that Has Raised Money for Convicted Murderers, Will Draw the Line at Abortion and 'Sorcery,'" *Washington Post,* September 9, 2014, https://www.washingtonpost.com/news/the-intersect/wp/2014/09/09/gofundme-the-site-that-has-raised-money-for-convicted-murderers-will-draw-the-line-at-abortion-and-sorcery/.

3. Jeffery Scott, "New Miss America Kira Kazantsev Slammed for Planned Parenthood Internship," *Christian Post,* September 17, 2014, http://www.christianpost.com/news/new-miss-america-kira-kazantsev-slammed-for-planned-parenthood-internship-126563/#VqVMUY7xTShzbBH6.99.

4. The song lyrics are available at http://www.azlyrics.com/lyrics/nickcannon/canilive.html. See also Annette John–Hall, "Rapper's Abortion-Themed Video Is Striking a Chord," *Philadelphia Inquirer,* August 2, 2005, p. E01; Kelefa Sanneh, "An Unborn Fetus with a Message for Mom," *New York Times,* June 26, 2005, p. 1.

5. Zayda Rivera, "Nicki Minaj Raps About Losing a Child as a Teen in 'All Things Go,'" *New York Daily News,* December 3, 2014, http://www.nydailynews.com/entertainment/music/nicki-minaj-raps-losing-child-teen-article-1.2032038.

6. See "How TV Shows Deal with Abortion: A Timeline," *Week,* April 24, 2012, http://theweek.com/article/index/227153/how-tv-shows-deal-with-abortion-a-timeline.

7. "'The Most Dangerous Place for an African American Is in the Womb': Black Politician Criticises Anti-Abortion Billboard," *Daily Mail,* February 24, 2011, http://www.dailymail.co.uk/news/article-1360125/The-dangerous-place-African-American-womb-Black-politician-criticises-antiabortion-billboard.html.

8. Shaila Dewan, "To Court Blacks, Foes of Abortion Make Racial Case," *New York Times,* February 27, 2010, p. A1. But see Joerg Dreweke, "No Conspiracy Theories Needed: Higher Abortion Rates among Women of Color Reflect Higher Rates of Unintended Pregnancy," Guttmacher Institute, August 13, 2008, http://www.guttmacher.org/media/nr/2008/08/13/.

9. Erin Einroch and Rich Schapiro, "Mother of Girl Featured in Shocking Anti-Abortion Billboard Is Outraged by Ad: 'I Want an Apology,'" *Daily News,* February 25, 2011, http://www.nydailynews.com/new-york/mother-girl-featured-shocking-antiabortion-billboard-outraged-ad-apology-article-1.135168.

10. Susan Berry, "Black Pro-Life Leader: 'Planned Parenthood Kills Over 266 Unarmed Black Lives' Each Day," *Breitbart,* July 8, 2016, http://www.breitbart.com/big-government/2016/07/08/black-pro-life-leader-planned-parenthood-kills-266-unarmed-black-lives-day/; see also Renee B.

Sherman, "Does an Antiabortion Bill Co-Opt Black Lives Matter's Slogan?," *EBONY,* January 28, 2016, http://www.ebony.com/news-views/abortion-black-lives-matter-slogan#axzz42S93JtH5; Paige W. Cunningham, " 'Black Babies Matter': The Black Anti-Abortion Movement's Political Problems," *Washington Examiner,* September 28, 2015, http://www.washingtonexaminer.com/black -babies-matter-the-black-antiabortion-movements-political-problems/article/2572869. During the late nineteenth century, there was also concern about "race suicide," although the worry was the demise of the *white* population through the use of abortion by native-born white women. See Margarete J. Sandelowski, "Failures of Volition: Female Agency and Infertility in Historical Perspective," *Signs* 15 (1990): 486–489; Linda Gordon, *Woman's Body, Woman's Right: A Social History of Birth Control in America* (New York: Penguin Books, 1977), 95–185.

11. Richard R. Sharp et al., "Moral Attitudes and Beliefs among Couples Pursuing PDG for Sex Selection," *Reproductive Biomedicine Online* 21 (2010): 842, http://www.rbmojournal.com/article /S1472-6483(10)00623-1/abstract.

12. Jason Abrevaya, "Are There Missing Girls in the United States? Evidence from Birth Data," *American Economic Journal: Applied Economics* 1, no. 2 (2009): 1–34; see also Sharp et al., "Moral Attitudes," 838–847. But see Brian Citro et al., "Replacing Myth with Facts: Sex-Selective Abortion Laws in the U.S.," *Cornell Law Faculty Publications,* June 2014, https://napawf.org/wp-content/ uploads/2014/06/Replacing-Myths-with-Facts-final.pdf.

13. See Steven D. Levitt and Stephen J. Dubner, *Freakonomics: A Rogue Economist Explores the Hidden Side of Everything* (New York: William Morrow, 2006) and John J. Donohue III and Steven D. Levitt, "The Impact of Legalized Abortion on Crime," *Quarterly Journal of Economics* 116 (2001): 379–420. But see Ted Joyce, "Did Legalized Abortion Lower Crime?" *Journal of Human Resources* 39 (2004): 1–28. The dispute has gone many rounds: see John J. Donohue III and Steven D. Levitt, "Further Evidence that Legalized Abortion Lowered Crime: A Reply to Joyce," *Journal of Human Resources* 39 (2004): 29–49; Steven D. Leavitt, "Understanding Why Crime Fell in the 1990s: Four Factors that Explain the Decline and Six that Do Not," *Journal of Economic Perspectives* 18 (2004): 186. More recent studies are summarized in Theodore J. Joyce, "Abortion and Crime" (National Bureau of Economic Research Working Paper No. 15098, June 2009), http://www.nber.org/papers/w15098.

14. See Carol Sanger, " 'The Birth of Death': Stillborn Birth Certificates and the Problem for Law," *California Law Review* 100 (2012): 269–312; see also "MISSing Angels Bill (MAB) Legislation State—Chart," *M.I.S.S Foundation,* http://missingangelsbill.org/index.php?option =com_content&view=article&id=76&Itemid=61, accessed February 10, 2016 (as of July 25, 2011, thirty-two states have enacted Missing Angel bills); see also Allison Stevens, "The Politics of Stillbirth," *American Prospect,* July 13, 2007, http://prospect.org/article/politics -stillbirth.

15. See Sanger, " 'Birth of Death,' " 306.

16. The states are Alaska, Arizona, Indiana, and Missouri.

17. F. Gary Cunningham et al., eds., *Williams Obstetrics* (New York: McGraw-Hill, 2010), 3.

18. Lisa B. Haddad and Nawal M. Nour, "Unsafe Abortion: Unnecessary Maternal Mortality," *Reviews in Obstetrics and Gynecology* 2 (2009): 122.

19. *Roe v. Wade,* 410 U.S. 113 (1973).

20. Ibid., 125, 153.

21. Mary Anne Glendon, *Abortion and Divorce in Western Law* (Cambridge, MA: Harvard University Press, 1987), 30.

22. Steven Ertelt, "2012 GOP Candidates Sign Pro-Life Pledge; Romney, Cain Decline," *LifeNews.com,* June 17, 2011, http://www.lifenews.com/2011/06/17/2012-gop-candidates-sign-pro -life-pledge-romney-cain-refuse/.

23. *Roe v. Wade,* 129.

24. John H. Ely, "The Wages of Crying Wolf: A Comment on *Roe v. Wade*," *Yale Law Journal* 82 (1973): 947.

25. See Jack. M. Balkin, ed., *What Roe v. Wade Should Have Said: The Nation's Top Legal Experts Rewrite America's Most Controversial Decision* (New York: New York University Press, 2005), particularly Reva B. Siegel's concurring opinion, 63–85; see also Reva B. Siegel, "Sex Equality Arguments for Reproductive Rights: Their Critical Basis and Evolving Constitutional Expression," *Emory Law Journal* 56 (2007): 815–842. Jack M. Balkin, "The New Originalism and the Uses of History," *Fordham Law Review* 82 (2013): 641–719.

26. *Alyne da Silva Pimentel Teixeria (deceased) v. Brazil,* CEDAW/C/49/D/17/2008, August 10, 2011; Corte Constitucional (Constitutional Court), May 10, 2006, Sentencia C-355/2006, Gaceta de la Corte Constitucional (Colombia) (partial translation is available in Women's Link World-wide, *C-355/2006: Excerpts of the Constitutional Court's Ruling that Liberalized Abortion in Colombia* (2007)); *Karen Noelia Llantoy Huamán v. Peru,* Communication No. 1153/2003, U.N. Doc. CCPR/C/85/D/1153/2003 (2005). See also Christina Zampas and Jaime M. Gher, "Abortion as a Human Right: International and Regional Standards," *Human Rights Law Review* 8 (2008): 250.

27. See Robert Post, "Informed Consent to Abortion: A First Amendment Analysis of Compelled Physician Speech," *University of Illinois Law Review* 2007 (2007): 940–944. For an argument on behalf of abortion patients required to listen to the legislative scripts, see Caroline M. Corbin, "The First Amendment Right against Compelled Listening," *Boston University Law Review* 89 (2009): 939–1016.

28. See "Church and Medicine: An Overview," *Physicians for Reproductive Health,* January 8, 2009, http://www.prch.org/church-and-medicine-an-overview.

29. See *State Policies in Brief: Refusing to Provide Health Services,* Guttmacher Institute, November 1, 2015, http://www.guttmacher.org/statecenter/spibs/spib_RPHS.pdf. See also 42 U.S.C. § 300a-7 (1973); Jody Feder, "The History and Effect of Abortion Conscience Clause Laws," Congressional Research Service Report for Congress, February 27, 2006, http://research .policyarchive.org/3696.pdf.

30. See Elizabeth Sepper, "Taking Conscience Seriously," *Virginia Law Review* 98 (2012): 1501–1575; Bernard M. Dickens, "The Right to Conscience," in *Abortion Law in Transnational Perspective,* ed. Rebecca J. Cook, Joanna N. Erdman, and Bernard M. Dickens (Philadelphia: University of Pennsylvania Press, 2014), 210; Carole E. Joffe, *Doctors of Conscience: The Struggle to Provide Abortion before and after Roe v. Wade* (Boston: Beacon Press, 1995).

31. *Planned Parenthood v. Casey,* 505 U.S. 833, 846 (1992).

32. Pope John Paul II's encyclical *Evangelium Vitae,* March 25, 1995, para. 101, 12. "Among all the crimes which can be committed against life," said the Pope, "procured abortion has characteristics making it particularly serious and deplorable. The Second Vatican Council defines abortion, together with infanticide, as an 'unspeakable crime'" (ibid., para. 58).

33. Joseph Cardinal Ratzinger's letter to bishops, "Worthiness to Receive Holy Communion: General Principles," July 2004; see generally Gregory C. Sisk and Charles J. Reid Jr., "Abortion, Bishops, Eucharist, and Politicians: A Question of Communion," *Catholic Lawyer* 43 (2004): 255–288.

34. Laurie Goodstein, "Bishop Would Deny Rite for Defiant Catholic Voters," *New York Times,* May 14, 2004, p. A16; Laurie Goodstein et al., "Vatican Cardinal Signals Backing for Sanctions on Kerry," *New York Times,* April 24, 2004, p. A13.

35. Most Reverend Michael J. Sheridan, "A Pastoral Letter to the Catholic Faithful of the Diocese of Colorado Springs on the Duties of Catholic Politicians and Voters," May 1, 2004.

36. Claire Chretien, "Catholics Rally outside Richmond Bishop's Office Urging him to Deny Communion to Tim Kaine," *Life Site,* September 30, 2016, https://www.lifesitenews.com/news /catholics-rally-outside-diocese-of-richmond-asking-bishop-to-enforce-canon.

37. Laurie Goodstein, "Pope Says Church Is 'Obsessed' with Gays, Abortion and Birth Control," *New York Times,* September 20, 2013, p. A1; Adam Withnall, "Pope Francis Denounces Abortion as 'Horrific,'" *Independent,* January 23, 2014, http://www.independent.co.uk/news/people /news/pope-francis-denounces-abortion-as-horrific-9058040.html; Tim Hume, "Pope Francis Extends Catholic Priests' Power to Forgive Abortion," *CNN,* November 21, 2016, http://www.cnn. com/2016/11/21/europe/pope-francis-absolve-abortion/. His earlier statements on absolution had been criticized for reinforcing abortion status as a sin: Jill Filipovic, "The Pope's Unforgiving Message of Forgiveness on Abortion," *New York Times,* September 11, 2015, p. A29.

38. Cathleen Kaveny, *A Culture of Engagement: Law, Religion, and Morality* (Washington, DC: Georgetown University Press, 2016), 123.

39. See generally *Catholics for Choice,* http://www.catholicsforchoice.org/, accessed October 24, 2016; *Jewish Pro-Life Foundation,* http://www.jewishprolifefoundation.org/, accessed October 24, 2016.

40. Mario M. Cuomo, "Religious Belief and Public Morality: A Catholic Governor's Perspective," *Notre Dame Journal of Law, Ethics & Public Policy* 1 (1984): 16. See also Robert Wuthnow, *Rough Country: How Texas Became America's Most Powerful Bible-Belt State* (Princeton, NJ: Princeton University Press, 2014), 418–419.

41. See the "Resolution on Abortion: Kansas City, Missouri—1984," *Southern Baptist Convention,* http://www.sbc.net/resolutions/21/resolution-on-abortion, accessed February 10, 2016.

42. Wuthnow, *Rough Country,* 366. Wuthnow notes that "a conservative person of faith knew that Republicans were now the ones who offered respect."

43. Marcia Pally, *The New Evangelicals: Expanding the Vision of the Common Good* (Grand Rapids, MI: William B. Eerdmans, 2011), 224–229.

44. See Elizabeth Wicks, *The Right to Life and Conflicting Interests* (Oxford: Oxford University Press, 2010), 5–9, 17–20. On consciousness, see Hugo Lagercrantz and Jean-Pierre Changeux, "The Emergence of Human Consciousness: From Fetal to Neonatal Life," *Pediatric Research* 65 (2009): 255–260; on sentience, see Jeff McMahan, *The Ethics of Killing: Problems at the Margins of Life* (New York : Oxford University Press, 2002), 268–300; on conception see Christopher Kaczor, *The Ethics of Abortion: Women's Rights, Human Life, and the Question of Justice* (New York: Routledge, 2011), 100–113.

45. See generally Louis Pojman and Francis J. Beckwith, eds., *Abortion Controversy: 25 Years after Roe vs. Wade—A Reader* (Belmont, CA: Wadsworth, 1998); John T. Noonan Jr., ed., *The Morality of Abortion: Legal and Historical Perspectives* (Cambridge, MA: Harvard University Press, 1970); David Boonin, *A Defense of Abortion* (Cambridge: Cambridge University Press, 2003).

46. Rosalind Hursthouse, "Virtue Theory and Abortion," *Philosophy & Public Affairs* 20 (1991): 237–238.

47. *R. B. v. Mississippi,* 790 So.2d 830, 835 (Miss. 2001) (Easley, J., concurring).

48. See Joffe, *Doctors of Conscience.*

49. Ann Furedi, "Wrong but the Right Thing to Do: Public Opinion and Abortion," in *Abortion Law and Politics Today,* ed. Ellie Lee (New York: St. Martin's Press, 1998), 159–171; Sepper, "Taking Conscience Seriously," 1529.

50. *R. B. v. Mississippi,* 835.

51. John Finnis, "Law, Morality and 'Sexual Orientation,'" in *Same Sex: Debating the Ethics, Science, and Culture of Homosexuality,* ed. John Corvino (Lanham, MD: Rowman & Littlefield, 1997), 34.

52. Kristin Luker, *Abortion and the Politics of Motherhood* (Berkeley: University of California Press, 1984), 165.

53. See *State Policies in Brief: State Funding of Abortion under Medicaid,* Guttmacher Institute, November 1, 2012, http://www.guttmacher.org/statecenter/spibs/spib_SFAM.pdf. To avoid the

problem of women claiming rape just to get an abortion, some cling to the pseudo-scientific view that "real" rape doesn't result in pregnancy anyway: as Representative Todd Aiken of Missouri explained in 2012, in cases of "legitimate rape," the female body has "ways to try to shut that whole thing down." Aaron Blake, "Todd Akin, GOP Senate Candidate: 'Legitimate Rape' Rarely Causes Pregnancy," *Washington Post,* August 19, 2012, https://www.washingtonpost.com/news/the-fix/wp/2012/08/19/todd-akin-gop-senate-candidate-legitimate-rape-rarely-causes-pregnancy/. On this account, pregnancy results only from voluntary sex, with abortion serving as an undeserved "get out of jail free" card.

54. Marc Santora, "Police to Limit Street Seizures of Condoms for Evidence," *New York Times,* May 13, 2014, p. A17.

55. See 42 U.S.C. § 710(b)(2)(C)–(D) (2000). See also *Silver Ring Thing,* http://www.silverringthing.com, accessed November 12, 2015; Cathryn Creno, "School Board Will Yank Abortion Mention in Biology Book," *Arizona Republic,* October 30, 2014, http://www.usatoday.com/story/news/nation/2014/10/30/biology-textbook-abortion/18171511/.

56. "Dr. Peter Baerman: Do Virginity Pledges Work?," *pbs.org,* April 13, 2005, http://www.pbs.org/pov/shelbyknox/special_pledges_1.php.

57. Rebecca Schleifer et al., "Ignorance Only: HIV/AIDS, Human Rights and Federally Funded Abstinence-Only Programs in the United States," *Human Rights Watch* 14 no. 5 (2002), https://www.hrw.org/reports/2002/usa0902/USA0902.pdf.

58. Laurie S. Zabin et al., "To whom Do Inner-City Minors Talk about Their Pregnancies? Adolescents' Communication with Parents and Parent Surrogates," *Family Planning Perspectives* 24 (1992): 148–154, 173.

59. Tracey E. George and Albert H. Yoon, "The Gavel Gap: Who Sits in Judgment on State Courts?," *American Constitution Society for Law and Policy,* http://gavelgap.org/pdf/gavel-gap-report.pdf, 2.

60. The exact number introduced between January 1, 2011, and April 21, 2011, was 916. See *State Legislative Trends: Hostility to Abortion Rights Increases,* Guttmacher Institute, April 12, 2011, http://www.guttmacher.org/media/inthenews/2011/04/12/. For a detailed analysis, see *Laws Affecting Reproductive Health and Rights: Trends in the First Quarter of 2011,* Guttmacher Institute, 2011, http://www.guttmacher.org/statecenter/updates/2011/statetrends12011.html.

61. Katharine Q. Seelye, "Voters Defeat Many G.O.P.-Sponsored Measures," *New York Times,* November 8, 2011, p. A20.

62. This was not always the case. In 1972 a majority of Democrats and Republicans agreed with the proposition that a decision about abortion should be left to the pregnant woman and her doctor. See Jill Lepore, "Birthright: What's Next for Planned Parenthood," *New Yorker,* November 14, 2011.

63. Lydia Saad, "U.S. Still Split on Abortion: 47% Pro-Choice, 46% Pro-Life," *Gallup,* May 22, 2014, http://www.gallup.com/poll/170249/split-abortion-pro-choice-pro-life.aspx.

64. Jessica Bulman-Pozen, "Partisan Federalism," *Harvard Law Review* 127 (2014): 1077–1147.

65. See generally Heather D. Boonstra, "Off Base: The U.S. Military's Ban on Privately Funded Abortions," *Guttmacher Policy Review* 13, no. 3 (2010): 2–7.

66. See 10 U.S.C. § 1093(b).

67. Boonstra, "Off Base," 1–3.

68. See generally Susan A. Cohen, "U.S. Overseas Family Planning Program, Perennial Victim of Abortion Politics, Is Once Again under Siege," *Guttmacher Policy Review* 14, no. 4 (2011): 7.

69. Richard P. Caldarone, Brandice Canes-Wrone, and Tom S. Clark, "Partisan Labels and Democratic Accountability: An Analysis of State Supreme Court Abortion Decisions," *Journal of Politics* 71 (2009): 560–573; Melinda Gann Hall, "State Supreme Courts in American Democracy: Probing the Myths of Judicial Reform," *American Political Science Review* 95 (2001): 315–330.

70. *Deters v. Judicial Retirement & Removal Commission,* 873 S.W.2d 200, 201 (Ky. 1994). But see *Republican Party of Minnesota. v. White,* 536 U.S. 765, 788 (2002) (holding in a 5–4 decision that that the prohibition violated the First Amendment rights of judicial candidates). Although it is unclear if *White,* which dealt with an "announce" clause, necessarily invalidates the "commit clauses" that were at issue in the Kentucky *Deters* case, it seems quite clear that judicial candidates after *White* are freer to express their views—if not their commitment regarding future cases—about abortion.

71. *Deters v. Judicial Retirement & Removal Commission,* 202.

72. Ibid., 201–203.

73. Sarah Palin, *Going Rogue: An American Life* (New York: Harper, 2009), 171–172.

74. *Roe v. Wade,* 152–153.

75. Susan M. Okin, *Justice, Gender, and the Family* (New York: Basic Books, 1989), 134–169.

76. Luker, *Abortion and the Politics of Motherhood,* 158–175.

77. *Planned Parenthood v. Casey,* 856.

78. Naomi Cahn and June Carbone, *Red Families v. Blue Families: Legal Polarization and the Creation of Culture* (Oxford: Oxford University Press, 2010); Susan Moller Okin, *Justice, Gender, and the Family* (New York: Basic Books, 1989), 134–169.

79. Rayna Rapp, *Testing Women, Testing the Fetus: The Social Impact of Amniocentesis in America* (New York: Routledge, 1999), 131.

80. See Angel M. Foster, Jane van Dis, and Jody Steinauer, "Educational and Legislative Initiatives Affecting Residency Training in Abortion," *Journal of the American Medical Association* 290 (2003): 1777–1778; see also *State Policies in Brief: Refusing to Provide Health Services,* Guttmacher Institute, November 1, 2015, http://www.guttmacher.org/statecenter/spibs/spib_RPHS.pdf.

81. *Burwell v. Hobby Lobby Stores, Inc.,* 134 S. Ct. 2751 (2014).

82. Frank Davidoff and James Trussell, "Plan B and the Politics of Doubt," *Journal of the American Medical Association* 296 (2006): 1775.

83. See "Statement on the So-Called 'Morning-After Pill,'" Vatican, Pontifical Academy for Life, Oct. 31, 2000, http://www.vatican.va/roman_curia/pontifical_academies/acdlife/documents/rc_pa_acdlife_doc_20001031_pillola-giorno-dopo_en.html. This was the basis of Governor Mitt Romney's 2005 veto of Massachusetts legislation authorizing specially trained pharmacists to prescribe emergency contraception to teenagers; Pam Belluck, "Massachusetts Veto Seeks to Curb Morning-After Pill," *New York Times,* July 26, 2005, p. A10. The Massachusetts legislature overrode Romney's veto (the Senate voted unanimously 37–0 to override the veto). "Mass. Lawmakers Override 'Morning After' Veto—Measure Would Expand Access to Emergency Contraception Drug," *NBC News,* September 15, 2005, http://www.nbcnews.com/id/9357672/ns/health-womens_health/t/mass-lawmakers-override-morning-after-veto/#.VjE3Y7TFsdU.

84. Davidoff and Trussell, "Plan B," 1775; Food and Drug Administration, *Decision Process to Deny Initial Application for Over-the-Counter Marketing of the Emergency Contraceptive Drug Plan B Was Unusual* (U.S. Government Accountability Office Report to Congressional Requesters GAO-06-109, November 2005), http://www.gao.gov/assets/250/248498.pdf.

85. See Ellie Lee, *Abortion, Motherhood, and Mental Health: Medicalizing Reproduction in the United States and Great Britain* (New York: Aldine de Gruyter, 2003).

86. Peggy Hau, "The Politics of Law, Language, & Morality: Thucydides & the Abortion Debate," *Southern California Interdisciplinary Law Journal* 8 (1999): 736.

87. On the constitutional complications of officially themed license plates, see Caroline Mala Corbin, "Mixed Speech: When Speech Is Both Private and Governmental," *New York University Law Review* 83 (2008): 641–644.

88. "In Touch Exclusive Interview & Photos: Sarah & Bristol Palin, 'We're Glad We Chose Life,'" *In Touch*, January 13, 2010, http://www.intouchweekly.com/posts/in-touch-exclusive -interview-photos-sarah-bristol-palin-we-re-glad-we-chose-life-21780.

89. *Abortion Changes You*, http://www.abortionchangesyou.com, accessed November 13, 2015.

90. Gillian Aldrich and Jennifer Baumgardner, *I Had an Abortion* (New York: Women Make Movies, 2005), DVD.

91. Janelle Sue Taylor, "The Public Fetus and the Family Car: From Abortion Politics to a Volvo Advertisement," *Public Culture* 4 (1992): 67.

92. Rachel Fuller, *Waiting for Baby* (Swindon, UK: Child's Play International Limited, 2009).

93. *Dillon v. Legg*, 68 Cal. 2d 728, 740 (1968).

94. See Carol Sanger, "Legislating with Effect: Emotion and Legislative Law Making," in *Passions and Emotions*, ed. James E. Fleming (New York: New York University Press, 2013), 38–76. See also Elizabeth G. Porter, "Taking Images Seriously," *Columbia Law Review* 114 (2014): 1687–1782.

95. Lindy West, "I Set Up #ShoutYourAbortion Because I am Not Sorry, and I Will Not Whisper," *Guardian*, September 22, 2015, https://www.theguardian.com/commentisfree/2015/sep /22/i-set-up-shoutyourabortion-because-i-am-not-sorry-and-i-will-not-whisper.

96. *Greenville Women's Clinic v. Commissioner, S.C. Department of Health*, 317 F.3d 357, 377 (4th Cir. 2002).

97. Samuel W. Buell, "Criminal Abortion Revisited," *New York University Law Review* 66 (1991): 1774–1831.

98. Malcolm Feeley, *The Process Is the Punishment: Handling Cases in a Lower Criminal Court* (New York: Russell Sage Foundation, 1979).

99. Reva B. Siegel, "The New Politics of Abortion: An Equality Analysis of Woman-Protective Abortion Restrictions," *University of Illinois Law Review* 2007 (2007): 991–1053.

Chapter 2 THE LAW FROM *ROE* FORWARD

1. See Carole Joffe, *Doctors of Conscience: The Struggle to Provide Abortion before and after Roe v. Wade* (Boston: Beacon Press, 1995). See also Leslie J. Reagan, *When Abortion Was a Crime: Women, Medicine, and Law in the United States, 1867–1973* (Berkeley: University of California Press, 1997).

2. Linda Greenhouse and Reva Siegel, eds., *Before Roe v. Wade: Voices that Shaped the Abortion Debate before the Supreme Court's Ruling* (New York: Kaplan, 2010), 7–8; David J. Garrow, *Liberty and Sexuality: The Right to Privacy and the Making of Roe v. Wade* (Berkeley: University of California Press, 1998), 486–487; Laura Kaplan, *The Story of Jane: The Legendary Underground Feminist Abortion Service* (New York: Pantheon Books, 1995).

3. Beth Palmer, "Lonely, Tragic, but Legally Necessary Pilgrimages: Transnational Abortion Travel in the 1970s," *Canadian Historical Review* 92 (2011): 638.

4. See Reagan, *When Abortion Was a Crime*, 193–215.

5. Susan B. Hansen, "State Implementation of Supreme Court Decisions: Abortion Rates since *Roe v. Wade*," *Journal of Politics* 42 (1980): 378.

6. Edward Weinstock et al., "Legal Abortions in the United States since the 1973 Supreme Court Decisions," *Family Planning Perspectives* 7 (1975): 28.

7. Willard Cates Jr. and Roger Rochat, "Illegal Abortions in the United States: 1972–1974," *Family Planning Perspectives* 8 (1976): 87.

8. James C. Mohr, *Abortion in America: The Origins and Evolutions of National Policy, 1800–1900* (New York: Oxford University Press, 1978), 200–245; Reva Siegel, "Reasoning from the Body:

A Historical Perspective on Abortion Regulation and Questions of Equal Protection," *Stanford Law Review* 44 (1992): 261–381; Reagan, *When Abortion Was a Crime*, 113–131; Janet F. Brodie, *Contraception and Abortion in Nineteenth-Century America* (Ithaca, NY: Cornell University Press, 1994).

9. Linda Gordon, *Woman's Body, Woman's Right: Birth Control in America* (New York: Penguin Books, 1990); Garrow, *Liberty and Sexuality*.

10. Philippa Strum, *Louis D. Brandeis: Justice for the People* (Cambridge, MA: Harvard University Press, 1984); Daniel K. Williams, *Defenders of the Unborn: The Pro-Life Movement before* Roe v. Wade (New York: Oxford University Press, 2016); David J. Garrow, "How *Roe v. Wade* Was Written," *Washington and Lee Law Review* 71 (2014): 893–924.

11. Linda Greenhouse, *Becoming Justice Blackmun: Harry Blackmun's Supreme Court Journey* (New York: Times Books, 2005), 94–95.

12. See Human Rights Act 1998, Section 19; New Zealand Bill of Rights Act 1990, section 7.

13. *Roe v. Wade*, 410 U.S. 113, 164 (1973).

14. Heather D. Boonstra, "The Heart of the Matter: Public Funding of Abortion for Poor Women in the United States," *Guttmacher Policy Review* 10 (2007): 12–16.

15. *Maher v. Roe*, 432 U.S. 464, 474 (1977).

16. Ibid.

17. Ibid., 474, 465.

18. *Harris v. McRae*, 448 U.S. 297, 316 (1980).

19. Ibid.

20. Ibid., 318.

21. Rickie Solinger, " 'A Complete Disaster': Abortion and the Politics of Hospital Abortion Committees, 1950–1970," *Feminist Studies* 19 (1993): 258–259.

22. Ibid., 250–254.

23. Mary Ziegler, *After Roe: The Lost History of the Abortion Debate* (Cambridge, MA: Harvard University Press, 2015), 29.

24. See Leslie Bennttes, "Anti-Abortion Forces in Disarray Less than a Year after Victories In," *New York Times,* September 22, 1981, p. B5; John G. Ferreira, "The Human Life Bill: Personhood Revisited, or Congress Takes Aim at *Roe v. Wade*," *Hofstra Law Review* 10 (1982): 1269–1295; Robert A. Destro, "Abortion and the Constitution: The Need for a Life Protective Amendment," *California Law Review* 63 (1975): 1321–1325.

25. Ziegler, *After Roe*, 30; see also Ronald Reagan, *Abortion and Conscience of the Nation* (Nashville: T. Nelson, 1984).

26. *City of Akron v. Akron Center for Reproductive Health Inc.*, 462 U.S. 416, 442–449 (1983).

27. Ibid., 442–449.

28. Ibid., 444.

29. Ibid.

30. Ibid., 438.

31. Ibid., 444.

32. Ibid., 444–445.

33. *Thornburgh v. American College of Obstetricians & Gynecologists,* 476 U.S. 747, 750 (1986).

34. Ibid., 763.

35. Ibid.

36. Ibid., 764.

37. Ibid., 762.

38. Ibid.

39. See Michael J. Graetz and Linda Greenhouse, *The Burger Court and the Rise of the Judicial Right* (New York: Simon & Schuster, 2016), 133–161, 148–154.

40. Susan R. Estrich and Kathleen M. Sullivan, "Abortion Politics: Writing for an Audience of One," *University of Pennsylvania Law Review* 138 (1989): 119–155; *Webster v. Reproductive Health Services,* 492 U.S. 490 (1989).

41. *Planned Parenthood v. Casey,* 505 U.S. 833 (1992).

42. Ibid., 846.

43. Ibid., 860.

44. Ibid., 869, 701.

45. Ibid., 872.

46. Ibid., 878.

47. Ibid., 882.

48. *Thornburgh v. American College of Obstetricians & Gynecologists,* 763.

49. *Planned Parenthood v. Casey,* 882.

50. See Michael Dorf, "Symposium: Abortion is Still a Fundamental Right," *SCOTUSblog,* January 4, 2016, http://www.scotusblog.com/2016/01/symposium-abortion-is-still-a-fundamental-right/.

51. *Planned Parenthood v. Casey,* 877.

52. Ibid.

53. See Gillian E. Metzger, "Unburdening the Undue Burden Standard: Orienting 'Casey' in Constitutional Jurisprudence," *Columbia Law Review* 94 (1994): 2029–2036.

54. *Planned Parenthood v. Casey,* 882.

55. See, for example, Merrit Kennedy, "Indiana Governor Signs New Abortion Restrictions Into Law," *The Two-Way,* March 25, 2016, http://www.npr.org/sections/thetwo-way/2016/03/25/471842196/indiana-governor-signs-new-abortion-restrictions-into-law; see also Jill Lepore, "Birthright: American Chronicles," *New Yorker,* November 14, 2011.

56. Justice Antonin Scalia, a ferocious detractor of *Roe v. Wade,* had died a few months earlier, and Congress refused to act on President Obama's nomination of Judge Merrick Garland.

57. *Whole Woman's Health v. Lakey,* 46 F. Supp. 3d 673, 684 (W.D. Tex. 2014).

58. *Gonzales v. Carhart,* 550 U.S. 124, 165 (2007).

59. *Whole Woman's Health v. Hellerstedt,* 136 S. Ct. 2292, 2318 (2016).

60. *Miller v. Albright,* 523 U.S. 420 (1998).

61. Ibid., 423.

62. Ibid., 438.

63. Ibid.

64. Ibid., 433–434.

65. See Mei Fong, *One Child: The Story of China's Most Radical Experiment* (Boston: Houghton Mifflin Harcourt, 2016), x, 60–62, 74–81.

66. 141 Cong. Rec. H72, 94 (daily ed. July 20, 1995) (statement of Rep. Ros-Lehtinen).

67. 8 U.S.C. § 1101 (a) (42) (1957).

68. See *Xin-Chang Zhang v. Slattery,* 55 F.3d 732, 737–739 (2nd Cir. 1995).

69. Ibid., 738.

70. 8 U.S.C. §1 101 (a) (42) (B) (1957).

71. *Matter of C-Y-Z-,* 21 I. & N. Dec. 915, 918 (B.I.A. 1997).

72. Mona Ma, "A Tale of Two Policies: A Defense of China's Population Policy and an Examination of U.S. Asylum Policy," *Cleveland State Law Review* 59 (2011): 264 (fn. 219); See also Ko-Lin Chin, *Smuggled Chinese: Clandestine Immigration to the United States* (Philadelphia: Temple University Press, 1999), 188–189.

73. *Shi Liang Lin v. United States Department of Justice,* 494 F.3d 296 (2nd Cir. 2007).

74. *Matter of J-S-,* 24 I. & N. Dec. 520, 523 (B.I.A. 2008).

75. *Cleveland Bar Association v. Cleary,* 93 Ohio St. 3d 191 (2001).

76. Ibid., 192.

77. Ibid., 193.

78. Ibid., 196.

79. Ibid.

80. Ibid., 201. See also the Associated Press, "Judge Who Jailed Pregnant Woman Disciplined," *USA Today,* September 19, 2001, http://usatoday30.usatoday.com/news/nation/2001/09/19/abortion-judge.htm.

81. *Cleveland Bar Association v. Cleary,* 196.

82. Ibid., 201.

83. *In re Bourisseau,* 480 N.W.2d 270, 271 (Mich. 1992).

84. *In re Disciplinary Proceeding against Sanders,* 135 Wash. 2d 175, 180 (1998).

85. Ibid.

86. *Pell v. Procunier,* 417 U.S. 817, 822 (1974). See Claire Deason, "Unexpected Consequences: The Constitutional Implications of Federal Prison Policy for Offenders Considering Abortion," *Minnesota Law Review* 93 (2009): 1377–1409.

87. *Roe v. Crawford,* 514 F.3d 789 (8th Cir. 2008).

88. Diana Kasdan, "Abortion Access for Incarcerated Women: Are Correctional Health Practices in Conflict with Constitutional Standards?," *Perspectives on Sexual and Reproductive Health* 41 (2009): 59.

89. *Roe v. Crawford,* 798.

90. *Victoria W. v. Larpenter,* 369 F.3d 475 (5th Cir. 2004).

91. "Ex-Inmate Can Sue La. Prison Officials Who Blocked Her Abortion," *Health Law Litigation Reporter* 9 (2002).

92. *Sherron v. State,* 959 So.2d 30 (Miss. App. 2006).

93. Ibid., 32.

94. Ibid., 35.

95. *Reese v. State,* 33 S.W.3d 238, 239 (Tex. Crim. App. 2000).

96. Ibid., 242.

97. Ibid.

98. Ibid., 240.

99. Ibid., 242. See also *Erazo v. State,* 167 S.W.3d 889 (Tex. App. 2005).

100. Ibid., 243.

101. *People v. Rios,* No. G031541, 2004 Cal. App. Unpub. LEXIS 6026 (Cal. Ct. App. Jun. 24, 2004); *Hicks v. Commonwealth,* No. 0430-06-4, 2007 Va. App. LEXIS 177 (Ct. App. May 1, 2007); and *Rogers v. State,* Nos. 05-05-00283-CR, 05-05-00284-CR, 2006 Tex. App. LEXIS 1609 (App. Mar. 1, 2006).

102. Susan A. Bandes and Jessica M. Salerno, "Emotion, Proof and Prejudice: The Cognitive Science of Gruesome Photos and Victim Impact Statements," *Arizona State Law Journal* 46 (2014): 1022.

103. *Steele v. Atlanta Maternal-Fetal Medicine P.C.,* 271 Ga. App. 622, 630 (2005).

104. Ibid.

105. *Wilson v. U.S. West Communications,* 58 F.3d 1337 (8th Cir. 1995).

106. Ibid., 1339.

107. Ibid., 1341.

108. *Wishnatsky v. Schuetzle,* No. 97-1130, 1998 U.S. App. LEXIS 5966, at *1–2 (8th Cir. Mar. 27, 1998).

109. See, for example, "Business Cards," *Abortion No,* http://www.abortionno.org/product-category/business-cards/, accessed May 7, 2016; and "Free Postcards: Unborn Persons," *Pro-Life Future,* http://prolifefuture.org/free-postcards-unborn-persons/, accessed May 7, 2016.

110. *Wishnatsky v. Schuetzle,* 2.

111. Ibid., 2.

112. Ibid., 1–2.

113. Ibid., 3.

114. *World Wide St. Preachers' Fellowship v. City of Owensboro,* 342 F. Supp. 2d 634 (W.D. Ky. 2004); see also "Graphic Anti-Abortion Billboard Disturbs Orlando Residents," *WFTV.com,* May 11, 2005, http://www.freerepublic.com/focus/f-news/1401500/posts (reporting on neighborhood distress caused after a Center for Bio-Ethical Reform [CBR] poster of a "fetus, torn into pieces and covered in blood" was displayed on a residential street).

115. *World Wide St. Preachers' Fellowship v. City of Owensboro,* 639.

116. *State v. Otterstad,* 734 N.W.2d 642 (Minn. 2007).

117. Ibid., 646 (fn. 2). See also *Center for Bio Ethical Reform, Inc. v. City of Springboro,* 477 F.3d 807 (6th Cir. 2007) (acknowledging that the CBR's free exercise rights were not infringed by police stopping a billboard truck out of concern for public safety after noticing drivers wearing helmets, body armor, and talking on the radio). The Sixth Circuit reversed summary judgment in favor of the officers and remanded the case on the grounds that CBR's Fourth Amendment rights may have been violated by the length of the stop. (Ibid., 825–827).

118. *Claudio v. United States,* 836 F. Supp. 1230, 1232 (E.D.N.C. 1993).

119. *R v. British Broadcasting Corporation Ex Parte Prolife Alliance* |2004| 1 A.C. 185 (U.K.).

120. Ibid., 223–224, 236.

121. Ibid., 185; for a critical analysis of the decision, see Jesse Elvin, *"R v. British Broadcasting Corporation Ex Parte Pro Life Alliance:* The Right to Free Speech Standards of Taste and Decency, and the 'Truth' about Abortions," *Web Journal Current Legal Issues* 1 (2004).

122. *Gillett Communications v. Becker,* 807 F. Supp. 757 (N.D. Ga. 1992); see Milagros Rivera-Sanchez and Paul H. Gates Jr., "Abortion on the Air: Broadcasters and Indecent Political Advertising," *Federal Communications Law Journal* 46 (1994): 267–287; Hille von Rosenvinge Sheppard, "The Federal Communications Act and the Broadcast of Aborted Fetus Advertisements," *University of Chicago Legal Forum* 1993 (1993): 393–415.

Chapter 3 ABORTION PRIVACY / ABORTION SECRECY

1. *Roe v. Wade,* 410 U.S. 113, 120 (1973).

2. Ibid., fn. 4. On Henry Wade, see Wolfgang Saxon, "Henry Wade Prosecutor in National Spotlight, Dies at 86," *New York Times,* March 2, 2001, p. B8. For more on Jane Roe, see David J. Garrow, *Liberty and Sexuality: The Right to Privacy and the Making of* Roe v. Wade (Berkeley: University of California Press, 1998); Norma McCorvey with Andy Meisler, *I Am Roe: My Life,* Roe v. Wade, *and Freedom of Choice* (New York: HarperCollins, 1994).

3. *Cox Broadcasting Corp. v. Cohn,* 420 U.S. 469, 492 (1975).

4. *Doe v. Blue Cross & Blue Shield United,* 112 F.3d 869, 872 (7th Cir. 1997).

5. *Doe v. Steagall,* 653 F.2d 180, 185 (5th Cir. 1981).

6. *Doe. v. Rostker,* 89 F.R.D. 158, 161 (N.D. Cal. 1981).

7. Ibid.

8. Beth M. Merfish, "My Mother's Abortion," *New York Times,* July 8, 2013, p. A21.

9. Ibid. (emphasis added).

10. Health Insurance Portability and Accountability Act of 1996, Pub. L. No. 104–191, 110 Stat. 1936 (1996) (codified as amended in scattered sections of Title 42). J. Andrew Lee et al., "Insured Women and Payment for Elective Abortion," *Women's Health Issues* 18 (2008): 347–350; Rachel K. Jones, Ushma D. Upadhyay, and Tracy A. Weitz, "At What Cost? Payment for Abortion Care by U.S. Women," *Women's Health Issues* 23 (2013): 173–178; Kate Cockrill and Tracy A. Weitz, "Abortion Patients' Perceptions of Abortion Regulation," *Women's Health Issues* 20 (2010): 12–19.

11. Susan Sugarman et al., "Family Planning Clinic Patients: Their Usual Health Care Providers, Insurance Status, and Implications for Managed Care," *Journal of Adolescent Health* 27 (2000): 25–33; Rachel B. Gold, "Unintended Consequences: How Insurance Processes Inadvertently Abrogate Patient Confidentiality," *Guttmacher Policy Review* 12 (2009): 12–16.

12. Tara Shochet and James Trussell, "Determinants of Demand: Method Selection and Provider Preference among U.S. Women Seeking Abortion Services," *Contraception* 77 (2008): 397–404.

13. Tracy A. Weitz and Kate Cockrill, "Abortion Clinic Patients' Opinions about Obtaining Abortions from General Women's Health Care Providers," *Patient Education and Counselling* 81 (2010): 409–414.

14. John Leland, "Under Din of Abortion Debate, an Experience Shared Quietly," *New York Times,* September 18, 2005, p. 1.

15. Patricia Hersch, *A Tribe Apart: A Journey into the Heart of American Adolescence* (New York: Fawcett Columbine, 1998), 195.

16. Helen S. Edelman, "Safe to Talk: Abortion Narratives as a Rite of Return," *Journal of American Culture* 19 (1996): 31.

17. Ibid., 35.

18. Sarah A. Leavitt, " 'A Private Little Revolution': The Home Pregnancy Test in American Culture," *Bulletin of the History of Medicine* 80 (2006): 317–345.

19. Sarah Todd, "Secrecy and Safety: Health Care Workers in Abortion Clinics," *Labour* 52 (2003): 353–361.

20. *Whole Woman's Health v. Hellerstedt,* 136 S. Ct. 2292 (2016).

21. Bernard Williams, "The Logic of Abortion," in *Essays and Reviews: 1959–2002* (Princeton, NJ: Princeton University Press, 2014), 152.

22. Report of the South Dakota Task Force to Study Abortion Submitted to the Governor and Legislature of South Dakota (Dec. 2005), http://www.dakotavoice.com/Docs/South%20 Dakota%20Abortion%20Task%20Force%20Report.pdf, 6.

23. Ibid., 7.

24. *Bellotti v. Baird,* 443 U.S. 622, 655 (1979) (Stevens, J., concurring). Justices Brennan, Marshall, and Blackmun joined Justice Stevens's concurrence. See also Alice Clapman, "Privacy Rights and Abortion Outing: A Proposal for Using Common-Law Torts to Protect Abortion Patients and Staff," *Yale Law Journal* 112 (2003): 1575.

25. Clapman, "Privacy Rights and Abortion Outing."

26. *National Abortion Federation v. Ashcroft,* No. 04 C 55, 2004 U.S. Dist. LEXIS 1701, at 18–19 (N.D. Ill. Feb. 5, 2004).

27. *Thornburgh v. American College of Obstetricians & Gynecologists,* 476 U.S. 747, 766 (1986).

28. Ibid., 750.

29. *Thorne v. El Segundo,* 726 F.2d 459 (9th Cir. 1983).

30. Shelia H. Byrd, "Tuck Signs 'No Abortion' Affidavit," *djournal.com,* October 29, 2003, http://djournal.com/news/tuck-signs-no-abortion-affidavit/.

31. Alan F. Westin, *Privacy and Freedom* (New York: Atheneum, 1967), 7.

32. Restatement (Second) of Torts § 652D (1977) comment (a).

33. *Y.G. v. Jewish Hospital of St. Louis,* 795 S.W.2d 488 (Mo. Ct. App. 1990). Note the use of initials.

34. Ibid., 503, 491.

35. *Doe v. Mills,* 212 Mich. App. 73 (1995).

36. Ibid., 83.

37. Ibid., 84.

38. Ibid.

39. Leslie J. Reagan, *When Abortion Was a Crime: Women, Medicine, and Law in the United States, 1867–1973* (Berkeley: University of California Press, 1997), 151.

40. Ibid., 129–131.

41. Ibid., 167.

42. Ibid., 125.

43. Gillian Aldrich and Jennifer Baumgardner, *I Had an Abortion* (New York: Women Make Movies, 2005), DVD.

44. David Segal, "Mugged by a Mug Shot," *New York Times,* October 6, 2013, p. BU1. Over time, marriage and divorce also became part of the public record. As legal historian Hendrik Hartog has shown, in the nineteenth century, when divorce was rare, both men and women often concealed earlier marriages (some still in effect) and simply they moved west to get on with new lives; see Hendrik Hartog, *Man and Wife in America: A History* (Cambridge, MA: Harvard University Press, 2000). Women sometimes presented themselves as widowed rather than divorced; see Barbara Babcock, *Women Lawyer: The Trials of Clara Foltz* (Stanford, CA: Stanford University Press, 2011).

45. S. Rep. No. 139, at 29469 (1993) (Statements of Senators Robb and Harkin).

46. *Sipple v. Chronicle Publishing Co.,* 154 Cal. App. 3d 1040, 1044 (1984).

47. *Chico Feminist Women's Health Center v. Scully,* 208 Cal. App. 3d 230, 242 (1989).

48. Indeed, with the "easing" of Facebook's privacy rules—posts on one's own page may now be seen by anyone and not just one's "friends"—online posting now promises uncontained publicity. Vindu Goel, "Facebook Eases Privacy Rules for Teenagers," *New York Times,* October 17, 2013, p. A1.

49. *Protecting Access to Clinics,* Guttmacher Institute, October 1, 2016, https://www.guttmacher.org/state-policy/explore/protecting-access-clinics.

50. *McCullen v. Coakley,* 134 S. Ct. 2518 (2014). See also *Hill v. Colorado,* 530 U.S. 703 (2000).

51. Kashmir Hill, "How Target Figured out a Girl Was Pregnant before Her Father Did," *Forbes,* February 16, 2012, http://www.forbes.com/sites/kashmirhill/2012/02/16/how-target-figured-out-a-teen-girl-was-pregnant-before-her-father-did/#580cccd134c6.

52. Ibid.

53. Ibid. See also Charles Duhigg, "Psst, You in Aisle 5," *New York Times Magazine,* February 19, 2012, p. MM30.

54. "NSA's Goal Is Elimination of Individual Privacy Worldwide—Greenwald to EU," *RT: Question More,* December 18, 2013, http://on.rt.com/dgton5.

55. Sharona Coutts, "Anti-Choice Groups Use Smartphone Surveillance to Target 'Abortion-Minded Women' During Clinic Visits," *Rewire,* May 25, 2016, https://rewire.news/article/2016/05/25/anti-choice-groups-deploy-surveillance-target-abortion-minded-women-clinic-visits/.

56. See *Sidis v. F-R Publishing Company,* 113 F.2d 806 (2nd Cir. 1940).

57. Sissela Bok, *Secrets: On the Ethics of Concealment and Revelation* (New York: Pantheon Books, 1982), 11.

58. Restatement (Second) of Torts § 652D (1977).

59. Cornelia H. Dayton, *Women before the Bar: Gender, Law, and Society in Connecticut, 1639–1789* (Chapel Hill: University of North Carolina Press, 1995); see also Mary B. Norton, "Gender and Defamation in Seventeenth Century Maryland," *William & Mary Quarterly* 44 (1987): 3–39.

60. Segal, "Mugged by a Mug Shot."

61. See *Cox Broadcasting Corp. v. Cohn.* See also Deborah W. Denno, "Perspectives on Disclosing Rape Victims' Names," *Fordham Law Review* 61 (1993): 1113–1132.

62. Clapman, "Privacy Rights and Abortion Outing."

63. *Glover v. Herald Co.,* 549 S.W.2d 858, 860 (Mo. 1977).

64. Ibid.

65. *Russell v. Thomson Newspapers, Inc.,* 842 P.2d 896 (Utah, 1992); *Davis v. Bostick,* 282 Or. 667 (1978).

66. *Thornburgh v. American College of Obstetricians & Gynecologists,* 766; overruled on other grounds by *Planned Parenthood v. Casey,* 505 U.S. 833 (1992).

67. Ariz. Rev. Stat. Ann. 36-2152(E) (LexisNexis 2000).

68. Ariz. Rev. Stat. Ann. 36-2152(D) (LexisNexis 2000).

69. *Planned Parenthood of Southern Arizona v. Lawall,* 307 F.3d 783, 789 (9th Cir. 2002).

70. Ibid., 788–790.

71. *In re Kline,* 298 Kan. 96, 100 (2013).

72. For the procedural history, see *In re Kline,* 105–107 (2013).

73. Patricia M. Spacks, *Privacy: Concealing the Eighteenth-Century Self* (Chicago: University of Chicago Press, 2003), 228.

74. Ferdinand D. Schoeman, "Privacy and Intimate Information," in *Philosophical Dimensions of Privacy: An Anthology,* ed. Ferdinand D. Schoeman (Cambridge: Cambridge University Press, 1984), 416.

75. Ibid., 413.

76. Kim L. Scheppele, *Legal Secrets: Equality and Efficiency in the Common Law* (Chicago: University of Chicago Press, 1988), 303.

77. Spacks, *Privacy,* 2.

78. Ibid.

79. Bok, *Secrets,* 97.

80. Restatement (Second) of Contracts § 175 (1981) comment (b). See also *In re Baby Boy L.,* 534 N.Y.S.2d 706, 708 (App. Div. 1988).

81. Georg Simmel, "The Sociology of Secrecy and of Secret Societies," *American Journal of Sociology* 11 (1906): 441–498.

82. Jane Austen, *Sense and Sensibility* (New York: New American Library, 1980), 108.

83. Oscar Wilde, *The Picture of Dorian Gray* (New York: Millennium Publications, 2014), 5.

84. Particular thanks to David Pozen for these points.

85. Bok, *Secrets,* 13.

86. Deborah Cohen, *Family Secrets: Shame and Privacy in Modern Britain* (New York: Oxford University Press, 2013), 4.

87. Eve K. Sedgwick, *Epistemology of the Closet* (Berkeley: University of California Press, 1990), 67–68.

88. Cohen, *Family Secrets,* 225.

89. Edgar L. Masters, *Spoon River Anthology* (New York: Macmillan, 1936), 24.

90. Sarah K. Cowan, "Secrets and Social Influence" (D.Phil. diss., University of California, Berkeley, 2013), 49; see also Margarete Sandelowski and Linda C. Jones, " 'Healing Fictions': Stories of Choosing in the Aftermath of Fetal Anomalies," *Social Science and Medicine* 42 (1996): 353–361.

91. *People v. Weaver,* 12 N.Y.3d 433, 441 (App. Div. 2009).

92. Ibid., 441–442 (emphasis added).

93. *Garcia v. Providence Medical Center,* 60 Wash. App. 635 (1991).

94. Ibid., 644.

95. Ibid.

96. *Schneider v. Tapfer,* 92 Or. 520, 524 (1919).

97. *Brock v. Wedincamp,* 253 Ga. App. 275, 276 (2002).

98. *Stephenson v. State,* 31 So.3d 847, 849 (Fla. Dist. Ct. App. 2010).

99. Ibid., 851.

100. Ibid.

101. *Collman v. State,* 116 Nev. 687, 703 (2000).

102. *Billett v. State,* 317 Ark. 346, 348 (1994).

103. Ibid., 349.

104. *People v. Morris,* 92 Mich. App. 747, 751 (1979).

105. Tara C. Ressler, "In an Ugly Custody Battle, Woman's Abortion Used as 'Proof She's Unfit to Raise Kids,' " *Think Progress,* October 18, 2013, http://thinkprogress.org/health/2013/10/18 /2804791/custody-battle-abortion-lisa-mehos/.

106. *Purser v. Owens,* 396 S.C. 531, 538 (Ct. App. 2011).

107. Ibid., 535.

108. *Stacey L.B. v. Kimberly R.L.,* 785 N.Y.S.2d 238, 240 (App. Div. 2004).

109. Reagan, *When Abortion Was a Crime,* 104.

110. *The Man Who Fell to Earth,* directed by Nicolas Roeg (British Lion Films, 1976).

111. See in Cohen, *Family Secrets,* "The Nabob's Secrets," 13–46; "Children Who Disappeared," 87–123; "Bachelor Uncles," 156–192.

Chapter 4 THE EYE OF THE STORM

1. The press release was sent in an email from Columbia Christians for Life to its members and was widely reported. See http://www.christianlifeandliberty.net/CCL05-14.doc; Alan Cooperman, "Where Most See a Weather System, Some See Divine Retribution," *Washington Post,* September 4, 2005, p. A27.

2. http://www.christianlifeandliberty.net/CCL05-14.doc.

3. See Theodore Steinberg, *Acts of God: The Unnatural History of Natural Disaster in America* (New York: Oxford University Press, 2000).

4. For more on the tendency to attribute "humanlike characteristics, motivations, intentions, or emotions" to nonhuman agents, see Nicholas Epley, Adam Waytz, and John T. Cacioppo, "On Seeing Human: A Three-Factor Theory of Anthropomorphism," *Psychological Review* 114 (2007): 864; see also Elizabeth Svoboda, "Faces, Faces Everywhere," *New York Times,* February 13, 2007, p. F1.

5. Margaret B. McNay and John E. E. Fleming, "Forty Years of Obstetric Ultrasound 1957–1997: From A-Scope to Three Dimensions," *Ultrasound in Medicine & Biology* 25 (1999): 50 (fig. 43). There are also personalized U.S. Postal Service–approved fetus-themed stamps from stores like Zazzle, http://www.zazzle.com/love_at_first_sight_pregnancy_announcement -161546319653049647, accessed May 8, 2016.

6. Janelle S. Taylor, "The Public Fetus and the Family Car: From Abortion Politics to a Volvo Advertisement," *Public Culture* 4 (1992): 67.

7. Ibid.

8. *Trends in the States: First Quarter 2015,* Guttmacher Institute, April 2, 2015, http://www .guttmacher.org/media/inthenews/2015/04/02/; Teddy Wilson, "235 Anti-Choice Bills Proposed in State Legislatures since January," *RH Reality* Check, March 31, 2015, http://rhrealitycheck.org /article/2015/03/31/235-anti-choice-bills-proposed-state-legislatures-since-january/.

9. Rosalind P. Petchesky, *Abortion and Woman's Choice: The State, Sexuality, and Reproductive Freedom* (Boston: Northeastern University Press, 1990), xiv.

10. *Doe v. Shalala,* 862 F. Supp. 1421, 1426 (D. Md. 1994) (quoting *Roe v. Wade*); see also *Sherely v. Sebelius,* 686 F. Supp. 2d 1, 5 (D.D.C. 2009).

11. *Doe v. Shalala,* 1426.

12. "The complexity of embryo-fetal development is almost beyond comprehension." F. Gary Cunningham et al., eds., *Williams Obstetrics* (New York: McGraw-Hill, 2013), 128.

13. Ibid., 129.

14. Ibid., text at Table 7-1.

15. S.D. Codified Laws § 34-23A-1 (2) (LexisNexis 1973).

16. S.D. Codified Laws § 34-23A-1.3 (LexisNexis 2005). See Caitlin E. Borgmann, "Rethinking Judicial Deference to Legislative Fact-Finding," *Indiana Law Journal* 84 (2009): 1–56.

17. *Roe v. Wade,* 410 U.S. 113 (1973).

18. "Judge Says Fetuses Don't Count as Passengers," *Los Angeles Times,* January 12, 2006, p. A9 (upholding woman's $367 fine); Rad Sallee, "Sorry, Ma'am: Fetuses Don't Count in HOV Lanes: More HOV Loners Caught in the Act," *Chron,* January 31, 2007, http://www.chron.com/news /houston-texas/article/Sorry-ma-am-Fetuses-don-t-count-in-HOV-lanes-1531485.php.

19. Ronald Dworkin, *Life's Dominion: An Argument About Abortion, Euthanasia, and Individual Freedom* (New York: Knopf, 1993), 10.

20. Ibid., 14.

21. S.D. Codified Laws § 34-23A-10.1 (1) (b) (LexisNexis 1980).

22. Vanessa R. Sasson and Jane Marie Law, eds., *Imagining the Fetus: The Unborn in Myth, Religion, and Culture* (Oxford: Oxford University Press, 2009), 3.

23. Ibid.

24. Nick Hopwood, "A Marble Embryo: Meanings of a Portrait from 1900," *History Workshop Journal* 73 (2012): 6.

25. Luke 1:39–45.

26. Gwynn Kessler, "'Famous' Fetuses in Rabbinic Narratives," in *Imagining the Fetus,* 185–202.

27. Vanessa R. Sasson, "A Womb with a View: The Buddha's Final Fetus Experiences," in *Imagining the Fetus,* 62; Robert Kritzer, "Life in the Womb: Conception and Gestation in Buddhist Scripture and Classical Indian Medical Literature," in *Imagining the Fetus,* 88.

28. See Daniel S. Dapaah, *The Relationship between John the Baptist and Jesus of Nazareth: A Critical Study* (Lanham, MD: University Press of America, 2005).

29. Catherine Playoust and Ellen Bradshaw Aitken, "The Leaping Child: Imagining the Unborn in Early Christian Literature," 157–183; and Marten Stol, "Embryology in Babylonia and the Bible," in *Imagining the Fetus,* 147.

30. Kessler, " 'Famous' Fetuses," 194.

31. Ibid., 201.

32. Barbara Duden, *Disembodying Women: Perspectives on Pregnancy and the Unborn,* trans. Lee Hoinacki (Cambridge, MA: Harvard University Press, 1993), 32.

33. Lynn M. Morgan, *Icons of Life: A Cultural History of Human Embryos* (Berkeley: University of California Press), 159–188.

34. See Alan W. Bates, "Good, Common, Regular, and Orderly: Early Modern Classifications of Monstrous Births," *Social History of Medicine* 18 (2005): 141–158.

35. George W. Bush, *Decision Points* (New York: Crown Publishers, 2010), 8. "I also never expected to see the remains of the fetus, which she had saved in a jar to bring to the hospital."

36. See Karen Newman, *Fetal Positions: Individualism, Science, Visuality* (Stanford, CA: Stanford University Press, 1996), 26–33.

37. Ibid., 33.

38. Ibid., 33–44.

39. Ibid.

40. Ibid., 63 (fig. 57).

41. Ibid., 86–87 (fig. 74, 75).

42. See Nick Hopwood, *Embryos in Wax: Models from the Ziegler Studio* (Cambridge: Whipple Museum of the History of Science, University of Cambridge, 2002).

43. See A. W. Bates, " 'Indecent and Demoralising Representations:' Public Anatomy Museums in Mid-Victorian England," *Medical History* 52 (2008): 1–22.

44. Hopwood, *Embryos in Wax.*

45. Sara Dubow, *Ourselves Unborn: Fetal Meanings in Modern America* (Oxford: Oxford University Press, 2011), 54–55; see also Lynn M. Morgan, "Materializing the Fetal Body, or, What Are Those Corpses Doing in Biology's Basement?," in *Fetal Subjects, Feminist Positions,* eds. Lynn M. Morgan and Meredith W. Michaels (Philadelphia: University of Pennsylvania Press, 1999), 43.

46. Dubow, *Ourselves Unborn,* 56.

47. See David Barboza, "China Turns out Mummified Bodies for Display," *New York Times,* August 8, 2006, p. A1; Andrew Jacobs, "Cadaver Exhibition Raises Questions beyond Taste, *New York Times,* November 18, 2005, p. B1.

48. See Barbara Duden, "Quick with Child: An Experience That Has Lost Its Status," *Technology in Society* 14 (1992): 341–343.

49. See Cathy McClive, "The Hidden Truths of the Belly: The Uncertainties of Pregnancy in Early Modern Europe," *Social History of Medicine* 15 (2002): 214–218; James C. Oldham, "On Pleading the Belly: A History of the Jury of Matrons," *Criminal Justice History* 6 (1985): 1–64.

50. Kathryn P. Addelson, "The Emergence of the Fetus," in *Fetal Subjects, Feminist Positions,* 29.

51. See Lennart Nilsson, "Photograph of Fetus at Fifteen Weeks," *Life,* April 30, 1965, 54–55; George P. Hunt, "Editor's Note: A Remarkable Photographic Feat," *Life,* April 30, 1965, 3.

52. Duden, *Disembodying Women*, 14.

53. Ibid., 11, 13, 17.

54. Nilsson, "Photograph of Fetus," 54.

55. Duden, *Disembodying Women*, 11–14.

56. Hunt, "Editor's Note," 3; Nathan Stormer, "Looking in Wonder: Prenatal Sublimity and the Commonplace 'Life,'" *Signs* 33 (2008): 647–673; Carol A. Stabile, "The Traffic in Fetuses," in *Fetal Subjects, Feminist Positions*, 133–158; Valerie Hartouni, "Epilogue: Reflections on Abortion Politics and the Practices Called Person," in *Fetal Subjects, Feminist Positions*, 296–303.

57. Nilsson, "Photograph of Fetus," 54.

58. Rosalind P. Petchesky, "Fetal Images: The Power of Visual Culture in the Politics of Reproduction," *Feminist Studies* 13 (1987): 264.

59. Lauren Berlant, "America, 'Fat,' the Fetus," *Boundary 2* 21 (1994): 177.

60. See *3D Babies*, http://www.3d-babies.com, accessed December 29, 2015.

61. "Baby in Sight FAQ," *Baby in Sight*, http://www.babyinsight3d.com/faq/, accessed December 29, 2015.

62. See generally, Lisa M. Mitchell, *Baby's First Picture: Ultrasound and the Politics of Fetal Subjects* (Toronto; Buffalo: University of Toronto Press, 2001), 3.

63. Duden, *Disembodying Women*, 7.

64. See Anne Higonnete, "A New Image of Childhood without the Maternal Body," in *Bodies and Borders: Negotiating Motherhood in the 21st Century*, ed. Yasmin Ergas, Jane Johnson, and Sonya Michel (forthcoming).

65. Rachel Quigley, "Foetus Defriended!," *Daily Mail*, June 3, 2011, http://www.dailymail.co.uk/news/article-1392918/New-craze-sweeping-parents-Giving-unborn-child-Facebook-page.html; Elizabeth Johnson, "Unborn Child Has Facebook Profile," *CNN*, May 31, 2011, http://news.blogs.cnn.com/2011/05/31/unborn-child-has-facebook-profile/; see also Bonnie Rochman, "'Expected: Child': Facebook Welcomes Fetuses to Social Media," *Time*, August 3, 2011, http://healthland.time.com/2011/08/03/expected-child-facebook-welcomes-unborn-babies-to-social-media/.

66. Carol Sanger, "Infant Safe Haven Laws: Legislating in the Culture of Life," *Columbia Law Review* 106 (2006): 801–803.

67. Unborn Victims of Violence Act of 2004 (also entitled "Laci and Connor's Law"), Pub. L. No. 108-212, 118 Stat. 568 (2004) (to be codified at 18 U.S.C. §1841 & 10 U.S.C. §919(a)); Born-Alive Infants Protection Act of 2002, 1 U.S.C. § 8; Unborn Child Pain Awareness Act of 2007, 110 H.R. 3442 (statement of Sen. Brownback) (proposing requirement that women seeking late-term abortions be given information about fetal pain and be offered "the opportunity to choose anesthesia for the unborn child in order to lessen its pain"); see also Dubow, *Ourselves Unborn*, 153–154.

68. Search of CONG-BILLTXT on Westlaw for the term "unborn" (yielding 113 bills).

69. 42 CFR 457.10 (2001).

70. H.R. Rep. No. 119-108 (2003).

71. Monica Casper, *The Making of the Unborn Patient: A Social Anatomy of Fetal Surgery* (New Brunswick, NJ: Rutgers University Press, 1998); Diana Bianchi et al., eds., *Fetology: Diagnosis and Management of the Fetal Patient* (New York: McGraw-Hill Medical Pub. Division, 2010).

72. Kate Atkinson, *Behind the Scenes at the Museum* (New York: St. Martin's Press, 1996), 11.

73. Laurence Sterne, *Life and Opinions of Tristram Shandy, Gentleman*, ed. Howard Anderson (New York: Norton, 1980), 4.

74. Ibid., 4–5.

75. Ian McEwan, *Nutshell* (New York: Nan A. Talese / Doubleday, 2016), 1.

76. Ibid., 6.

77. *Doe v. Shalala,* 1426.

78. Alabama has since codified the holding. Ala. R. Civ. P. Rule 17 (d) (LexisNexis 1995).

79. Amy Bach, "No Choice for Teens," *Nation,* October 11, 1999, p. 7; see also Helena Silverstein, "In the Matter of Anonymous: Fetal Representation in Hearing to Waive Parental Consent for Abortion," *Cornell Journal of Public Policy* 11 (2001): 69–111.

80. Stills from the film are available at "The Silent Scream Script and Photos," *The Silent Scream,* http://silentscream.org/silent_e.htm, accessed December 29, 2015. The movie itself is also available online: "The Silent Scream," YouTube video, 28:39, posted by Rachel Lubbe, January 27, 2012, https://www.youtube.com/watch?v=gON-8PP6zgQ.

81. Berlant, "America, 'Fat', the Fetus," 150.

82. Ibid.

83. David Lodge, *Changing Places: A Tale of Two Campuses* (New York: Penguin Books, 1992). His seatmate inquires whether he bought "the whole package—round trip, surgeon's fee, five days nursing with private room and excursion to Stratford-on-Avon" (p. 30).

84. Ibid., 31.

85. Robert P. George and Christopher Tollefsen, *Embryo: A Defense of Human Life* (New York: Doubleday, 2008), 1. For an excellent discussion of embryo ethics in relation to abortion politics, see June Carbone and Naomi Chan, "Embryo Fundamentalism," *William & Mary Bill of Rights Journal* 18 (2010): 1015–1052.

86. George and Tollefsen, *Embryo,* 1.

87. Ibid., 2.

88. Dworkin, *Life's Dominion,* 13.

89. See Sheri Fink, *Five Days at Memorial: Life and Death in a Storm-Ravaged Hospital* (New York: Random House, Inc., Crown Publishing Group, 2013).

90. Katherine Verdery, *The Political Lives of Dead Bodies: Reburial and Postsocialist Change* (New York: Columbia University Press, 1999), 33.

91. Ibid., 27.

92. Ibid., 25.

93. See, for example, Ryszard Kapuściński, *Shah of Shahs,* trans. William R. Brand and Katarzyna M. Brand (New York: Vintage International, 1992), 41–43. A ninety-day period of mourning created a rhythmic pattern of solidarity and public funereal protest.

94. "Ted Cruz Blasts Obama's Plan for Empty SOTU Seat in Pro-Life Tweet," *Washington Times,* January 8, 2016, http://www.washingtontimes.com/news/2016/jan/8/ted-cruz-blasts-obamas-plan-for-empty-sotu-seat-in/.

95. Micheal Wilson, "After an Open-Coffin Funeral, a Shock: That Wasn't Mom," *New York Times,* March 22, 2016, p. A19.

96. See Leslie J. Reagan, "From Hazard to Blessing to Tragedy: Representations of Miscarriage in Twentieth-Century America," *Feminist Studies* 29 (2003): 357–378; Toby Ord, "The Scourge: Moral Implications of Natural Embryo Loss," *American Journal of Bioethics* 8, no. 7 (2008): 12–19.

97. *Margaret S. v. Treen,* 597 F. Supp. 636, 668 n.26 (E.D. La. 1984).

98. Ibid., 644–645.

99. Ibid., 670.

100. Caitlin E. Borgmann and Bonnie S. Jones, "Legal Issues in the Provision of Medical Abortion," *American Journal of Obstetrics and Gynecology* 183 (2000): S91–S92.

101. Liam Stacknov, "Texas Will Require Burial of Aborted Fetuses," *New York Times,* November 30, 2016, http://www.nytimes.com/2016/11/30/us/texas-burial-aborted-fetuses.html?_r-0; for the proposed rules see *Texas Register—Proposed Rules,* July 1, 2016, http://www.sos.state.tx.us/texreg/pdf /backview/0701/0701prop.pdf.

102. Morgan, "Materializing the Fetal Body," 44.

103. Ibid., 51. To obtain embryos at the earliest stages of development, women scheduled for hysterectomies were urged by physician researchers to have unprotected intercourse just before their scheduled surgeries.

104. Ibid., 55.

105. Erik Cohen, "Fetuses in Thai Temple as Chaotic Irruption and Public Embarrassment," *Asian Anthropology* 11 (2012): 1–20.

106. Ibid., 9.

107. Ibid.

108. Ibid.

109. Morgan, *Icons of Life,* 163–168.

110. Ibid., 167.

111. Ibid., 167.

112. Celeste M. Condit, *Decoding Abortion Rhetoric: Communicating Social Change* (Urbana: University of Illinois Press, 1990), 89.

113. *Juno,* directed by Jason Reitman (Fox Searchlight Pictures, 2007).

114. Ziv Eisenberg, " 'The Whole Nine Months': Women, Men and the Making of Modern Pregnancy in America," (D.Phil. diss., Yale University, New Haven, 2013), 262.

115. *Cleveland Board of Education v. LaFleur,* 414 U.S. 632 (1974). For helpful discussion of *LaFleur,* see Michael Graetz and Linda Greenhouse, *The Burger Court and the Rise of the Judicial Right* (New York: Simon & Schuster, 2016).

116. See also Ame M. Beanland and Emily M. Terry, *Postcards from the Bump: A Chick's Guide to Getting to Know the Baby in Your Belly* (Cambridge, MA: Da Capo Press, 2009); Jessica Denay, *The Hot Mom to Be Handbook: Look and Feel Great from Bump to Baby* (New York: HarperCollins Publishers, 2010).

117. *Bump It Up,* http://www.bumpitupstyle.com, accessed March 15, 2016.

118. Berlant, "America, 'Fat', the Fetus," 146. See Sandra Matthews and Laura Wexler, *Pregnant Pictures* (New York: Routledge, 2000), 94–98, 195–218; see also Imogen Tyler, "Skin-Tight: Celebrity, Pregnancy and Subjectivity," in *Thinking through the Skin,* eds. Sara Ahmed and Jackie Stacie (London: Routledge, 2001), 69–83.

119. Eric Metaxas, "Bad Boy Does Good: Damien Hirst and Those Giant Fetus Sculptures," *Life Site,* October 23, 2013, https://www.lifesitenews.com/opinion/bad-boy-does-good-damien-hirst-and -those-giant-fetus-sculptures.

120. Carol Vogel, "From Conception to Birth in Qatar: Damien Hirst's Anatomical Sculptures Have Their Debut," *New York Times,* October 8, 2013, p. C1.

121. "14 Giant Sculptures of Fetuses Attract Praise from Pro-Life Supporters," *Huffington Post,* October 24, 2013, http://www.huffingtonpost.com/2013/10/24/damien-hirst-fetus_n_4151500.html.

122. Vogel, "From Conception to Birth in Qatar," C1. For more on Sheikha al Mayassa, see *Qatar Museums,* http://www.qm.org.qa/en/her-excellency-sheikha-al-mayassa, accessed December 30, 2015.

123. "14 Giant Sculptures of Fetuses Attract Praise" (quoting Independent Catholic News).

124. Ibid., calling the work "Hirst's homage to the gestation process."

125. "Damien Hirst News," *Damien Hirst,* http://www.damienhirst.com/news/2013/miraculous -journey, accessed December 30, 2015.

126. Martine Powers, "For Senior, Abortion a Medium for Art, Political Discourse," *Yale Daily News,* April 17, 2008.

127. Elizabeth K. Menon, "Anatomy of a Motif: The Fetus in Late 19th Century Graphic Art," *Nineteenth-Century Art Worldwide: A Journal of Nineteenth-Century Visual Culture* 3 (2004): 13.

128. Ibid., 11. In another drawing, "Lucian's Strange Creatures," a priestess holds up a fetus amidst a crowd of strangers and menacing sorts (ibid.). See also Milly Heyd, *Aubrey Beardsley: Symbol, Mask, and Self-Irony* (New York: Peter Lang, 1986), 55–92.

129. Lisa J. Rogers, " 'Abortion,' 'Miscarriage,' or 'Untitled'? A Frida Kahlo Lithograph's Complicated History," *Hypoallergetic,* April 29, 2015, http://hyperallergic.com/202802/abortion -miscarriage-or-untitled-a-frida-kahlo-lithographs-complicated-history/.

130. "Tracy Emin, Terribly Wrong 1997," *Tate,* http://www.tate.org.uk/art/artworks/emin -terribly-wrong-p11565/text-display-caption, accessed May 8, 2016.

131. Carolyn E. Tate, "The Colossal Fetuses of La Venta and Mesoamerica's Earliest Creation Story," in *Imagining the Fetus,* 223.

132. Ibid., 225.

133. Carolyn E. Tate, *Reconsidering Olmec Visual Culture: The Unborn, Women, and Creation* (Austin: University of Texas Press, 2012), 37. The neonatologists were brought in to establish that the sculptures were in fact fetuses and not dwarves or midgets, as earlier scholars had asserted.

134. Tate, "Colossal Fetuses," 223.

135. Vernon L. Scarborough and David R. Wilcox, eds., *The Mesoamerican Ballgame* (Tucson: University of Arizona Press, 1991).

136. Tate, "Colossal Fetuses," 229, 225.

137. Ibid., 254; Tate, *Reconsidering Olmec,* 57.

138. Tate, *Reconsidering Olmec,* 64.

139. Nick Hopwood, " 'Giving Body' to Embryos: Modeling, Mechanism, and the Microtome in Late Nineteenth Century Anatomy," *Isis* 90 (1999): 464.

140. Morgan, *Icons of Life,* 63–69.

141. Hopwood, "Giving Body," 476. The microtome was described by an American contemporary as having "a place in the zoological laboratory second in importance only to the microscope."

142. This progression is shown in Figure 10.2 in Nick Hopwood, *Haeckel's Embryos: Images, Evolution, and Fraud* (Chicago: University of Chicago Press, 2015), 174. The process was later simplified by His's invention of a special machine, the embryograph, in the early 1880s.

143. Hopwood, "A Marble Embryo," 17.

144. Ibid., 22.

145. Ibid., 15.

146. Morgan, "Materializing the Fetal Body," 43–45. Explanations given for the disappearance of the bottled fetuses at Mount Holyoke included student health (the proximity of formaldehyde), not enough shelf space, and the connection between sexual intercourse and embryo creation. Lynn Morgan further suggests that the fetus specimens, however instructionally sound they may have been, originated in abortions, and that present sensibilities about that override any pedagogical or historiographic benefit the collections might have.

147. Hopwood, "A Marble Embryo," 13.

148. Ibid.

149. Ibid., 21.

150. *Taylor v. Roswell Indep. Sch. Dist.*, 713 F.3d 25, 29–30 (10th Cir. 2013).

151. Ibid., 30.

152. Ibid., 30.

153. Ibid., 31.

154. Ibid., 31.

155. Ibid.

156. *Heritage House: Protecting and Changing Lives,* http://www.heritagehouse76.com/details.aspx?prod_id=3378, accessed December 30, 2015.

157. Andrew Bair, "Abortion Advocates Go Nuts over Pro-Lifers Distributing Fetal Models," *LifeNews.com,* July 26, 2013, http://www.lifenews.com/2013/07/26/abortion-advocates-go-nuts-over-pro-lifers-distributing-fetal-models/; Katie J. M. Baker, "Worst State Fair Ever Has Squishy Fetus Toys for Unsuspecting Kids," *Jezebel,* July 24, 2013, http://jezebel.com/worst-state-fair-ever-has-squishy-fetus-toys-for-unsusp-882405859.

158. *One Tiny Life,* http://www.onetinylife.org/menu.htm, accessed December 30, 2015.

159. Ibid.

160. Doug Bailey, "Touch and the Cheirotic Apprehension of Prehistoric Figurines," in *Sculpture and Touch,* ed. Peter Dent (Burlington, VT: Ashgate, 2014), 27–44.

161. Ibid., 29. See also Alberto Gallace and Charles Spence, "The Neglected Power of Touch: What the Cognitive Neurosciences Can Tell Us about the Importance of Touch in Artistic Communication," in *Sculpture and Touch,* 107–124.

162. William R. LaFluer, "Abortion in Japan: Towards a 'Middle Way' for the West?," in *Buddhism and Abortion,* ed. Damien Keown (London: Macmillan, 1998), 67–92; Elizabeth G. Harrison, "I Can Only Move My Feet toward Mizuko Kuyo: Memorial Services for Dead Children in Japan," in *Buddhism and Abortion,* 93–120.

163. LaFluer, "Abortion in Japan," 75–76.

164. Tiana Norgren, "Abortion before Birth Control: The Interest Group Politics behind Postwar Japanese Reproduction Policy," *Journal of Japanese Studies* 24 (1998): 59–94.

165. Marc L. Moskowitz, *The Haunting Fetus: Abortion, Sexuality, and the Spirit World in Taiwan* (Honolulu: University of Hawai'i Press, 2001).

166. Helen Hardacre, *Marketing the Menacing Fetus in Japan* (Berkeley: University of California Press, 1999).

167. Ibid., 117.

168. See Carol Sanger, "The Birth of Death: Stillborn Birth Certificates and the Problem for Law," *California Law Review* 100 (2012): 269–311.

169. Tate, "Colossal Fetuses," 223.

170. Doris Lessing, *The Fifth Child* (New York: Knopf, 1988).

171. Ibid., 38.

172. Ibid., 40–41.

173. Ibid., 42.

174. Doris Lessing, *Ben, in the World: The Sequel to The Fifth Child* (New York: HarperCollins, 2000).

175. Daniel Sullivan and Jeff Greenberg, "Monstrous Children as the Harbinger of Mortality: A Psychological Analysis of Doris Lessing's *The Fifth Child,*" *LIT: Literature Interpretation Theory* 22 (2011): 113–133; Sarolta Marinovich, "The Discourse of the Other: Female Gothic in Contemporary Women's Writing," *Neohelicon* 21 (1994): 189; Richard Brock, "'No Such Thing as Society': Thatcherism and Derridean Hospitality in *The Fifth Child,*" *Doris Lessing Studies* 28 (2009): 7–13;

Emily Clark, "Re-Reading Horror Stories: Maternity, Disability, and Narrative in Doris Lessing's *The Fifth Child*," *Feminist Review* 98 (2011): 173–189; Kun Zhao, "A Narrative Analysis of Lessing's *The Fifth Child*," *Theory and Practice in Language Studies* 2 (2012): 1498–1502; Mica Hilson, "'The Odd Man out in the Family?': Queer Throwbacks and Reproductive Futurism in *The Fifth Child*," *Doris Lessing Studies* 30 (2010): 18–22.

176. See generally A. Robin Hoffman, "How to See the Horror: The Hostile Fetus in *Rosemary's Baby* and *Alien*," *LIT: Literature Interpretation Theory* 22 (2011): 239–261; Karyn Valerius, "'Rosemary's Baby,' Gothic Pregnancy, and Fetal Subjects," *College Literature* 32 (2005): 116–135. Dead fetuses were also thought to have magical powers; see David Frankfurter, "Fetus Magic and Sorcery Fears in Roman Egypt," *Greek, Roman, and Byzantine Studies* 46 (2006): 37–62.

177. Hardacre, *Menacing Fetus*, 80, 86 (fig. 6).

178. Ibid., 87 (fig. 7).

179. Ibid, 86 (fig. 6).

180. Ibid., 83 (fig. 4).

181. Ibid., 91.

182. Ibid., 216.

183. Harrison, "Toward Mizuko Kuyo," 114.

184. See Carl Ingram, "Mother Strives to Save Unwanted Babies," *Los Angeles Times*, April 23, 2000, p. A28; see also S. 116, 2005–2006 Leg., Reg. Sess. (Cal. 2005), 1–2, available at http://info.sen.ca.gov/pub/bill/sen/sb_101-0150/sb_116_cfa_20050316_153453_sen_comm.html (crediting "a group that retrieved dead abandoned babies from county morgues" as spurring legislation).

185. Anne Rice, *The Witching Hour* (New York: Knopf, 1990), 64–65 (paragraphs omitted).

186. Sally G. McMillen, *Motherhood in the Old South: Pregnancy, Childbirth, and Infant Rearing* (Baton Rouge: Louisiana State University Press, 1990), 54.

187. Nancy F. Cott, *The Bonds of Womanhood: "Woman's Sphere" in New England, 1780–1835* (New Haven, CT: Yale University Press, 1997), 90–91. In 1813 Susan Huntington wrote in her diary that "the idea of soon giving birth to my 3rd child & the consequent duties I shall be called to discharge distress me so I felt as if I should sink. . . . [I] see so many defects in my conduct to my offspring *now*, that I know not how it will be *possible* for me to do my duty then. Oh God! Strengthen me" (p. 91).

188. Insight Team of the *Sunday Times of London*, *Suffer the Children: The Story of Thalidomide* (New York: Viking Press, 1979), 112–121, 115.

189. Robert D. McFadden, "Frances Kelsey, 101, Dies; Exposed Dangerous Drug," *New York Times*, August 8, 2015, p. A1.

190. Leslie J. Reagan, *Dangerous Pregnancies: Mothers, Disabilities, and Abortion in Modern America* (Berkeley: University of California Press, 2010), 55–104.

191. Abortion Act, 1967, c. 87 (Eng.) section 1 (1)(a) (emphasis added).

192. Ibid., section 1(1)(d).

193. Jennifer Baumgradner, *Abortion & Life* (New York: Akashic Books, 2008), 89.

194. Newman, *Fetal Positions*, 2–3.

195. Rogers, "A Frida Kahlo Lithograph's Complicated History"; Heyd, *Aubrey Beardsley*, 55–92.

196. Chris Sims, "Utterly Disturbing Super-Hero Fetus Sculptures Are Things that Exist," *Comics Alliance*, September 20, 2011, http://comicsalliance.com/super-hero-fetus-sculptures/.

197. See, for example, *Shutterstock*, http://www.shutterstock.com/s/fetus/search-vectors.html, accessed April 15, 2016.

198. Ann Pellegrini, "'Signaling through the Flames': Hell House Performance and Structures of Religious Feeling," *American Quarterly* 59 (2007): 912 (emphasis added).

Chapter 5 FACING YOUR FETUS

1. *Dillon v. Legg,* 68 Cal. 2d 728 (1968).

2. *Amaya v. Home Ice, Fuel & Supply Co.,* 59 Cal. 2d 295 (1963).

3. Appellant's Opening Brief at 16, *Dillon v. Legg,* 68 Cal. 2d 728 (1968).

4. *Dillon v. Legg,* 731.

5. Ibid., 741.

6. Ibid., 747. See generally Martha Chamallas and Linda K. Kerber, "Women, Mothers, and the Law of Fright: A History," *Michigan Law Review* 88 (1990): 814–864.

7. Woman's Right to Know Act, Code of Ala. § 26-23A-4 (b) (4) (LexisNexis 2002).

8. Ibid.

9. N.C. Gen. Stat. § 90-21.85 (a) (2); (4) (LexisNexis 2011).

10. See *State Policies in Brief: Requirements for Ultrasound,* Guttmacher Institute, March 1, 2016, https://www.guttmacher.org/sites/default/files/pdfs/spibs/spib_RFU.pdf.

11. A.C.A. § 20-16-602 (b); (c) (LexisNexis 2003); Tex. Health & Safety Code § 171.0121 (b) (1) (LexisNexis 2011).

12. Ibid.

13. Richard Fausset, "Law on Ultrasounds Reignites Abortion Battle in North Carolina," *New York Times,* January 11, 2016, p. A12.

14. See, for example, the best seller of John Medina, *Brain Rules for Baby: How to Raise a Smart and Happy Child from Zero to Five* (Seattle, WA: Pear Press, 2014).

15. See generally F. Rene Van De Carr and Marc Lehrer, *While You Are Expecting: Creating Your Own Prenatal Classroom* (Atlanta GA: Green Dragon Publishing Group, 1996).

16. Woman's Right to Know Act, Code of Ala. § 26-23A-2 (LexisNexis 2002).

17. *Texas Medical Providers Performing Abortion Services v. Lakey,* 667 F.3d 570, 579 (5th Cir. 2012).

18. *Stuart v. Camnitz,* 774 F.3d 238, 246, 254 (4th Cir. 2014).

19. Susan Sontag, *On Photography* (New York: Farrar, Straus and Giroux, 1977), 3.

20. See Sheryl G. Stolberg, "Senate Backs Ban on Photos of G.I. Coffins," *New York Times,* June 22, 2004, p. A17.

21. Jay Ruby, *Secure the Shadow: Death and Photography in America* (Cambridge, MA: MIT Press, 1995), 6.

22. Ibid.

23. Lisa M. Mitchell, *Baby's First Picture: Ultrasound and the Politics of Fetal Subjects* (Toronto: University of Toronto Press, 2001), 27, 142.

24. Margaret B. McNay and John E. E. Fleming, "Forty Years of Obstetric Ultrasound 1957–1997: From A-Scope to Three Dimensions," *Ultrasound in Medicine and Biology* 25 (1999): 50, fig. 43. For an excellent account of the development of ultrasound technology and corporate investment in its manufacture, see especially Stuart S. Blume, *Insight and Industry: On the Dynamics of Technological Change in Medicine* (Cambridge, MA: MIT Press, 1992), 74–118.

25. Donald later observed, "there is not so much difference after all between a fetus in utero and a submarine at sea." See Ian Donald, "On Launching a New Diagnostic Science," *American Journal of Obstetrics and Gynecology* 103 (1969): 618. See also John MacVicar and Ian Donald, "Sonar in the Diagnosis of Early Pregnancy and Its Complications," *Journal of Obstetrics and Gynaecology of the British Commonwealth* 70 (1963): 387–395; Ian Donald, J. MacVicar, and T. G. Brown, "Investigation of Abdominal Masses by Pulsed Ultrasound," *Lancet* 1 (1958): 1192. For feminist critiques of the masculinist origins of the technology, see Rosalind P. Petchesky, "Foetal Images: The Power of

Visual Culture in the Politics of Reproduction," in *Reproductive Technologies: Gender, Motherhood and Medicine,* ed. Michelle Stanworth (Minneapolis: University of Minnesota Press, 1987), 57–80.

26. McNay and Fleming, "Forty Years of Obstetric Ultrasound," 28, 39–40.

27. Blume, *Insight and Industry,* 115; McNay and Fleming, "Forty Years of Obstetric Ultrasound," 27.

28. Blume, *Insight and Industry,* 108.

29. John C. Fletcher and Mark I. Evans, "Maternal Bonding in Early Fetal Ultrasound Examinations," *New England Journal of Medicine* 308 (1983): 392–393.

30. Janelle S. Taylor, "Image of Contradiction: Obstetrical Ultrasound in American Culture," in *Reproducing Reproduction: Kinship, Power, and Technological Innovation,* eds. Sarah Franklin and Helena Ragoné (Philadelphia: University of Pennsylvania Press, 1998), 19.

31. Fletcher and Evans, "Maternal Bonding," 392–393.

32. Ibid., 393.

33. Ibid.

34. See generally Pierre Coste, "An Historical Examination of the Strategic Issues Which Influenced Technologically Entrepreneurial Firms Serving the Medical Diagnostic Ultrasound Market" (Ph.D. diss., Claremont Graduate School, 1989).

35. McNay and Fleming, "Forty Years of Obstetric Ultrasound," 7.

36. Taylor, "Image of Contradiction," 25–26.

37. Margarete Sandelowski and Linda C. Jones, " 'Healing Fictions': Stories of Choosing in the Aftermath of the Detection of Fetal Anomalies," *Social Science & Medicine* 42 (1996): 356.

38. Melanie S. Watson et al., "Psychological Impact of the Detection of Soft Markers on Routine Ultrasound Scanning: A Pilot Study Investigating the Modifying Role of Information," *Prenatal Diagnosis* 22 (2002): 570.

39. "About Us," *Baby in Sight,* http://www.babyinsight3d.com/about/, accessed May 9, 2016.

40. Sontag, *On Photography,* 24

41. Ibid., 153–154.

42. Sallie Han, "The First Picture Show: A Media Anthropology Approach to the Ultrasound," (2001) (copy on file with author).

43. Mary Bouquet, "The Family Photographic Condition," *Visual Anthropology Review* 16 (2000): 2–19.

44. Marianne Hirsch, *Family Frames: Photography, Narrative, and Postmemory* (Cambridge, MA: Harvard University Press, 1997), 10.

45. Mitchell, *Baby's First Picture,* 3.

46. Paula A. Treichler, Lisa Cartwright, and Constance Penley, eds., "Introduction: Paradoxes of Visibility," in *The Visible Woman: Imaging Technologies, Gender, and Science* (New York: New York University Press, 1998), 4.

47. Gayle Kirshenbaum, "Caught in the Act of Becoming: 'Baby's First Picture' Is Now in Utero, but What If You Don't Feel Like a Mom?," *Newsweek,* May 23, 2005, p. 18–19.

48. Lynne S. Milne and Olive J. Rich, "Cognitive and Affective Aspects of the Responses of Pregnant Women to Sonography," *Maternal-Child Nursing Journal* 10 (1981): 27.

49. Stuart Campbell, "The Picture That Made Me Change My Mind about Abortion," *Daily Mail,* April 1, 2005, p. 31.

50. Lisa M. Mitchell and Eugenia Georges, "Cross-Cultural Cyborgs: Greek and Canadian Women's Discourses on Fetal Ultrasound," *Feminist Studies* 23 (1997): 376.

51. Janelle Sue Taylor, "The Public Fetus and the Family Car: From Abortion Politics to a Volvo Advertisement," *Public Culture* 4 (1992): 76.

52. Janelle S. Taylor, "The Public Life of the Fetal Sonogram and the Work of the Sonographer," *Journal of Diagnostic Medical Sonography* 18 (2002): 369.

53. See "Sonographer Testimonials in the Field," *American Registry for Diagnostic Sonography*, http://www.ardms.org/Discover-ARDMS/careers-in-sonography/Pages/Sonographer%20 Testimonials.aspx, accessed April 7, 2016.

54. For information regarding Windows to the Womb, see "About Unborn.com: The 25 Year Journey of Sound Wave Images with Shari Richard," *About Unborn.com*, http://sharirichard.com /about-unborn-com/, accessed April 7, 2016; Miguel A. Ruiz and Kathleen Murphy, "Sonographer–Fetus Bonding," *Journal of Diagnostic Medical Sonography* 8 (1992): 273.

55. See Marveen Craig, "Pro-Life/Pro-Choice: A New Dilemma for Sonographers," *Journal of Diagnostic Medical Sonography* 9 (1993): 152–158; Patricia A. Sullivan, "Public Perceptions and Politics: When Diagnostic Medical Ultrasound Is Employed as a Nondiagnostic Tool," *Journal of Diagnostic Medical Sonography* 18 (2002): 216–217.

56. See Craig, "Pro-Life/Pro-Choice," 153.

57. See John R. Pierson, Response, in Craig, "Pro-Life/Pro-Choice," 156: "If we are going to continue to move toward professional status we, as a profession, must discourage our members from sermonizing, professing, or openly trying to inflict their personal opinions and values on patients." Richard Taylor, Letter to Editor, "'A Few Good Men' (and Women) Looking for a Profession," *Journal of Diagnostic Medical Sonography* 9 (1993): 209–212. For critical analyses of earlier forms of imaging the body such as X-rays, see Lisa Cartwright, *Screening the Body: Tracing Medicine's Visual Culture* (Minneapolis: University of Minnesota Press, 1995); and Blume, *Insight and Industry*.

58. K. Dykes and K. Stjernqvist, "The Importance of Ultrasound to First-Time Mothers' Thoughts about Their Unborn Child," *Journal of Reproductive and Infant Psychology* 19 (2001): 95; Milne and Rich, "Cognitive and Affective Aspects," 33.

59. See Lisa M. Mitchell, "Women's Experiences of Unexpected Ultrasound Findings," *Journal of Midwifery and Women's Health* 49 (2004): 228–234.

60. See Margarete Sandelowski and Julie Barroso, "The Travesty of Choosing after Positive Prenatal Diagnosis," *Journal of Obstetric, Gynecologic, & Neonatal Nursing* 34 (2005): 310.

61. Taylor, "Image of Contradiction," 24–25.

62. See, Barbara K. Rothman, *The Tentative Pregnancy: How Amniocentesis Changes the Experience of Motherhood* (New York: W. W. Norton, 1993) and Rayna Rapp, *Testing Women, Testing the Fetus: The Social Impact of Amniocentesis in America* (New York: Routledge, 1999), 126.

63. Woman's Right to Know Act, Code of Ala. § 26-23A-3 (10) (LexisNexis 2002); O.C.G.A. § 31-9A-2 (7) (LexisNexis 1981); KRS § 311.720 (6) (LexisNexis 1974); N.D. Cent. Code, § 12.1-17.1-01 (3) (LexisNexis 1987); 63 Okl. St. § 1-730 (4) (LexisNexis 2007); Tex. Fam. Code § 33.001 (2) (LexisNexis 1999).

64. *Planned Parenthood v. Casey*, 505 U.S. 833, 852 (1992).

65. See Aaron G. Sheinin, "Bill Clears Early Hurdle—S.C. House: View Fetal Image Prior to Abortion," *State* (S.C.), March 22, 2007, p. A1. See also Matthew Gordon, "Recent Developments in Health Law—State Attempts to Expand Abortion Informed Consent Requirements: New Life after *Gonzales v. Carhart?*," *Journal of Law, Medicine & Ethics* 3 (2007): 751–752.

66. *Stuart v. Loomis*, 992 F. Supp. 2d 585, 601 (M.D.N.C. 2014).

67. Faye D. Ginsburg, *Contested Lives: The Abortion Debate in an American Community* (Berkeley: University of California Press, 1989), 104–105.

68. Nathan Stormer, "Looking in Wonder: Prenatal Sublimity and the Commonplace 'Life,'" *Signs* 33 (2008): 647–673.

69. Particular thanks to Robert Ferguson for discussion on this point.

70. See Susan Dominus, "The Mysterious Disappearance of Young Pro-Choice Women," *Glamour,* August 2005, p. 200.

71. *Roe v. Wade,* 410 U.S. 113, 150, 154, 156, 163 (1973).

72. Sontag, *On Photography,* 155–156.

73. Woman's Right to Know Act, Code of Ala. § 26-23A-2 (LexisNexis 2002).

74. *Ex parte Anonymous,* 803 So.2d 542, 561 (Ala. 2001) (Johnstone, J., dissenting).

75. *Texas Medical Providers Performing Abortion Services. v. Lakey,* 667 F.3d 570, 576 (5th Cir. 2012).

76. See generally Gary L. Wells and Eric P. Seelau, "Eyewitness Identification: Psychological Research and Legal Policy on Line-Ups," *Psychology, Public Policy, and Law* 1 (1995): 769.

77. A.C.A. § 20-16-602 (a) (LexisNexis 2003).

78. See A. Edelman, L. Thomas, and J. Jensen, "Transvaginal Ultrasound and the Success of Medical Abortion," *International Journal of Gynecology and Obstetrics* 85 (2004): 62–63 (discussing transvaginal ultrasound's use in confirming the success of a medical abortion by imaging the now empty uterus).

79. Maureen Paul, Eric Schaff, and Mark Nichols, "The Roles of Clinical Assessment, Human Chorionic Gonadotropin Assays, and Ultrasonography in Medical Abortion Practice," *American Journal of Obstetrics and Gynecology* 183 (2000): S37 (showing ultrasound images in the early weeks of pregnancy); Caitlin E. Borgmann and Bonnie S. Jones, "Legal Issues in the Provision of Medical Abortion," *American Journal of Obstetrics and Gynecology* 183 (2000): S84–S94.

80. One measure of enthusiasm for ultrasound is found in a study that reports that 37 percent of pregnant women are willing to pay for ultrasound out of pocket. See Mark B. Stephens, "Majority of Pregnant Women Want Prenatal Ultrasound," *American Family Physician* 62 (2000): 2665.

81. Sallie Han, "Seeing the Baby in the Belly: Family and Kinship at the Ultrasound Scan," in *The Changing Landscape of Work and Family in the American Middle Class: Reports from the Field,* eds. Elizabeth Rudd and Lara Descartes (Lanham, MD: Lexington Books, 2008), 250; see also Nancy Press and C. H. Browner, "Why Women Say Yes to Prenatal Diagnosis," *Social Science & Medicine* 45 (1997): 985 (observing that beginning prenatal care "in a timely manner . . . is a maternal responsibility").

82. See Jeremy Waldron, *God, Locke, and Equality: Christian Foundations of John Locke's Political Thought* (Cambridge: Cambridge University Press, 2002), 210–211.

83. John Locke, *A Letter Concerning Toleration,* ed. James H. Tully (Indianapolis: Hackett, 1983), 38.

84. *Stuart v. Loomis,* 589.

85. N.C. Gen. Stat. § 90-21.85 (2); (4) (LexisNexis 2011).

86. *Rochin v. California,* 342 U.S. 165, 173 (1952).

87. Leslie J. Reagan, *When Abortion Was a Crime: Women, Medicine, and Law in the United States, 1867–1973* (Berkeley: University of California Press, 1997), 168–171.

88. *People v. Stanko,* 407 Ill. 624 (1950).

89. Okla. Stat. tit. 63, § 1-738.3d. (LexisNexis 2010).

90. Ewen MacAskill, "*Doonesbury* Strip on Texas Abortion Law Dropped by Some US Newspapers," *Guardian,* March 11, 2012, http://www.theguardian.com/world/2012/mar/11/doonesbury-strip-texas-abortion-law.

91. Okla. Stat. tit. 63, § 1-738.3d. (LexisNexis 2010).

92. *Hill v. Colorado,* 530 U.S. 703, 757 (2000) (Scalia, J., dissenting).

93. Ellen R. Wiebe and Lisa Adams, "Women's Perceptions about Seeing the Ultrasound Picture before an Abortion," *European Journal of Contraception and Reproductive Healthcare* 14 (2009): 97–102.

94. Mitchell, *Baby's First Picture,* 6.

95. Kirshenbaum, "Caught in the Act of Becoming," 18–19.

96. *Planned Parenthood v. Casey,* 851.

97. Ibid.

98. Bruno Latour, "Visualization and Cognition: Thinking with Eyes and Hands," *Knowledge and Society: Studies in the Sociology of Culture Past and Present* 6 (1986): 3.

Chapter 6 "You Had Body, You Died"

1. *In re Doe,* 19 S.W.3d 346, 361 (Tex. 2000).

2. Carol Sanger, "Decisional Dignity: Teenage Abortion, Bypass Hearings, and the Misuse of Law," *Columbia Journal of Gender and Law* 18 (2009): 409–499; see also *The Judicial Bypass: Report on a Meeting* (National Partnership for Women & Families no. 8, 2008), 8.

3. See Stephen A. Tyler, "The Vision Quest in the West, or What the Mind's Eye Sees," *Journal of Anthropological Research* 40 (1984): 23.

4. *Fact Sheet: Induced Abortion in the United States,* Guttmacher Institute, March 2016, https://www.guttmacher.org/fact-sheet/induced-abortion-united-states.

5. Jen Gish, *Tiger Writing: Art, Culture, and the Interdependent Self* (Cambridge, MA: Harvard University Press, 2013).

6. Carol Sanger, "Seeing and Believing: Mandatory Ultrasound and the Path to a Protected Choice," *University of California Law Review* 56 (2008): 351–408.

7. Anne Higonnet, "A New Image of Childhood without the Maternal Body," in *Bodies and Borders: Negotiating Motherhood in the 21st Century,* eds. Yasmin Ergas, Jane Johnson, and Sonya Michel (forthcoming).

8. Susan Sontag, *On Photography* (New York: Farrar, Straus and Giroux, 1977), 8.

9. Mary Bouquet, "The Family Photographic Condition," *Visual Anthropology Review* 16 (2000): 2–19.

10. Roland Barthes, *Camera Lucida: Reflections on Photography*, trans. Richard Howard (New York: Hill and Wang, 2010), 81.

11. Ibid., 5.

12. *Gonzales v. Carhart,* 550 U.S. 124, 159 (2007).

13. Elaine G. Gerber, "Deconstructing Pregnancy: RU 486, Seeing 'Eggs,' and the Ambiguity of Very Early Conception," *Medical Anthropology Quarterly* 16 (2002): 94.

14. See Regina Austin, "Sapphire Bound," *Wisconsin Law Review* 1989 (1989): 539–578.

15. Governor and Legislature of South Dakota, *Report of the South Dakota Task Force to Study Abortion,* December 2005.

16. Linda L. Layne, *Motherhood Lost: A Feminist Account of Pregnancy Loss in America* (New York: Routledge, 2003), 83.

17. Lynn M. Morgan, "Strange Anatomy: Gertrude Stein and the Avant-Garde Embryo," *Hypatia* 21 (2006): 30.

18. Pierre Apraxine and Sophie Schmit, "Photography and the Occult," in *The Perfect Medium: Photography and the Occult* (New Haven, CT: Yale University Press, 2005), 14.

19. Ibid.

20. Roland Barthes, *Camera Lucida,* 86.

21. "Brady's Photographs; Pictures of the Dead at Antietam," *New York Times,* October 20, 1862, http://www.nytimes.com/1862/10/20/news/brady-s-photographs-pictures-of-the-dead-at

-antietam.html?pagewanted=all. Quoted in Beaumont Newhall, *The History of Photography: From 1839 to the Present* (New York: Museum of Modern Art, 1982), 91.

22. Keith F. Davis, "'A Terrible Distinctiveness': Photographs of the Civil War Era," in *Photography in Nineteenth Century America,* ed. Martha A. Sandweiss (Fort Worth, TX: Amon Carter Museum, 1991), 143; see also Newhall, *History of Photography,* 32.

23. Edward L. Wilson, "To My Patrons (1871)," in *Photograph: Essays and Images, Illustrated Readings in the History of Photography,* ed. Beaumont Newhall (New York: Museum of Modern Art, 1980), 129–133. See also Rees V. Jenkins, "Technology and the Market: George Eastman and the Origins of Mass Amateur Photography," *Technology and Culture* 1616 (1975): 1–19.

24. Wilson, "To My Patrons," 130.

25. Matthew R. Isenburg, "The Wonder of the American Daguerreotype," in *American Daguerreotypes: From the Matthew R. Isenburg Collection,* ed. Richard S. Field (New Haven, CT: Yale University Art Gallery), 10.

26. Phoebe Lloyd, "Posthumous Mourning Portraiture," in *A Time to Mourn: Expressions of Grief in Nineteenth Century America,* eds. Martha V. Pike and Janice G. Armstrong (Stony Brook, NY: Museums at Stony Brook, 1980), 71–89.

27. See Robert Woods, *Children Remembered: Responses to Ultimately Death in the Past* (Liverpool: Liverpool University Press, 2006), 166; Rosemary Mander and Rosalind K. Marshall, "An Historical Analysis of the Role of Paintings and Photographs in Comforting Bereaved Parents," *Midwifery* 19 (2003): 230–242; Nigel Llewellyn, "'[An] Impe Entombed Here Doth Lie': The Beresford Triptych and Child Memorials in Post-Reformation England," in *Representations of Childhood Deaths,* eds. Gillian Avery and Kimberley Reynolds (New York: St. Martin's Press, 2000), 52–64; and Raymond A. Anselment, *The Realms of Apollo: Literature and Healing in Seventeenth-Century England* (Newark: University of Delaware Press; London; Cranbury, NJ: Associated University Presses, 1995), 59–61.

28. See Anton Pigler, "Portraying the Dead: Painting—Graphic Art," in *Acta Historiae Artium. Academiae Scientiarum Hungaricae, vol. 4,* ed. Lajos Fülep (Budapest: Akadémiai Kiadó, 1956), 1–75.

29. See Phoebe Lloyd, "A Young Boy in His First and Last Suit," *Minneapolis Institute of Arts Bulletin* 64 (1978–1980): 104–111, http://www.artsconnected.org/resource/93906/a-young-boy-in-his-first-and-last-suit.

30. Ibid.

31. Phoebe Lloyd, "A Death in the Family," *Philadelphia Museum of Art Bulletin* 78, no. 335 (1982): 2–13.

32. David E. Stannard, "Sex, Death, and Daguerreotypes," in *America and the Daguerreotype,* ed. John Wood (Iowa City: University of Iowa Press, 1991), 91.

33. Lloyd, "A Death in the Family."

34. See Phoebe Lloyd's discussion of Charles Wilson Peale's Portrait of Rachel Weeping: ibid., 2–3.

35. Stannard, "Sex, Death, and Daguerreotypes," 95.

36. Jay Ruby, *Secure the Shadow: Death and Photography in America* (Cambridge, MA: MIT Press, 1995), 32.

37. Ruby offers a moving *carte-de-visite* of a baby with the inscription "Taken when dying" written on the back. Ibid., 179.

38. Collections are found in Ruby, *Secure the Shadow;* Stanley Burns, *Sleeping Beauty: Memorial Photography in America* (Altadena, CA: Twelvetrees Press, 1990); and Stanley Burns, *Sleeping Beauty II: Grief, Bereavement in Memorial Photography American and European Traditions* (New York: Burns Archive Press, 2002). See also Dan Meinwald, *Memento Mori: Death and Photography in*

Nineteenth Century America (Berkeley, CA: University of California, 1990), available at http://vv .arts.ucla.edu/terminals/meinwald/meinwald1.html.

39. In his 1938 history of photography, historian Robert Taft described the images as "too gruesome to contemplate with pleasure." Robert Taft, *Photography and the American Scene* (New York: Dover, 1964), 196, quoted in Kent N. Bowser, "An Examination of Nineteenth Century American Post-Mortem Photography" (Master's thesis, Ohio State University, 1983), 2.

40. Anne Douglas, "Heaven Our Home: Consolation Literature in the Northern United States, 1830–1880," in *Death in America,* ed. David E. Stannard (Philadelphia: University of Pennsylvania Press, 1975, 1974), 49, 50. "A lock of hair from the head of some beloved one is often prized above gold or gems, for it is . . . a portion of themselves, present with us when they are absent, surviving while they are moldering in the silent tomb." Kathryn Beattie, "Aspects of Acceptance and Denial in Painted Posthumous Portraits and Postmortem Photographs of Nineteenth-Century Children" (Master's thesis, Concordia University, 2006), 35 (quoting Ann S. Stephens).

41. Stannard, "Sex, Death, and Daguerreotypes," 95.

42. Beattie, "Aspects of Acceptance," 52.

43. See Diane Waggoner, "Photographic Amusement: 1888–1919," in *The Art of the American Snapshot, 1888–1978: From the Collection of Robert E. Jackson* (Washington, DC: National Gallery of Art, 2007), 7.

44. Ruby, *Secure the Shadow,* 7–11.

45. Ibid., 7.

46. Philippe Ariès, *Western Attitudes toward Death: From the Middle Ages to the Present* (Baltimore: Johns Hopkins University Press, 1974), 94.

47. Ibid.

48. James Van Der Zee et al., *The Harlem Book of the Dead* (Dobbs Ferry, NY: Morgan & Morgan, 1978), 83.

49. Ruby, *Secure the Shadow,* 209. Anton Pigler concluded much the same with regard to sixteenth-century Dutch funeral paintings of children. Pigler, "Portraying the Dead," 43.

50. Rosanne Cecil, "Memories of Pregnancy Loss: Recollections of Elderly Women in Northern Ireland," in *The Anthropology of Pregnancy Loss: Comparative Studies in Miscarriage, Stillbirth and Neonatal Death,* ed. Rosanne Cecil (Washington, DC: Berg, 1996), 186.

51. Margaret Godel, "Images of Stillbirth: Memory, Mourning and Memorial," *Visual Studies* 22 (2007): 253–269. See also Ingela Rådestad et al., "Long-Term Outcomes for Mothers who Have or Have Not Held Their Stillborn Baby," *Midwifery* 25 (2009): 422–429; Carol Sanger, "'The Birth of Death': Stillborn Birth Certificates and the Problem for Law," *California Law Review* 100 (2012): 272.

52. Godel, "Images of Stillbirth," 257.

53. "Now I Lay Me Down to Sleep | Angela Lynn Portraits Selma, TX," January 29, 2013, http://angelalynnportraits.com/2013/01/now-i-lay-me-down-to-sleep-angela-lynn-portraits-selma-tx//.

54. See Rachel Meredith, "The Photography of Neonatal Bereavement at Wythenshawe Hospital," *Journal of Visual Communication in Medicine* 23 (2000): 162–164; *Touching Souls: Healing with Bereavement Photography,* http://www.toddhochberg.com/about.html, accessed April 29, 2016.

55. See *Share Pregnancy and Infant Loss Support,* http://nationalshare.org, accessed April 29, 2016; *Sands: Stillbirth & Neonatal Death Charity,* http://www.uk-sands.org, accessed April 29, 2016; Judith Schott, Alix Henley, and Nancy Kohner, *Pregnancy Loss and the Death of a Baby: Guidelines for Professionals* (Sands, UK: Bosun-Publications, 2007).

56. Elizabeth McCracken, *An Exact Replica of a Figment of My Imagination: A Memoir* (New York: Little, Brown, 2008), 14. But see Layne, *Motherhood Lost,* 142. Layne notes that traditional social disregard of pregnancy loss has contributed to the need for fetishization.

57. Godel, "Images of Stillbirth."

58. Clement Cheroux, "Ghost Dialectics: Spirit Photography in Entertainment and Belief," in *The Perfect Medium: Photography and the Occult* (New Haven, CT: Yale University Press, 2005), 46.

59. Oliver W. Holmes, "Doings of the Sunbeam," in *Soundings from the Atlantic* (Boston: Ticknor and Fields, 1864), 276–277.

60. Crista Cloutier, "Mumler's Ghosts," in *The Perfect Medium: Photography and the Occult* (New Haven, CT: Yale University Press, 2005), 26–27.

61. See Tom Patterson, *100 Years of Spirit Photography* (London: Regency Press 1965), 8.

62. Tom Gunning, "Haunting Images: Ghosts, Photography, and the Modern Body," in *The Disembodied Spirit* (Brunswick, ME: Bowdoin College Museum of Art, 2003), 20.

63. Jay Winter, *Sites of Memory, Sites of Mourning: The Great War in European Cultural History* (Cambridge: Cambridge University Press, 2014), 6.

64. Gunning, "Haunting Images," 53.

65. Louis Kaplan, *The Strange Case of William Mumler, Spirit Photographer* (Minneapolis: University of Minnesota Press, 2008), 4; Thomas J. Brown, ed., *Remixing the Civil War: Meditations on the Sesquicentennial* (Baltimore: Johns Hopkins University Press, 2011), 152; Arthur C. Doyle, *The Case for Spirit Photography* (New York: George H. Doran, 1923); Winter, *Sites of Memory*.

66. See Martyn Jolly, *Faces of the Living Dead: The Belief in Spirit Photographs* (West New York, NJ: Mark Batty, 2006), 9.

67. Ibid., 144–145.

68. Cheroux, "Ghost Dialectics," 46.

69. Linda L. Layne, "He Was a Real Baby with Baby Things," *Journal of Material Culture* 5 (2000): 322.

70. Ellen Hopkins, "Tales from the Baby Factory," *New York Times Magazine*, March 15, 1992, p. 80.

71. Barbara Duden, *Disembodying Women: Perspectives on Pregnancy and the Unborn*, trans. Lee Hoinacki (Cambridge, MA: Harvard University Press, 1993), 53.

72. Rayna Rapp, *Testing Women, Testing the Fetus: The Social Impact of Amniocenteses in America* (New York: Routledge, 1999), 96.

73. Gerald Epstein, *Healing Visualizations: Creating Health through Imagery* (New York: Bantam Books, 1989), 137.

74. Kathy Freston, *Visualizing Pregnancy*, CreateSpace, 2009, audio CD, 20 min.

75. See Teresa Robertson, "Fertility and the Mind Body Connection," *Tony Crisp*, http://dreamhawk.com/pregnancy-childbirth/fertility-and-the-mind-body-connection/, accessed April 29, 2016.

76. Layne, *Motherhood Lost*, 8.

77. See Kenneth B. Schechtman et al., "Decision-Making for Termination of Pregnancies with Fetal Anomalies: Analysis of 53,000 Pregnancies," *Obstetrics & Gynecology* 99 (2002): 217.

78. Margarete Sandelowski and Linda C. Jones, " 'Healing Fictions': Stories of Choosing in the Aftermath of the Detection of Fetal Anomalies," *Social Science & Medicine* 42 (1996): 356.

79. See Lisa M. Mitchell, "Women's Experiences of Unexpected Ultrasound Findings," *Journal of Midwifery and Women's Health* 49 (2004): 228–234.

80. Rapp, *Testing Women*, 131.

81. Barbara K. Rothman, *The Tentative Pregnancy: How Amniocentesis Changes the Experience of Motherhood* (New York: W. W. Norton, 1993).

82. Janelle S. Taylor, "Image of Contradiction: Obstetrical Ultrasound in American Culture," in *Reproducing Reproduction: Kinship, Power, and Technological Innovation,* eds. Sarah Franklin and Helena Ragoné (Philadelphia: University of Pennsylvania Press, 1998), 24–25.

83. Rothman, *Tentative Pregnancy,* 86–116.

84. Philippe Ariès, *Centuries of Childhood,* trans. Robert Baldick (New York: Knopf, 1962), 38.

85. Ibid.

86. See Margarete Sandelowski and Julie Barroso, "The Travesty of Choosing after Positive Prenatal Diagnosis," *Journal of Obstetric, Gynecologic, & Neonatal Nursing* 34 (2005): 310.

87. Rita B. Black, "Seeing the Baby: The Impact of Ultrasound Technology," *Journal of Genetic Counseling* 1 (1992): 48.

88. Sandelowski and Jones, "Healing Fictions," 357–358.

89. Layne, *Motherhood Lost,* 97, quoting Mickey Hoch, "A Miscarriage Hurts, Too," *UNITE Notes* 8 no. 1 (1988): 3.

90. Ellen R. Wiebe and Lisa C. Adams, "Women's Experience of Viewing the Products of Conception after an Abortion," *Contraception* 80 (2009): 575.

91. Karen Pazol, Andreea A. Creanga, and Denise J. Jamieson, "Abortion Surveillance: United States, 2012," *Surveillance Summaries* 64 (2015): 1.

92. Wiebe and Adams, "Viewing the Products of Conception," 576.

93. Ibid., 577.

94. Ibid.

95. Ibid.

96. Ibid.

97. Ibid.

98. Brenna Donnelly, "AZ Legislator Wants Requirement to Watch Abortion," *WSMV,* March 21, 2012, http://www.wsmv.com/story/17215824/legislator-wants-requirement-to-watch -abortion#ixzz47KdoqWVh.

99. *Stenberg v. Carhart,* 530 U.S. 914 (2000).

100. *Gonzales v. Carhart,* 132.

101. Ibid., 139 (paragraphs omitted).

102. Ibid., 158.

103. Ibid., 161.

104. Ibid., 158.

105. Ibid., 157.

106. Ibid., 159–160.

107. Larry Neumeister, "Doctor: Aborting Intact Fetus Can Shorten Grieving Period," *Seattle Times,* March 31, 2004, http://community.seattletimes.nwsource.com/archive/?date =20040331&slug=abortion31.

108. Ibid.

109. Jennifer Kerns et al., "Women's Decision Making Regarding Choice of Second Trimester Termination Method for Pregnancy Complications," *International Journal of Gynecology and Obstetrics* 116 (2012): 247.

110. Transcript of Trial Proceedings at 57–58, *Carhart v. Ashcroft,* 331 F. Supp. 2d 805 (D. Neb. 2004) (No. 4:03CV3385).

111. Frances E. Casey et al., "Elective Abortion Treatment and Management," *Medscape,* February 29, 2016, http://emedicine.medscape.com/article/252560-treatment#d6.

112. Transcript of Trial Proceedings at 57, *Carhart v. Ashcroft.*

113. Rapp, *Testing Women,* 243.

114. Barry Yeoman, "I Had an Abortion When I Was Six Months Pregnant," *Barry Yeoman—Journalist,* October 1, 2001, http://www.barryyeoman.com/articles/gina.html (by Gina Gonzales as told to Barry Yeoman, originally published in *Glamour*). See also Suzanne R. Trupin and Carey Moreno, "Medical Abortion: Overview and Management," *Medscape Women's Health* 7 (2002): 4–18.

115. See Michael S. Harper and Anthony Walton, eds., *Every Shut Eye Ain't Asleep: An Anthology of Poetry by African Americans since 1945* (Boston: Little, Brown, 1994), 151; Anne Sexton, *The Complete Poems* (Boston: Houghton Mifflin, 1981), 61.

116. Barbara Johnson, "Apostrophe, Animation, and Abortion," *Diacritics* 16 (1986): 35.

117. Ibid., 46.

118. Ibid., 29–30.

119. Ibid., 32.

120. Ibid., 34.

121. Karen Houle, "Abortion as the Work of Mourning," *Canadian Journal of Continental Philosophy* 11 (2007): 141.

122. From "The Mother," in Gwendolyn Brooks, *Selected Poems* (New York: Harper & Row, 1963), 4–5.

Chapter 7 Sending Pregnant Teenagers to Court

1. Twenty-five states require parental consent and twelve require notification. See "Restrictions on Young Women's Access to Abortion," *NARAL Pro-Choice America,* http://www.prochoiceamerica.org/what-is-choice/fast-facts/young-women.html, accessed February 8, 2016.

2. *Bellotti v. Baird,* 443 U.S. 622 (1979).

3. *Roe v. Wade,* 410 U.S. 113, 153 (1973); *Doe v. Bolton,* 410 U.S. 179 (1973).

4. *Bellotti v. Baird,* 647.

5. *In re Gault,* 387 U.S. 1, 13 (1967).

6. *Bellotti v. Baird,* 642.

7. Ibid., 634.

8. Martin Guggenheim argues that the bypass procedure itself violates *Roe* in that it gives one person, the judge, a veto over the girl's decision. Martin Guggenheim, "Minor Rights: The Adolescent Abortion Case," *Hofstra Law Review* 30 (2002): 589–646.

9. *In re Anonymous,* 684 So.2d 1337, 1338 (Ala. Civ. App. 1996).

10. *In re Anonymous,* 905 So.2d 845, 848 (Ala. Civ. App. 2005).

11. Ibid.

12. *In re A.W.,* 826 So.2d 1280, 1282 (Miss. 2002).

13. *In re Jane Doe,* 613 N.E.2d 1112, 1114–1115 (Ohio Ct. App. 1993).

14. *In re Doe,* 19 S.W.3d 346, 358 (Tex. 2000).

15. *In re Anonymous,* 515 So.2d 1254, 1255 (Ala. Civ. App. 1987).

16. Ibid., 1256.

17. Brian K. Landsberg, "Sumter County, Alabama and the Origins of the Voting Rights Act," *Alabama Law Review* 54 (2003): 904.

18. Malcolm M. Feeley, *The Process Is the Punishment: Handling Cases in a Lower Criminal Court* (New York: Russell Sage Foundation, 1992), 33.

19. See *Hodgson v. Minnesota,* 497 U.S. 417, 436 n.21 (1990) (nine out of 3,573 petitions were denied, six withdrawn, and 3,558 were granted); *Planned Parenthood League of Mass. Inc. v. Attorney General,* 424 Mass. 586, 592 (1997) (out of 15,000 cases in Massachusetts heard by 2000, thirteen were denied and eleven of those were reversed); and "Report: Arizona Judges OK Most Minors' Abortion Requests," *Arizona Daily Star,* http://tucson.com/news/local/report-arizona-judges-ok -most-minors-abortion-requests/article_476f23f2-631c-524a-8ffc-ef133d916073.html. (Arizona judges approved three-fourths of all petitions filed in 2012). Susan H. Friedman et al., "Judicial Bypass of Parental Consent for Abortion: Characteristics of Pregnant Minor 'Jane Doe's," *Journal of Nervous and Mental Disease* 203 (2015): 401–403 (over a three-year period in one Ohio juvenile court, fifty-two out of fifty-five petitions were granted, one was denied, and two were withdrawn). The director of Reproductive Rights Project in Chicago stated that she has never had a petitioner client turned down since judicial bypass hearings came to Illinois in 2013. Barbara Brotman, "Bypassing Parents on Abortions Strain to All," *Chicago Tribune,* October 11, 2015, p. 1.

20. *Planned Parenthood v. Casey,* 505 U.S. 833, 899 (1992).

21. Samantha Luks and Michael Salamone, "Abortion," in *Public Opinion and Constitutional Controversy,* eds. Nathaniel Persily, Jack Citrin, and Patrick J. Egan (Oxford: Oxford University Press, 2008), 84–107.

22. See Rickie Solinger, "'A Complete Disaster': Abortion and the Politics of Hospital Abortion Committees, 1950–1970," *Feminist Studies* 19 (1993): 240–268.

23. 1997. AK. ALS14.

24. *In re Anonymous,* 720 So.2d 497, 502–503 (Ala. 1998) (Hooper, C. J., concurring in part and dissenting in part).

25. *In re Doe,* 19 S.W.3d 346, 364 (Tex. 2000) (Enoch, J., concurring).

26. Feeley, *Process Is the Punishment,* 5.

27. J. Shoshanna Ehrlich, *Who Decides? The Abortion Right of Teens* (Westport, CT: Praeger Press, 2006), 133.

28. *The Judicial Bypass: Report on a Meeting* (National Partnership for Women & Families no. 8, 2008) (on file with author), 17.

29. Avishai Margalit, *The Decent Society* (Cambridge, MA: Harvard University Press, 1996), 210.

30. *Planned Parenthood v. Casey,* 851.

31. *Tyrer v. United Kingdom,* 26 Eur. Ct. H.R. (ser. A) at 32–33 (1978).

32. Ibid., 32 (emphasis added).

33. Alastair Fowler, *Kinds of Literature: An Introduction to the Theory of Genre and Modes* (Oxford, UK: Clarendon Press, 1982), 20.

34. *Bellotti v. Baird,* 644.

35. Ibid.

36. *Glick v. McKay,* 937 F.2d 434, 441 (9th Cir. 1991), overruled on other grounds by *Lambert v. Wicklund,* 520 U.S. 292 (1997).

37. Texas Supreme Court, *Instructions for Applying to the Court for a Waiver of Parental Notification and Consent* (forms 2A and 2B promulgated pursuant to Texas Fam. Code §§ 33.003(1), 33.004(c) (1999)), http://www.txcourts.gov/media/1240926/Parental-Notification-Forms-2015.pdf.

38. Tex. Fam. Code § 33.003 (g-1) (LexisNexis 2016).

39. N.C. Gen. Stat. § 90-21.8 (f) (LexisNexis 1995).

40. *Planned Parenthood of Central New Jersey v. Farmer,* 165 N.J. 609, 638 (2000).

41. Ibid. In Massachusetts, minors are at the courthouse for approximately two hours and before a judge for between fifteen and thirty minutes. *Planned Parenthood League of Mass. Inc. v. Attorney General,* 424 Mass. 586, 592 (1997).

42. Tex. Fam. Code § 33.003(b)(1) (LexisNexis 2015).

43. Tex. Fam. Code § 33.003(b)(2), (b)(3) (LexisNexis 2015).

44. *In re Doe,* 19 S.W.3d 346, 363 (Tex. 2000) (Enoch, J., concurring).

45. Ibid., 363. Justice Enoch felt particularly stymied by Hecht's practices, stating that "[Hecht's] disclosures leave the Court in an untenable position. The Court cannot respond because to do so would require it to reveal whatever other pieces of the record remain confidential."

46. *North Western Memorial Hospital v. Ashcroft,* 362 F.3d 923, 929 (7th Cir. 2004).

47. See Patricia M. Spacks, *Gossip* (New York: Knopf, 1985); Mary Beth Norton, "Gender and Defamation in Seventeenth-Century Maryland," *William and Mary Quarterly* 44 (1987): 3–39.

48. *In re T. H.,* 484 N.E.2d 568, 569–570 (Ind. 1985).

49. Ibid.

50. Catherine Candisky and Randall Edwards, "Pregnant Jane Does Often Intelligent, Scared," *Columbus Dispatch,* February 28, 1993, p. 5B (quoting Juvenile Court Judge Katherine Liss).

51. Cornelia H. Dayton, "Taking the Trade: Abortion and Gender Relations in an Eighteenth-Century New England Village," *William and Mary Quarterly* 48 (1991): 23.

52. Ibid.

53. *Bellotti v. Baird,* 644.

54. Miss. Code Ann. § 41-41-55 (3) (LexisNexis 1986); N.C. Gen. Stat. § 90-21.8 (d) (LexisNexis 1995).

55. Miss. Code Ann. § 41-41-55 (3) (LexisNexis 1986).

56. Tex. Fam. Code § 33.003 (LexisNexis 2015).

57. *Ohio v. Akron Center for Reproductive Health,* 497 U.S. 502, 532 (1990) (Blackmun, J., dissenting).

58. Pregnant women who learn their fetus is no longer alive, and must schedule a procedure to remove or evacuate it, describe the waiting period between decision and procedure as terribly hard. See Elizabeth McCracken, *An Exact Replica of a Figment of My Imagination: A Memoir* (New York: Little, Brown, 2008).

59. *Ex parte Anonymous,* 889 So.2d 518, 520 (Ala. 2003) (Johnstone, J., concurring).

60. See Helena Silverstein, *Girls on the Stand: How Courts Fail Pregnant Minors* (New York: New York University Press, 2007), 52.

61. See, for example, Texas Supreme Court, *Instructions for Applying for a Waiver.*

62. *In re Doe,* 19 S.W.3d 346, 358 (Tex. 2000).

63. Women's Law Project, *Young Women's Guide to Abortion in Pennsylvania* (2009), http://www.womenslawproject.org/brochures/wlp_teen_piece.pdf, 2. A few private organizations offer abortion funding for indigent women, young and old; for more, see *National Network of Abortion Funds,* https://fundabortionnow.org, accessed February 15, 2016.

64. *Bellotti v. Baird,* 643 n.23.

65. 18 Pennsylvania Cons. Stat. § 3206(f) (2009). See also Satsie Veith, "The Judicial Bypass Procedure and Adolescents' Abortion Rights: The Fallacy of the 'Maturity' Standard," *Hofstra Law Review* 23 (1994): 453–481.

66. *In re Doe,* 19 S.W.3d 249, 255 (Tex. 2000).

67. See Catherine Candisky and Randall Edwards, "Abortion Waivers Are a Judicial Crapshoot," *Columbus Dispatch,* February 29, 1993, p. 1A. See also Suellyn Scarnecchia and Julie K. Field, "Judging Girls: Decision Making in Parental Consent to Abortion Cases," *Michigan Journal of Gender & Law* 41 (1995): 75–123.

68. *In re Doe,* 19 Kan. App. 2d 204, 210 (1994).

69. *In re Doe,* 19 S.W.3d 249, 256 (Tex. 2000).

70. *In re Anonymous,* 964 So.2d 1239, 1243 (Ala. Civ. App. 2007) (affirming denial of petition of a minor whose testimony "did not indicate that she had discussed with a doctor, a nurse, or a counselor any potential psychological or emotional problems that might arise after having an abortion").

71. *Ex parte Anonymous,* 803 So. 2d 542, 564 (Ala. 2001) (Johnstone, J., dissenting).

72. Ibid., 561.

73. *In re Anonymous 1,* 251 Neb. 424, 428 (1997).

74. *In re Matter of B. S.,* 74 P.3d 285, 289, 290 (Ariz. Ct. App. 2003).

75. Ibid., 289.

76. Fowler, *Kinds of Literature,* 55.

77. Ala. Code § 26-21-4 (j) (LexisNexis 1987).

78. Natalie Z. Davis, *Fiction in the Archives: Pardon Tales and Their Tellers in Sixteenth-Century France* (Stanford, CA: Stanford University Press, 1987).

79. Ibid., 4.

80. Ibid.

81. *Judicial Bypass Report,* 5.

82. Silverstein, *Girls on the Stand,* 100–103.

83. Candisky and Edwards, "Pregnant Jane Does," 5B.

84. *In re Doe,* 645 N.E.2d 134, 134–135 (Ohio Ct. App. 1994). See generally *In re Anonymous,* 964 So.2d 1239 (Ala. Civ. App. 2007); *In re Anonymous 2,* 253 Neb. 485, 486 (1997); *In re Anonymous,* 515 So.2d 1254, 1255 (Ala. Civ. App. 1987).

85. Johanna Schoen, *Abortion After Roe* (Chapel Hill: University of North Carolina Press, 2015), 2.

86. Ibid., 1–3.

87. *Planned Parenthood v. Casey,* 891–894.

88. *In re Anonymous,* 806 So.2d 1269, 1274 (Ala. 2001).

89. Silverstein, *Girls on the Stand.*

90. *Hodgson v. Minnesota,* 648 F. Supp. 756, 766 (D. Minn. 1986), reversed, 853 F.2d 1452 (8th Cir. 1988).

91. Ibid.

92. J. Shoshanna Ehrlich, "Grounded in the Reality of Their Lives: Listening to Teens Who Make the Abortion Decision without Involving Their Parents," *Berkeley Women's Law Journal* 18 (2013): 141.

93. *In re Anonymous 1,* 251 Neb. 424, 427 (1997).

94. Ibid., 430.

95. *Ex parte Anonymous,* 803 So.2d 542, 564 (Ala. 2001).

96. *In re Doe,* 973 So.2d 548, 564 (Fla. Dist. Ct. App. 2008).

97. Ibid., 573.

98. *In re Jane Doe 4,* 19 S.W.3d. 337, 344 (Tex. 2000).

99. Ibid.

100. *In re Jane Doe,* 141 Ohio App. 3d 20, 23 (2001).

101. John Locke, *Two Treatises of Government* (London: Printed for Awnsham and John Churchill, 1698), 205.

102. Robert A. Ferguson, *The Trial in American Life* (Chicago: University of Chicago Press, 2007), 31.

103. *In re in re Doe*, 973 So.2d 548, 565 (Fla. Dist. Ct. App. 2008). The denial of the petition was upheld on appeal.

104. *In re Doe*, 924 So.2d 935, 940 (Fla. Dist. Ct. App. 2006) (reversing the trial court's decision to deny the petition for waiver).

105. *Ex parte Anonymous*, 803 So.2d 542, 561 (Ala. 2001).

106. Davis, *Fiction in the Archives*, 103–104.

107. Ibid., 85. See generally David I. Kertzer, *Sacrificed for Honor: Italian Infant Abandonment and the Politics of Reproductive Control* (Boston: Beacon Press, 1993).

108. Davis, *Fiction in the Archives*, 87.

109. See generally Columbia Human Rights Law Review, *Jailhouse Lawyer's Manual* (2009), 937; Lisa F. Orenstein, "The Maryland Survey: 1995–1996—Recent Decisions: The Maryland Court of Appeals," *Maryland Law Review* 56 (1997): 780–793.

110. *Del Piano v. United States*, 575 F.2d 1066, 1069 (3d Cir. 1978).

111. *Judicial Bypass Report*, 14.

112. *In re Doe*, 967 So.2d 1017, 1020 (Fla. Dist. Ct. App. 2007).

113. *In re Doe*, 19 S.W.3d 346, 361 (Tex. 2000).

114. See generally Herbert Jacob, *Silent Revolution: The Transformation of Divorce Law in the United States* (Chicago: University of Chicago Press, 1988); Walter Wadlington, "Divorce without Fault without Perjury," *Virginia Law Review* 52 (1966): 33–34.

115. *Report of the Governor's Commission on the Family* (California: Governor's Commission on the Family, 1966).

116. Ibid., 267–270.

117. *In re June Doe 4*, 19 S.W.3d 322, 324 (Tex. 2000).

118. *In re in re Doe*, 973 So.2d 548, 557 (Fla. Dist. Ct. App. 2008).

119. *Ex parte Anonymous*, 812 So.2d 1234, 1236 (Ala. 2001). See also Khiara M. Bridges, "An Anthropological Meditation on Ex Parte Anonymous: A Judicial Bypass Procedure for an Adolescent's Abortion," *California Law Review* 94 (2006): 215–242.

120. *Ex parte Anonymous*, 1239 (Houston, J., dissenting).

121. *Hodgson v. Minnesota*, 648 F. Supp. 756, 766 (D. Minn. 1986), reversed, 853 F.2d 1452 (8th Cir. 1988).

122. Ibid.

123. Victor S. Navasky, *Naming Names* (New York: Viking Press, 1980), 317.

124. Ibid., 318.

125. See Jeremy Waldron, "Lucky in Your Judge," *Theoretical Inquiries in Law* 9 (2008): 185–216.

126. Candisky and Edwards, "Abortion Waivers," 1A.

127. Phil Trexler, "Abortion Fiery Issue for Judges," *Akron Beacon Journal*, November 9, 2003, p. A1 (quoting Franklin County Juvenile Court Judge Lias). See also Larry Cunningham, "Can a Catholic Lawyer Represent a Minor Seeking a Judicial Bypass for an Abortion? A Moral and Canon Law Analysis," *Journal of Catholic Legal Studies* 44 (2005): 379–410. For the argument that granting a bypass petition is from a pro-life perspective cooperating in evil, see Eric P. Babbs, "Pro-Life Judges and Judicial Bypass Cases," *Notre Dame Journal of Law, Ethics & Public Policy* 22 (2008): 489–497.

128. See generally *Ex parte Anonymous*, 810 So.2d 786, 789 (Ala. 2001); Helena Silverstein, "In the Matter of Anonymous, a Minor: Fetal Representation in Hearings to Waive Parental Consent for Abortion," *Cornell Journal of Law & Public Policy* 11 (2001): 77–80.

129. See *In re Doe*, 866 P.2d 1069, 1074 (Kan. 1994); see also *In re T. H.*, 484 N.E.2d 568 (Ind. 1985) (upholding trial court's denial of petition on ground that the fetus might be viable, despite

medical testimony stating it was not viable); *In re L. D. F.*, 820 A.2d 714 (Pa. 2003) (extramedical grounds).

130. *In re Anonymous,* 905 So.2d 845, 850 (Ala. Civ. App. 2005). The minor had testified that she worked part-time at two restaurants during the preceding year-and-a-half; that the father of the child no longer speaks to her; and that she planned to tell her parents about the abortion in the future when she felt more comfortable.

131. Ibid. (emphasis added).

132. *In re Bourisseau,* 480 N.W.2d 270, 271 (Mich. 1992). See *New Mexico Judicial Ethics Handbook: Judicial Ethics for New Mexico Courts,* New Mexico Judicial Education Center, Institute of Public Law, University of New Mexico School of Law, April 2011, http://jec.unm.edu/manuals -resources/manuals/Judicial%20Ethics%20Handbook.pdf.

133. *In re Bourisseau,* 271.

134. Jeff Holyfield, "Michigan's Highest Court Censures Judge for Racial Rape Remark," *Associated Press,* March 3, 1992; see also "Judge Apologizes for Racial Remarks on Youth Abortion," *Baltimore Sun,* May 3, 1991.

135. See Richard Briffault, "Judicial Campaign Codes after Republican Party of *Minnesota v. White,*" *University of Pennsylvania Law Review* 153 (2004): 181–238; Brandice Canes-Wrone and Tom S. Clark, "Judicial Independence and Nonpartisan Elections," *Wisconsin Law Review* 21 (2009): 31–33.

136. Carol Sanger, "Decisional Dignity: Teenage Abortion, Bypass Hearings, and the Misuse of Law," *Columbia Journal of Gender and Law* 18 (2009): 492.

137. Canes-Wrone and Clark, "Judicial Independence," 34.

138. Ibid. See generally Anthony Champagne, "Television Ads in Judicial Campaigns," *Indiana Law Review* 35 (2002): 669–689 (particularly 676).

139. *State ex rel. Cincinnati Post v. Court of Appeals,* 65 Ohio St. 3d 378 (1992).

140. Mark Donald, "Dissent over Consent: Outing Judges, Changing Venue? Parental Consent Bill Has Something for Everyone," *Texas Lawyer,* March 7, 2005 (quoting attorney Susan Hays).

141. Adam Liptak, "On Moral Grounds, Some Judges Are Opting out of Abortion Cases," *New York Times,* September 4, 2005, p. S1; Helena Silverstein, " 'Honey, I Have No Idea': Court Readiness to Handle Petitions to Waive Parental Consent for Abortion," *Iowa Law Review* 88 (2002): 102 n.121.

142. *Judicial Bypass Report,* 15–16.

143. Stephen Koff, "Judges Set Own Abortion Consent Rules: Some Girls Try Court-Shopping," *Plain Dealer,* January 17, 1993, p. 1B.

144. Frank I. Michelman, "The Supreme Court and Litigation Access Fees: The Right to Protect One's Own Rights—Part I," *Duke Law Journal* 1973 (1974): 1173.

145. James Q. Whitman, "What Is Wrong with Inflicting Shaming Sanctions?," *Yale Law Journal* 107 (1998): 1090.

146. *Boddie v. Connecticut,* 401 U.S. 371, 372 (1971).

147. Ibid., 377.

148. Ibid., 376.

149. Joan Biskupic, "Ginsburg: Court Needs Another Woman," *USA Today,* May 5, 2009, http://usatoday30.usatoday.com/news/washington/judicial/2009-05-05-ruthginsburg_N.htm.

150. *In re Anonymous,* 678 So.2d 783 (Ala. Civ. App. 1996) (fourteen-year-old petitioner testified that "her pregnancy resulted from sexual abuse practiced upon her by her father"); *In re Jane Doe 1,* 57 Ohio St. 3d 135, 138 (1990) (petition denied); See *In re Complaint of Doe,* 96 Ohio App. 3d 435 (1994) (denial reversed on appeal); *In re Anonymous,* 711 So.2d 475, 475 (Ala. Civ. App. 1998).

151. *In re A. W.,* 826 So.2d 1280, 1282 (Miss. 2002); *In re Doe,* 2002-Ohio-6081, ¶ 6 (Ct. App.); *In re in re Doe,* 973 So.2d 548, 550 (Fla. Dist. Ct. App. 2008).

152. Donald, "Dissent over Consent."

153. See *Cleveland Surgi-Center Inc. v. Jones,* 2 F.3d 686, 689 (6th Cir. 1993).

154. *Judicial Bypass Report,* 2. See also (sadly) Amber Hausenfluck, "A Pregnant Teenager's Right to Education in Texas," *Scholar* 9 (2006): 169.

155. *Tyrer v. United Kingdom,* 31.

156. Ibid.

157. *Bellotti v. Baird,* 643 n.22.

158. Ibid.

159. Del. Code Ann. tit. 24, § 1783 (1) (LexisNexis 2009).

160. Me. Rev. Stat. tit. 22, § 1597-A (LexisNexis 1992).

161. Ibid.

162. See Lee-Ann Banaszak, Karen Beckwith, and Dieter Rucht, eds., *Women's Movements Facing the Reconfigured State* (New York: Cambridge University Press, 2003), 152. See also Nanette Funk, "Abortion Counseling and the 1995 German Abortion Law," *Connecticut Journal of International Law* 12 (1996): 33–65. In 1999 Pope John Paul II ordered the German bishops to withdraw Catholic agencies from such counseling, declaring that "In the defense of life, it is essential that bishops of the entire church speak unanimously and with one voice." Alessandra Stanley, "Pope Lectures German Bishops on Abortion," *New York Times,* November 21, 1999, p. A9. In response, Catholic laypeople used private counseling organizations, such as Donum Vitae and Caritas.

163. *In re R. B.,* 790 So.2d 830 (Miss. 2001), *In re Anonymous,* 812 So.2d 1221 (Ala. Civ. App. 2001); *In re A. W.,* 826 So.2d 1280 (Miss. 2002); *Ex parte Anonymous,* 531 So.2d 901 (Ala. 1988).

164. *Judicial Bypass Report,* 10–12.

165. *In re Anonymous,* 678 So.2d 783 (Ala. Civ. App. 1996).

166. *Sherron v. State,* 959 So.2d 30 (Miss. App. 2006).

167. Del. Code Ann. tit. 24, § 1783 (6) (LexisNexis 2009). With regard to other areas of (more or less) adult life, such as working, leaving school, and engaging in consensual sex, sixteen-year-olds are treated as adults; West Virginia Code § 16-2F-2 (2009).

168. Davis, *Fiction in the Archives,* 6.

169. Ibid., 57–58.

170. Ibid.

Chapter 8 FATHERS AND FETUSES—WHAT WOULD MEN DO?

1. Sarah A. Leavitt, "'A Private Little Revolution': The Home Pregnancy Test in American Culture," *Bulletin of the History of Medicine* 80 (2006): 317–345.

2. Olga Kenyon, *800 Years of Women's Letters* (London: Alan Sutton, 1992), 118–119. For accounts of other couples sympathetic to one another, see Margarete Sandelowski and Linda C. Jones, "'Healing Fictions': Stories of Choosing in the Aftermath of the Detection of Fetal Anomalies," *Social Science & Medicine* 42 (1996): 353–361.

3. Kenyon, *800 Years,* 118–119.

4. Ibid., 118–119.

5. See Rachel A. Camp, "Coercing Pregnancy," *William and Mary Journal of Women and the Law* 21 (2015): 275–318; Rachel K. Jones, Ann M. Moore, and Lori F. Frohwirth, "Perceptions of

Male Knowledge and Support among U.S. Women Obtaining Abortions," *Women's Health Issues* 21 (2011): 117–123 (study of 9,493 women); Barbara Ryan and Eric Plutzer, "When Married Women Have Abortions: Spousal Notification and Marital Interaction," *Journal of Marriage and Family* 51 (1989): 41–50 (study of 505 women); H. W. Smith and Cindy Kronauge, "The Politics of Abortion: Husband Notification Legislation, Self-Disclosure, and Marital Bargaining," *Sociological Quarterly* 31 (1990): 585–598 (study of 1,004 married Canadian women); Karuna S. Chibber et al., "The Role of Intimate Partners in Women's Reasons for Seeking Abortion," *Women's Health Issues* 21 (2014): e131–e138 (study of 954 women).

6. Meaghan Winter, "My Abortion," *New York Magazine,* November 10, 2013, http://nymag .com/news/features/abortion-stories-2013-11/.

7. Richard Yates, *Revolutionary Road* (New York: Knopf Doubleday, 2008), 229.

8. Ibid., 237.

9. See Margarete Sandelowski, "Failures of Volition: Female Agency and Infertility in Historical Perspective," *Signs* 15 (1990): 477–478.

10. Margarete Sandelowski, "Separate, but Less Unequal: Fetal Ultrasonography and the Transformation of Expectant Mother / Fatherhood," *Gender and Society* 8 (1994): 233–234.

11. *Planned Parenthood v. Danforth,* 428 U.S. 52, 69 (1976). Some men even develop physical symptoms that mimic their wife's pregnancy. See W. H. Terthowan and M. F. Conlon, "The Couvade Syndrome," *British Journal of Psychiatry* 111 (1965): 57–66.

12. *Planned Parenthood v. Danforth,* 71.

13. *Planned Parenthood v. Casey,* 505 U.S. 833 (1992).

14. See Dominique Bourassa and Jocelyn Bérubé, "The Prevalence of Intimate Partner Violence among Women and Teenagers Seeking Abortion Compared with Those Continuing Pregnancy," *Journal of Obstetrics and Gynaecology Canada* 29 (2007): 415–423.

15. *Planned Parenthood v. Casey,* 843.

16. Sandelowski, "Separate, but Less Unequal," 234.

17. Barack Obama, "How the Presidency Made Me a Better Father," June 21, 2015, *Huffington Post,* http://www.huffingtonpost.com/barack-obama/how-the-presidency-made-me-a-better-father _b_7632178.html.

18. *Knussman v. Maryland,* 272 F.3d 625 (4th Cir. 2001). But see Catherine R. Albiston, *Institutional Inequality and the Mobilization of the Family and Medical Leave Act: Rights on Leave* (New York: Cambridge University Press, 2010).

19. Reva Siegel, "Reasoning from the Body: A Historical Perspective on Abortion Regulation and Questions of Equal Protection," *Stanford Law Review* 44 (1992): 265.

20. Barbara Ehrenreich and Deirdre English, *For Her Own Good: 150 Years of the Experts' Advice to Women* (Garden City, NY: Anchor Press, 1978), 211–239.

21. Ruth H. Bloch, "American Feminine Ideals in Transition: The Rise of the Moral Mother, 1785–1815," *Feminist Studies* 4 (1978): 100–126.

22. Rita Rhodes, "Women, Motherhood, and Infertility: The Social and Historical Context," *Journal of Social Work and Human Sexuality* 6 (1988): 10 (quoting psychologist G. Stanley Hall in the 1903 address to the National Education Association).

23. *Bradwell v. State,* 83 U.S. 130, 141 (1873). This is antique phrasing to be sure, yet current practices of egg freezing by twenty-somethings in order not to interrupt their careers may be an updated version of securing that the sacred is not put at risk by careerist success.

24. Winter, "My Abortion."

25. Carol Gilligan, *In a Different Voice: Psychological Theory and Women's Development* (Cambridge, MA: Harvard University Press, 1982).

26. "Anti-Pregnancy Poster from 1970," *Flashbak*, October 31, 2012, http://flashbak.com/anti-pregnancy-poster-from-1970-14485/.

27. YouTube video, 0:40, posted by "!!omgblog!!," May 4, 2007, https://youtu.be/2gLlBv_SrZw.

28. Mary W. Shelley, *Frankenstein: Or, The Modern Prometheus* (London: G. Routledge & Sons, 1891), 231.

29. Ibid., 232.

30. Ibid., 233.

31. Anne K. Mellor, "Making a 'Monster,'" in *The Cambridge Companion to Mary Shelley*, ed. Esther Schor (Cambridge: Cambridge University Press, 2003), 10.

32. Ellen Moers, "Female Gothic," in *The Endurance of 'Frankenstein': Essays on Mary Shelley's Novel*, eds. George Levine and U. C. Knoepflmacher (Berkeley: University of California Press, 1979), 86–87. For thoughts on Mary Shelley's tribulations as a daughter, see U. C. Knoepflmacher, "Thoughts on the Aggression of Daughters," in *Endurance of 'Frankenstein,'* 88–119. See also Marc A. Rubenstein, "'My Accursed Origin': The Search for the Mother in *Frankenstein*," *Studies in Romanticism* 15 (1976): 165–194.

33. Anne K. Mellor, "Making a 'Monster,'" 10.

34. Shelley, *Frankenstein*, 73; Alan Bewell, "An Issue of Monstrous Desire: Frankenstein and Obstetrics," *Yale Journal of Criticism* 2 (1988): 116.

35. Judith J. Thomson, "A Defense of Abortion," *Philosophy & Public Affairs* 1 (1971): 47–66.

36. See, for example, *L. Pamela P. v. Frank. S.*, 59 N.Y.2d 1 (1983). See also Anita M. Hodgson, "The Warranty of Sperm: A Modest Proposal to Increase the Accountability of Sperm Banks and Physicians in the Performance of Artificial Insemination Procedures," *Indiana Law Review* 26 (1993): 357–386; Michael S. Schmidt, "Pentagon to Offer Plan to Store Eggs and Sperm to Retain Young Troops," *New York Times*, February 3, 2016, http://www.nytimes.com/2016/02/04/us/politics/pentagon-to-offer-plan-to-store-eggs-and-sperm-to-retain-young-troops.html?_r=0; Robin Romm, "All His Children: A Sperm Donor Discovers His Rich, Unsettling Legacy," *Atlantic*, December 2011, http://www.theatlantic.com/magazine/archive/2011/12/all-his-children/308714/; David Margolick, "15 Vials of Sperm: The Unusual Bequest of an Even More Unusual Man," *New York Times*, April 29, 1994, p. B18; Henry Weinstein, "Judges Rule Man Can Bequeath Sperm in Will," *Los Angeles Times*, June 19, 1993, p. 1.

37. See Sally Sheldon, "'Sperm Bandits,' Birth Control Fraud and the Battle of the Sexes," *Legal Studies* 21 (2001): 460–480.

38. Scott D. Johnson and Lindy B. Williams, "Deference, Denial, and Exclusion: Men Talk about Contraception and Unintended Pregnancy," *International Journal of Men's Health* 4 (2005): 230.

39. Amanda J. Miller, "Cohabiting Men's Preferences for and Roles in Determining the Outcomes of Unexpected Pregnancies," *Sociological Forum* 27 (2012): 711.

40. Jennifer A. Reich, "Not Ready to Fill His Father's Shoes," *Men and Masculinities* 11 (2008): 3–21; Miller, "Cohabiting Men's Preferences," 711.

41. See Elizabeth Emens, "Admin," *Georgetown Law Journal* 103 (2015): 1409–1481.

42. Robert P. George and Christopher Tollefsen, *Embryo: A Defense of Human Life* (New York: Doubleday, 2008), 1–6.

43. For a detailed backstory, see Margaret F. Brinig, "The Story of Mary Sue and Junior Davis," in *Family Law Stories*, ed. Carol Sanger (New York: Foundation Press, 2008), 195–217.

44. Ibid., 196.

45. Ibid.

46. *Davis v. Davis*, No. E-14496, 1989 Tenn. App. LEXIS 641, at *59 (Ct. App. Sep. 21, 1989).

47. Ibid., 60.

48. *Davis v. Davis,* 842 S.W.2d 588 (Tenn. 1992).

49. *Kass v. Kass,* 663 N.Y.S.2d 581 (App. Div. 1997).

50. Ibid., 595 (Miller, J., dissenting).

51. Ibid.

52. *Cahill v. Cahill,* 757 So.2d. 465 (Civ. App. Ala. 2000).

53. Associated Press, "Couple Fighting in Court over Frozen Embryos," *Times Daily,* August 10, 1998; P. Douglas Filaroski, "Frozen Assets," *Florida Times-Union,* August 20, 1998, http://jacksonville.com/tuonline/stories/082098/met_2A1mainc.html#.VvSjAmOCzzI.

54. *In re Johnson,* 2012 MT 140N.

55. Appellee / Cross–Appellant's Brief, *In re Marriage of Witten,* 672 N.W.2d 768 (Iowa 2003). The Iowa court forbade the use or disposition of the Wittens' embryos unless they reached an agreement, and until then, whichever party opposed embryo destruction was responsible for storage fees.

56. *Kass v. Kass,* 601.

57. *Karmasu v. Karmasu,* 2009-Ohio-5252, ¶ 26 (Ct. App.).

58. Ibid.

59. Ibid.

60. "Johnston: It's Been Very Difficult for Me," *Telegraph,* April 10, 2007, http://www.telegraph.co.uk/news/uknews/1548117/Johnston-Its-been-very-difficult-for-me.html.

61. Ibid. See *Evans v. United Kingdom,* 43 E.H.R.R. 21 (2006).

62. Rebecca English, "Couple at War over Frozen IVF Embryos," *Daily Mail,* http://www.dailymail.co.uk/news/article-132714/Couple-war-frozen-IVF-embryos.html#ixzz4Og3b7svh.

63. Filaroski, "Frozen Assets"; P. Douglas Filaroski, "Deadline Nearing in Embryo Appeal," *Florida Times-Union,* July 11, 1999, http://jacksonville.com/tuonline/stories/071199/met_2b2Embry.html#.VwFUAmOCzzI.

64. "Divorced Couple Battles over Frozen Embryos," *Today News,* May 31, 2007, http://www.today.com/news/divorced-couple-battles-over-frozen-embryos-1C9013805.

65. Appellate Brief in *Reber v. Reiss,* 2012 WL 1119939 (Pa. Super.), 30.

66. Reich, "Not Ready to Fill His Father's Shoes."

67. Louise Farr, "Whose Egg Is It, Anyway? An Embryo-Custody Battle," *MORE,* 2006, http://gayreitz.com/images/PDF/Whose_egg_more.com.pdf.

68. Appellate Brief in *Reber v. Reiss,* 29.

69. Ibid.

70. "Understanding Costs," *Growing Generations,* https://www.growinggenerations.com/surrogacy-program/intended-parents/surrogacy-cost/, accessed May 11 2016.

71. *In re Baby M,* 109 N.J. 396, 473 (1988).

72. *In re Baby "M,"* 217 N.J. Super. 313, 375 (1987). For the argument that a promise to abort made in the context of gestational surrogacy should be enforced, see Kevin Yamamoto and Shelby A. D. Moore, "A Trust Analysis of a Gestational Surrogate's Right to Abortion," *Fordham Law Review* 70 (2001): 93–186.

73. See Katie M. Brophy, "A Surrogate Mother Contract to Bear a Child," *Journal of Family Law* 20 (1982): 263–291; Martha A. Bohn, "Contracts Concerning Abortion," *Journal of Family Law* 31 (1991): 515–534; Carmen Y. D'Aversa, "The Right of Abortion in Surrogate Motherhood Arrangements," *Northern Illinois University Law Review* 7 (1987): 1–39.

74. See Sample Gestational Surrogacy Contract at *Choice Surrogacy,* http://www.allaboutsurrogacy.com/sample_contracts/GScontract1.htm, accessed April 30, 2016.

75. Ibid.

76. Elizabeth Cohen, "Surrogate Offered $10,000 to Abort Baby," *CNN,* March 6, 2013, http://www.cnn.com/2013/03/04/health/surrogacy-kelley-legal-battle/index.html.

77. Ibid.

78. *Stiver v. Parker,* 975 F.2d 261 (6th Cir. 1992); see "Surrogate Mother's Deformed Baby Rejected," *New York Times,* January 22, 1983, http://www.nytimes.com/1983/01/23/us/surrogate -mother-s-deformed-baby-rejected.html.

79. See *Choice Surrogacy*'s sample agreement.

80. Ibid.

81. *L. G. v. F. G. H.,* 729 S.W.2d 634 (Mo. Ct. App. 1987).

82. Ibid., 639.

83. See Lindsay Rovegno, "Athletes Often Forced into Heartbreaking Decisions," *ESPN,* May 12, 2007, http://espn.go.com/college-sports/news/story?id=2865230.

84. *L. G. v. F. G. H.,* 640.

85. See generally Daniel Sperling, *Management of Post-Mortem Pregnancy: Legal and Philosoph-ical Aspects* (Burlington, VT: Ashgate, 2006).

86. Robert M. Sade, "Brain Death, Cardiac Death, and the Dead Donor Rule," *Journal of the South Carolina Medical Association* 107 (2011): 146.

87. Melissa C. Bush et al., "Pregnancy in a Persistent Vegetative State: Case Report, Comparison to Brain Death, and Review of the Literature," *Obstetrical & Gynecological Survey* 58 (2003): 739.

88. Sperling, *Management of Post-Mortem Pregnancy,* 1.

89. Antara Mallampalli and Elizabeth Guy, "Cardiac Arrest in Pregnancy and Somatic Support after Brain Death," *Critical Care Medicine* 33 (2005): S325–S331. See also P. W. McKeown, R. S. Bonser, and J. A. Kellum, "Management of the Heartbeating Brain-Dead Organ Donor," *British Journal of Anaesthesia* 108 (2012): 196–1107.

90. See Alexis Gregorian, "Post-Mortem Pregnancy: A Proposed Methodology for the Resolution of Conflicts over Whether a Brain Dead Pregnant Woman Should Be Maintained on Life-Sustaining Treatment," *Annals of Health Law* 19 (2010): 401–424; Sperling, *Management of Post-Mortem Pregnancy,* 92–93; Robert M. Veatch, "Maternal Brain Death: An Ethicist's Thoughts," *Journal of the American Medical Association* 248 (1982): 1102–1103.

91. Gregorian, "Post-Mortem Pregnancy," 421–422.

92. See, for example, Stephanie McCrummen, "Brain-Dead Mother Is Taken off Life-Support," *Washington Post,* August 4, 2005, p. A1; *In re A. C.,* 573 A.2d 1235 (D.C. 1990); *University Health Services v. Piazzi,* No. CV86-RCCV-464 (Ga. Super. Ct. Aug. 4, 1986).

93. Manny Fernandez and Erik Eckholm, "Pregnant, and Forced to Stay on Life Support," *New York Times,* January 8, 2014, p. A1.

94. Tex. Health & Safety Code § 166.040 (LexisNexis 1989).

95. Tex. Health & Safety Code § 166.049 (LexisNexis 1989).

96. *Munoz v. John Peter Hospital,* 2014 WL 285057 (Tex. Dist. 2014).

97. Ibid.

98. Ibid.

99. *University Health Services Inc. v. Piazzi.*

100. Ibid., 418.

101. Ibid.

102. Ibid., 416. For a contrary holding under Florida law, see *In re Guardianship of J. D. S.,* 865 So.2d 534 (Fla. App. 5th Dist. 2004).

103. "Brain-Dead Mom's Baby Also Dies," *SunSentinel,* August 17, 1986, http://articles.sun-sentinel.com/1986-08-17/news/8602180736_1_david-hadden-donna-piazzi-2-ounce-baby.

104. Jeffrey L. Ecker, "Death in Pregnancy—An American Tragedy," *New England Journal of Medicine* 370 (2014): 890.

105. Mich. Comp. Laws Serv. § 700.5507 (4) (LexisNexis 1998).

106. Minn. Stat. Ann. § 145B.13 (3) (LexisNexis 1989).

107. James M. Jordan, "Incubating for the State: The Precarious Autonomy of Persistently Vegetative and Brain-Dead Pregnant Women," *Georgia Law Review* 22 (1988): 1111–1112.

108. See James Kunen, "Fertility Rights," *People Weekly* 49 (1998): 179–182. See also Brinig, "Story of Mary Sue and Junior Davis."

109. See Robert F. Kelly and Shawn L. Ward, "Allocating Custodial Responsibilities at Divorce: Social Science Research and the American Law Institute's Approximation Rule," *Family Court Review* 40 (2002): 350–370. Also see Margaret F. Brinig, "Does Parental Autonomy Require Equal Custody at Divorce?," *Louisiana Law Review* 65 (2005): 1345–1378.

110. *Re Stephen E. Findley v. Lee,* 2015 WL 7295217 (Cal. Super. Nov. 18, 2015).

111. *Kass v. Kass,* 601.

112. M. Antonia Biggs, Heather Gould, and Diana G. Foster, "Understanding Why Women Seek Abortions in the US," *BMC Women's Health* 13 (2013): 35.

113. Lawrence B. Finer et al., "Reasons U.S. Women Have Abortions: Quantitative and Qualitative Perspectives," *Perspectives on Sexual and Reproductive Health* 37 (2005): 110–118.

114. Winter, "My Abortion."

115. Ibid.

116. Joyce Maynard, "Mother of Three, Two Children Short," in *About What Was Lost: 20 Writers on Miscarriage, Healing, and Hope,* ed. Jessica B. Gross (New York: Penguin, 2006), 45.

117. Rachel K. Jones, Lori F. Frohwirth, and Ann M. Moore, "I Would 'Want to Give My Child, Like, Everything in the World,'" *Journal of Family Issues* 29 (2008): 95; see also Biggs, Gould, and Foster, "Understanding Why Women Seek Abortions," 37.

118. Biggs, Gould and Foster, "Understanding Why Women Seek Abortions," 33.

119. Jones, Frohwirth, and Moore, "I Would 'Want to Give My Child, Like, Everything in the World,'" 91.

120. Ibid., 92.

121. Biggs, Gould, and Foster, "Understanding Why Women Seek Abortions," 35.

122. Finer et al., "Reasons U.S. Women Have Abortions," 110.

123. Winter, "My Abortion."

124. Finer et al., "Reasons U.S. Women Have Abortions," 114–115; Biggs, Gould and Foster, "Understanding Why Women Seek Abortions," 35; Jones, Frohwirth and Moore, "I Would 'Want to Give My Child, Like, Everything in the World,'" 95.

125. Biggs, Gould, and Foster, "Understanding Why Women Seek Abortions," 34; Finer et al., "Reasons U.S. Women Have Abortions," 112.

126. Abortion Act, 1967, c. 87 (Eng.) section 1 (1)(a).

127. Jones, Frohwirth, and Moore, "I Would 'Want to Give My Child, Like, Everything in the World,'" 90.

128. For a discussion of other contractual issues, see Thomas W. Mayo, "Medical Decision Making during a Surrogate Pregnancy," *Houston Law Review* 25 (1988): 609–622.

129. Carline Mansfield et al., "Termination Rates after Prenatal Diagnosis of Down Syndrome, Spina Bifida, Anencephaly and Turner and Klinefelter Syndromes: A Systematic Literature Review," *Prenatal Diagnosis* 19 (1999): 808–812.

130. Sandelowski and Jones, "'Healing Fictions.'"

131. Roy Weatherford, "Philippa Foot and the Doctrine of Double Effect," *Personalist* 60 (1979): 105–113.

132. Leavitt, "'A Private Little Revolution,'" 335. See also "Your Stories," *A Thin Blue Line: The History of the Pregnancy Test Kit,* http://history.nih.gov/exhibits/thinblueline/survey.html, accessed January 11, 2016.

133. See *Davis v. Davis.*

134. *Stuart v. Camnitz,* 774 F.3d 238 (4th Cir. 2014). Statement is available at https://acluofnorthcarolina.org/files/Lawsuits/Declaration_of_Dr__James_R__Dingfelder.pdf.

135. Charles C. Camosy, *Beyond the Abortion Wars: A Way Forward for a New Generation* (Grand Rapids, MI: Eerdmans, 2015), 5.

136. Jean Hampton, "Selflessness and the Loss of Self," *Social Philosophy and Policy* 10 (1993): 135–165.

137. Ibid., 148.

138. Ibid., 146.

139. Ibid., 148.

140. Ibid., 163 (emphasis added).

141. Thomson, "Defence of Abortion," 64.

142. Elaine Showalter, *The Civil Wars of Julia Ward Howe: A Biography* (New York: Simon & Schuster, 2016), 83.

143. Pamela S. Karlan and Daniel R. Ortiz, "In a Different Voice: Relational Feminism, Abortion Rights, and the Feminist Legal Agenda," *Northwestern Law Review* 87 (1993): 890, 885–890.

144. Ibid., 889.

145. See, for example, Robin West, *Caring for Justice* (New York: New York University, 1997); Janet Halley, "The Politics of Injury: A Review of Robin West's Caring for Justice," *Unbound: Harvard Journal of the Legal Left* 1 (2005): 65–93; Robin West, "Desperately Seeking a Moralist," *Harvard Journal of Law & Gender* 29 (2006): 1–50.

146. Yates, *Revolutionary Road,* 254.

147. Ibid., 256.

Chapter 9   Normalizing Abortion

1. Siddhartha Mukherjee, *The Emperor of All Maladies: A Biography of Cancer* (New York: Scribner, 2011), 26–27.

2. Angelina Jolie, "My Medical Choice," *New York Times,* May 14, 2013, p. A25. Ten years earlier the cover of the *New York Times Magazine* featured a photograph of the scarred and breastless chest of cancer activist Matuschka with the headline "You Can't Look Away Anymore"; see Samantha King, "Pink Ribbons Inc.: Breast Cancer Activism and the Politics of Philanthropy," *International Journal of Qualitative Studies in Education* 17 (2004): 475.

3. Edwin Cameron, *Justice: A Personal Account* (Cape Town: Tafelberg, 2014), 68; see also Josh Gamson, "Silence, Death, and the Invisible Enemy: AIDS Activism and Social Movement 'Newness,'" *Social Problems* 36 (1989): 351–367.

4. Cameron, *Justice,* 68.

5. Edwin Cameron, *Witness to AIDS* (Cape Town: Tafelberg, 2005), 63.

6. Gordon W. Allport, *The Nature of Prejudice* (Garden City, NY: Doubleday, 1958).

7. Ibid., 261–282.

8. Sarah K. Cowan, "Secrets and Social Influence" (D.Phil. diss. University of California, Berkeley, 2013).

9. See Linda L. Layne, *Motherhood Lost: A Feminist Account of Pregnancy Loss in America* (New York: Routledge, 2003); Jessica B. Gross, ed., *About What Was Lost* (New York: Penguin, 2007).

10. Anita L. Vangelisti, Lindsay Timmerman, and John P. Caughlin, "Criteria for Revealing Family Secrets," *Communication Monographs* 68 (2001): 1–27.

11. Primo Levi, *The Mirror Maker: Stories & Essays* (New York: Schocken Books, 1989), 147. Stephanie R. Chaudoir and Diane M. Quinn, "Revealing Concealable Stigmatized Identities: The Impact of Disclosure Motivations and Positive First Disclosure Experiences on Fear of Disclosure and Well-Being," *Journal of Social Issues* 66 (2010): 570–584.

12. Cowan, "Secrets and Social Influence," 2.

13. Ibid., 5.

14. Ibid., 73.

15. *Fact Sheet: Induced Abortion in the United States,* Guttmacher Institute, March 2016, https://www.guttmacher.org/fact-sheet/induced-abortion-united-states.

16. This point aligns with human rights advocacy research, see generally Jonathan Baron, "Parochialism as a Result of Cognitive Biases," in *Understanding Social Action, Promoting Human Rights,* eds. Ryan Goodman, Derek Jinks, and Andrew K. Woods (Oxford; New York: Oxford University Press, 2012), 204–237.

17. Kristin Luker, *Abortion and the Politics of Motherhood* (Berkeley: University of California Press, 1984).

18. Cowan, "Secrets and Social Influence," 2.

19. See "Abortion Statistics: United States Data & Trends," *NRLC,* http://www.nrlc.org/uploads /factsheets/FS01AbortionintheUS.pdf; Cowan, "Secrets and Social Influence," 4.

20. Thanks to Jane Caldercott Norton for pressing this point.

21. Sheryl Sandberg, *Lean In: Women, Work, and the Will to Lead* (New York: Alfred A. Knopf, 2013). But see Anne-Marie Slaughter, "Yes, You Can," *New York Times,* March p. 10, 2013, p. BR1.

22. "Answers," *Billy Graham Evangelistic Association,* http://billygraham.org/answer/i-have-had -an-abortion-and-feel-so-guilty-can-god-forgive-me/, accessed May 10, 2016. See also "Are you a Christian Woman Who Has Had an Abortion?," *Christian Apologetics & Research Ministry,* http://carm.org/are-you-christian-woman-who-has-had-abortion, accessed May 10, 2016.

23. Emily Bazelon and Dahlia Lithwick, "I Went Full Out," in *About What Was Lost,* ed. Jessica B. Gross (New York: Penguin, 2007), 54.

24. *Exhale,* https://exhaleprovoice.org/, accessed May 10, 2016.

25. "Times Will Begin Reporting Gay Couples' Ceremonies," *New York Times,* August 18, 2002, http://www.nytimes.com/2002/08/18/us/times-will-begin-reporting-gay-couples-ceremonies.html ?pagewanted=print.

26. Ibid.

27. Linda Marx, "Taking Their Very Sweet Time," *New York Times,* September 1, 2013, p. ST14.

28. Ibid. For a discussion of whether Udonis was in Sarah Silverman's term "bro-choice," see Lauren Enriquez, "NYT Gushes over NBA Couple Who Put Sports ahead of Their Child's

Life," *Live Action News,* September 3, 2013, http://liveactionnews.org/nyt-gushes-nba-couple -put-sports-ahead-childs-life/; Katie Mcdonough, "There's Nothing Wrong with Being 'Bro-choice,'" *Salon,* July 17, 2013, http://www.salon.com/2013/07/17/theres_nothing_wrong _with_being_bro_choice/.

29. Dave Andrusko, "Another Attempt to 'Normalize' Abortion," *National Right to Life News,* September 3, 2013, http://www.nationalrighttolifenews.org/news/2013/09/another-attempt-to -normalize-abortion/#.Vy9nuIQrLcs; Cynthia Greenlee, "An Abortion Story Both Radical and Ordinary," *Rewire,* September 4, 2013, https://rewire.news/article/2013/09/04/the-abortion-story-in -this-weekends-vows-column-is-both-radical-and-ordinary/.

30. For an historical example, see David Kertzer, *Sacrificed for Honor: Italian Infant Abandon- ment and the Politics of Reproductive Control* (Boston: Beacon Press, 1993).

31. See *In re Kline,* 298 Kan. 96, 100 (2013).

32. Carol Smart, "Families, Secrets and Memories," *Sociology* 45 (2011): 539–553.

33. Doris Lessing, *The Real Thing: Stories and Sketches* (New York: HarperCollins, 1992), 1.

34. Ibid., 22.

35. Ibid., 23.

36. See Judith Modell, *Kinship with Strangers: Adoption and Interpretations of Kinship in American Culture* (Berkeley: University of California Press, 1994); E. Wayne Carp, *Family Matters: Secrecy and Disclosure in the History of Adoption* (Cambridge, MA: Harvard University Press, 1998)

37. *Does 1–7 v. State,* 330 Or. 138, 6 P.3d 1098 (2000).

38. Tasha N. Dubriwny, "Constructing Breast Cancer in the News," *Journal of Communication Inquiry* 33 (2009): 116. See also Susan Braun, "The History of Breast Cancer Advocacy," *Breast Journal* 9 (2003): S101–S103.

39. Bijou Hunt, Steve Whitman, and Marc S. Hurlbert, "Increasing Black: White Disparities in Breast Cancer Mortality in the 50 Largest Cities in the United States," *Cancer Epidemiology* 38 (2014): 118–123.

40. Paul Longmore, "'Heaven's Special Child': The Making of Poster Children," in *The Disability Studies Reader,* ed. Lenard J. Davis (New York: Routledge, 2013), 34–41.

41. Sherri C. Finkbine, "The Lesser of Two Evils," in *Before Roe v. Wade: Voices that Shaped the Abortion Debate before the Supreme Court's Ruling,* eds. Linda Greenhouse and Reva Siegel (New York: Kaplan, 2010), 11–18.

42. Thalidomide had not been approved for sale in the United States due to the diligence of Dr. Frances Kelsey at the Food and Drug Administration. W. Lenz, "A Short History of Thalido- mide Embryopathy," *Teratology* 38 (1988): 203–215.

43. Finkbine, "Lesser of Two Evils," 13–14.

44. See Edward Stein, "*The Story of Goodridge v. Department of Public Health*: The Bumpy Road to Marriage for Same-Sex Couples," in *Family Law Stories,* ed. Carol Sanger (New York: Founda- tion Press, 2008), 27–49.

45. Norma McCorvey and Andy Meisler, *I Am Roe: My Life, Roe v. Wade, and Freedom of Choice* (New York: HarperCollins, 1994), 154. See also Brief of Sandra Cano, the Former "Mary Doe" of *Doe v. Bolton,* and 180 Women Injured by Abortion as Amici Curiae in Support of Petitioner, *Gonzales v. Carhart,* 550 U.S. 124 (2007) (no. 05-380).

46. Brief for Janice MacAvoy, Janie Schulman, and Over 110 Other Women in the Legal Profession Who Have Exercised Their Constitutional Right to an Abortion as Amici Curiae Supporting Petitioners, *Whole Woman's Health v. Cole* (No. 15-274) (U.S. argued March 2, 2016).

47. Linda H. Edwards, "Hearing Voices: Non-Party Stories in Abortion and Gay Rights Advocacy," *Michigan State Law Review* 2015 (2015): 1327–1357.

48. Andrea L. Irwin, "Maine Voices: Why I'm Not Shy about Telling the Supreme Court about My Abortion," *Portland Press Herald,* March 2, 2016, http://www.pressherald.com/2016/03/02 /maine-voices-why-im-not-shy-about-telling-the-supreme-court-about-my-abortion/. See also Janice MacAvoy, "I'm a Successful Lawyer and Mother Because I Had an Abortion, *Charlotte Observer,* January 28, 2016, https://charlotteobserver.relaymedia.com/amp/opinion/article57065938 .html.

49. Robert B. Voas and James C. Fell, "Mothers Against Drunk Driving (MADD): The First 25 Years," *Traffic Injury Prevention* 7 (2006): 197.

50. See Celeste M. Condit, *Decoding Abortion Rhetoric: Communicating Social Change* (Urbana: University of Illinois Press, 1990); Nick Hopkins and Steve Reicher, "Social Movement Rhetoric and the Social Psychology of Collective Action: A Case Study of Anti-Abortion Mobilization," *Human Relations* 50 (1997): 261–286; Myra M. Ferree, "Resonance and Radicalism: Feminist Framing in the Abortion Debates of the United States and Germany," *American Journal of Sociology* 109 (2003): 304–344.

51. Tracy A. Weitz, "Rethinking the Mantra that Abortion Should be 'Safe, Legal, and Rare,'" *Journal of Women's History* 22 (2010): 162.

52. See William Saletan, *Bearing Right: How Conservatives Won the Abortion War* (Berkeley: University of California Press, 2003), 140–157; Robin Toner, "Settling In: Easing Abortion Policy; Clinton Orders Reversal of Abortion Restrictions Left by Reagan and Bush," *New York Times,* January 23, 1993, p. 1.

53. Weitz, "Rethinking the Mantra," 163.

54. Ibid., 168.

55. Michael McGough, "Hillary Clinton Tweaks Her 'Safe, Legal and Rare' Abortion Mantra," *Los Angeles Times,* February 9, 2016, http://www.latimes.com/opinion/opinion-la/la-ol -hillaryclinton-abortion-campaign-20160209-story.html.

56. "Lovingly Dedicated to All Who Have Made 'A Heartbreaking Choice,'" *A Heartbreaking Choice,* http://www.aheartbreakingchoice.com/, accessed May 13, 2016; see also Christie Brooks, ed., *Our Heartbreaking Choices: Forty-Six Women Share Their Stories of Interrupting a Much-Wanted Pregnancy* (Bloomington, IN: iUniverse, 2008).

57. Brooks, *Our Heartbreaking Choices,* 2.

58. Beth Ann Pentney, "Feminism, Activism, and Knitting: Are the Fibre Arts a Viable Mode for Feminist Political Action?," *Third Space* 8 (2008): 12. See also generally Maura Kelly, "Knitting as a Feminist Project?," *Women's Studies International Forum* 44 (2014): 133–144.

59. Lindy West, "I Set up #ShoutYourAbortion Because I Am Not Sorry, and I Will Not Whisper," *Guardian,* September 22, 2015, https://www.theguardian.com/commentisfree/2015/sep /22/i-set-up-shoutyourabortion-because-i-am-not-sorry-and-i-will-not-whisper.

60. Gloria Steinem, *My Life On the Road* (New York: Random House, 2015).

61. West, "I Set up #ShoutYourAbortion."

62. Ibid.

63. Tamar Lewin, "#ShoutYourAbortion Gets Angry Shouts Back," *New York Times,* October 2, 2015, p. A1.

64. Ibid.

65. Ibid.

66. *1 in 3,* http://www.1in3campaign.org/, accessed October 18, 2016; "Tell Your Story," *NARAL: Pro-Choice America,* http://www.prochoiceamerica.org/womens-voices/tell-your-story .html, accessed October 18, 2016; *Silent No More Awareness,* http://www.silentnomoreawareness.org/, accessed October 18, 2016; Share Your Abortion Story, http://shareyourabortionstory.tumblr

.com/, accessed October 18, 2016; "The Shirt," *Abortion and Life,* http://abortionandlife.com/p/the
-shirt/, accessed October 30, 2016.

67. Jennifer Baumgardner, *Abortion and Life* (New York: Akashic Books, 2008), 73–129.

68. Cornelia H. Dayton, "Taking the Trade: Abortion and Gender Relations in an Eighteenth-
Century New England Village," *William & Mary Quarterly* 48 (1991): 19–49.

69. Ibid., 24.

70. Daniel Grossman et al., "Self-Induction of Abortion among Women in the United States,"
Reproductive Health Matters 18 (2010): 136–146; Carla Zanoni, "Women Resort to Over-the-
Counter Remedies to End Pregnancies in WaHi," *DNAinfo,* December 20, 2011, https://www
.dnainfo.com/new-york/20111220/washington-heights-inwood/women-resort-overthecounter
-remedies-end-pregnancies-wahi.

71. Grossman et al., "Self-Induction of abortion," 142–144.

72. Carla Zanoni, Shayna Jacobs, and Ben Fractenberg, "Mother of Fetus Found in
Alley Charged with Self-Abortion," *DNAinfo,* December 1, 2011, https://www.dnainfo.com/new
-york/20111201/washington-heights-inwood/mother-of-fetus-found-alley-charged-with-selfabortion.

73. Ricki Sollinger, *Wake up Little Susie: Single Pregnancy and Race before Roe v. Wade* (New
York: Routledge, 1992), 103–147.

74. Timur Kuran, *Private Truth, Public Lies: The Social Consequences of Preference Falsification*
(Cambridge, MA: Harvard University Press, 1997), 261.

75. Ibid., 20.

76. Ibid., 21.

77. See "Defending Life 2015: Celebrating Ten Years of Defending Life," *Americans United for
Life,* http://aul.org/downloads/defending-life-2015/AUL_Defending_Life_2015.pdf.

78. *Planned Parenthood of the Heartland, Inc. v. Iowa Board of Medicine,* 865 N.W.2d 252, 255
(Iowa 2015).

79. See Daniel Grossman et al., "Effectiveness and Acceptability of Medical Abortion Provided
through Telemedicine," *Obstetrics and Gynecology* 118 (2011): 296–303; see also Alana Semuels, "The
Safer, More Affordable Abortion Only Available in Two States," *Atlantic,* October 10, 2014,
http://www.theatlantic.com/business/archive/2014/10/the-safer-more-affordable-abortion-only
-available-in-two-states/381321/.

80. *Planned Parenthood of the Heartland, Inc. v. Iowa Board of Medicine,* 256.

81. Tony Leys, "Iowa Supreme Court: Ban on Telemed Abortion Unconstitutional," *Des Moines
Register,* June 19, 2015, http://www.desmoinesregister.com/story/news/politics/2015/06/19/iowa
-supreme-court-approves-planned-parenthood-heartland-telemedicine-abortion-system/28973085/.

82. West, "I Set up #ShoutYourAbortion."

83. Iowa Admin. Code r. 653-13.10.

84. "Arkansas Telemedicine Ban (HB 1076)," *Rewire,* https://rewire.news/legislative-tracker/law
/arkansas-telemedicine-ban-hb-1076/, accessed May 13, 2016.

85. *Planned Parenthood of the Heartland, Inc. v. Iowa Board of Medicine;* Leys, "Iowa Supreme
Court: Ban on Telemed Abortion Unconstitutional."

86. Leslie J. Reagan, *Dangerous Pregnancies: Mothers, Disabilities, and Abortion in Modern
America* (Berkeley: University of California Press, 2010), 160–161.

87. "Facts about Microcephaly," *Centers for Disease Control and Prevention,* https://www.cdc.gov
/ncbddd/birthdefects/microcephaly.html.

88. Mitch Smith and Erik Eckholm, "Federal Judge Blocks Indiana Abortion Law," *New York
Times,* July 1, 2016, p. A15.

89. "Attorney General Strange Comment on Impact of U.S. Supreme Court Abortion Decision On Alabama," *State of Alabama: Office of the Attorney General,* June 27, 2016, http://www.ago.state .al.us/News-863.

90. "Virginia Rescinds Strict Building Codes for Abortion Clinics," *U.S. News,* October 24, http://www.usnews.com/news/us/articles/2016-10-24/virginia-rescinds-strict-building-codes-for -abortion-clinics.

91. Blythe Bernhard, "Clinic Vows to Resume Abortions in Columbia After Supreme Court Ruling," *St. Louis Post-Dispatch,* June, 29, 2016, http://www.stltoday.com/lifestyles/health-med-fit /health/clinic-vows-to-resume-abortions-in-columbia-after-supreme-court/article_09414645-e606 -5888-b9a3-a329ed7d07e0.html.

92. Alexa Ura, "Texas Won't Give Up on Fetal Burial Rule," *Washington Post,* September 23, 2016, https://www.washingtonpost.com/news/post-nation/wp/2016/09/23/texas-wont-give-up-on -fetal-burial-rule/?utm_term=.c3efbc62b24f; see also *Texas Register—Proposed Rules,* July 1, 2016, http://www.sos.state.tx.us/texreg/pdf/backview/0701/0701prop.pdf.

93. "Standards for Licensing Abortion Clinic," *Department of Health and Environmental Control,* September 23, 2016, http://shrbeta.brack.net/wp-content/uploads/2016/10/4669.pdf, 42.

94. Ibid., 5.

95. Andy Brack, "Time to Say the Heck with DHEC," *Statehouse Report,* October, 21, 2016, http://www.statehousereport.com/2016/10/21/brack-the-heck-with-dhec/.

96. Ibid.

97. *Gonzales v. Carhart,* 550 U.S. 124 (2007).

98. Sherry F. Colb and Michael C. Dorf, *Beating Hearts: Abortion and Animal Rights* (New York: Columbia University Press, 2016), 15.

99. *Whole Woman's Health v. Hellerstedt,* 136 S. Ct. 2292, 2316 (2016).

100. Ibid., 2318.

101. Richard Yates, *Revolutionary Road* (New York: Knopf Doubleday, 2008), 327.

Acknowledgments

I would like to thank the colleagues and institutions who have supported my work on this book. Over the last few years, a small group of colleagues read chapter after chapter with patience and great care. Their friendship, criticisms, and huzzahs were key to making this a better book and me a better writer. My thanks to Richard Brooks, Victoria de Grazia, Jean Howard, Martha Howell, Alice Kessler-Harris, Susan Rieger, and Holly Sanger. For early encouragement to take on the topic of abortion directly, I thank Martha Minow and Elizabeth Knoll.

I have also benefited greatly from exchanges with many readers and interlocutors: Erez Aloni, Rosalind Ballaster, Susan Bandes, Barbara Black, Emily Braun, Jessica Bulman-Pozen, June Carbone, Brett Dignam, Michael Dorf, Nancy Dowd, Elizabeth Emens, Robert Ferguson, Jill Fisch, Ruth Fletcher, Katherine Franke, Jesse Fried, Philip Genty, Marie-Amélie George, Suzanne Goldberg, Imogen Goold, Jeffrey Gordon, Michael Graetz, Kent Greenawalt, Carol Greenhouse, Bernard Harcourt, Cecilia Heyes, Susan Hays, Carole Joffe, Avery Katz, Lisa Kelly, Linda Kerber, Sarah Knuckey, Jennifer Laurin, Liora Lazarus, Sara Lipton, Solangel Maldonado, Kent McKeever, Gillian Metzger, Siobhán Mullally, Claire Murray, Madeline Naegle, Luke Norris, Jane Caldercott Norton, Lucy Painter, David Pozen, Alexander Pulte, Alex Raskolnikov, Lomin Saayman, Michael Sanger, Elizabeth Scott, Anna Sochynsky, Michael Sochynsky, Nomita Sonty, Amia Srinivasan, Lawrence Stanberry, Jonny Steinberg, Eric Talley, Caroline Tate, Kendall Thomas, Hendrik Wendland, Mary Zulack, and three anonymous reviewers whose detailed comments were extraordinarily helpful.

While writing this book, several institutions at Oxford University provided me with office space, libraries, collegiality, and critical conversation. I would like to thank Warden John Vickers, Professor Simon Hornblower, and the Fellows of All Souls College; former Dean Timothy Endicott, Faculty of Law; Principal Helena Kennedy and the Fellows of Mansfield College; former Principal Tim Gardam and the Fellows of St Anne's College; and Nigel Bowles, former Director of the Rothermere American Institute. I have been lucky indeed in these associations, and I am most grateful to them all. Appreciative thanks are also given on this side of the Atlantic to Dean Gillian Lester and Dean David Schizer of Columbia Law School for their kind support, including summer stipends and research leaves.

I would also like to thank the participants at workshops at Chicago-Kent College of Law, the Centre for Law and Society at Edinburgh Law School, University of Florida Levin College of Law, Whittier Law School, Birmingham Law School (United Kingdom), University of Arizona James E. Rogers College of Law, West Virginia University College of Law, the Center for Reproductive Rights, and the British Pregnancy Advisory Service.

An early version of Chapter 1 was previously published as the University of Arizona Law School Isaac Marks Memorial Lecture, "About Abortion: The Complications of the Category," *Arizona Law Review* 54, no. 4 (2013): 849–78. A version of Chapter 7 was previously published as "Decisional Dignity: Teenage Abortion, Bypass Hearings, and the Misuse of Law," *Columbia Journal of Gender and Law* 18 (2009): 409–499. A version of Chapter 5 was previously published as "Seeing and Believing: Mandatory Ultrasound and the Path to a Protected Choice," *UCLA Law Review* 56 (2008): 351–408.

Three young women took responsibility for the production of this book, turning the manuscript into a bound volume. Their help was invaluable in every aspect of the process, including excellent editorial suggestions and months of searching for the right image for the book jacket: the face of a woman who could carry the weight of abortion in America today with grace and intelligence. My deepest thanks then to Marianne Carroll, Francesca Cocuzza, and Nofar Yakovi Gan-Or.

Many thanks as well to the student research assistants at Columbia who worked on this project: Aliza Hochman Bloom, Emily Brailey, Jenny Ding, Shreya Fadia, Madeline Gomez, Elizabeth Howell, Samantha Harper Knox, Jenny Ma, Jaclyn Neely, Anya Crosby Olsen, Sarah Rosenbluth, Kirby Tyrrell, Laura Flahive Wu, Jean Zachariasiewicz, and Joy Ziegeweid. I hope they see their contributions in the final product.

Joyce Seltzer, my editor at Harvard University Press, wielded a mighty and unerring pencil, and I am deeply grateful for her close reading of this text. Thanks also to Kate Brick and Kimberly Giambattisto for their steady guidance.

I thank Caroline Lukaszewski and her staff—Taylor Cook, Christopher Mark, and Claire Merrill—at Columbia Law School for terrific administrative support. The staff of the Arthur W. Diamond Law Library at Columbia Law

School, particularly Philip Greene and Dana Neacsu, were of tremendous help collecting resource material.

Finally, I want to acknowledge two others. The first is my sister-in-law, Anne Kathleen Elliot (1955–1992), whose presence has been much missed. Second, Jeremy Waldron has been the best companion throughout this long process, as he is even when no book is on the horizon. I am grateful for his kindness and thoughtful counsel during the thick and thin of the last several years. I thank him for everything. And, dear readers, he did my index.

Illustration Credits

Chapter 1

Ultrasound before the Ohio House Health and Aging Committee. Photo by Fred Squillante / *The Columbus Dispatch*, March 3, 2011.   3

"Is that the baby inside your tummy?" Illustration © Rachel Fuller, from *Waiting for Baby* (Swindon, UK: Child's Play (International) Ltd, 2009). Courtesy of the illustrator.   20

Chapter 4

The Visitation (detail). Museum für Angewandte Kunst, Frankfurt am Main, Inv. Nr. 6810. Digital image reproduction via Wikimedia Commons.   75

"The Byrthe," Eucharius Rösslin. *The Byrthe of Mankynde, Otherwyse Named the Womans Booke*, 1545. Wellcome Library, London, folio 102r; EPB / 7358 / B. L0041839 (CC BY 4.0).   78

Damian Hirst, *The Miraculous Journey* (night). Photo © Penny Yi Wang.   88

Damian Hirst, newborn sculpture. Doha, Qatar. Photo © Alexey Sergeev.   89

Aubrey Vincent Beardsley (1872–1898). "Incipit Vita Nova."   91

Olmec fetus sculpture. Drawing by Carolyn E. Tate from *Reconsidering Olmec Visual Culture: The Unborn, Women, and Creation* by Carolyn E. Tate. Copyright © 2012 by the University of Texas Press. Courtesy of the author and the University of Texas Press.   92

Precious Ones. Photo by Danielle Burgos.   95

A statue of Jizō. Photo Wikimedia Commons / Jonny-mt (CC BY-SA 3.0).   97

Fetal superhero figures. Courtesy of the artist, Alexandre Nicolas.   104

Public health poster, "Zika Virus causes microcephaly." © Fang Chun Liu / Shutterstock / Image ID: 369618797.   105

Chapter 6

Mother and lifeless child, ambrotype, circa 1857. Stanley B. Burns, MD and the Burns Archive.   138

Mary Todd Lincoln. Photograph by William H. Mumler, Boston, Massachusetts, 1872. Digital image from the Lincoln Financial Foundation Collection, courtesy of the Indiana State Museum and Allen County Public Library.   142

Mrs. French. Photograph by William H. Mumler. Boston, Massachusetts, ca. 1870. The J. Paul Getty Museum, Los Angeles. Digital image courtesy of the Getty's Open Content Program.   143

Index